COLONIAL FAMILIES
OF
CAPE MAY COUNTY,
NEW JERSEY

2nd Edition (Revised)

F. Edward Wright

HERITAGE BOOKS
2017

HERITAGE BOOKS
AN IMPRINT OF HERITAGE BOOKS, INC.

Books, CDs, and more—Worldwide

For our listing of thousands of titles see our website at www.HeritageBooks.com

Published 2017 by
HERITAGE BOOKS, INC.
Publishing Division
5810 Ruatan Street
Berwyn Heights, Md. 20740

International Standard Book Number
Paperbound: 978-1-58549-443-9

CONTENTS

PREFACE to Second Edition

This is the Second Edition to *Colonial Families of Cape May County, New Jersey*. This edition contains additional information in the Appendix based on Bible records of Cape May County. These Bible records were recently published in a book titled *New Jersey Bible Records, Volume 1: Atlantic, Burlington, Cape May, and Gloucester Counties*, edited by Anna Miller Watring. We are indebted to Ms. Watring and to members of Red Bank Chapter, D.A.R. who contributed records and who preserved the enormous number of records collected by Timothy Chalkley Matlack, to members of the Cape May Patriots Chapter, and to others, who contributed family records.

F. Edward Wright
Lewes, Delaware
2002

INTRODUCTION

A great deal has been printed on the early families of the county. Numerous articles have appeared in *The Cape May County Magazine of History and Genealogy* (shown below), oft times dealing with a branch of the family and leaving the reconstruction of other branches to future genealogists. A few books have appeared which cover all the branches of particular family, notably the Corsons and Hughes families.

I have attempted to organize past research into one package, performing additional research when necessary to fill the gaps. In those cases when a female has married into another Cape May County family her descendancy is followed only down the husband's line, rather than repeat the same information down both lines. The reader is reminded of this by the use of an asterisk (*) indicating that more information is available on the spouse's lineage; that family's entry should then be consulted.

I have summarized the research done by others in reconstructing the pre-Cape May County history of families. It is recommended that the researcher avail himself of these published sources followed by an examination of the original sources whenever possible. I noted instances of apparent discrepancies and conflicts of information. As one would expect of any publication, there are a number of errors and omissions in the Calendar of New Jersey Wills, Administrations, etc. of the First Series of the *New Jersey Archives*. In this study it was not possible to verify the accuracy of each will found in the Archives series, against the original will.

Variations in spelling usually reflect the spelling of the name as found in the original source.

Whenever possible the family has been traced up to the time of the Revolutionary War.

F. Edward Wright
Westminster, Maryland
1997

SOURCES

(1) The Pilgrim Ancestry of Cape May County," *The Cape May County Magazine of History and Genealogy*, p. 9. April 1931. By Rev. Paul Sturtevant Howe, Ph.D., Rector of the Church of the Advent, Cape May.

(2) "Descendants of Esther Learning," *The Cape May County Magazine of History and Genealogy*, p. 59. June 1932. By Rev. Paul Sturtevant Howe, Ph.D.

(3) "Diaries of Aaron Learning," *The Cape May County Magazine of History and Genealogy*, p. 69. June 1932. Copied by Lewis T. Stevens. [The diary of Aaron Learning is held by the Historical Museum of Cape May County.]

(4) "Some of the Descendants of Abraham Bennett, Member of Committee of Safety, Captain of the Randolph, Used as a Privateer in Revolution, *The Cape May County Magazine of History and Genealogy*, p. 108. June 1933. Genealogy Notes, by Rev. Paul Sturtevant Howe.

(5) "Memorandum book of Jacob Spicer, 1757-1764," *The Cape May County Magazine of History and Genealogy*, p. 112. June 1933.

(6) "Genealogical Abstracts From Early Cape May County Deeds," *The Cape May County Magazine of History and Genealogy*, p. 229. June 1936. By William Evans Price.

(7) "John Townsend - An Historical and Genealogical Records of One of the Original English Settlers of Cape May County, *The Cape May County Magazine of History and Genealogy*, p. 122. June 1933. By Lewis Townsend Stevens.

(8) "First Public Records of Cape May County," *The Cape May County Magazine of History and Genealogy*, p. 269. June 1937.

(9) "First Official Records of Cape May County," *The Cape May County Magazine of History and Genealogy*, p. 316.

(10) "The Stillwells - A Patriotic Family, And Their Descendants, *The Cape May County Magazine of History and Genealogy*, p. 51. June 1940. By William Evans Price.

(11) "Origin of the Hughes Family in Cape May County, N.J. - and Seven Humphreys," *The Cape May County Magazine of History and Genealogy*, p. 143. June 1942. By Stanley Williamson.

(12) "The, Eldridge Family," *The Cape May County Magazine of and Genealogy*, p. 157. June 1942. By H. S. Campion, Jr.

(13) "The Account Book of John Parsons, With Notes," *The Cape County Magazine of History and Genealogy*, p. 166. June 1942. By Norman Harvey Vanaman.

(14) "Comments on Townsend," *The Cape May County Magazine History and Genealogy*, p. 174. June 1942. By H. C. Campion, Jr.

(15) "Timothy Brandreth," *The Cape May County Magazine of j tistory and Genealogy*, p. 191. June 1943. By H. Clifford Campion, Jr.

(16) "William Golding (Gelder, Golden, Goulding) of Cape May County," *The Cape May County Magazine of History and Genealogy*, p. 289. June 1944. By H. Clifford Campion, Jr.

(17) "Ancestry of Christopher Hand, of Hand's Mill," *The Cape May County Magazine of History and Genealogy*, p. 255. June 1944. By H. Clifford Campion, Jr.

(18) "Caleb Carmen (Whaler, Millwright and Miller) (Builder of the first Mill in Cape May County)," *The Cape May County Magazine of History and Genealogy*, p. 283. June 1944. By H. Clifford Campion, Jr.

(19) "Concerning Ellis Hughes, Son of Uriah," *The Cape May County Magazine of History and Genealogy*, p. 78. June 1949.

(20) "Some Old Houses of Cape May County," *The Cape May County Magazine of History and Genealogy*, p. 103. June 1950.

(21) "Bible Records (The Town-Corgie Bible and Eliza Bennett Bible)", *The Cape May County Magazine of History and Genealogy*, p. 225. June 1952.

(22) "Swain Family," *The Cape May County Magazine of History and Genealogy*, p. 251. June 1953. By Margaret Irwin McVickar.

(23) "Izard Family," *The Cape May County Magazine of History and Genealogy*, p. 301. June 1954. By Margaret Irwin McVickar.

(24) "The Pierson Family," *The Cape May County Magazine of History and Genealogy,* p. 6. June 1955. By Margaret Irwin McVickar.

(25) "A True Copy of the Complete List of Marriages from the 'First Writings' of the First Baptist Church of Cape May Cape May Court House, New Jersey," *The Cape May County Magazine of History and Genealogy*, p. 23. June 1955. Transcribed by M. Catharine Stauffer.

(26) "The Historic Baptist Burial Yard - Cape May Court House New Jersey," *The Cape May County Magazine of History and Genealogy,* p. 63. June 1956. By M. Catharine Stauffer.

(27) "The Leamings - Some Historical Notes of a Family and the Times," *The Cape May County Magazine of History and Genealogy*, p. 85. June 1956. By Karl A. Dickinson.

(28) "Records of The Hildreth Family," *The Cape May County Magazine of History and Genealogy*, p. 82. By Alice G. Stathem (Mrs. Paul Woodson Stathem). These are records copied on 20 March 1956 by Alice G. Stathem from the Bible then owned by Paul Woodson Stathem.

(29) "Bible Records, *The Cape May County Magazine of History and Genealogy*, p. 111. June 1957. By Margret Irwin McVickar. Edward Irwin, Jr.'s Bible.

(30) "Early West Creek Settlers," *The Cape May County Magazine of History and Genealogy*, p. 142. June 1958. Roy Hand.

(31) "Rem and Rebekah Erritsen Cape May County Pioneers," *The Cape May County Magazine of History and Genealogy*, p. 156. June 1958. By Marie E. Garretson.

(32) "Sketch on the Early Life and Ancestry of John I. Corson," *The Cape May County Magazine of History and Genealogy,* p. 205. June 1959. As Contained In An Old Book Evidently His Property And Written By Him. By Grace Gallaher.

(33) "Irwin Family," *The Cape May County Magazine of History and Genealogy*, p. 215. June 1959.

(34) "The Mills of East and West Creek," Part II, *The Cape May County Magazine of History and Genealogy*. p. 273. June 1961. By Dr. Hand. The Hoffmans.

(35) "The Jenkins Family of Cape May County, New Jersey," *The Cape May County Magazine of History and Genealogy*, p. 369. June 1963. By Grace C. Gallaher.

(36) "The Tomlin Family," *The Cape May County Magazine of History and Genealogy*, p. 409. June 1963. Comments based on excerpts from the book, *The Tomlin Family*, by Rachel Tomlin Rankin, Torch Press, Cedar Rapids, Iowa, 1932.

(37) "The Pierson Family," *The Cape May County Magazine of History and Genealogy*, p. 423. June 1963. By Dr. Roy Hand.

(38) "The Goff and Bishop Families," *The Cape May County Magazine of History and Genealogy*, p. 45. June 1964. By Dr. Roy Hand.

(39) "The Cresse Family of New Jersey," *The Cape May County Magazine of History and Genealogy*, p. 79. June 1964. By Claude Young.

(40) "The Other Osborne Family," *Genealogies of New Jersey Families*[1], by Richard W. Cook, assisted by Donald Lines Jacobus. Vol. 1, p. 682. Gen. Mag. of NJ: Vol. XXVI (1961), 3-7.

(41) "Richard Somers Family," *Genealogies of New Jersey Families*, Vol. 1, p. 790. Gen. Mag. of NJ: Vol. 57 (1982), 38.

---

[1] A collection of articles from the Genealogical Magazine of New Jersey published by Genealogical Publishing Co., Inc., 1996.

(42) "Job Somers," *Genealogies of New Jersey Families*, Vol. 1, 790. Gen. Mag. of NJ: Vol. 61 (1986), 128.

(43) "Andrews," *Genealogies of New Jersey Families*, by John Dornan. Vol. 2, p. 378. Gen. Mag. of NJ: Vol. XXIV (1949), 51-56; V XXV (1950), 10-12, 35-41, 55-60, 76-83; [Correction, Vol. XXVI (195: 24]; Vol. XXV I (1951), 4-6.

(44) "Townsend Family Record," *Genealogies of New Families,* Vol. 2, p. 619. Gen. Mag. of NJ: 58 (1983), 113-116.

(45) "Jesse Hand," *Genealogies of New Jersey Families*, Thomas Van Fleet. Vol. 2, p.819. Gen. Mag. of NJ: Vol. 64 (1989), 39-40.

(46) 'William And Esther Eldredge," *Genealogies of New Jersey Families*, Vol. 2, p. 821. Gen. Mag. of NJ: Vol. 64 (1989), 50.

(47) "Savage - Stillwell," *Genealogies of New Jersey Families*, Vol. 2, p. 829. Gen. Mag. of NJ: Vol. 65 (1990), 9-10.

(48) "Bible Records in Rutgers University Library," ... Townsend Family. *Genealogies of New Jersey.Families*, Vol. 2, p. 890. Gen. Mag. NJ: Vol. XVM (1943), 96.

(49) "Corson Family Genealogical Samplers," *Genealogies of New Jersey Families*, Vol. 2, p. 935. Gen. Mag. of NJ: Vol 44 (1969), 75-76.

(50) "The Stites Family," *Genealogies of Long Island Families*, p. 123. By Edmund J. James. Genealogical Publishing Co., Inc., 1987. From *The New York Genealogical and Biographical Record,* Vol. XXVIII (July 1897), 165-166; (Oct. 1897), 237-239; Vol. XXIX (April 1898), 93-98.

(51) *Three Hundred Years with the Corson Families in America*. By Orville Corson, Middletown, Ohio. 1939. 2 volumes. The author discusses in detail his reconstruction of this family, covering the reasoning and logic of his conclusions.

(52) *Hughes Family of Cape May County, New Jersey 1650-1950. A Genealogy of descendants of Humphrey Hughes of Long Island 1650 and later of Cape May County, New Jersey*. Privately printed (1950) for Raymond Finley Hughes, 3561 Monteith Ave., Cincinnati, 8, OH. Copies Cape May County Library and Cape May County Historical Society.

(53) *Mayflower Pilgrim Descendants In Cape May County New A Record of the Pilgrim Descendants who early in its History in Cape May County, and some of their children throughout the States of the Union at the present time.* By Rev. Paul Sturtevant LL., B., Ph.D. Originally published Cape May, New Jersey, 1921. Reprinted Genealogical Publishing Co., Inc. Baltimore, 1977.

(54) *Encyclopedia of American Quaker Genealogy*, Vol., III, New Fork. William Wade Hinshaw. Thomas Worth Marshall, Editor and Compiler. Originally published: Ann Arbor, Michigan, 1940. Reprinted Genealogical Publishing Co., Inc., Baltimore, 1969, 1991.

(55) *Early Church Records of Atlantic & Cape May Counties, New Jersey*. By Barbara Epler Wright. Westminster, Maryland: Family Line Publications, 1995.

(56) *Early Church Records of Salem County, New Jersey*. By Charlotte D. Meldrum. Westminster, Maryland: Family Line Publications, 1996.

(57) *Early Church Records of Gloucester County, New Jersey*. By Charlotte D. Meldrum and John Pitts Launey. Westminster, Maryland: Family Line Publications, 1996.

(58) *Cumberland County (New Jersey) Marriages*. Compiled by H. Stanley Craig. Published by author, Merchantville, NJ, 1932. Reprinted by Gloucester County Historcial Society, 1981.

(59) *Cumberland County New Jersey Genealogical Data. Records Pertaining to Persons Residing in Cumberland County Prior to 1800*. Compiled by H. Stanley Craig. Published by author, Merchantville, NJ, 1930s. Reprinted by Gloucester County Historcial Society, 1981.

(60) *History And Genealogy Of Fenwick's Colony*. By Thomas Shrouds. Originally published Bridgetown, NJ, 1876. Reprinted by Genealogical Publishing Co., Inc., Baltimore, 1976.

(61) *The Records of the Court of Sessions of Suffolk County in the Province of New York,* 1670-1 688. By Thomas W. Cooper. Bowie, MD: Heritage Books, Inc., 1993.

(62) *Patents and Deeds and Other Early Records of New Jersey, 1664-1703.* Edited by William Nelson. The Patterson New Jersey Press Printing and Publishing Co., 1899.

(63) *New Jersey Biographical and Genealogical Notes. From the volumes of the New Jersey Archives with additions and supplements.* William Nelson. Originally published as *Collections of the New Jersey Historical Society*, Volume IX, Newark, 1916. Reprinted by Genealogical Publishing Co., Inc. Baltimore, 1973.

(64) *The History of Cape May County, New Jersey, From The Aboriginal Times to The Present Day ...* Lewis T. Stevens. Cape May City, NJ, 1897.

ABBREVIATIONS USED TO IDENTIFY SOURCES

Baptists- Records of First Baptist Church, Cape May Court House.

Baptist Burials - Most of this information was taken from "The Historic Baptist Burial Yard - Cape May Court House, New Jersey," *The Cape May County Magazine of History and Genealogy*, p. 63. June 1956. By M. Catharine Stauffer. Some information not found in this article was taken directly from the tombstones. "First Baptist Cemetery," founded in 1766, located on Church Street, Cape May Court House.

Book of Mortgages A. See "Genealogical Abstracts From Early Cape May .County Deeds," *The Cape May County Magazine of History and Genealogy.* (Following last entries of deeds) By William Evans Price.

CMDB - Cape May County Deed Book.

Cold Spring Cemetery - Based on inscriptions at the cemetery. Many are difficult to read and oft times misread. Often discrepancies occur with the numbers 3 and 5; and 1 and 4.

Co. Clerk Reds-Book A - County Clerk Records, Book A.

Cumberland Wills - Wills of Cumberland County.

Deeds - "Genealogical Abstracts From Early Cape May County Deeds," *The Cape May County Magazine of History and Genealogy*, p. 229. By William Evans Price.

EVMM - Evesham Monthly Meeting records. The Evesham Monthly Meeting was established in 1760 out of Haddonfield Monthly Meeting.

First Official Rcds - "First Official Records of Cape May County," The Cape May County Magazine of History and Genealogy, p. 316.

First Public Rcds - "First Public Records of Cape May County," The Cape May County Magazine of History and Genealogy, p. 269. June 1937.

GEMM - Great Eggharbor Monthly Meeting. This monthly meeting of the Society of Friends (Quakers) was established in 1726 by Salem Quarterly Meeting to include the meetings at Great Egg Harbor and Cape May. The records are available at Friends Historical Society, Swarthmore College, Swarthmore, Pennsylvania.

Genealogies of New Jersey Families - *Genealogies of New Jersey Families*, published by Genealogical Publishing Co., Inc., Baltimore, 1966. Excerpts from *Genealogical Magazine of New Jersey* from the first issue through the end of Volume 65.

Hildreth Bible - taken from "Records of The Hildreth Family," *The Cape May County Magazine of History and Genealogy*, p. 82. By Alice G. Stathem (Mrs. Paul Woodson Stathem). These are records copied on 26 March 1956 by Alice G. Stathem from the Bible then owned by Paul Woodson Stathem.

History of Fenwick's Colony - *History And Genealogy Of Fenwick's Colony*. By Thomas Shrouds.

Hughes - *Hughes Family of Cape May County, New Jersey 1650-1950. A Genealogy of descendants of Humphrey Hughes of Long Island 1650 and later of Cape May County, New Jersey.* Raymond Finley Hughes

Learning Diaries - Information taken from "Diaries of Aaron Leaming," *The Cape May County Magazine of History and Genealogy*, p. 69. June 1932. Copied by Lewis T. Stevens. [The diary of Aaron Leaming is held by the Historical Museum of Cape May County.]

LEMM - Little Egg Harbor Monthly Meeting records.

Ltrs&Inv A(Rev) - Letters and Inventories (reverse of book). Records held by the Cape May County Surrogate Court, 9 North Main St., Cape May Court House.

MLNJ - Marriage Licenses from *New Jersey Archives* (dates given by month-day-year).

Nelson - William Nelson in *New Jersey Biographical and Genealogical Notes*.

NJCW - New Jersey Wills. As published in the *New Jersey Archives* series. The original wills or original recorded wills should be consulted when possible.

NYMM - New York Monthly Meeting records.

Old Cohansey Bur. Ground - Old Cohansey Burying Ground. Held in collection of Vineland Historical and Antiquarian Society.

Orphans Courts minutes, loose papers - Held by the Cape May County Surrogate Court.

Parsons Account Bk - Excerpts from "The Account Book of John Parsons, With Notes," *The Cape May County Magazine of History and Genealogy*, p. 166. June 1942. By Norman Harvey Vanaman.

Phila ... Ledger - *Philadelphia & Great Egg Harbor Journal & Ledger* of 28 Oct 1782 as reprinted *Genealogies of New Jersey Families*, published by Genealogical Publishing Co. (1996), Vol. 1, p. 790.

Pierson Article - Based on the article, "The Pierson Family," *The Cape May County Magazine of History and Genealogy,* p. 6. June 1955. By Margaret Irwin McVickar.

P1MM - Pilesgrove Monthly Meeting records. This monthly meeting was established in 1794. Eventually the name of Woodstown Monthly Meeting was adopted.

SAMM - Salem Monthly Meeting records. The Quakers at Salem formed a meeting for worship in 1676 coincident with the establishment of a monthly meeting.

The Sayre Family - Banta. Cited as a Genealogy in H. Stanley Craig, *Cumberland County (New Jersey) Marriages,* p. 248.

Sheppard Papers - Charles E. Sheppard Papers. A collection of genealogies of Cumberland County, held by the Vineland Historical and Antiquarian Society.

Stevens - *The History of Cape May County, New Jersey, From The Aboriginal Times to The Present Day* ... Lewis T. Stevens.

BADCOCK

First Generation

1. JOSEPH BADCOCK registered his ear mark on 18 April 1694. The same mark was registered to his grandson Joseph in 1760.{First Public Rcds}

On 26 June 1694 Joseph Badcock, cordwainer, gave power of attorney to John Crafford, "provided ye sd. badock should deceace, or not come a gaine to Cape May, then this my attorney is to sell all that ... " the said Badcok ownes, "and to pay for my land and that to reserve for my eldest son."{First Public Rcds}

John Townsend was appointed to take charge of the real and personal estate of Joseph Badcock for the benefit of Ester Badcock, Joseph Badcock having "absented this Countey with a dysine not to return a gaine but hass left ye sd. Ester Badcock in a distressed condition and in danger of being a charge to ye county." 18 Dec 1694. Recorded 15 March 1694/5.{First Official Rcds}

Letters of administration were granted to John Townsend, exec. to and for Easter Badcock, dec. 17 March 1696.{First Official Rcds}

Joseph Badcock of Cape May, shoemaker, d. leaving a will dated 30 Aug 1709, proved 25 Sep 1710. Mentioned were wife Mary and children: George, Jacob, Joseph, Retorn, Mary, Elizabeth, Sarah. Son Jacob to be apprenticed to John Dole until of age. The execs. were Rem Garison and Timothy Brandreth. The will was witnessed by Thomas Gandy, Silvanus Townsend and Rem Gerretson. On 4 March 1709/10 the personal estate was inventoried by John Townsend and William Goldin, appraised by Richard Townsend and Joseph Ludlow.{NJCW 2:75}

Joseph Badcock was the father of the following children: GEORGE; JACOB; JOSEPH; RETORN; MARY; ELIZABETH; SARAH[1].

Second Generation

2. JACOB BADCOCK of Gloucester Co., probable son of Joseph (1) Badcock, husbandman, d. leaving a will dated 30 Oct 1716, proved 15 Dec 1716. Legatees included William Hunt, aunt Mary Dolle, Tobias Holloway, brother-in-law John Cock, exec. The will was witnessed by Frances Collins and Samuel Shivers.{NJCW 2:75} An inventory was filed (£37.11.9} on 15 Dec 176 by George Hamuck and Robrd. Champion. An

---

1 Gloucester County Court Records show the marriage of Nehemiah Nicholson of Great Eggharbour, Gloucester Co., Gent., and Sarah Badcock of same, spinster, dated 1 June 1739.

account was filed on 14 Dec 1717 by exec. John Cock, showing payments to John Dole, John Walker, Elin Cox, Richard Townsend, Thomas Chakley, John Wright, Sarah Michell, Ezeakell Sidells and John Keyn.

3. JOSEPH BADCOCK, of Cape May Co., yeoman, probable son of Joseph (1) Badcock, d. leaving a will dated 2 Sep 1753, proved 3 June 1755. Mentioned were wife Mary and children: Joseph, Rachel, Hannah, Naomi, Sarah and Mary. Execs. were wife and Jeremiah Hand. The will was witnessed by William Evans, Daniel Gerretsen and Job Garretson.{NJCW 8:172} On 28 June 1755 an inventory of the estate was filed by Richard Smith and Jacob Spicer. An account of the estate was made 5 April 1759 by execs. who had increased the value of the estate by £40 for land sold and £18 for sundries.

Mary Badcock of Cape May Co., d. leaving a will dated 1 Oct 1765 and proved 11 April 1778. Mentioned were son, Joseph Badcock and daus.: Hannah Evins and Sarah Smith; granddau. Vialete Smith; grandsons: Joseph Smith; Jeremiah Leaming. Said Joseph Smith and Jeremiah Leaming were under 21. Execs. were son Joseph Badcock and son-in-law, John Evins. The will was witnessed by Joseph Corson, Isaac Baner and Lydia Baner. On 11 April 1778 it was recorded that both execs. were dead; Jeremiah Smith of Gloucester Co. was appointed admin. with will annexed. Fellowbondsman: Joseph Edwards of Cape May Co. Witnessed by Joseph Corson and Isaac Baner. On 3 April 1778 an inventory was made by Joseph Corson and Joseph Edwards.{NJCW 22:44}

Joseph Badcock was the father of the following children: JOSEPH; RACHEL; HANNAH, m. John Evins; NAOMI; SARAH, m. (N) Smith; MARY.

4. RETURN BADCOCK, son of Joseph (1) Badcock, m. Abigail Cresse by license dated 22 April 1733.{MLNJ}

Return Badcock of Great Egg Harbor, Gloucester Co., d. leaving a will dated 13 April 1781. Mentioned were wife Abigail; children: John, David, Jonathan, Abigail Scull; grandchildren, Return and Judith, children of Gideon and Rebecah his wife and their half-brother Gideon Badcock; other grandchildren: John Nicelson and Marget his sister, Return Brookfield and his sister Sarah.{CWNJ Lib. 31:25}

Return was father of the following children: JOHN; DAVID; JONATHAN; ABIGAIL, m. (N) Scull; GIDEON, m. 1st Rebecah and m. 2nd Margaret (N).

5. JOSEPH BADCOCK of Cape May Co., probable son of Joseph (3)

Badcock, d. prior to 27 March 1777 when Lydia Badcock, widow of Joseph, was appointed admx. Fellowbondsman: Joseph Edwards, both of said county. Witness: James Godfrey. On 18 March 1777 an inventory was made by James Godfrey and Joseph Edwards.

Lydia Badcock m. Christopher Smith 25 Oct 1774.{Baptists} Badcock; their marriage license was dated 24 Oct 1774.{MLNJ}

6. JOHN BADCOCK, probable son of Return (3) Badcock, had the following children: SARAH, b. 13th day, 2nd mo., 1751; MILLISENT, b. 28th day, 7th mo., 1752; JOHN, b. 29th day, 9th mo., 1754; REBECKAH, b. 9th day, 12th mo., 1756.{GEMM}

7. GIDEON BADCOCK, son of Return (4) Badcock, m. 1st, Rebecca Townsend by license dated 23 Aug 1768 in Gloucester Co.{MLNJ} and m. 2nd, Margaret (N).

Gideon Badcock of Great Egg Harbor, Gent., d. leaving a will dated 19 Nov 1773, proved 11 Jan 1774. The estate was to be sold and wife Margaret was to have 1/3. The other 2/3 to be divided between son and dau. which are born and the other child that is to be born. Exec. was father Return Badcock. The will was witnessed by Andrew Blackman, Andrew Blackman, Jr. and Catharine Bright. On 12 Dec 1773 an inventory was filed (£292.0.3 1/2) by Gideon Scull, Andrew Blackman, Jr. and John Scull.{NJCW 15:497, 17:49}

By his 1st wife, Rebecca, he had children: RETURN; JUDITH.

By his 2nd wife, Margaret, he had a son GIDEON.

8. JOHN BADCOCK, probable son of John (6) Badcock, m. Abiah Badcock, 16 Nov 1778.{MLNJ}

9. RACHEL BADCOCK, probable dau. of Joseph (2) Badcock, m. Jacob Richards, by marriage license issued 26 Sep 1754.{MLNJ}

10. MARY BADCOCK, probably dau. of Joseph (3) Badcock, m. Peter Corson by license dated 15 Jan 1761.{MLNJ}

BANCROFT

Relationships have not been established.

THOMAS BANCROFT d. ca. Feb 1694/5. A jury was impaneled

concerning the death of Thomas Bancroft. They found on ca. 20 Feb 1694/5 that said Bancroft being sick and weak, went forth of the house where he was and went to the waterside, put of[f] his clothes, went into the sea and was drowned, accidental or purposely, they do not understand.{First Public Rcds}

THOMAS BANCROFT and Elizabeth Mathews m. by Justice of the Peace, Cape May Co., 6 April 1715. Witnesses: John Paige, Richard Downes, John Taylor, John Buck, John Hughes, Mary Mathews, John Cresse, Zelophead Hand, William Segrave. Entered 30 May 1715.{First Official Rcds}

In the Diaries of Aaron Leaming, he mentioned the death of Thomas Bancroft of pleurisie on 13 March 1761. On 25 June 1761 John Bancraft was appointed admin. of the estate of Thomas Bancroft. Fellowbondsman: John Eldredge. Witnesses: Elizabeth Stillwell and Elijah Hughes. On 25 June 1761 an inventory was made (£69.9.3} by John Eldredge and Isaac Newton.{NJCW 11:73}

DAVID BANCROFT, brother of Ephraim, m. Abigail Stites* by license dated 6 Nov 1752.{MLNJ} She was the sister of Richard Stites* (see will below).

David Bancraft of Cape May Co., blacksmith, d. leaving a will dated 19 March 1761, proved 25 June 1761. Mentioned were wife Abigail; eldest son David to whom was devised his house and land when David was age 21, he to pay his brother Samuel, £10. The rest of the estate was to be sold and used for son Samuel Bancraft and Margaret Bancraft; they to have principal, the son when 21 and dau. when 18. To son David, the shop and tools but brother Ephraim to have the use of them until David was 21 and Ephraim to pay 40 shillings each year to "my widow Abigail, and to take my son David at age 16 years and teach him the smith trade." ... "Whereas I have left an account against my father's estate, and I give them 10 years before it is paid." Execs. were brother-in-law, Richard Stites and wife Abigail. The will was witnessed by Aaron Eldredge, Mary Simpkins and Frances Taylor. The inventory (£83.3.3) was made on 25 April 1761 by John Eldredge and Isaac Newton.{NJCW 11:76}

David was the father of the following children: DAVID; SAMUEL, d. by 10 Feb 1794 when Charles Allen was appointed admin. {NJCW 35:109, File 599E}; MARGARET.

JOHN BANCROFT d. prior to 11 April 1768 when Phebe Bancraft, relict of said John, was appointed admx. Fellowbondsmen: John Eldredge and

John Newton, both of said county. Witnesses: Nathan Church and Seth Whilldin. On 6 April 1768 an inventory was made of the estate (£107.6.8) by John Eldredge and John Newton.{NJCW 13:332}

SAMUEL BANCROFT of Cape May Co., d. leaving a will dated 4 July 1759, proved 25 June 1761. (His death was mentioned in the Leaming diary as occurring in 1760.) Mentioned were wife Margrate, son David to whom was devised land on east side of the Kings road; sons David and Ephraim; daus. Sarah Buck, Phebe Bancraft, Elizabeth Reeves and Johannah Bancraft; grandson John Newton. The execs were wife and son Ephraim. The will was witnessed by Benjamin Laughton, Elizabeth Stillwell and John Leek. On 9 Nov 1760 an inventory (£55.10.0) was made by Isaac Newton and John Eldredge.{NJCW 11:69}

Samuel was the father of the following children: DAVID; EPHRAIM; SARAH, m. (N) Buck[2]; PHEBE; ELIZABETH, m. (N) Reeves; JOHANNAH.

EPHRAIM BANCROFT m. Elizabeth Crowell by license dated 8 June 1763.{MLNJ}

ELISHA BANCROFT m. Susannah Hughes, by license dated 7 April 1773.{MLNJ}

MARTHA BANCROFT m. Silas Church by license dated 1 Aug 1770. {MLNJ}

BENNETT

See "Some of the Descendants of Abraham Bennett, Member of Committee of Safety, Captain of the Randolph, Used as a Privateer in the Revolution," *The Cape May County Magazine of History and Genealogy*, p. 108. June 1933. Genealogy Notes, by Rev. Paul Sturtevant Howe. This article traces some lines into the late 1800s. The following entries are based on this article.

1. ABRAHAM BENNETT was b. ca. 1740, d. 1804, leaving a will dated 11 June 1804; m. by license of 6 Nov 1759, Levice Stevens{MLNJ}, who

2 Probably Thomas Buck. See The Buck Family.

was b. 1741 and d. 19 March 1814, bur. Cold Spring Cemetery. They were parents of the following children: AARON, b. 11 Sep 1764, d. 8 Aug 1840; possibly JUDITH, who according to Hughes[3] was b. 1774, d. 1 June 1858, dau. of Capt. Abraham and Louisa (Stevens) Bennett and m. Joseph Buck Hughes.*

2. AARON BENNETT, son of Abraham (1) and Louisa (Stevens) Bennett, b. 10 Sep 1764, d. 8 Aug 1840, m. by license of 6 Nov 1759, Mary (N) who was b. 23 Dec 1769, d. 27 Jan 1820{Cold Spring Cemetery}; they were the parents of the following children: SOPHIA, b. 10 Jan 1792, m. Aaron Schellinger{Sheppard Papers} and ABRAHAM, b. 17 Feb 1795, d. 18 Jan 1852, m. Louisa (N) (d. 19 March 1814, age 73.{Cold Spring Cemtery}

3. JUDITH BENNETT, dau. of Capt. Abraham (1) and Louisa (Stevens) Bennett, b. 1774, d. 1 June 1858, m. 1793, Joseph Buck (b. 10 Nov 1772, d. 13 March 1813).

Unplaced

WILLIAM BENNET m. Hannah Hand by license dated 8 Sep 1752.{MLNJ}

FULKIT BENNET m. Phebe Jenkins 31 March 1771.{Baptists}

BILLINGS

Joshua Smith & CHARITY BILLINGS m. 4 Dec 1770.{Baptists}
A marriage license was issued to Charity BILLINGS and Joshua Smith on 3 Dec 1770.{MLNJ}

JUDITH BILLINGS m. Elihu Smith 20 Sep 1774.{Baptists}

A marriage license was issued to TEMPERANCE BILLINGS and Daniel Johnson on 5 March 1765.{MLNJ}

---

3 See *Hughes Family of Cape May County* by Raymond Finley Hughes.

A marriage license was issued to WILLIAM BILLINGS and Charity Ingram, 19 Feb 1736.{MLNJ}

A marriage license was issued to WILLIAM BILLINGS and Rhoda Hand, 20 Feb 1763.{MLNJ}

WILLIAM BILLINGS d. prior to 8 July 1789 when Joshua Billings was appointed admin. of his estate. Witnesses: Sarah Hand and Betsy Griffing. On 19 Oct 1789 an inventory was filed (£151.14.9) by Philip Hand and Benjamin Stites.{NJCW 31:370}

BISHOP

See "The Goff and Bishop Families," *The Cape May County Magazine of History and Genealogy*, p. 45. June 1964. By Dr. Roy Hand. According to Dr. Hand,

1. RICHARD BISHOP was living in Salem, Massachusetts in 1635.

2. NATHANIEL BISHOP, son of Richard (1), settled in the Cohansey District of Salem Co. (now Cumberland) before 1710.

3. SAMUEL BISHOP, son of Nathaniel (2) and Sarah Bishop, m. Mary (N) and had children: JOHN, bapt. 31 Jan 1742; NAOMI, bapt. 15 May 1743; MARY, bapt. 12 Aug 1744; SARAH, b. 21 Feb 1744, bapt. 27 April 1746, d. 3 Aug 1831, m. 13 July 1766, John Goff (b. 22 April 1743, d. 15 Oct 1809); SAMUEL, bapt. 4 Sep 1748.{The children were baptized in the Presbyterian congregation at Pilesgrove. See these records.}

4. SAMUEL BISHOP, son of Samuel (3) and Mary Bishop, moved to Cape May Co., before 1774. He m. Sarah (N) and had the following children: SAMUEL, m. Lydia Crandle; SOSTHEMUS.

Samuel Bishop of Cape May Co. d. prior to 26 May 1778 when Sarah Bishop was appointed admx. Fellowbondsman: Reuben Ludlam, both of said county. On 26 May 1778 an inventory was made by Hance Peterson and Thomas Campbell.{NJCW 22:41}

5. JOHN BISHOP, son of Samuel (3) and Mary Bishop, m. Rachel (N)

and had the following children: MARY; NAOMI, b. 6 Jan 1775, d. 14 Sep 1841, m. Robert Wilson (b. 6 June 1776, d. 10 May 1849) 14 Nov 1798, son of William and Isabella Wilson of County Antrim, Ireland; SARAH, b. 26 Jan 1777, d. 18 May 1857, m. Daniel Goff* (b. 16 Feb 1778), 16 Dec 1798; RACHEL, m. John Dennis, 19 Sep 1798; GIDEON, b. 27 Jan 1783, d. before 1837, m. Mary McCarty (b. 1786), 1814; SAMUEL, b. 20 Jan 1785, d. 25 March 1837, m. Sarah Goff (b. 1 July 1787, d. 14 April 1808) and m. 2nd Phebe Steelman (b. Oct 1792, d. 26 May 1871).

6. NAOMI BISHOP, dau. of John (5) and Rachel Bishop, m. Robert Wilson by license dated 14 Nov 1798.{Co. Clerk Rcds - Book A}

7. SARAH BISHOP, dau. of John (5) and Rachel Bishop, m. Daniel Goff by 26 Dec 1798.{Co. Clerk Rcds - Book A}

Unplaced

RACHEL BISHOP, b. 1769, d. 30 Nov 1839.{Cold Spring Cemetery}

BRANDRETH

Based partially on the article in *The Cape May County Magazine of History and Genealogy*, p. 191, June 1943, titled, "Timothy Brandreth," by H. Clifford Campion, Jr. For more details and proof, see this article.

According to Mr. Campion,

1. TIMOTHY BRANDRETH, cordwainer, was living in Burlington Co., NJ, in March 1683/4 when his name was recorded in the court records as witness to the marriage of Peter Jennings and the widow Ann Nott. His name also appears in 1685 when he entered his ear mark for cattle. His name appears in Cape May County in July 1691. He was Sheriff of the county on 20 March 1693/4, later serving as clerk of the court, 1695, 1696, 1697 and 1699 - succeeding George Taylor.

He m. 1st Catherine Rodman (bapt. 2 May 1665 in Christ Church Parish, Barbados, d. ca. 1690), dau. of John Rodman by his wife Anna.[4] Her name (single) appears in the Friends Meeting records of Newport, R.I., as witness to the marriage of her older brother Dr. Thomas Rodman in 1682. Timothy and Catherine Brandreth had one child: MARY, m. 1709, Jonathan Huestis [Hewstis] of Westchester Co.{NYMM} by whom she had a dau. Katherine who probably m. John Green ca. 1st mo., 1744/5 and a son Joseph who probably m. ca. 11th mo., 1748, Sarah Lord, dau. of Samuel and Mary Lord.{HAMM minutes, 2nd intentions}

Timothy Brandreth m. 2nd, after his move to Cape May Co., Sarah, eldest dau. of William Golding by his first wife Margaret Lake, who was born according to the Gravesend, Long Island Town Records, 14th day of 12th month 1676/7. Her father William Golding having been an early whaler in Cape May Co. evidently settled there by 1693 when he purchased his first land. Sarah, d. ca. 1701.

Timothy and Sarah Brandreth were the parents of the following children: SARAH, b. ca. 1695, m. William Middleton by whom she had a son Timothy who m. Elizabeth Barton and a dau. Elizabeth who m. Edward Barton[5]; DANIEL, m. Catharine (N); MARGARET, probably m. her foster brother Benjamin Shaw, son of Edward and Sarah (Holmes) Shaw; PENELOPE, d. 1759, may have been the wife of Benjamin Johnson* of Cape May who d. in 1759 leaving a will.

Timothy Brandreth m. 3rd ca. 1706, Sarah Shaw, widow of Edward Shaw (d. 1705), and dau. of Obediah and Elizabeth (Cook) Holmes of Salem Co. Timothy and Sarah were the parents of the following children: TIMOTHY, m. Mary (N), may have moved to Mays Landing in Gloucester Co.; ELIZABETH.

Timothy Brandreth of Cape May d. leaving a will dated 3 July 1714, proved 10 May 1715. Mentioned were wife Sarah and children: Timothy, minor, Mary Hughestis (Huestis), Sarah Middleton, Daniel, Margrate, Penelopey and Elizabeth Brandreth. Sons-in-law (stepsons):

---

4 See the will of John Rodman dated 7th month 1686 in which mentions his dau. Catharine Brandreth.

5 On 13th da, 8th mo, 1746 it was announced in Haddonfield Monthly Meeting that Timothy Middletown, son of William and Sarah (Brandreth) Middleton and Elizabeth Barton continued their intentions of marriage. {Haddonfield Monthly Meeting}

Benjamin Shaw and Obadiah Shaw. 400 a. bought of John Lad on Middle Creek of Great Egg Harbour, dwelling house and land between Joseph Ludlow and Richard Townsend. The execs. were John Page, Joseph Ludlow and Daniel Wells. The will was witnesses by John, Robert and Mary Townsend. On 15 Feb 1716/18 an inventory of the estate was made by Thomas Leamying and Nathaniel Jenkins.{NJCW: 2:25 and 89}

2. MARY BRANDRETH, dau. of Timothy (1) and Catherine Brandreth, m. 1709, at the Flushing Meeting, Jonathan Huestis of Westchester Co. She and her husband, then of Newport, R.I., conveyed land in 1710 to her uncle Dr. Thomas Rodman of Newport, R.I. for 4 1/4 acres in the Barbados which she inherited from her mother Catharine (Rodman) Brandreth as her only child, and which her mother received by the Will of her father John Rodman. In exchange for this her uncle Dr. Thomas Rodman conveyed to her 500 acres in Evesham Township, Burlington Co., where she moved and resided for the remainder of her life.

3. SARAH BRANDRETH, dau. of Timothy (1) and Sarah Brandreth, b. ca. 1695, m. William Middleton of Cape May and later Evesham Township, Burlington Co. Sarah m. 2nd John Shipton of Gloucester Co.

4. DANIEL BRANDRETH, son of Timothy (1) and Sarah Brandreth, m. Catharine (N); moved from Cape May Co. to Lower Penns Neck, Salem Co. ca. 1738.

On 5th day, 12th mo., 1738/9 Daniel Brandreth, requested a certificate for himself and wife to remove to within the compass of another meeting.{GEMM} On 3rd day, 7th mo., 1739 he and his wife were received into Salem Monthly Meeting.{SAMM} Their dau. Elizabeth m. David Townsend of Cape May Co. on 2nd day, 7th mo., 1760.{SAMM}

5. On 26th day, 5th mo., 1708 TIMOTHY BRANDRITH, probably son of Timothy (1) Brandreth, produced an acknowledgment condemning his unbecoming behavior before the Salem Monthly Meeting.{Salem Monthly Meeting}

Unplaced

On 7th day, 2nd mo., 1735, the marriage of Richard Townsend, Jr., and SARAH BRANDRATH, was reported orderly accomplished.{GEMM}

TIMOTHY BRANDRETH m. Elizabeth Hughes by license dated 11 Dec 1776.{MLNJ}

BRIGGS

1. JAMES BRIGGS m. Margery Taylor, dau. of John Taylor. They were m. by Thomas Hand, Justice, 22 March 1713. Their children: MARY, b. 19 Aug 1715; ELIZABETH, b. 3 July 1717; KESIAH, b. 30 Aug 1719; MARTHA, b. 10 Aug 1721; SARAH, b 31 May 1724.{First Official Rcds}

James Briggs and wife Margery are shown in the land records of 1724.{Deeds B:194}

2. ELIZABETH BRIGGS, probable dau. of James (1) Briggs, m. Benjamin Hollden* by license dated 18 Dec 1739.{MLNJ}

Unplaced

JOHN BRIGS of Cape May, yeoman, d. leaving a will dated 4 Dec 1690, proved 14 March 1690/1. Mentioned were wife Elizabeth, sole heiress and extx. The will was witnessed by Joseph Houldin, Henry Gray, Sarah Marsh and George Taylor.{NJCW: Burlington Records:16}

BUCK

1. JOHN BUCK of Cape May, mariner, d. of small pox, leaving a will dated 4 Nov 1716. Mentioned were wife Annie and children: Joseph, John, Thomas, Mary. The exec. was John Taylor with Jonathan Swain and Christopher Church as overseers. The estate was inventoried on 22 Nov 1716 by Christopher Church and Nathaniel Jenkins.{NJCW} John Taylor, admin of John Buck, dec. by consent of Jonathan Swaine and Mr. Christofor Church, trustees, agreed with Jeremiah Hand that he should have £4.10 proclamation money for keeping Mary Buck, dau. of John Buck, one year after her father's death.{First Public Rcds} In the deed book is shown John Buck, wife Anna in 1715; also Jacob Dayton, father-in-law of Richard Downs.{Deeds B:183}

John was the father of the following children: JOSEPH; JOHN;THOMAS; MARY.

2. JOSEPH BUCK of Cape May Co., probable son of John (1) Buck, d. leaving a will dated 17 July 1734, proved 9 Aug 1734. Mentioned were wife Lydia, extx. and brothers: Thomas and John Buck. The will was witnessed by William Johnson, Frs. Taylor, Thomas Stonebanks.{NJCW 3:443} The estate was inventoried on 20 July 1734, containing cattle, horses, sheep and swine. It was appraised by Ebenezer Swaine and William Johnson.{NJCW}

Lydia Buck m. Annanias Osborne* by license dated 9 June 1738.{MLNJ}

3. JOHN BUCK, possible son of John (1) Buck, had sons, William and Andrew, as mentioned in deeds dated 1794.{Deeds E: 295} A marriage license was issued to John Buck and Elizabeth Wheaton, 25 Jan 1766.{MLNJ}

4. MARY BUCK, probable dau. of John (1) Buck, m. Hope Willets* (Burlington Co.) by license dated 20 June 1730.{MLNJ}

5. THOMAS BUCK of Cape May Co., yeoman, probable son of John (1) Buck, d. leaving a will dated 23 Nov 1768, proved 17 Dec 1772. Mentioned was son Thomas Buck to whom was devised land where testator lived in the Lower Precinct, at Coldspring, bounded by Aaron Eldredge on the west and Seth Whilldin on the east, and other lands, provided he pay all debts; otherwise to grandson, Swain Buck. To his children: Marcy Taylor, Abigail Eldredge, Elihu, Mary, Sarah, Seth, Esther, Elizabeth and William Buck, he left 5 shillings each. Grandchildren Armelia and Rhoda Buck were to receive 5 shillings each. Wife Sarah, 1/3 of land during her life. Execs. were wife and son Thomas Buck. The will was witnessed by Nathaniel Foster, Jr., Aaron Eldredge and Elizabeth Mills. On 17 Dec 1772 an inventory was made by Aaron Eldredge and Daniel Crowell.{NJCW 16:48}

Thomas was the father of the following children: THOMAS; MARCY, m. John Taylor (marriage license dated 29 Dec 1759); Abigail, m. (N) Eldredge; ELIHU; MARY; SARAH; SETH; ESTHER; ELIZABETH; WILLIAM.

6. JOSEPH BUCK of Cape May Co., son of Thomas (5) Buck[6], d. leaving a will dated 27 May 1768, proved 5 July 1768. Mentioned were wife Lydia; daus.: Judath and Theody; sons: Swain and Lamuel. Execs. were wife Lydia and Levi Eldredge. The will was witnessed by Daniel Mulford, Elizabeth Reeves and Nathaniel Foster. The inventory (£278.8.8) was filed on 5 Nov 1764 by James Whilldin and Henry Hand.{NJCW 13:527}

7. THOMAS BUCK, son of Thomas (5) Buck, d. 2 Feb 1790, age 46.{Cold Spring Cemetery} He m. Judith Edmunds by license dated 9 Jan 1771.{MLNJ} AARON, son of Thomas and Judith Buck, d. 12 Feb 1790, age 16 years, 10 months.{Cold Spring Cemtery}

On 26 Jan 1791 Ellis Hughes was appointed admin. of his estate. Fellowbondsman: Jeremiah Edmunds of Cape May Co. Witnesses: Jeremiah Eldredge and Sarah Hand.{NJCW 32:301}. On 11 June an inventory was filed (£270.5.6) by Jeremiah Eldredge and Ebenezer Newton.{NJCW File 8555-8558L}

UNPLACED

ABIGAIL BUCK m. Samuel Crowell by license dated 29 Dec 1763.{MLNJ}

ENOS BUCK m. Elizabeth Crawford by license dated 3 May 1773.{MLNJ}

FREDERICK BUCK, d. 2 Sep 1828, age 68 years, 5 mos.{Cold Spring Cemetery} He probably m. Tabitha (N), who d. 21 May 1836, age 68 years, 5 mos. who is buried next to him.{Cold Spring Cemetery}

IRA BUCK m. Sarah Hand by license dated 14 Jan 1760.{MLNJ}

JOSEPH BUCK m. Elizabeth Eldridge by license dated 10 July 1759.{MLNJ}

LIDIA BUCK m. Azariah Hewet* by license dated 12 June 1775.{MLNJ}

MARY BUCK m. John Hand by license dated 28 July 1769.{MLNJ}

---

6 Noting that Swain Buck was mentioned as grandson in the will of Thomas (5) and was mentioned as son in the will of Joseph (6).

CARMAN (CARMEN)

See "Caleb Carmen (Whaler, Millwright and Miller) (Builder of the first Mill in Cape May County)," *The Cape May County Magazine of History and Genealogy*, p. 283. June 1944. By H. Clifford Campion, Jr. See this article for more details on the early years of this family. According to Mr. Campion,

1. CALEB CARMEN, son of John and Florence Carmen, was b. 1st day, 1st month (March) 1639.[7] His father and Rev. Robert Fordam, bought from the Indians a large tract on Long Island, the patent granted on 16 Nov 1644. The town of Hempstead was settled on the tract. His father d. 1653 and his widowed mother m. John Hicks. Caleb Carmen and his older brother John and his brother-in-law, Benjamin Coe, husband of Abigail Carmen, on 7 April 1661, petitioned the government at New Amsterdam that John Hicks, who m. their mother, be made accountable for her estate.

On 25 March 1688 the province gave a 7-year lease to Caleb Carmen for 1200 acres along Cold Spring Creek near Cape May with the right to purchase.

Caleb Carman, Sr., d. leaving a nuncupative will dated 5 Aug 1693. Affidavits of John Gervis and Caleb Carman, stating he left all to his wife Elizabeth; sons were mentioned. The estate was inventoried 7 July 1693 by Shamgar Hand and Jacob Dayton. Letter of administration granted to his widow Elizabeth on 16 Aug 1693.{NJCW}

Caleb Carman m. Elizabeth (N). An indenture was made on 11 April 1694, between Caleb Carman and his wife Elizabeth Carman, and Jacob Spicer. For £25 Carman and wife agreed to sell to Spicer all their right to their house and lot in the town of Portsmouth in Cape May Co.{First Official Rcds:324}

Elizabeth, widow of Caleb Carman, was deceased in 1700.{Deeds B:34}

According to Campion,

Caleb was the father of the following children: JOHN, b. 1663, d. 1696, m. 1683/4, Elizabeth Ludlam; JOSHUA,[8] b. 1665, m.

---

7 According to Rev. John Elliott's records of the Roxbury Church.

8 Mentioned in Deeds B:23.

Lueo (N)[9] prior to 1701; ELIZABETH, b. ca. 1667, d. before 1742, m. 1st Jonathan Forman ca. 1683, m. 2nd John Parsons ca. 1700; ROBERT (said to be a son in some accounts); CALEB, m. Elizabeth (N) before 1694; ABIGAIL, m. 1st Jonathan Pine, m. 2nd probably William Sharwood[10]; JAMES,[11] b. 1677, d. 28 Oct 1756, m. 1st Margaret Duwys, m. 2nd Sara Frazier; DANIEL, living in 1700; EPHRIAM, living in 1723.[12]

2. JOHN CARMAN, son of Caleb (1) Carman, d. before 23 April 1696. On that date an inventory of the estate of John Carman was recorded as appraised by Samll. Mathews, Jonathan Forman and Timothy Brandreth.{First Official Rcds:332} Letters of administration were granted to Elisabeth Carman, widow and relict of John Carman, dec., by Mr. Sam. Crowell and John Jervis. 15 Dec 1696.{First Official Rcds:326}

On 12 April 1716 a deed of sale was recorded; Elizabeth Carman, widow and relict of John Carman, dec., of Cape May, being left whole and sole exec. of all the estate, for £7 sold to John Crafford, all her right to a water mill on Cold Spring Creek, the 1/2 given by her husband, John Carman by his will.{First Official Rcds:324}

In the record of deeds are shown Caleb Carmen, son of John, dec. in 1716; John Carmen, son of John, dec. in 1707; Benjamin and William Carman, now of Long Island, sons of John Carman, dec., in 1720.{Deeds B:106, 109, 135}

John Carman was the father of the following sons: JOHN; CALEB; BENJAMIN; WILLIAM.

Unplaced

ELIZABETH CARMAN m. Samuel Richardson by license dated 4 June 1731.{MLNJ}

---

9 See Deeds B:34.

10 See Deeds B:53, showing Wm. Sharwood and wife Abigail, formerly wife of Jonathan Pine.

11 According to Stevens, James was pastor of the Baptist Church at Cranbury, NJ.

12 See also Deeds B:57 showing Ephraim son of Elizabeth in 1703.

On 8 Oct 1718 Thomas Langley recorded his ear mark, "formerly JOSHUA CARMAN, he decerted the Countey." {First Official Recds}

CHAMPION

First Generation

1. JOHN CHAMPION of Waterford, Gloucester Co. d. leaving a will dated 11 Nov 1717, proved 21 Aug 1727. Mentioned were children: THOMAS; ROBERT; NATHANIEL; SARAH; MARY, m. 1698, Jarvis Martin; ELIZABETH and PHOEBE. Land was devised on Cooper's Creek adjoining John Wright, John Shivers and Henry Jonston. Execs. were son Robert and son-in-law John Wright. The will was witnessed by John Kaighin, John Dole and Elizabeth Kaighin. The will was proved by witness Elizabeth Kaighin, now signing as Eliz. Wills.{NJCW 2:437 and Gloucester Wills} An inventory was filed (£33.8.7) on 15 Aug 1727 by Martyn Jervis. On 16 Aug 1727 John Wright stated he was too sickly to continue as exec., leaving Nathaniel Champion acting alone. On 21 Aug 1727 a bond was issued to Nathaniel Champion as admin. cum test. ann.{NJCW 2:441 and Gloucester Wills}

The records of Westbury Monthly Meeting (New York) reveal John and Sarah Champion with the following children: Mary, who m. 1698, Jarvis Martin and Sarah who was granted a certificate to Newton Monthly Meeting, West Jersey on 6th mo., 25th day, 1708.

Second Generation

2. ROBERT CHAMPION, son of John (1) and Sarah (Williams) Champion, m. Mary Carson, dau. of Peter Carson [Corson], widow of Joseph Mapes, "marrying out" of the Society of Friends.{Reported in Haddonfield Monthly Meeting minutes, dated 11th mo., 1715}.

Robert m. Mary Mayps (Maypes) before John Townsend, Justice of the Peace, 17 June 1715. Witnesses: John Champion, Peter Corson, Deborah Corson, Christian Corson, Samuell Champion, Anne Corson, Catren Corson, Abigal Young, Elizabeth Corson, Henry Young, Robert Townsend, Joseph Goldin, John Corson, Samuel Shivers, Thomas Gandey.{First Public Rcds:276}

Robert and Mary had a son PETER.

3. NATHANIEL CHAMPION, probable son of John (1) and Sarah

Champion, m. Mary Combe.[13] They were parents of the following children: BENJAMIN who probably m. Amy Hughet as they announced their intentions to marry for the second time on 9th mo., 14th day, 1748.{Haddonfield Monthly Meeting minutes}; ELIZABETH, probably m. in 1750, sometime following the death of her father, John Barton, son of John and Ann (Butcher) Barton.{Haddonfield Monthly Meeting minutes}; THOMAS, m. Deborah Clark, dau. of William and Phillis (Ward) Clark{Haddonfield Monthly Meeting minutes of 10th mo., 13th day, 1760}

4. MARY CHAMPION of Gloucester County, possible dau. of John (1) Champion, m. Joshua Belange by license dated 15 April 1751.{MLNJ}

5. ELIZABETH CHAMPION, dau. of John (1) Champion, m. John Wright. Elizabeth, dau. of John and Elizabeth (5) (Champion) Wright of Gloucester Co., m. William Mickle, son of John and Hannah (Cooper) Mickle of Gloucester Co., with consent of their parents at Haddonfield on 8th mo., 19th day, 1732.{Haddonfield Monthly Meeting}

Third Generation

6. THOMAS CHAMPION, son of Nathaniel (3) Champion, m. Deborah Clark, dau. of William and Phillis (Ward) Clark{Haddonfield Monthly Meeting Minutes of 10th mo., 13th day, 1760}. Their dau. SARAH, of Haddonfield, m. at Haddonfield on 11th mo., 13th day, 1788, Caleb Atkinson of Newton Twp., bricklayer, son of Samuel and Esther (Evans) Atkinson.{Haddonfield Monthly Meeting}

Thomas Champion of Haddonfield, Gloucester Co., innholder, d. by 1 Dec 1766 when his widow, Deborah, was appointed admx. On 25 Nov 1766 an inventory was filed (£830.17.3 3/4) by Jacob Clement and Josiah Shivers.{NJCW 12:439}

CHESTER

SAMUEL and JOHN CHESTER

Reference was made to Samuel Chester and his brother John ca. 16 Jan 1758, in "Memorandum book of Jacob Spicer, 1757-1764," *The Cape May County Magazine of History and Genealogy*, p. 112. June 1933.

---

13 On 12th da, 7th mo, 1715 Nathaniel Champion of Haddonfield Monthly Meeting requested a certificate signifying his clearness from marriage engagements. {Haddonfield Monthly Meeting minutes}

A marriage license was issued to John Chester and Sarah Long, 13 April 1741.{MLNJ}

A marriage license was issued to John Chester and Sarah Vanluden, 11 Aug 1761.{MLNJ}

John Chester of Cape May Co. d. leaving a will dated 7 Dec 1773, proved 14 March 1775. Mentioned was dau. Lydia who was devised 8 1/4 acres in the Lower Precinct of the county and his right on the Five Mile Beach, when 18; also to have personal estate. Exec. was Downes Edmunds. The will was witnessed by Elizabeth Reeves, Lydia Buck and Thomas Ewing. On 21 Dec 1773 the estate was inventoried by Ephraim Kent and Abraham Woolson.{NJCW 17:182}

A marriage license was issued to SAMUEL CHESTER and --- Young on 5 Jan 1748{MLNJ Gloucester Co.}

Samuel Chester of Greenwich Twp., Gloucester Co., d. leaving a will dated 13 Aug 1759, proved 2 March 1764. Execs. were wife Amy and friend, Thomas Denny. On 27 Jan 1764 an inventory was filed (£34.17.2} by Thomas Roberts and Mathew Gill.{NJCW 11:519}

WILLIAM CHESTER m. Lydia Jordan of Cape May 4 Jan 1750/1. {Baptists}

On 27 Feb 1777 it was reported that Wm. Chester had taken sick of a pleurisye.{Leaming Diaries}

CHURCH

1. CHRISTEFER CHURCH recorded his ear mark in May 1713; later belonging to his son Jeremiah Church.{First Official Rcds}

2. JEREMIAH CHURCH of Cape May Co., yeoman, son of Christopher (1) Church, d. prior to 1 Nov 1740 when Rebeckah Church was appointed admx. Fellow bondsmen: Elisha Hand, John Stites of the same county. The will was witnessed by Jeremiah Leaming and Jacob Spicer.{NJCW 4:257} The estate was inventoried on 22 Sep 1740 and appraised by Elisha Hand and Thomas Beck. The estate included cattle, sheep and swine.{NJCW}

Unplaced

The following appears to be closely related to the above Church family.

CHRISTOPHER CHURCH of Philadelphia, sadler, d. leaving a will dated 10 Nov 1710, proved at Philadelphia on 26 Feb 1729/30. Brother Edward Church of Philadelphia, cordwainer, exec. He left to brother Edward and brother John Church of the same place, cordwainer, all goods, chattels and money. The will was witnessed by John Simes, John Russel and John Cadwalader.{NJCW 3:80} On 23 May 1729 an inventory was made by John Mackey and Barnabas Crowell. On 14 July 1729 Else Church as admx. of the estate and Nathaniel Jenkins and George Hand, fellowbondsmen, all of Cape May Co.{NJCW 3:33} On 16 June 1730 an account was filed by the admx., Alice Church, now wife of John Flower, she having paid debts to John Hands, Samuel Eldregge, Moses Crosby, Nicholas Johnson, Benjamin Hand, Rand'l Huet, Henry Noden, Thomas Langley, Isaac Wildin, John Hughs, Wm. Smith, Humphry Hughs, John Parsons, Nath'l Resque, Benjamin Stites, John Stillwell, and for the maintenance of Rode, Nathan, Silas, Patience and Susannah, children, and of the widow of the dec.

LYDIA CHURCH m. Thomas Paige by license dated 7 Aug 1766.{MLNJ}

PATIENCE CHURCH m. Silas Hand by license issued 28 March 1746.{MLNJ}

PRUDENCE CHURCH m. Henry Schellinger by license issued 21 Jan 1760.{MLNJ}

REBECCA CHURCH m. Thomas Johnson* by license dated 30 Dec 1741.{MLNJ}

SILAS CHURCH m. by license issued 1 Aug 1770, Martha Bancroft.{MLNJ}

Silas Church of Fairfield, Cumberland Co., weaver, d. leaving a will dated 7 April 1761, proved 22 April 1761. Mentioned were wife Martha and children: Joseph, Christopher (to whom was devised lands at Cape May), Deborah and Alice; father, John Page; brother-in-law, Benjamin Stites. On 17 April 1761 an inventory was filed (£144.17.2) by David Shepherd and Stephen Clerk.{NJCW 11:169}

On 15 Nov 1762 a marriage license was issued to Martha Church and Recompence Hand.{MLNJ}

Silas was the father of the following children: JOSEPH; CHRISTOPHER; DEBORAH; ALICE.

SUSANNAH CHURCH m. Jeremiah Richardson by license dated 8 Sep

1764.{MLNJ}

CORSON

See *Three Hundred Years with the Corson Families in America*. By Orville Corson, Middletown, Ohio. 1939. 2 volumes. The author discusses in detail his reconstruction of this family, covering the reasoning and logic of his conclusions.

See also "Sketch on the Early Life and Ancestry of John I. Corson, As Contained In An Old Book Evidently His Property And Written By Him." *The Cape May County Magazine of History and Genealogy*, p. 205. June 1959. By Grace Gallaher. In this book John I. Corson (b. 12 Feb 1823) recounts his line as follows: his father is John M. Corson (b. 29 Dec 1795) whose father was Joseph Corson, whose father was Joseph (b. 6 Sep 1716), whose father was Christopher, whose father was Peter. This agrees with other information except for the name Christopher which otherwise is given as Christian.

A sketch of some of the Corsons is given in "Early West Creek Settlers," *The Cape May County Magazine of History and Genealogy*, p. 142. June 1958. By Roy Hand. See "The Corsons," p. 144.

First Generation

1. According to Orville Corson, in *Three Hundred Years with the Corson Families in America*, the progenitor of the Cape May Corson families was CARSTEN (or CORSTEN) JANSEN,

his signature is preserved in many of the early records of Gravesend and Flatbush, Long Island [in the 1660s and later].

The first record of Carsten Jansen, occurs under date of 1656 in a list of persons who were inhabitants and probably freeholders of Gravesend, Long Island, in that year.

Carsten Jansen m. Barbara (N) and they had sons: Jan or JOHN Carstensen and PETER Carstensen.

Second Generation

2. JOHN CORSON, was probably the eldest son of Carsten (1) Jansen and Barbara, and b. probably not later than 1660 as he had m. Maria Eliase Daas or Daws ca. 1680. He baptized a son Andries, 23 Jan 1681, recorded in the records of the Flatbush Dutch Reformed Church.

John Corson of Cape May Co., yeoman, d. leaving a will dated 11 Jan 1721/2, proved 6 May 1728. Mentioned were wife Mary and children: Andrew, Hannah, Martha, Jacob and John[14]. The execs. were wife and son Jacob. The will was witnessed by Peter Corson, David Gandy, Nathaniel Jenkins. An inventory was made by Robert Townsend and John Willets, both Quakers.{NJCW: 2:534 and Cape May Wills}

John Corson was the father of the following children: ANDREW; HANNAH, MARTHA, m. John Willets* 5 Oct 1716{First Public Rcds}; JACOB; JOHN.

3. PETER CARSTENSEN, Carsten or Corson, son of Carsten (1) Jansen and Barbara, m. Deborah (N). He moved to Cape May Co. in 1694. A deed dated 25 Sep 1694, recorded in Gravesend Book VI, p. 136 refers to "Peeter Carsten living now in the County of Cape May in ye province of West Jersey ..." and mentioned his brother John Carsten.

Children of Peter and Deborah Corson: CHRISTIAN, b. between 1680 and 1685, d. ca. 1731, (the inventory of his estate was returned 22 April 1731, three days before the inventory of his father's estate was filed); ABIGAIL, m. Shamger Hand, son of Shamgar; MARY, m. 1st Joseph Mapes and 2nd Robert Champion*; PETER, JR.

Third Generation

4. JACOB CORSON of Cape May Co., yeoman, son of John Corson (1), d. leaving a will dated 12 Dec 1736, proved 25 April 1737. Mentioned were wife Amy; sons: Jacob, Peter and Jeremiah Corson (to whom was devised 100 acres "at the place called the 'fast Landing'"); daus.: Rachel, Amy and Martha (minors). Execs. were wife Amy and son Jacob. The will was witnessed by John Willets, Joseph Badcock, Rich. Hoe. Letters were granted to Naomi Corson, widow.{NJCW 4:103} The estate was inventoried 4 April 1737 by Henry Young and John Willets.

Jacob m. Amy (also Naomi) (N).

Jacob was the father of the following children: JACOB; PETER; JEREMIAH; RACHEL; AMY; MARTHA.

---

14 The name John does not appear in the abstract given in the New Jersey Archives, although mentioned twice in the original will.

According to Orville Corson,

5. CHRISTIAN CORSON, son of Peter (3) and Deborah Corson, m. Ann (N) and had: CHRISTIAN; CATREN; JOHN; ELIZABETH; ANDREW; JOSEPH, b. 6 Sep 1716.

Christian (of Upper Precinct, Cape May Co., husbandman), d. prior to 28 April 1731 when Ann Corson, spinster, was appointed admx. Fellow bondsman Peter Corson.{NJCW 3:101} The estate was inventoried on 22 April 1731; it included smith's tools, 1/4 of a shallop, oxen, cows, etc. Appraisers: Robert Townsend and Henry Young.

6. ABIGAIL CORSON, dau. of Peter (3) and Deborah Corson, b. 1680-90, widow with five children in 1709, identified as dau. of Peter Corson by the will of her first husband, Shamgar Hand, Jr., son of Shamgar, dated 4 June 1707. Mentioned in the will were his wife Abigail, sons, Cornelius, William and other children.

Shamgar and Abigail Hand were parents of the following children: CORNELIUS, m. Deborah (Garrison) Taylor, widow of John Taylor, who d. ca. 1728; WILLIAM; SHAMGAR III; ICHOBOD; JAMAMIE.

Abigail m. 2nd Henry Young (as proved by ear mark record of Shamgar Hand, Jr. "Shamgar hand, juner, records his ear mark Apr. 30, 1707, late Henry Young's his suckseeder." Their children: STEPHEN, m. Anne (N); DEBORAH, m. Clement Daniels, 24 Oct 1737; TABITHA, b. 27 Oct 1718, m. John Townsend*; PHOEBE, m. William Robinson, 20 June 1738; (N), m. (N) Godfrey and had a dau. Mehetibel; ABIGAIL, m. 1st Joseph Ludlam 17 Aug 1747, 2nd Jonathan Smith, 27 June 1758; ELIZABETH, m. John Mackey, 25 April 1746; JOB, m. Mary Norton 26 April 1757, dau. of Nathaniel Norton and Eunice Hand, dau. of George Hand, Sr.

Henry Young d. 8 April 1767, in his 77th year. In his will dated 17 July 1762, proved 2 June 1767, are mentioned sons, Stephen and Job, daus. Tabitha Townsend, Abigail Smith, Elizabeth Mackey, granddau. Mehetibel Godfrey.

7. MARY CORSON, dau. of Peter (3) and Deborah Corson, m. 1st Joseph Maypse* and had a son Joseph; m. 2nd Robert Champion and had Peter; m. 3rd by license dated 19 April 1728 (Gloucester Co.) Jonathan Belldon by whom she had the following children: SYDONIA; MARY; HEZEKIAH. He d.

leaving a will proved 7 April 1737. Mary m. 4th John Eastlack of Gloucester Co. by license of 27 June 1737.

8. PETER CORSON, son of Peter (3) Corson, was the father of the following children: BENJAMIN, b. 20th day, 8th mo., 1722, d. 28th day, 8th mo., 1722; ZIBIAH, b. 24th day, 6th mo., 1723, m. Joseph Hildreth* by license dated 16 Feb 1748{MLNJ}; DARIUS, b. 14th day, 11th mo., 1726; DEBORAH, b. 27th day, 1st mo., 1728; REM, b. 31st day, 5th mo., 1730; PETER, b. 9th day, 6th mo., 1732; REBECKAH, b. 11th day, 5th mo., 1735, m. Daniel Townsend*[15]; LEVI, b. 17th day, 11th mo., 1737; RACHEL, b. 21st day, 4th mo., 1741, m. Isaac Dole* by license dated 28 Oct 1761; JESSE, b. 6th day, 5th mo., 1743; ELIZABETH, b. 18th day, 4th mo., 1744.{GEMM}

Peter Corson, of Cape May, d. 29th day, 12th mo., 1763.{GEMM}

Peter Corson of Upper Precinct, Cape May Co., Gent., d. leaving a will dated 12 Dec 1760, proved 4 April 1764. Mentioned were son Levy to whom land was devised by Rem Corson's and 1/3 of 47 acres at the head of the said land and 1/3 of the land joining James Hathorn. Son Jesse was to receive the rest of the home tract and a tract lying between sons, Peter and Levi, 80 acres; also 1/2 of the land lying back of James Godfrey and 1/3 of the 41 acres. Son Darius received 8 shillings, dau. Rachel Corson, £17, dau. Elizabeth Corson, £17. Execs. were wife Rachel and son Darious. The will was witnessed by Joseph Corson, Jacob Corson and Peter Corson. An inventory (£106.17.1) was made by Joseph Corson and Daniel Townsend on 3 April 1764.{NJCW 11:505}

Fourth Generation

9. PETER CORSON, Upper Precinct, Cape May Co., yeoman and probable son of Jacob (4) Corson, d. prior to 25 April 1731 when the estate was inventoried and appraised by Robert Townsend and Henry Young. Bondsmen: Peter Corson, Jr., and Christian Corson. Admx. Deborah Corson, spinster, appointed admx. by 29 April 1731. Fellow bondsmen: Peter Corson and Jacob Corson. Witnessed by Henry Young, Mary Corson and Jacob Spicer.{NJCW 3:101}

10. JEREMIAH CORSON, probable son of Jacob (4) Corson, d. by 27 Dec 1776 when Jacob Corson was appointed admin. of his estate.

15 On 2nd da, 2nd mo, 1756, the marriage of Daniel Townsend and Rebekah Corson was reported as orderly accomplished. {GEMM}

Witnesses: Hugh Hathorn and Daniel Steelman. On 18 Dec 1776 an inventory was made by Joseph Edwards and Hugh Hathorn.{NJCW 22:43}

11. JOSEPH CORSON, son of Christian (5) Corson, m. by license dated 22 Jan 1759, Rachel Corson.

Joseph d. leaving a will dated 19 March 1793, proved 7 May 1793. Mentioned were wife Rachel; eldest son Parmenas, youngest son Joseph. Land was left to son Joseph which was purchased by grandfather Peter Corson.{NJCW 33:276} An inventory was filed (£324.10.8 1/2) by Eli Townsend and Daniel Townsend on 7 Aug 1793.{NJCW File:585E}

12. PETER CORSON, probable son of Peter (8) Corson, m. Martha Edwards by license dated 1 Feb 1757.{MLNJ}

On 1st day, 10th mo., 1759, Peter Corson, Jr., was spoken to concerning his taking oaths and bearing arms.{GEMM}

Peter d. by 18 Jan 1797 when Martha Corson was appointed admx. of his estate. Fellowbondsman was Elias Corson of Cape May Co.{NJCW 37:166} An inventory was filed (£734.19) on 12 Jan 1797 by John Townsend.{NJCW File:677E}

13. REM CORSON, son of Peter (8) Corson, b. 31st day, 5th mo., 1730, d. 8 April 1797, m. by license dated 17 Jan 1759{MLNJ}, Hannah, dau. of Nicholas and Sarah Stillwell*.

Rem and Hannah, among others, were mentioned as execs. to the estate of Sarah Stillwell at October Court 1787.{Ltrs&Inv A (Rev):16}

Rem and Hannah Corson were parents of the following children: AMELIA, m. --- Pederick; HANNAH; SOPHIA, b. 22 April 1769, d. 8 Nov 1848, m. 23 April 1789 Uriah Smith; LEWIS, d. ca. 1848, m. 1st 15 Sep 1790, Martha Baker, m. 2nd 28 June 1801, Rebecca (Mattox) Townsend and m. 3rd 11 March 1824 Hannah (Ford) Townsend; AMOS, b. 1774, d. 20 Aug 1843, m. 5 Oct 1812, Mary (Polly) Garretson.[16]

On 7 May 1797 Amos Corson, son of Rem Corson, dec., chose as his guardian Lewis Corson.{NJCW 37:166, File 675E}

Fifth Generation

14. DARIAS CORSON, probable son of Peter (8) m. Hannah Willits.

---

16 See "The Stillwells - A Patriotic Family, And Their Descendants," *The Cape May County of History and Genealogy*, p. 51. June 1940, by William Evans Price. Most of the information here on the family of Rem (13) and Hannah Corson is based on this article.

Children of Darius Corson: SON, b. 24th day, 8th mo., 1752, d. without a name, 1st day, 10th mo., 1732; DARIUS, b. 2nd day, 9th mo., 1757(new stile), probably m. Martha Mackey*, dau. of John Mackey.{GEMM}

On 5th day, 4th mo., 1756, Dorias Corson was spoken to concerning his marrying out of unity.{GEMM}

Hannah Corson, wife of Darias Corson, dau. of John Willits, d. 26th day, 7th mo., 1777.{GEMM}

15. JESSE CORSON, probable son of Peter Corson (8), m. Martha (N). They were the parents of the following children{GEMM}: SAMUEL, b. 26th day, 4th mo., 1768; HANNAH, b. 25th day, 10th mo., 1770; ZIBIAH, b. 8th day, 2nd mo., 1773; MARTHA, b. 16th day, 5th mo., 1776; MELISCENT, b. 26th day, 11th mo., 1778; JESSE, b. 26th day, 2nd mo., 1781; RACHEL, b. 2nd day, 8th mo., 1783; EDITH, b. 26th day, 2nd mo., 1786; SOMERS, b. 9th day, 2nd mo., 1789; AARON, b. 3rd day, 10th mo., 1792; REM, b. 15th day, 4th mo., 1797.{GEMM}

16. JOHN CORSON of Cape May Co. d. prior to April 1739 when the estate was inventoried. On 31 March 1740 Susannah Corson had been appointed admx.{NJCW 4:227} The estate was inventoried by Henry Young and John Willets on 23 April 1739.{NJCW} A marriage license was issued to James Conaway and Susannah Corson on 14 May 1741.{MLNJ}

17. JACOB CORSON (probable son of Jacob (2)) & Charity Stillwell of Cape May, m. 15 Oct 1750.{Baptists}

The following entries (18-20) are based on the work of Orville Corson:

18. SOPHIA CORSON, dau. of Rem (13) and Hannah Corson, b. 22 April 1769, d. 8 Nov 1848, m. 23 April 1789 Uriah Smith. They were the parents of the following children: REM; SAMUEL G., b. 27 March 1792; RACHEL; SARAH; SOPHIA; URIAH; RICHARD; JANE; REUBEN.

19. LEWIS CORSON, son of Rem (13) and Hannah Corson, d. ca. 1848, m. 1st 15 Sep 1790, Martha Baker, m. 2nd 28 June 1801, Rebecca (Mattox) Townsend and m. 3rd 11 March 1824 Hannah (Ford) Townsend.

By his first wife Martha Baker, Lewis Corson had the following children: MILES; REM; LEWIS.

By his second wife Rebecca Mattox Townsend, he had the following children: MARTHA, b. 27 Feb 1802, m. (N) Gandy; STILLWELL, m. Elizabeth Ford and left numerous issue; FRANKLIN.

By his third wife Lewis Corson had no issue.

20. AMOS CORSON, son of Rem (13) and Hannah Corson, b. 1774, d. 20 Aug 1843, m. 5 Oct 1812, Mary (Polly) Garretson. They were the parents of the following children: HANNAH FIRMAN, b. 1815; MARY; TRIPHENA; ABIGAIL; AMELIA; RACHEL; HENRIETTA, b. 1831.

Unplaced

A marriage license was issued to John Leonard and ANN CORSON, 29 Dec 1732.{MLNJ}

A marriage license was issued to ABNER CORSON and Mary Smith, 5 April 1773.{MLNJ}

Abner Corson and Mary Smith m. 8 March 1773. {Baptists}

Abner d. leaving a will dated 22 Sep 1798, proved 28 May 1799. Mentioned were sons: Nathan, Abner, Christian; daus.: Judith Eldredge and Jean Orum; dau. Jean Orum's three children: Charlotte Cresse, Daniel Hildreth and Benjamin Orum.{NJCW 38:421}

DAVID CORSON & Phebe Isard, both of this county of Cape May, 13 Oct 1751.{Baptists}

A marriage license was issued to Jotham Townsend and ELIZABETH CORSON, 21 May 1776. {MLNJ}

A marriage license was issued to JEREMIAH CORSON and Mary Creasey, 24 Sep 1763.{MLNJ}

Jeremiah d. by 2 Aug 1791 when Mary Corson was appointed admx.{NJCW 32:302} An inventory was filed (£21.14.1) by Moses Williams and John Goff on 14 May 1791.{NJCW 547E}

A marriage license was issued to JOHN CORSON, Jr., and Mary Goff of Cumberland Co., 19 Dec 1761.{MLNJ}

JOHN CORSON & MARTHA CORSON, m. 3 Dec 1765. {Baptists}

A marriage license was issued to LEVI CORSON and Margaret Hand, 23 Dec 1766.{MLNJ}

A marriage license was issued to Isaac Binar and LYDIA CORSON, 20 June 1740.{MLNJ}

In the home of Mr. and Mrs. Charles Wendell Holmes, 11 Poplar Street, Cape May Courthouse, hang two samplers concerning Mrs. Holme's ancestors. They were copied in July 1966 by Kenn Stryker-Rodda. PARMENAS CORSON, b. 23 Jan 1760, and Rachel Willits, b. 9 Aug 1762, m. 18 Oct 1778. Amos, b. 4 Aug 1779; Anthea, b. 2 Feb 1784.{p. 935, Genealogies of New Jersey Families}

A marriage license was issued to PARMENAS CORSON and Mary Lea, 12 April 1774.{MLNJ}

A marriage license was issued to PARMENAS CORSON and Priscilla Cresse, 1 Nov 1774. {MLNJ}

A marriage license was issued to PETER CORSON and Mary Badcock, 15 Jan 1761.{MLNJ}

A marriage license was issued to PETER CORSON and Elizabeth Godfrey*, 20 July 1763.{MLNJ}

A marriage license was issued to Isaac Dole and RACHEL CORSON, 28 Oct 1761.{MLNJ}

A marriage license was issued to Tomson, Richard, and RAAMAH CORSEN, 19 Dec 1741.{MLNJ}

Robinson, William, and ROADA CORSON, 13 Aug 1754.{MLNJ}

On 1st day, 8th mo., 1757 REM CORSON was spoken to concerning his bearing of arms.{GEMM}

A marriage license was issued to THOMAS CARSON and Elizabeth Murray, 26 April 1730.{MLNJ}

CRANDALL

Relationships have not been established.

JOHN CRANDALL of Cape May, blacksmith, d. prior to 4 April 1730 when his estate was inventoried by Nathaniel Rusco and Nathaniel Foster. On 20 Oct 1730 a bond was issued to Elizabeth Crandol to administer his estate. {NJCW}

A marriage licenses was issued to WILLIAM CRANDEL and Thankful Williams 22 Dec 1777.{MLNJ}

JOHN CRANDOL (Crandell) of Cape May Co. d. leaving a will dated 5 April 1775, proved 2 June 1775. Mentioned were Levi Crandol, son Reubin's elder son, 10 shillings. Son, John, estate. Exec. was son John. On 26 May 1775 an inventory was made by Nathaniel Foster and Richard Edmunds.{NJCW 17:162}

John was father of the following children: REUBIN, in the 1751 tax list; JOHN, d. prior to 22 June 1785 when Mary Crandal, widow, was appointed admx. {NJCW 38:79}

CRAWFORD (CRAFFORD)

1. JOHN CRAWFORD of Cape May Co. d. before 11 Dec 1705 when his estate was inventoried by his son George and delivered to the appraisers John Townsend and John Page. On 23 Nov 1721 his son and admin., George Crawford made an account of the estate, including two coffins, one for his father and one for his father's wife who d. a month before him. 14 shillings for wine at the funeral to Ezekell Eldridge. £1.4 to Ezekell Eldridge for wine at the funeral. Reference was made to Jacob Spicer, Capt. Andrew Gravenrod, Capt. John Bown, George Allen, Henry Buck and Richard Whitacer, exec. of James Townsend of Boston, Thomas Laytropp of Boston, Alexander Griffith, Edward Smouth, Humphrey Hughes.{NJCW}

John Crafford's ear mark was recorded 3 Jan 1694; "George Crafford takes his father's mark" 25 March 1707.{First Public Rcds}

John Crawford was father of GEORGE; probably JOSHUA; and probably BENJAMIN.

2. JOSHUA CRAFFORD of Cape May Co., probable son of John (1) Crawford, d. leaving a will dated 8 April 1731, proved 30 April 1733. He

left his house and land to his brother Benjamin Crafford's son, Eleser. Exec. was brother Benjamin. The will was witnessed by John Flower, Jonathan Fourman and Thomas Hand.{NJCW 3:340} The estate was inventoried on 25 April 1733 by Richard Downes and Elisha Hand.{NJCW}

3. BENJAMIN CRAWFORD of Cape May Co., yeoman, probable son of John (1), d. leaving a will dated 31 July 1746, proved 6 Aug 1746. Mentioned were son Richard, 100 acres (the plantation whereon the testator lived) and 40 acres adjoining Christopher Lupton's. He was to bring up testator's dau., Elizabeth until age 18. Legacies were bestowed on son Eliezer and daus.: Rachel, Sarah, Mary, Priscilla, Judith and Elizabeth. Execs. were son Richard and Elisha Hand. The will was witnessed by Reuben Crandol, Elisha Eldredge and Richd. Ball.{NJCW 5:312} The estate was inventoried on 12 Aug 1746 by John Eldredge and James Whildin. On 13 Nov 1748 an account of the estate was made.{NJCW}

Benjamin Craford's ear mark was recorded on 18 April 1715; later Issachar Crafford's.{First Official Rcds}

Benjamin Crawford was father of the following children: RICHARD; ELIZABETH, m. by license dated 17 Dec 1756, John Richardson*{MLNJ}; ELIEZER; RACHEL; SARAH, m. Ezekiel Eldridge by license dated 14 April 1741; MARY; PRISCILLA; JUDITH.

4. RICHARD CRAWFORD, probable son of Benjamin (3) Crawford, of Cape May Co. d. leaving a will dated 16 June 1751, proved 6 Aug 1751. Mentioned were wife Rachel and sons: Issachar and Benjamin (under age). Execs. were wife and James Whilldin. The will was witnessed by James Hedges, Loes Crowel and Peter Toullard.{NJCW 14:536, 15:517} On 17 Oct 1751 an inventory was filed by Elisha Hand and Ebenezer Johnson which included an old Negro.{NJCW} Richard m. Rachel Whilldin*, dau. of Joseph Whilldin.

Richard was father of the following children: ISSACHAR; BENJAMIN. (Sheppard Papers also show WILLIAM as son of Richard.)

5. RACHEL CRAWFORD, probable dau. of Benjamin (3) Crawford m. Jeremiah Hand* by license dated 17 March 1739.{MLNJ}

Unplaced

At court convened on 20 March 1693/4 ELIZABETH CRAFFORD complained regarding that no one ought to sell strong drink to inhabitants of Cape May without license.{First Public Rcds:274}

On 1 May 1706 Abraham Bener recorded his ear mark "formerly belonging to RICHARD CRAFORD, desesed [deceased]." {First Official Recds}

RICHARD CRAWFORD, b. 1766, d. 9 Nov 1811.{Cold Spring Cemetery}

CRESSE

See "The Cresse Family of New Jersey," *The Cape May County Magazine of History and Genealogy*, p. 79. June 1964. By Claude Young.

According to Mr. Young,

> Arthur Cresse is the founder of the New Jersey branch of the family. In 1692 he purchased from the West Jersey Society, 350 acres in Cape May Co. and that same year he and John Townsend, became the first collectors of the county. This position they held until 1700, when they were succeeded by his brother John Cresse, and Jacob Spicer. The first ear mark in the archives of the Cape May county courts was recorded by Arthur Cresse, 13 July 1692. Both Arthur and his son John were prominent in establishing the First Baptist Society of Cape May County. Of Lewis, a younger son of Arthur Cresse, little is known except that he was a planter of the county ca. 1713.

1. ARTHUR CRESSE of Cape May, yeoman, d. leaving a will dated 5 Sep 1711, proved 18 Feb 1714/5. Mentioned were wife Mary and sons: John, Arthur, Aepath(?), Lewes; daus.: Abigall, Sarah, Elsbeth, Darbrow (Deborah), Paththeyah. The will was witnessed by Richard Downes, Thomas Hand and Christopher Church. An inventory was made on 17 Jan 1714/5 by Richard Downes and John Taylor. On 20 Oct 1715 son John Cresse filed an account of the estate showing payments to David Wills, Ceaser Godfrey, Jacob Spicer, Josiah Bishop, David Cresse, Sarah Johnson, Lewis Cresse, Samuel Johnson, Buthia Cresse, Zelophehead Hand and Mercy Eldridge.{NJCW}

Another source states Arthur Cresse of Cape May Co., yeoman, d. leaving a will dated 1 Sep 1711, proved 18 Feb 1714/5. Mentioned were wife Mary and children: John, Arthur, David, Seejah(?), Lewis, Abigail, Sarah, Elizabeth, Deboraw, Pathegah. No exec. named. The will was witnessed by Richard Downes, Thomas Hand, Christopher Church.{NJCW 1:505}

Stevens in his *History of Cape May County* states Arthur Cresse came from Long Island about 1692. This compiler notes that Arthur Cresey had an account with John Parsons, 19 Feb 1674, placing him in the Long Island area. {Parsons Account Bk} His name is shown in the Cape May Co. deed book as early as 15 Jan 1694/5 in a return of survey of 150 acres called Shoemakers' Hall. The name of Arthur Cressy appears in the land records on 20 April 1695 owing quitrent on 350 acres.{Deeds A:445}

Arthur Cresse was the father of the following children: JOHN; ARTHUR; DAVID; SEEJAH(?); LEWIS; ABIGAIL; SARAH; ELIZABETH; DEBORAH; PATHEGAH.

Second Generation

2. JOHN CRESSE of Cape May Co., yeoman, son of Arthur (1) Cresse, d. leaving a will dated 31 March 1729, proved 22 June 1729. Mentioned were children: Robert, John, Hannah, Penelope, Comfort, Eunice, Josiah (under 20). Son Robert exec. with Aaron Leaming as trustee and overseer. The will was witnessed by Nathaniel Jenkins, David Hildreth, Ester Jenkins. On 1 May 1729 inventory of the personal estate was made, £143.14.11 made by Nathaniel Jenkins and Aaron Leaming.{NJCW}

John Cresse recorded his ear mark on 4 April 1709; later on 9 Feb 1740 it was recorded by his son Robert Cresse.{First Official Rcds}

John was the father of the following children: ROBERT; JOHN; HANNAH; PENELOPE; COMFORT, m. Elias Steelman of Great Eggharbour on 16 Dec 1732{Gloucester Co. Court records dated 16 Dec 1732}; EUNICE, m. Job Sommers of Great Egg Harbor, Gloucester Co.{Gloucester Co. Court records dated 2 Jan 1732}; JOSIAH.

3. ARTHUR CRESSE, Jr. of Cape May Co., weaver, son of Arthur (1) Cresse, d. leaving a will dated 31 Dec 1714, proved 9 May 1715. His wife Marcy was extx. Mentioned were the children: James, Zebulon, Elizabeth, Lydia, Marcy. Land at Indian Neck. The will was witnessed by Nathaniel Jenkins, John Bradner and John Taylor. According to Young the above named Zebulon changed his name to Arthur at the father's desire. Inventory was made on 20 Jan 1714/5 by Nathaniel Jenkins and John Taylor.

Arthur was the father of the following children: JAMES, recorded his ear mark, 13 July 1693; ZEBULON; ELIZABETH; LYDIA; MARCY.

4. DAVID CRESSE of Cape May Co., probable son of Arthur (1) Cresse,

d. prior to 23 Oct 1755 when an inventory was filed by James Cresse and John Shaw. On 28 Oct 1755 a bond was issued for Lewis Cresse as admin; James Cresse fellowbondsman, both of Cape May Co.{NJCW Cape May Wills:170E}

David Cresse recorded his ear mark on last day of Sep 1712; later recorded by Lewis Cresse.{First Official Rcds: 336}

5. LEWIS CRESSE of Cape May Co., probable son of Arthur (1) Cresse, d. prior to 1 May 1733 when Abigail Cresse had been appointed admx. Fellow bondsman: Ephraim Edwards, all of the county afsd. Witnesses: John Jones, Wm. Barlow and Jacob Spicer, Jr.{NJCW Cape May Wills:64E} An inventory was made on 18 April 1733 by John Jones and Ephraim Edwards. A second inventory was taken by Elijah Hughes and John Eldredge on 23 March 1747/8.{NJCW}

Third Generation

6. ROBERT CRESSE, Gent., probable son of John (2) Cresse, d. leaving a will dated 27 April 1768, proved 20 June 1768. Mentioned were wife Mary; son Robert to whom was devised a piece of land on Wills Creek, and was along land that belonged to brother John Cresse. To dau. Hannah Cresse was devised a piece of land on Wills Creek and was along Jesse Hand's line. Dau. Esther Cresse received land. Son Jonathan received the rest of lands adjoining where testator lived. Execs. were wife and son Jonathan. The will was witnessed by Samson Hawks, Zeruiah Hedges and Thomas Smith. On 6 June 1768 an inventory was filed (£96.0.3) by John Leonard and Thomas Smith.{NJCW 15:243}

Robert was father of the following children: ROBERT; HANNAH; ESTHER; JONATHAN.

7. JOSIAH CRESSE of Cape May Co., probable son of John (2) Cresse, m. Mary Holding by license issued 26 Sep 1737.{MLNJ}

Josiah Cresse d. leaving a will dated 15 May 1758, proved 3 Aug 1758. Mentioned were wife Mary and children: Aaron, Salathiel, Israel, Unis and Ruth, the last two under age. The execs were wife and son Israel. The will was witnessed by William Goff, John Smith and Nathaniel Jenkins.{NJCW Cape May Wills:185E} On 31 July 1758 an inventory was filed by William Goff and Nathaniel Jenkins.{NJCW}

Josiah was father of the following children: AARON; SALATHIEL; ISRAEL; UNIS; RUTH.

8. JAMES CRESSE, probable son of Arthur (3) Cresse, d. prior to 17 July

1764 when Elizabeth Cresse was appointed admx. Fellowbondsmen: Joseph Hildreth and Joshua Hildreth, all of Cape May Co. Witnesses: William Billings, Jr., and John Cresse.{NJCW 12:333}

9. ZEBULON CRESSE, son of Arthur (3) Cresse, m. Rhoda Goff* by license dated 14 Sep 1764.{MLNJ}

Zebulon d. by 3 Feb 1796 when Rhoda Cresse was appointed admx. of his estate.{NJCW 36:275} On 11 Feb 1796 an inventory was filed (£136.16.6) by Eli Townsend and Clark Nottingham.{NJCW File:641E}

At August Term of 1797 Zebulun Cresse of Cape May Co., dec., stood seized of three tracts in the upper precinct of the county. The first was part of the homestead whereon Arther Cresse dec. last dwelt who devised a part of the tract to his son Zebulun Cresse. The second tract was purchased of Jacob Spicer, dec., 46 acres. The third tract was a part of the land which Jacob Cresse purchased of the execs. of Jacob Spicer, dec. and Jacob Cresse conveyed same to Zebulun Cresse. And Zebulun Cresse seized of this land d. intestate leaving issue: Sarah Smith, Arthur, Hannah, Priscilla, William, Rhoda and Elizabeth Cresse. Among these heirs a division of the land remained to be made.{Ltrs&Inv A(Rev):151}

Enoch Smith Jr., and wife Sarah, heirs of Zebulon Cresse (1796).{Deeds B:242}

Zebulon was the father of the following children: SARAH, m. Enoch Smith, Jr.; ARTHUR; HANNAH; PRISCILLA; WILLIAM; RHODA; ELIZABETH.

Fourth Generation

10. ISRAEL CRESSE, probable son of Josiah (7) Cresse, m. Hannah Goff by license dated 3 Nov 1761.{MLNJ}

Israel d. prior to 19 April 1766 when his widow, Hannah, was appointed admx. Fellowbondsman was William Goff of Cape May Co. Witness: Margaret Goff. The inventory (£73.0.1) was made on 18 April 1766 by John Shaw and Lewis Cresse.{NJCW 12:357}

11. ARTHUR CRESSE, probable son of Zebulon (9) Cresse, m. ca. 1737, (N) (N).

On Oct 11 [1777], Arthur Cresse's wife died. They were married about 40 years.{Leaming Diaries}

Arthur Cresse of Upper Precinct, Cape May Co., d. leaving a will dated 13 Feb 1790, proved 4 May 1790. Mentioned were children: ZEBULON, JACOB, MARCY, MARY, RACHEL and ELIZABETH;

granddau. Mary Stites; grandson James Corson. The will was witnessed by Thomas Scott, Ann Cresse and Nathan Cresse. Execs. were Jonathan Hildreth and Eli Eldredge. On 4 March 1790 an inventory was filed (£127.0.3) by Richard Townsend and Elijah Townsend.{NJCW 31:544}

Unplaced

A marriage license was issued to Return Badcock and ABIGAIL CRESSE, 22 Feb 1733.{MLNJ}

ANTHONY CRESSE, b. 4 Jan 1773, d. 23 Jan 1834.{Cold Spring Cemetery}

DANIEL CRESSE m. Mary Goff Dec 12, 1749, of Cape May.{Baptists}

Daniel Cresse of Middle Precinct, Cape May Co., yeoman, d. leaving a will dated 14 Dec 1786, proved 4 June 1789. Mentioned were wife Mary; grandson Cresse Townsend under age 21, son of Jotham Townsend and Rachel Townsend; Japhet Ireland, son of Thomas Ireland and Mary Ireland of Great Egg Harbor in Gloucester Co.; Israel Cresse, son of Israel Cresse and his wife Hanah. On 3 June 1789 an inventory was filed (£355.14.4) by Humphry Stites and Eli Eldredge.{NJCW 31:359}

A marriage license was issued to DAVID CRESSE and Patience Stites*, 27 Sep 1769.{MLNJ}

Patience was the dau. of Benjamin Stites.{Deeds A:137}[17]

Sons of David Cresse: Anthony (wife Judith), Richard and George. (1800){Deeds B:80}

David d. by 24 April 1795 when Patience Cresse was appointed admx. of his estate. Fellow bondsman was Humphrey Stites of Cape May Co.{NJCW 36:189}

A marriage license was issued to Richard Edmunds and ESTHER CRESSE, 21 June 1769.{MLNJ}

A marriage license was issued to Thomas Matthews and HANNAH CREESE, 8 Jan 1768.{MLNJ}

---

17 Benjamin Stites had the following children: Humphrey; Philip; Joshua; Patience, wife of David Cresse; Ellizabeth, widow of Eli Eldredge. Benjamin Stites also had two grandchildren, Silsby and Eli, both sons of Nathaniel Jenkins. (1791) {Deeds A:137}

A marriage license was issued to Thomas Pratten and HANNAH CRESSE, 21 June 1769.{MLNJ}

A marriage license was issued to Isaiah Stites and HANNAH CRESSEY, 19 Dec 1770.{MLNJ}

JOHN CRESSE of Cape May Co. d. prior to 24 May 1745 when Priscilla Cresse[18] had been appointed admx. Fellow bondsman: Jeremiah Hand of the county afsd. Witnessed by Robert Cresse and Nathl. Jenkins, Jr.{NJCW Cape May Wills:116E} On 2 May 1745 an inventory was made by Jeremiah Hand and Nathl. Jenkins, Jr.{NJCW}

The deed book shows living in 1761: Jacob Spicer, wife Deborah; Aaron Cresse (no issue); Keziah, wife of Daniel Swain, children of John Cresse (living in 1744, now dec.).

A marriage license was issued to JOHN CRESSE and Beulah Ludlam, 18 May 1739.{MLNJ}

JOHN CRESSE & Rachel Goff, m. 12 Nov 1767.{Baptists}

John d. leaving a will dated 20 April 1788, proved 26 June 1788. Mentioned were wife Rachel and the Baptist Society of Cape May Co. to which he left 1/3 of his estate. Execs. were wife Rachel and Amos Cresse. On 10 June 1788 an inventory was filed (£224.17.7) by Philip Hand and David Cresse.{NJCW 31:79}

A marriage license was issued to Jeremiah Corson and MARY CREASEY, 24 Sep 1763.{MLNJ}

A marriage license was issued to Parmenas Corson and PRISCILLA CRESSE, 1 Nov 1774.{MLNJ}

Joatham Townsend and RACHEL CRESSEY, 14 Nov 1768.{MLNJ}

A marriage license was issued to JONATHAN CRESSE and Naomi Hand, 1 July 1763.{MLNJ}

---

18 Noting that Charles Dennis, husband of Priscilla, had at the time of his death in 1747-49, sons-in-law [probably step-sons] John Cresse (minor) and Joseph Ludlam, it is likely that Priscilla was the Priscilla Ludlam, widow of Anthony Ludlam who d. 1736/7 and Priscilla Cresse, the widow of John Cresse who d. in 1745.

JONATHAN CRESSE and Naomi Hand, both of Cape May, m. 1 July 1763.{Baptists}

JUDITH CRESSE, b. 21 March 1773, d. 25 Jan 1843.{Cold Spring Cemetery}

LEWIS CRESSE of Cape May Co., yeoman, d. leaving a will dated 22 Dec 1766, proved 29 July 1769. Mentioned were son Philip; son David. The right in the islands and marshes lying near Five Mile Beach was given to his five sons: Philip, David, Anthony, Amos and Nathan. Wife Elizabeth was given £10 over her rights. Dau. Hannah received movables. Son Philip to be guardian of Nathan. Execs. were wife and son Philip. The will was witnessed by Abner Corson, Shamgar Hand, Jemima Hand and Martha Smith. On 11 Aug 1769 an inventory (£495.14.0 1/2) was filed by Thomas Smith and John Smith.{NJCW 14:184}

A marriage license was issued to Lewis Cresse and Elizabeth Ludlam*, 1 Sep 1740.{MLNJ} Elizabeth was probably the dau. of Anthony Ludlam.

Elizabeth Cresse of Cape May Co. d. prior to 4 Aug 1772 when Phillip Cresse and Isaiah Stites were appointed admins. Fellowbondsmen: Zebulon Swain and Abner Corson, all of said county, gent. Witnesses: Jacob Harris and James Miller. On 22 June 1772 an inventory was made by Abner Corsen and Zebulon Swain. (£180.0.7 3/4){NJCW 14:507}

Lewis was father of the following children: PHILIP; DAVID; ANTHONY; AMOS; NATHAN; HANNAH.

LEWIS CRESSE of Cape May Co.,yeoman, d. leaving a will dated 29 Jan 1788, proved 10 March 1788. Mentioned were son Daniel; granddau. Ellenner, dau. of son Daniel under age of 18; grandson Ebinnezer Shaw; grandson Aaron Shaw, sons of Hosea Shaw; son Lewis; dau. Abigail Shaw. On 27 Feb 1788 an inventory was filed (£294.0.7) by John Cresse and David Cresse.{NJCW 31:77}

Reeves Iszard and MARY CRESSEY, 12 Jan 1761.{MLNJ}

A marriage license was issued to NATHAN CRESSE and Annie Errexison, 24 Dec 1774.{MLNJ}

NATHAN CRESSE and Anne Erickson, Dec 25, 1774.{Baptists}

A marriage license was issued to PHILIP CRESSE and Experience Smith,

20 Feb 1763.{MLNJ}

RICHARD CRESSE m. by license issued 7 Feb 1798, Mary Foster, dau. of Constantine and Bethia Foster.{Co. Clerk Rcds - Book A; Deeds B:68}

SAMUEL CROWELL

1. SAMUEL CROWELL was witness to the marriage of Joseph Crowell in 1709/10. The record of deeds shows a Samuel Crowell, son of Samuel, of age, in 1701.{Deeds B:45}

On 26 June 1694/5 Samuell Crowell recorded his ear mark (later Barnabas Crowel's).

Samuel Crowell m. Phebe Smith by license dated 7 Nov 1759.{MLNJ}

Samuel Crowell of Cape May d. at an advanced age leaving a will dated 3 Jun 1765, proved 14 March 1768. Mentioned were son Josiah to whom was left lands where testator lived. Son Thomas was devised land bought of Elisha Eldredge and Silas Hand. Son Mathew was devised land bought of Eleazer Crawford at Fishing Creek, near Nathaniel Foster. Son David was devised land bought of James Hedges and Ellis Hughes. Sons to have the lands when age 21. Wife Phebe was left what the law directs. The rest of the moveable estate was left to son Seale Crowell and 4 daus.: Mary Eldredge, Elizabeth Bancraft, Ruth Crowell and Lowes Crowell. Execs. were son Josiah Crowell and Thomas Crowell. The will was witnessed by John Eldredge, John Eldredge, Jr. and Elizabeth Jenkins. On 19 March 1768 an inventory was filed (£184.7.6} by John Eldredge and Ezekiel Eldredge.{NJCW 13:378}

Samuel was father of the following children: JOSIAH; THOMAS; MATHEW; DAVID; SEALE; MARY, m. (N) Eldredge; ELIZABETH, m. Ephraim Bancraft by license dated 8 June 1763{MLNJ}; RUTH; LOWES.

2. JOSIAH CROWELL, probable son of Samuel (1) Crowell, m. Mary Whilldin, dau. of Joseph Whilldin, of the same place on 17 Dec 1708. Witnesses: Joseph Whillden, Hannah Whillden, Ezekell Eldredge, John Page, Elizabeth Page, Sarah Eldredge, Samuell Crowell, Arthur Cresse, Mercy Cresse, Marcy Bell, Experience Whillden, Experience Crowell, Elizabeth Taylor, Sarah Mason, Ephraim Edwards, Cesar Godffrey, George Crafford, John Roberts, John Taylor, Joseph Whillden, John Mathews, David Cresse, Samuell Eldrege. Entered 10 Jan 1708.{First Official Rcds: 323}

Josiah Crowell recorded his ear mark 1 May 1708; later recorded by Saml. Crowell in 1734.{First Official Rcds}

BARNABAS CROWELL

1. BARNABAS CROWELL, yeoman, of Cape May Co., possible son of Samuel (1) Crowell, d. leaving a will dated 9 July 1740, proved 30 March 1748. Mentioned were wife Abigail and son Barnabas to have all lands. Dau. Martha Havens. Rest to my six children: Barnabas, Elisha, Daniel, Marey, Lydia and Sarah Crowell. The will was witnessed by Nathaniel Hand, Joanna Hand and Abiah Ross.{NJCW 5:453}

Barnabas was the father of the following children: BARNABAS, b. 1766; MARTHA, m. (N) Havens; ELISHA; DANIEL; MAREY; LYDIA; SARAH, probably m. Silas Hand* by license dated 22 April 1751.{MLNJ}

2. BARNABAS CROWELL, son of Barnabas (1), was mentioned in Book of Mortgages A: 64 dated 1768.

The deed book shows a Barnabas Crowell, wife Rebecca in 1770.{Deeds A:51}

In "Diaries of Aaron Leaming," he mentions the death of Mrs. Crowell, wife of Barnabas in 1761.

3. DANIEL CROWELL, probable son of Barnabas (1) Crowell, d. leaving a will dated 8 Jan 1777, proved 19 Feb 1780. Mentioned were wife Hannah; son Barnabas, under age 20; Daniel, land where testator lived near Cold Spring, bounded by lands of Thomas Buck, John Eldredge, the Parsonage tract, Constantine Frosting and Jacob Hughes, in which tract is included those tracts I bought of Barnabas Crowell and Mark Hewlings; also the use of 1/2 the water mill, till son Barnabas is 21. Son Barnabas when 21 to have the said water mill and the lands whereon it stands, which were purchased of Elisha Crowell. Son Joshua to have a new suit of clothes in case he returns from his voyage at sea. Dau. Abigaill Crowell to have £15. Dau. Judith to have £15 when 18. Dau. Hannah to have £15. Execs. were wife Hannah and son Daniel. The will was witnessed by James Watt, James Cochran and Phebe Crowell. On 18 Feb 1780 an inventory was filed (£9,908.9.6) by Henry Hand and Silas Swain.{NJCW 21:319}

Daniel was the father of the following children: BARNABAS, b. 1766, d. 5 March 1819, m. Elizabeth (N) who. d. 15 Jan 1836, age 68.{Cold Spring Cemetery}; DANIEL; JOSHUA; ABIGAILL; JUDITH; HANNAH.

4. DANIEL CROWELL, probable son of Daniel (3) Crowell, b. 1751, d. 16 Nov 1815.{Cold Spring Cemetery}

Unplaced

Levi Eldridge and ABIGAIL CROWELL, 7 Aug 1766.{MLNJ}

AARON CROWELL, d. 15 Jan 1860, age 89 years, 2 mos., 26 days; m. Sarah (N) (b. 8 July 1777, d. 6 June 1857).{Cold Spring Cemetery}

Jacob Hand* and EXPERIENCE CROWEL, 8 June 1748.{MLNJ}

Jonathan Whildin and HANNAH CROWELL, 16 Nov 1772.{MLNJ}

A marriage license was issued to JACOB CROWELL and Jane Edwards, 15 Jan 1731.{MLNJ}

JACOB CROWELL m. Rachel Edwards* by license dated 9 April 1764.{MLNJ} He d. prior to 22 Dec 1783 when Rachel Crowell was appointed admx. Fellowbondsman: Thomas Hand, Sr. of Cape May Co. Witnesses: Levi Eldredge and Jonathan Eldredge. On 24 June 1786 an inventory was filed (£143.2.10} by Jeremiah Eldredge and Abraham Woolson.{NJCW 38:79}

August Court 1787. Amos Cresse and Hanah Stites, admins. of Isaiah Stites, complained that Rachel Crow admx. of Jacob Crow, defrauds the creditors of sd. Jacob, particularly the execs. of Isaiah Stites. Dismissed.{Ltrs&Inv A(Rev):14}

Rachel Crow[ell] d. by 6 May 1788 when George Hand was appointed admin. of her estate. On 17 Jan 1788 an inventory was filed (£21.15.1) by David Hildreth and Jeremiah Richardson.{NJCW 31:93}

JOHN CROMWELL m. Ruth Hand by license dated 22 April 1737.{MLNJ}

John Cromwell (of Upper Precinct of Cape May Co.) d. leaving a will dated 22 Dec 1739, proved 11 Jan 1739. Mentioned were wife Ruth to have 1/2 of estate and son Olifer Cromal to have the other half. Execs. were wife Ruth and son Olifer. The will was witnessed by Will. Ball, William Allen, Barns Sifin and Joseph Woodward.{NJCW Cape May Wills:98E}

On 22 March 1740/1 letters testamentary were granted to Ruth Cromall, extx. On 24 May 1740 an inventory was made by Jeremiah Hand and Moses Crosle.{NJCW}

JOHN CROWELL and Experience Hughes m. 13 Feb 1770.

John Crowel of Cape May d. by 30 June 1786 when Experience Crowel was appointed admx. of his estate. Fellowbondsman: Jedidiah Hughes.{NJCW 28:187}

JOSEPH CROWELL m. Anne Eaglesfield before John Townsend, Justice of the Peace of Cape May Co., 2 March 1709/10. Witnesses: Jacob Spicer, Ezekiel Eldredge, John Parsons, Robert Townsend, Silvanes Townsend, Samuel Eldredge, Elizabeth Parsons, Sarah Eldredge, Mary Mathews, --- Crowell, Phebe Townsend, Sarah Townsend, Charytee Forman, Joseph Crowell, Ann Crowell, George Eaglesfield, Elizabeth Eaglesfield, Samuell Mathews, Samuell Crowell. Recorded 10 May 1711. Children of Joseph Crowell: MARY, b. 14 March 1711; EDWARD, b. 17[19] June 1713; JOSEPH, b. 6 Sep 1716.{First Official Rcds} Anne Eaglesfield was probably dau. of George Eaglesfield who was the original owner of Cape Island, late Cape May City.{See Townsend article, p. 85}

Joseph Crowel of Cape May Co., yeoman, d. leaving a will dated 14 Feb 1714/5, proved 25 Sep 1717. Wife Ann was extx. Mentioned were children: Edward, minor, to have all land and tenements at Goshen; dau. Mary, all land, etc., at New England in Cape May. The will was witnessed by Yelverton Crowel, Thomas Smith and Nathaniel Jenkins. Inventory of the personal estate was made by Samuel Johnson and Nathanial Jenkins on 17 Jan 1716/7.{NJCW 2:80}

JOSIAH CROWEL m. Temperance Richardson, dau. of Jacob Richardson, by 4 May 1777{See will of Jacob Richardson.} Josiah d. leaving a will dated 15 Sep 1781, proved 19 Oct 1781. Mentioned were an only son Humphrey to whom he left all his lands; wife Temperance; daus.: Gudith Crowell and Ruth Crowell. Execs. were wife Temperance and Jacob Richardson. The will was witnessed by Amelia Buck, Samuel Eldredge and Thomas Ewing.{NJCW 38:76}

At court during the August Term 1788, Temperance Crow applied for some person to be appointed guardian to her dau., an infant under 14, named Ruth.{Ltrs&Inv A(Rev):25} On 28 Sep 1788 a bond was

19 Stevens shows this date as 7 June 1713.

given of Temperance Crowel as guardian to her dau. Ruth.{Ltrs&Inv A:15}

In October Court 1788 Temperance Crowel prayed that Elis Hughes, Jr., be appointed guardianship of her son Humphry Crowel, minor about 9 years old, son of Josiah Crowel, dec.{Ltrs&Inv A(Rev):28}

At February Court 1789 Jacob Richardson was appointed guardian to Humphry Crow[el], minor son of Josiah Crowel, dec.{Ltrs&Inv A(Rev):30}

On 5 Feb 1789 Humphry, son of Josiah Crow[ell], dec. is under age 14, guardian Jacob Richardson.{NJCW 31:373} On 13 March 1790 Humphrey Crowell, son of Josiah Crowell, chose Richard Shaw as his guardian.{NJCW 33:280, File 594E}

On 14 Aug 1788, Ruth Crowel, dau. of Josiah Crowel, dec., was made a ward of her mother, Temperance Crowel until age 14.{NJCW 31:94}

Josiah was father of the following children: HUMPHREY, b. ca. 1779; JUDITH; RUTH, b. 1774 and 1777.

A marriage license was issued to JOSIAH CROWELL and Sarah Eldridge 28 Feb 1764.{MLNJ}

MATTHEW CROWELL of Cape May co. d. prior to 18 Oct 1751 when an inventory of the estate was filed by Elisha Hand and Ebenezer Johnson. On 28 Oct 1751 a bond was issued for Loes Crowell as admin; James Godfrey, fellowbondsman, both of said county.{NJCW Cape May Wills:151E}

Christopher Church, wife Sarah. Matthew Crowell (living 1746) had sisters Elishaba, Mary, Experience and Rhoda who m. Isaiah Stites. (1799){Deeds B:182}

A marriage license was issued to Eldridge, Ezekiel, and PHEBE CROWELL, 18 Oct 1768.{MLNJ}

William Stites & RACHEL CROWELL of Cape May m. 8 May 1751. {Baptists}

A marriage license was issued to Isaiah Stites* and RHODA CROWELL, 29 April 1738.{MLNJ}

A marriage license was issued to Reeves, Abraham, and RUTH CROWELL, 22 Oct 1765.{MLNJ}

A marriage license was issued to SAMUEL CROWELL and Abigail Buck, 29 Dec 1763.{MLNJ}

A marriage license was issued to THOMAS CROWELL and Sarah Shillinks, 15 Jan 1771.{MLNJ}

YELVERTON CROWELL of Cape May Co., yeoman, d. prior to 10 Jan 1723/4 when his personal estate was inventoried by Nathaniel Jenkins and Thomas Smith. On 15 July 1724 his estate was administered by his widow Elizabeth.{NJCW 2:265}

A cattle (ear) mark was recorded for Yelverton Crowell on 18 May 1696 and the same mark was later recorded for his son Jacob Crowell. {According to Stevens, p.12}

DANIELS

1. CLEMENT DANIELS, Sr., of Cape May Co. d. leaving a will dated 27 Dec 1746, proved 30 Jan 1746. Mentioned were wife Mary; dau. Martha Savage; sons: Clement, Thomas and Randal Daniels, to have equally cooper tools, cedar swamp and marsh excepting 5 acres adjoining Wigenses branch which he gave to his grandson, John Daniels. Execs. were sons Clement, Thomas and Randal. The will was witnessed by Robert Townsend (Quaker), Felix Fitz Summons (Quaker) and Nathaniel Morrison. On 30 Jan 1746/7 letters were granted to Clement and Randal Daniels.{NJCW 8:334} On 30 Jan 1746/7 an inventory was made including cooper tools and appraised by John Leonard and John Ireland.{NJCW}

Clement was father of the following children: MARTHA, m. Joseph Savage{MLNJ}; CLEMENT; THOMAS; RANDAL.

2. THOMAS DANIELS, probable son of Clement (1) Daniels, m. Mary Golding*, by license issued 2 July 1740.{MLNJ}

3. JOHN DANIELS and his brother, Clement Daniels, grandsons of Clement (1) Daniels, dec., were mentioned in the deeds dated 1756.{Deeds C:179}

John Daniels m. Phebe Stillwell by license of Gloucester Co. dated 10 Nov 1788. On 27 May 1789 Richard Summars, guardian to the estates of Anna and Sophia Stillwell, daus. of Enoch Stillwell, dec. against Phebe Stillwell now Daniels and John Daniels her husband, admins. of the estate of Enoch Stillwell, dec., next court.{Ltrs&Inv A(Rev):32}

4. CLEMENT DANIELS, possible grandson of Clement (1) Daniels, m. Deborah Young by license dated 24 Oct 1737.{MLNJ}

DENNIS

Charles and Philip Dennis (below) may have been the sons of Jonathan Dennes of Cohansey, Salem Co., yeoman, who d. leaving a will dated 9 Aug 1719., proved 31 May 1720. Mentioned in the will were wife Rachel and sons: Phillip, Charles and Samuel.{NJCW 2:160} On 28 April 1720 an inventory was filed (£186.7) by Thomas Craven and Enoch Moore.

1. CHARLES DENNES, brother of Philip Dennis, Cape May Co., Gent., d. leaving a will dated 9 Jan 1747, proved 16 May 1749. Mentioned were wife Priscilla[20]; sons-in-law: John Cresse (minor) and Joseph Ludlam. Son Charles Dennis to have plantation at Cohansey, Salem Co., at the upper end of the place called Beacken's Neck joining land of Nememiah Craven and land of Jonathan Stathem. Execs. were brother, Philip Dennis and Charles Davis. The will was witnessed by Henry Young, John Mackey and Elizabeth Mackey. Letters granted to Philip Dennis in Cumberland Co.{NJCW 6:223} An inventory was filed by Henry Young and Joseph Ludlam on 15 May 1749.{NJCW}

Charles was father of the following children: CHARLES.

2. PHILIP DENNIS, Greenwich, Cumberland Co., brother of Charles (1) Dennis, d. 15th day, 2nd mo., 1768, aged 66 years. He m. Luce Bacon by 28 Oct 1723.{SAMM}

He left a will dated 1 May 1767, proved 28 May 1768. Mentioned were wife Lucy and children: PHILIP, JONATHAN, PRUDENCE, ELIZABETH, GRACE Bowen and RACHEL, b. 6th day, 6th mo., 1743, m. Richard Smith, son of John and Sarah Smith{Salem Monthly Meeting}. In his will Philip mentioned his wife Lucy to whom he left a case of drawers that was left to her by her father. On 25 May 1768 an inventory was filed (£295.19.10) by Charles Davis and Mark Sheppard.{NJCW 13:414}

Philip and Lucy were parents of the following children: MARTHA, b. 15th day, 7th mo., 1724; PRUDENCE, b. 19th day, 9th mo., 1726; PHILIP, b. 19th day, 11th mo., 1731; GRACE, b. 7th day, 7th mo., 1740; RACHEL, b. 6th day, 4th mo., 1742; ELIZABETH, b. 29th day, 5th mo., 1747; JONATHAN, b. 4th day, 6th mo., 1750; MARTHA, b. 7th

---

20 Noting that Charles Dennis, husband of Priscilla, had at the time of his death, sons-in-law [probably step-sons] John Cresse (minor) and Joseph Ludlam, it is likely that Priscilla was the Priscilla Ludlam, widow of Anthony Ludlam who d. 1736/7 and Priscilla Cresse, the widow of John Cresse who d. in 1745.

day, 12th mo., 1760.{SAMM}

3. PHILIP DENNIS, son of Philip (2) Dennis, m. Hannah Thompson of Alloways Creek, Salem Co., on 4th day, 11th mo., 1751. They were parents of the following children: EDWARD, b. 13th day, 2nd mo., 1763; JOHN, b. 20th day, 10th mo., 1764; MARY, b. 13th day, 4th mo., 1767; PHILIP, b. 26th day, 7th mo., 1769; HANNAH, b. 20th day, 1st mo., 1772.{SAMM}

4. EDWARD DENNIS of Cumberland Co., probable son of Philip (3) Dennis, m. by license dated 22 March 1786, Jean Cook.{MLNJ}

DOLE

1. JOSEPH DOLE of Great Egg Harbour m. Hannah Somers*, b. (ca. 1691, d. 24th day, 2nd mo., 1737).

Joseph d. leaving a will dated 29 March 1727, proved 17 June 1727. Mentioned were wife Hannah, extx., to sell with the consent of brothers Richard Somers and James Somers, all real property, left by testator. Children mentioned (unnamed). The will was witnessed by Daniel Collings, Daniel Engorson and Bridget Somers.{NJCW 2:430} On 12th day, 3rd mo., 1727 an inventory was filed (£123.11). On 17 May 1729 an account of the estate was filed by Hannah Engersul, alias Dole, extx., and her husband Benjamin Engersul.

2. JOHN DOLE, possible son of Joseph (1) Dole, m. Hannah (N). They were the parents of the following children: MARY, b. 10th day, 1st mo., 1714, d. 26th day, 9th mo., 1720; JOHN, b. 9th day, 5th mo., 1716, d. 2nd day, 11th mo., 1748; SARAH, b. 16th day, 10th mo., 1718, d. 16th day, 10th mo., 1758; JOSEPH, b. 19th day, 3rd mo., 1721, d. 5th day, 1st mo., 1786, 65 years of age; SAMUEL, b. 23rd day, 11th mo., 1723, d. 3rd day, 12th mo., 1723; RICHARD, b. 28th day, 1st mo., 1725, d. 18th day, 6th mo., 1779; ISAAC, b. 9th day, 8th mo., 1727; d. 4th day, 9th mo., 1803.{GEMM}

John Dole of Great Egg Harbor, Gloucester Co., yeoman, d. by 10 April 1749 when Joseph Dole was appointed admin. of the estate.{NJCW 6:331; 7:88}

3. ISAAC DOLE, probable son of John (2) and Hannah Dole, m. Rachel Corson*, by license issued 28 Oct 1761. On 3rd day, 5th mo., Isaac Dole

acknowledged his going out in marriage.{GEMM} He and Rachel were parents of the following children{GEMM}: JOHN, b. 22nd day, 8th mo., 1762; ISAAC, b. 29th day, 2nd mo., 1764; PETER, b. 25th day, 11th mo., 1765; RICHARD, b. 22nd day, 2nd mo., 1768; RACHEL, b. 3rd day, 5th mo., 1770; SARAH, b. 15th day, 1st mo., 1773; ISAAC, b. 12th day, 6th mo., 1774; REBECAH, b. 1st day, 4th mo., 1776; JESSE, b. 19th day, 10th mo., 1778; HANNAH, b. 3rd day, 3rd mo., 1784.

On 9th day, 5th mo., 1786 the Woodbury Monthly Meeting was informed by Great Eggharbour Monthly Meeting that Isaac Dole had lived in the Woodbury area for some time.{Woodbury Monthly Meeting minutes}

4. REBECCA DOLE, probable dau. of Isaac (3) Dole m. Samuel Gandy, in 1799.{Co. Clerk Rcds - Book A}

5. JOSEPH DOLE, son of John (2), b. 19th day, 3rd mo., 1721, d. 5th day, 1st mo., 1786, 65 years of age. He is probably the same Joseph Dole who on 7th day, 3rd mo., 1763, acknowledged going out in marriage.{GEMM}

DOWNS

1. Capt. RICHARD DOWNS m. Elizabeth (N). He d. leaving a will dated 28 March 1747, proved 12 May 1747. Mentioned were Downs Edmons, grandson to whom was devised all lands and tenements, he to pay £20 to his brother Richard Edmons when 21. Part of the movables to dau. Mary Edmons and rest to grandchildren: Robert Edmon's children and Randal Hute's children (that he had by his first wife Hannah Downs). Execs. were Elisha Hand, Nathaniel Foster, Esq., both of Cape May. The will was witnessed by Josiah Cresse, Benjamin Shaw and Obed. Shaw.{NJCW 5:526} The estate of "Capt. Richard Downs" was inventoried on 1 May 1747 and included cattle and oxen. It was appraised by John Shaw and George Stites. On 13 Nov 1748 an account was rendered. Payments were made to Elijah Hughes, Thomas Johnson, John Garlick, Lory Hand, Uriah Hughes, Barnabas Crowele, Ebenezer Swaine, Ebenezer Johnson, George Stites, Jeremiah Leaming, Downes Edmuns, Elisha Crowele, John Robinson, Robert Edmunds, Zachariah Sickles, Josiah Cress, William Cooper, John Buck, Mary Edmunds, Samuel Leonard, Elizabeth Downs, widow of the dec., Robert Edmunds, Amey Edmunds, Rachele Hewit, Joseph Fancher (who m. one of the grandchildren of the dec.), Henry Young, Elisha Hand, etc.{NJCW}

Richard was father of the following children: MARY, probably

m. Robert Edmons; HANNAH, probably m. Randall Hewett.

2. WILLIAM DOWNS of Cape May Co., mariner, probable nephew of Richard (1) Downes, d. leaving a will dated 4 July 1741, proved 9 Dec 1741. Mentioned were Uncle Richard Downs, Esq., of Cape May, all estate, but "if my brother should come to this country, my will is that he should have and enjoy my house and land. Exec. was uncle Richard Downes. The will was witnessed by Robert Edmonds, Abigail Dagg and Fras. Taylor.{NJCW Cape May Wills:103E} On 8 Aug 1741 an inventory was made which included 1/4 of a schooner; appraised by John Dagg and Francis Taylor.

EDMONDS

1. ROBERT EDMANS recorded his ear mark on 26 Feb 1725/6.{First Public Rcds:276} Robert probably m. Mary Downes by whom he appears to have had the following sons: DOWNS; RICHARD, minor in 1747.

2. DOWNES EDMUNDS, son of Robert (1) Edmunds, m. 1st Experience Hand, by license issued 10 Aug 1752 and m. 2nd Mary Hand by license issued 18 Jan 1774.{MLNJ} According to Charles E. Sheppard Papers, Downes Edmunds was father of the following children: JUDITH, d. Aug 1795, age 40 years, 10 mos., 20 days, m. Thomas Buck, Jr. by license dated 9 Jan 1771; LOUISA, b. by 1758 (m. by license dated 30 May 1775, John Parsons); RACHEL, b. by 1758, m. George Foster*; ROBERT, b. 2 Oct 1760; JEREMIAH, b. 2 Oct 1760; AARON, b. 14 Sep 1766, d. 23 June 1844; DOWNES; PARSONS; EXPERIENCE; EVAN, b. 1781, d. 18 Nov 1844, m. Anna (N) who d. 10 Jan 1870, age 78.{Cold Spring Cemetery}

3. RICHARD EDMUNDS, probable son of Robert (2) Edmunds m. by license dated 21 June 1769, Esther Cresse.{MLNJ}

4. ROBERT EDMUNDS, son of Downes (2) Edmunds, b. 2 Oct 1760, d. 17 March 1822, age 61 years, 6 mos.{Cold Spring Cemetery} He m. 1st Thankful Bancroft (d. 19 March 1798, age 42) and m. 2nd Tryphenia Bancroft (d. 13 Sep 1821, in her 63rd year).{Sheppard Papers; Cold Spring Cemetery} Robert and Thankful were parents of the following children: JUDITH, d. 12 Aug 1794 in her 3rd year; JOHN, d. 11 Aug 1794, age 12 days.{Cold Spring Cemetery}

5. JEREMIAH EDMUNDS, son of Downes (2) Edmunds, b. 2 Oct 1760,

d. 22 Nov 1807, m. 1st Mrs. Jane Hughes, dau. of James Whilddin*, and were the parents of ELIZABETH, b. 4 Dec 1780, d. 11 Jan 1868, m. 10 April 1799, Levi Eldredge (b. 17 Oct 1776, d. 23 Nov 1822). Jeremiah later m. Mrs. Ann Hughes, widow of Jacob Hughes*.{Sheppard Papers, Cold Spring Cemtery}

6. AARON EDMONDS, son of Downes (2) Edmunds, b. 14 Sep 1766, d. 23 June 1844.{Cold Spring Cemetery} Aaron m. 1st Lydia Eldredge* (d. 23 June 1844) and m. 2nd her older sister, Sarah Eldredge*, b. 20 Feb 1767, d. 20 Jan 1846.{Cold Spring Cemetery}

Unplaced

William Simkins and MARY EDMUNDS, 10 Dec 1759.{MLNJ}

EDWARDS

1. JOSEPH EDWARDS, of Upper Precinct, brother of David Edwards, d. leaving a will dated 28 June 1782, proved 6 Sep 1782. To son James he devised the land bought of James Steelman, Jr., in Great Egg Harbor Township, Gloucester Co., he paying to son Enoch, £20, when he is 21. Son Joseph, 1/2 of plantation where testator dwelled and 1/2 of cedar swamp at Peach Orchard Neck, he paying to son Ebenezer, £15 when 21. Son David 1/2 of plantation and 1/2 of said swamp, he paying £10 to the child that wife is pregnant with. Wife Susannah to have 1/3 of estate. Daus. Elizabeth Edwards and Sarah Edwards, £36 when age 18. Daus. Ellenar Steelman, Naomah Steelman, Sarah Edwards and Elizabeth Edwards, rest of moveable estate. Brother David Edwards and son James, guardians of the rest of the children who are under age. Execs. were brother David and son James. The will was witnessed by Darius Corson, Rem Corson and Jesse Corson. On 16 July 1782 an inventory was made (£959.4.6) by Hugh Hathorn and John Baker.{NJCW 24:263}

Joseph apparently m. 1st Elizabeth Ingersol (Gloucester Co.) by license dated 1 Aug 1752.{MLNJ}

Joseph probably m. 2nd Susannah Ingersol 9 Dec 1776.{MLNJ}

Joseph was father of the following children: JAMES; ENOCH; JOSEPH; EBENEZER; ELIZABETH; SARAH; ELLENAR, m. (N) Steelman; NAOMAH, m. (N) Steelman.

2. DAVID EDWARDS, probable brother of Joseph (1) Edwards, m.

Deborah Thomson by license dated 20 Jan 1772.{MLNJ}

David Edwards of Upper Precinct d. leaving a will dated 7 July 1782, proved 6 Sep 1782. Mentioned were wife Deborah and his children: Sarah, David, Charles, Curtes and Mary, minors. Execs. were wife Deborah and John Baker and Hugh Hathorn of the same precinct, to be guardians of the children. On 23 Aug 1782 an inventory was filed (£789.13.1) by John Goldin and Jesse Corson.{NJCW 14:261}

David was father of the following children: SARAH; DAVID; CHARLES; CURTES; MARY.

3. JOSEPH EDWARDS, probable son (1) of Joseph Edwards, m. Sarah Willets, dau. of James.{Ltrs&Inv A(Rev):33} (plats shown)

Unplaced

EPHRAIM EDWARDS of Cape May Co. d. prior to 2 Jan 1715/6 when the estate was inventoried by John Taylor and George Hand. Administration was granted to Humphrey Hughes on 25 Aug 1717 who gave an account on 18 June 1718. Final account was made on 27 May 1726.{NJCW Admin bonds 1716-56 and Lib. 2:83}

WILLIAM EDWARDS of Cape May Co., yeoman, d. leaving a will dated 4 Jan 1733, proved 1749. Mentioned were wife Anne, extx. to have the estate. The will was witnessed by Henry Stites, Jr., Timothy Brandrof and Richard Robins, Jr.{NJCW 6:340} The estate was inventoried on 1 March 1749/50 by Frans. Taylor and Joseph Lord. Administration was granted to Joseph Savage of Cape May on 20 March 1749/50, the widow Anne, having renounced her right as extx. Fellow bondsman, Joseph Lord. Witnessed by Henry Young and Fras. Taylor.{NJCW}

William Edwards had an account with John Parsons, 30 March 1674.{Parsons Account Bk}

EPHRAIM EDWARDS recorded his ear mark on 7 June 1725.{First Public Rcds:274}

Ephraim Edwards of Cape May Co., yeoman, d. leaving a will dated 20 Feb 1777, proved 28 Nov 1777. Mentioned were son Daniel; dau. Jane Hildreth, to whom was devised the land which joined lands of James Edwards, dec.; dau. Esther Eldredge. On 28 Nov 1777 an inventory was filed (£192.2.9) by Henry Hand and Isaac Matthews.{NJCW 21:234}

ESTHER EDWARDS m. Robert Eldridge by license dated 11 Jan 1776.{MLNJ}

JAMES EDWARDS, Gent., d. leaving a will dated 15 Sep 1766, with codicils on 18 Sep 1766 (appointed Henry Hand of the Lower Precinct as guardian of dau. Elizabeth Edwards) and 31 Oct 1766 (son-in-law Jacob Crowell to be guardian of dau. Elizabeth, son-in-law Jacob Crowell, exec. instead of Mary Mulford, Ezekiel Mulford and Rachel Crowell), proved 24 Nov 1767. Mentioned in the will were dau. Mary Mulford to whom was devised 1/3 the plantation on northeast side and 1/3 the back land. Dau. Rachel Crowell to receive 1/3 of plantation to the southwest of Elizabeth Edwards and 1/3 of back lands, never to be sold. Rachel to be allowed to live in the lean-to for 10 years. Dau. Mary Mulford to pay granddau. Sarah Hand, £10 when 21. Execs. were dau. Mary Mulford, son-in-law Ezekiel Mulford, dau. Rachel Crowell, son-in-law Jacob Crowell. The will was witnessed by Abner Corson, Lewis Cresse and Anthony Cresse. On 29 Dec 1766 an inventory was filed £85.5.1) by John Eldredge and Lewis Cresse.{NJCW 13:361}

Ezekiel Mulford, wife Mary, dau. of James Edwards, mentioned in Book of Mortgages A: 56, dated 1767.

James was father of the following children: ELIZABETH; MARY, m. Ezekiel Mulford* by license dated 4 May 1762{MLNJ}; RACHEL, m. Jacob Crowell*, by license dated 9 April 1764.{MLNJ}

JANE EDWARDS m. David Hildreth by license dated 21 April 1769.{MLNJ}

JONATHAN EDWARDS m. Phebe Osbon by license dated 31 May 1766.{MLNJ}

MARCY EDWARDS m. John Gogin by license dated 1 June 1748.{MLNJ}

MARTHA EDWARDS m. Peter Corson* by license dated 1 Feb 1757.{MLNJ}

ELDREDGE (ELDRIDGE)

See Volume 1, No. 2 of the *Cape May County Magazine of History and Genealogy*, April 1931, p. 9, "The Pilgrim Ancestry of Cape May County," by Rev. Paul Sturtevant Howe, Ph. D. Cited hereafter as {Pilgrim Ancestry}.

See also *The Cape May County Magazine of History and Genealogy*, June 1942, p. 157, "The Eldridge Family," by H. S. Campion, Jr. in which addition material is added to the previous article and some corrections made.

See also Family Records, William and Esther Eldredge, p. 821, *Genealogies of New Jersey Families*. Cited here as {Eldredge Family Records}. The family record comes from a Bible printed in 1763, owned by Mrs. Cora Chambers of Dumont, NJ, when it was copied in the 1930s and is in a collection of the Genealogical Society of New Jersey. Bible Record number 4509.

First Generation

1. EZEKIEL ELDREDGE[21] of Yarmouth, Plymouth Colony, was one of the whalers who in 1690 made the first settlement of the Cape May County and founded the first village of thirteen houses at Town Bank on Delaware Bay, described by Aaron Leaming in his diary. "At the first settlement of the County, the chief whaling was in the Delaware Bay, and that occasioned the town to be built there, but there has not been one house in that town since my remembrance. In 1734 I saw the graves: Samuel Eldredge showed them to me. They were then about fifty rods from the Bay and the sand was blown to them. The town was between them and the water. There were some signs of the ruins of the houses."

On 17 Dec 1692 Ezekiel Eldredge of Cape May, weaver, for the sum of £12.10 bought 200 acres already in possession of said Eldredge, under lease dated 25 March 1688. {First Public Recds}

Ezekiel m. Sarah (N) (b. 1677, d. 25 July 1742).[22] Ezekiel died leaving a will dated 6 June 1710, proved 2 Feb 1711/12 in which he mentioned his wife Sarah and 5 sons and 3 daus., unnamed.

Ezekiel was the father of the following children: LYDIA, b. 1695, d. 1755, m. by license of 30 Aug 1736, as his 2nd wife, Elisha Hand*, son of John and Mercy Hand; EZEKIEL, b. ca. 1696, d. 1739 intestate, m. Elizabeth (N) who m. 2nd Nathaniel Norton*; WILLIAM, b. 18 April 1697/8, d. 7 Nov 1768, m. Esther Leaming* (b. 3 July 1702, d. 8 May 1773), dau. of Thomas and Hannah (Whilldin) Leaming; SAMUEL, b. ca. 1699, d. March 1745 leaving a will, m. Mercy Leaming*,

---

21 Probable son of William Eldredge of Yarmouth, Plymouth Colony.

22 Buried at Cold Spring Cemetery. Her tombstone is the oldest in the cemetery.

dau. of Thomas and Hannah (Whilldin) Leaming; ELISHA, b. ca. 1701, d. 1732 leaving a will, d. 1732, m. by license of 20 Sep 1729, Phebe Ludlam* (b. 1710, d. 23 Aug 1766, dau. of Joseph and Elizabeth (Ryder) Ludlam who m. 2nd Daniel Norton and m. 3rd Henry Young; SARAH, b. ca. 1703, m. by license dated 30 Oct 1727{MLNJ}, Henry Stites*, Jr., son of Henry and Hannah (Garlick) Stites; BETHIA, b. ca. 1705, m. 1st John Parsons, Jr.[23] (b. 7 March 1706, d. 1732), son of John and Elizabeth Parsons[24]; JOHN, b. ca. 1707.[25]

Sarah, widow of Ezekiel Eldredge, Sr., m. 2nd at the First Presbyterian Church, Philadelphia, 6 March 1715, Jacob Spicer* by whom she had a son: JACOB, Jr.

Second Generation

2. EZEKIAL ELDREDGE of Cape May Co., son of Ezekiel (1) Eldredge, d. prior to 30 Oct 1739 when administration was granted to Elizabeth, his widow, and son Ezekiel. Fellow bondsmen: Ephraim Edwards, John Eldredge. Witnesses: Samuel Eldredge, Robert Parsons and Jacob Spicer.{NJCW 4:200} An account was made on 7 Nov 1764 by Elizabeth Norton and Ezekial Eldredge, admins. Moneys were paid to Henry Young, Esq., Jonathan Pratt, John Eldredge, Joseph Page, Nathaniel Hand, Elisha Hand, Elijah Hughes, Sarah Parsons, Levi Eldredge, Nathan Eldredge, Elisha Eldredge, James Eldredge, Silas Eldredge, Nathaniel Forster,

---

23 Rev. Howe gave her husband as Robert Parsons.

24 Rev. Howe also names a second husband, Ezekiel Mulford.

25 Campion makes a case for another daughter. He notes that Lydia Eldridge Hand in her will dated 10 Nov 1754 makes bequests to persons who are mostly nieces and nephews. He infers from the bequest to Hannah, dau. of Nathan Hand, that Nathan's wife is Lydia's sister and notes that there is a Nathan who m. Hannah Eldredge by license dated 23 March 1742. The will of Nathan Hand, son of George, mentions a dau. Hannah and three other children: Japheth, Nathan and Stephen. These children are also named in the will of their grandfather, George Hand. However there is also a Nathan Hand, son of Zelophead Hand who in his will mentions a wife Hannah, suggesting that Campion's theory could be wrong. Campion notes that the will of Nathan of George mentions a wife Lydia and assumes that Hannah died earlier. Ezekiel Eldredge mentions only 3 daus. in his will (unnamed); Campion explains that Hannah could have been born after the writing of his will. One should also note that Elisha (5) Eldredge, presumed son of Ezekiel Eldredge, mentions in his will his brothers and the three sisters, Lydia Eldredge, Bethia Parsons and Sarah Stites and does not mention Hannah, further weakening Campion's case. The will of Elisha was written 1 Dec 1732.

Joseph Buck, Elizabeth Norton, Ezekiel Eldredge, etc. In the will was mentioned that Nathaniel Forster, Jr. was husband to the late Mary Eldredge and (1760) that Joseph Buck was husband of the late Elizabeth Eldredge.{NJCW}

Ezekiel's widow, Elizabeth, m. 2nd Nathaniel Norton*.

Ezekiel was father of EZEKIEL, who is probably the Ezekiel Eldridge who m. Sarah Crawford by license dated 14 April 1741{MLNJ}; possibly ELISHA.

3. WILLIAM ELDREDGE, son of Ezekiel (1) and Sarah Eldredge[26] of Yarmouth and Cape May, b. 2/18/1697/8, m. Esther Leaming*, dau. of Thomas and Hannah (Whilldin) Leaming (b. Cape May 3 July 1702, d. 5/8/1773).

William d. 11/7/1768, leaving a will dated 17 June 1765, proved 16 Jan 1769. Mentioned were wife Esther; sons: John and Eli; daus.: Esther Garison, Hannah Morris; grandsons: Elihu Eldredge, Daniel Eldredge and Thomas Eldredge; granddau. Mary Eldredge. Execs. were sons: Jehu and Eli. The will was witnessed by Daniel Hildreth, Joshua Hildreth, Jr. and Mary Peterson. On 25 Jan 1769 an inventory (£110.12.1 1/2) was filed by Zebulon Swain and Philip Godfrey.{NJCW 14:175}

Esther and William Eldredge were the parents of the following children{William Eldredge Bible; Eldredge Family Records}: DANIEL, b. 29 Sep 1721, d. 20 Sep 1758; ELIZABETH, b. 20 Aug 1723, d. 27 April 1753; THOMAS, b. 21 Sep 1725, d. Oct 1762; WILLIAM, Jr., b. 29 April 1727, d. 4 Oct 1752; ELIHU, b. 21 Sep 1731, d. 28 Nov 1755, drowned around the coast of Carolina; ESTHER, Jr., b. 25 Feb 1733/4, d. 29 Jan 1796; JEHU, b. 14 Nov 1736, d. 22 May 1800; ELI, b. 8 Feb 1738/9, d. 3 April 1791 about 4 o'clock in the afternoon; PRISCILLA, b. 19 Nov 1742, d. 26 Feb 1788, about 7 o'clock in the morning; HANNAH, b. 5/3/1746, m. 15 Dec 1764 Adam Morris by license.{MLNJ}

4. SAMUEL ELDREDGE, son of Ezekiel (1) and Sarah Eldredge, b. ca. 1699, d. March 1745 leaving a will, m. Mercy Leaming*, dau. of Thomas and Hannah (Whilldin) Leaming. They were the parents of the following children: SAMUEL, b. ca. 1730, d. 1796, m. Abigail, dau. of Thomas

---

26 Ezekiel Eldredge of Yarmouth, Plymouth Colony, was one of the whalers who in 1690 made the first settlement of the Cape May County and founded the first village of thirteen houses at Town Bank on the Delaware Bay.

Buck; SARAH[27], b. 23 Sep 1742, m. William Ewing; AARON, b. 2 Feb 1735, m. Cape May, 29 Jan 1761, Elizabeth Stillwell[28], dau. of Richard Stillwell; JACOB, b. ca. 1740, m. Sarah Covenover by 1769[29]; JEREMIAH, b. 5 Aug 1745, d. 28 April 1795{Cold Spring Cemetery}[30], m. Lydia Leaming, dau. of Thomas Leaming, no issue; PRISCILLA, m. by license of 12 April 1751, James Rayney (Raney, Reney)*{MLNJ} and later m. by license of 11 Aug 1775, Bartholomew McCormick.

Mercy m. 2nd Thomas Ross by whom she had no issue.

Samuel Eldredge, Esq., of Cape May Co., yeoman, d. leaving a will dated 23 Sep 1742, proved 22 May 1745. Mentioned were wife Mercy; eldest son Samuel, to whom he left the plantation where he lived, 100 acres adjoining James Page, southern half of Oyster Point and Negro man York; he to pay youngest dau. Sarah Eldredge, £10, when she arrives at age 17. Son Aaron to have 100 acres purchased of John Parsons and Christopher Church (both dec.), and execs. to Nathaniel Norton and 87 acres of woodland and other land (described). Son Jacob to have 100 acres purchased of Daniel Mulford and other land and lots (described). If wife delivered of a son, he to have plantation at Piles Grove in Salem. Execs. wife Mercy and son Samuel. Sons to have their lands at age 17. The will was witnessed by Abiah Ross, Jacob Spicer and William Ross. Letters granted to Samuel Eldredge on 11 June 1745.{NJCW 5:122} On 12 March 1744/5 an inventory was made by John Eldredge and Elisha Hand.{NJCW}

5. ELISHA ELDREDGE of Cape May, son of Ezekiel (1) and Sarah Eldredge, d. leaving a will dated 1 Dec 1732, proved 5 Jan 1732. Mentioned were brother Ezekiel Eldredge, exec. to whom was devised the estate, he to pay brothers Samuel and William £10, John £15, Jacob a cow and his mother £5. Sisters: Lydia Eldredge, Bethia Parsons and Sarah Stites. The will was witnessed by Huson Huse, Barnabas Crowell and James Flood.{NJCW 3:237} On 25 Dec 1732 an inventory was taken of

---

27 Of possible significance is the entry in the "Diaries of Aaron Leaming," in which he mentions delivering Jeremiah Leaming's wearing apparel to Nathan Shaw's children with added notation that "Priscilla Raney and Sarah Ewing appeard."

28 The marriage license was dated 1-25-1761 {MLNJ}

29 Deeds B:48.

30 Jeremiah d. leaving a will dated 12 April 1793 with a codicil. Not having issue he disposed of a large estate to his brothers and sisters and their representatives.

the estate which included half interest in a shallop. Appraisers: Thomas Ross and Richard Stites. An account of the estate was made on 19 March 1733. Payments were made to Huson Huse, Sarah Spicer, Thomas Ross, Lemuell Swain, James Flood, Richard Stites, John Eldridge, John Jones, Barnabas Crowell, William Eldridge, Sarah Spicer; pair of oxen delivered to Lydia Eldridge; two cows delivered to Bethia Parsons; one cow and a calf delivered to Jacob Spicer; one cow and a calf delivered to Sarah Spicer, etc.{NJCW}

6. JOHN ELDREDGE, son of Ezekiel (1) and Sarah Eldredge, b. ca. 1707, had a dau. named LYDIA. {Based on the will of John's sister Lydia}

Third Generation

7. EZEKIEL ELDREDGE of Cape May, yeoman, probable son of Ezekiel (2) Eldredge, d. leaving a will dated 18 May 1774, proved 4 Sep 1779. Mentioned were wife Sarah, children: Ezekiel, Ezra, Jonathan, Nathan, Hosea, Silas, Priscilla Eldredge, Mary Eldredge and Rachel Eldredge; cousin Elisha Eldredge, son of brother Elisha Eldredge, dec. On 5 Jan 1780 an inventory was filed (£5,416.5.10) by Levi Eldredge and Matthew Whilldin.{NJCW 21:257}

Ezekiel m. Sarah Crawford by license dated 14 April 1741. {MLNJ}

Ezekiel was father of the following children: EZEKIEL, EZRA, JONATHAN, NATHAN, HOSEA; SILAS; PRISCILLA; MARY; RACHEL.

8. DANIEL ELDREDGE, son of William (3) and Esther Eldredge, b. 9/29/1721, d. 9/20/1758 intestate. On 15 Aug 1759 an inventory of the estate was filed by John Leonard and Zebulon Swain which included half a vessel and debts. On 18 Aug 1759 a bond was issued to Thomas Eldredge as admin; Zebulon Swain, Gent., fellowbondsman, both of Cape May Co.{NJCW 9:313}

9. THOMAS ELDREDGE, son of William (3) and Esther Eldredge, b. 9/21/1725, d. 10/1762. Glory Eldredge (signed as Glory Aner Eldredge) was appointed admx. of his estate on 31 Jan 1763. Fellowbondsman: Eli Eldredge. Witnesses: Jacob Hand and Zebulon Swain. On 31 Jan 1763 an inventory (£228.14.7 1/2) was filed by Providence Ludlam and Zebulon Swain.{NJCW 11:414}

10. ELIHU ELDREDGE, son of William (3) and Esther Eldredge, d. 28 Nov 1755, drowned off the coast of Carolina. On 18 Sep 1756 a bond was issued to Daniel Eldredge as admin.; David Smith fellowbondsman, both

of Cape May Co.{NJCW 8:334} On 20 Sep 1756 an inventory was filed by Zebulon Swain and David Smith.{NJCW }

11. ESTHER ELDREDGE, dau. of William (3) and Esther Eldredge, b. 2/25/1733/4, d. 1/27/1796. She m. 1st by license of 18 Aug 1760, Abraham Hand, who d. after 12 Dec of the same year; in his will he mentions his wife Esther and "if I have no child then to fall to my cousin, Jesse Hand."

Esther m. 2nd by license of 13 Oct 1761, Rem Garrison, who d. leaving a will dated 10 Dec 1772, proved 30 April 1773 in which he named his wife Esther and daus.: Martha Garrison and Esther Garrison.

Esther m. 3rd by license of 8 Oct 1774, Daniel Hand. In her will Esther mentioned her dau. Martha Oram.

Children of Esther and Rem Garrison: MARTHA, b. 19 Nov 1763, d. 9 Oct 1819, m. by license of 16 Nov 1778, Samuel Oram who was b. 7 March 1755 and d. 19 Oct 1818; ESTHER. It appears that Esther had no issue by her first and third husbands.

12. JEHU ELDREDGE, son of William (3) and Esther Eldredge, b. 11/14/1736, d. 5/22/1800 intestate. His name is incorrectly recorded as John in the will of his father.

13. ELI ELDRIDGE, son of William (3) and Esther Eldredge, b. Cape May 8 Feb 1739, d. Cape May 3 April 1791, m. at Cape May by license of 20 June 1761{MLNJ}, Priscilla Leaming.

Eli Eldridge m. 2nd Elizabeth Stites*, dau. of Benjamin Stites, between 1788 and 1791.[31]

Eli d. by 31 May 1791 when Henry Stites was appointed admin of his estate.{NJCW 32:302} On 8 June 1791 an inventory was filed (£225.7.2) by Thomas Shaw and Richard Townsend.

At Court, May Term 1795 John Dickinson applied, on the part of the heirs of Priscilla Eldredge, dec., late wife of Eli Eldredge, Esqr., dec. for a division of her lands among her six children. The court decreed that a division of said land be made in such manner as to give to Priscilla Cresse, granddau. of the said Priscilla Eldredge and dau. of Lewes Cresse, 1/8 part of said land, and to John Dickinson the applicant who having bought the right, represents the other heirs, 7/8 thereof.{Ltrs&Inv A(Rev):99}

At Court, August Term 1795, Priscilla Eldredge, late the wife of

31 Mentioned in a deed as dau. of Benjamin Stites is Elizabeth, widow of Eli Eldredge (1791). {Deeds A:137}

Eli Eldredge, dec., in her lifetime stood seized of a tract of woodland in the Middle Precinct of Cape May Co. which she purchased of Jacob Spicer, dec., 100 acres. The said Priscilla Eldredge d. intestate and the same devolved to her six children, 2 sons and 4 daus. Priscilla Cresse the granddau. of said Priscilla Eldredge, being the heir of one of the devisees. The land was divided. (plat shown){Ltrs&Inv A(Rev):103}

At May Term 1794 John Dickinson applied on the part of the heirs of Priscilla Eldredge, dec. wife of Eli Eldredge, Esqr., dec. for the division of her lands among his 6 children, viz., Eli Eldredge, Zilpha Hand, Elizabeth Cresse, Esther Read, Jehu Eldridge, Priscilla Eldredge.{Ltrs&Inv A(Rev):95}

Eli and Priscilla Eldredge were the parents of the following children: ZILPHA, b. 11/10/1761, m. (N) Hand; ELIZABETH, b. 5/1/1763, m. Lewis Cresse and had a dau. Priscilla[32]; ELI, Jr., b. 5/10/1765, d. 1/25/1802; ESTHER, b. 7/13/1769, m. ca. 4 Jan 1786, Charles Reed[33]; JEHU, b. 5/5/1772, d. 11/6/1819; PRISCILLA, Jr., b. 8/17/1774; DEBORAH, b. 3/4/1778, d. 7/25/1783.{CMDB C:170}

14. SAMUEL ELDRIDGE, son of Samuel (4) and Mercy Eldridge, b. ca. 1730, d. 1796{inventory 12 March 1796}, m. Abigail, dau. of Thomas Buck. Their children mentioned in his will were: Hannah, wife of Joseph Greenway of Philadelphia; son David; heirs of Bethia Foster, wife of Constantine Foster[34]; heirs of Experience Albertson by right of their mother. All were mentioned as minors except Hannah Greenway. Division cited in deed of David Eldredge to Jacob Eldredge, 5 Dec 1800.{CMDB B:109}

At May and October Terms of court in 1796 Constantine Foster applied for a division of lands of Samuel Eldredge, dec., between Hannah Greenway, wife of Joseph Greenway, David Eldredge, the children of Bethia wife of Constantine Foster in right of their mother (Jacob, Mary and Richard Foster) and John Elbertson, son of John and Experience

---

32 In "The Pilgrim Ancestry of Cape May County," *The Cape May County Magazine of History and Genealogy*, April 1931, Rev. Howe cites Reports A, No. 1, Orphans' Court, et seq.

33 4 Jan 1786. Took bond of and granted marriage license to Charles Reed of Dividing Creek Cumberland County to take in marriage Esther Eldredge, dau. of Eli Eldredge, Cape May. {Ltrs&Inv A:9}

34 Mentioned in the land records of 1799, Deeds D: 1, is Richard Foster, son of Constantine and Lydia, and grandson of Samuel Eldredge. Deeds B:68 shows that in 1798 Samuel Eldredge had dau. Bethia Foster, who had children Jacob and Richard, and Mary who m. Richard Cresse.

Elbertson in right of his mother - all minors except Hannah Greenway. (plats shown){Ltrs&Inv A(Rev):118, 133}

Samuel was father of the following children: HANNAH; DAVID; BETHIA, m. Constantine Foster (by license dated 1 June 1773{MLNJ}) and had issue: Jacob, Richard and Mary; EXPERIENCE, m. John Elbertson [Albertson] and had a son John.

15. SARAH ELDREDGE, dau. of Samuel (4) and Mercy Eldridge, b. 23 Sep 1742, m. William Ewing. In the will of her brother, she is mentioned as the mother of Jeremiah, James, William, Elmer and Sarah Ewing. William Ewing d. leaving a will dated 10 May 1779. Sarah Ewing m. 2nd Jonathan Leaming. Sarah and William Ewing were parents of WILLIAM EWING, ship carpenter in Philadelphia, d. unmarried; JEREMIAH EWING, b. 1763, d. 11 Aug 1836, m. 1st Lydia Hand, dau. of Jeremiah Hand and m. 2nd Mary Nottingham; JAMES EWING, m. (N) Stites of Seaville, NJ, settled in Brownston, Indiana; THOMAS EWING, m. Lydia Rainey by whom he had Lydia who m. Noah Clarke, and Eliza Ewing; SARAH, m. David Ewing; ELMER EWING.{Pilgrim Ancestry}

16. AARON ELDREDGE, son of Samuel (4) and Mercy Eldridge, b. Cape May, 2 Feb 1735, d. 2 July 1785, m. Cape May, 29 Jan 1761, Elizabeth Stillwell (b. 27 June 1735, d. 23 April 1790). She was the dau. of Richard Stillwell*.{Book of Mortgages A:211, dated 1785}

Aaron d. by 27 June 1786 when Elizabeth Eldredge was appointed admx. of his estate. On 16 Aug 1785 an inventory was filed (£379.3.3) by Jacob Hughes and Matthew Whilldin.{NJCW 28:187}

Aaron was father of the following children: CHARLOTTA, b. 5 April 1765, m. ca. 1782, Persons Leaming; SARAH, b. 20 Feb 1767, d. 20 Jan 1846{Cold Spring Cemetery}, m. 3 June 1798, Aaron Edmunds* who previously m. 1st her sister; LYDIA, b. 4 March 1769, d. 29 Jan 1794, m. 25 June 1780, Aaron Edmunds*; AARON, d. 21 Aug 1819, age 48 years, 2 mos., 8 days, m. 17 June 1792, Hannah Langdon (d. 6 June 1846, age 61 years, 5 mos., 15 days){Cold Spring Cemetery}.

17. JACOB ELDREDGE, son of Samuel (4) and Mercy Eldredge, b. Cape May ca. 1740, m. Sarah Covenover, by license dated 21 Aug 1764, Gloucester Co., NJ. They had the following children: JACOB, m. Elizabeth (N); MARY (MERCY), m. (N) Smith, SARAH, probably m.

Josiah Crowellby license dated 28 Feb 1764; PRISCILLA, m. (N) Shaw.

Sarah Eldredge, possible wife of Jacob, b. 1747, d. 12 Feb 1804.{Cold Spring Cemetery}

18. JEREMIAH ELDREDGE, son of Samuel (4) and Mercy Eldredge, b. Cape May, 5 Aug 1745, d. Cape May, 28 April 1795, m. Lydia Leaming*, dau. of Thomas Leaming, by license dated 8 Sep 1775{MLNJ}; no issue.{Deeds A:178}

Jeremiah d. leaving a will dated 12 April 1793, proved 1 May 1795. Mentioned were wife Lydia; Jacob Eldredge, son of brother Jacob; brother Aaron Eldredge; Aaron Eldredge, son of brother Aaron; James Ewing, son of sister Sarah; Lydia Ewing, dau. of Thomas and Letty Ewing; Jeremiah Ewing, son of sister Sarah; brother Samuel; Letty Ewing, dau. of sister Priscilla; Eliza Ewing, granddau. of sister Sarah and dau. of David and cousin Sarah Ewing, dec.; Sarah Eldredge and Lydia Edmonds, daus. of brother Aaron; Charlott Leaming; William Ewing, son of sister Sarah; 3 daus. of brother Jacob: Mary Smith, Priscilla Shaw and Sarah Conell [probably Crowell]; John Albertson, son of Experience, dau. of brother Samuel; Mary Foster and Jacob Foster, dau. and son of Constant and Bethia Foster, the dau. of brother Samuel; Hannah Thomas, Jeremiah and James Thomas, children of Job and Hannah Thomas; cousins: Aaron Eldredge and Jacob Eldredge. Execs. were wife Lydia, cousin Aaron Eldredge and brother Thomas Leaming.{NJCW 36:171} An inventory was filed (£3051.17.7 1/2) by Jacob Hughes and Matthew Whilldin on 25 July 1795.{NJCW File:620E}

19. PRISCILLA BERTHOLAMA ELDREDGE, dau. of Samuel (4) and Mercy Eldredge, m. by license of 12 April 1751, James Rayney (Raney, Reney).* She later m. by license of 11 Aug 1775, Bartholomew McCormick.{MLNJ} Priscilla had a dau. LETTY who m. Thomas Ewing.

Fourth Generation

20. CHARLOTTA ELDREDGE, dau. of Aaron (16) and Elizabeth (Stillwell) Eldredge, b. 5 April 1765, m. ca. 1782, Persons Leaming (b. 1756, d. 9 March 1807[35]). They were the parents of the following children: AARON, b. 15 May 1784, d. 7 Jan 1836,[36] m. Hannah Stites (d. 12 April

---

35 Cold Spring Cemetery

36 Tabernacle Cemetery.

1862, aged 73 years, 6 months)[37]; FURMAN, b. 27 Sep 1786, d. 18 March 1832, m. Hannah Ludlam; MARY, b. 1778, d. 5 Feb 1861, m. Robert M. Holmes; PERSONS, b. 3 Sep 1790, d. 20 Nov 1820,[38] unmarried; JEREMIAH, b. 25 May 1792, d. at Dennisville, NJ, 26 April 1839, m. 3 Oct 1814, Abigail Falkenburge; JAMES RAINEY, b. 6 June 1794, m. 7 Aug 1814, Sarah Irwin.

21. AARON ELDREDGE, son of Aaron (16) Eldredge, on 17 Oct 1792 was granted a marriage license to marry Hannah Langdon.{Ltrs&Inv A:45}
Aaron, d. 21 Aug 1819, age 48 years, 2 mos., 8 days. Hannah Langdon d. 6 June 1846, age 61 years, 5 mos., 15 days.{Cold Spring Cemetery}.

Unplaced
ELISHA ELDREDGE[39] of Cape May Co. d. prior to 27 May 1758 when an inventory was filed by John Eldredge and Ebenezer Johnson. On 20 Aug 1759 a bond was issued for Persilah Eldredge as admx.; Daniel Hand fellowbondsman, both of Cape May Co.{NJCW 9:313}

A marriage license was issued to Joseph Buck and ELIZABETH ELDRIDGE, 10 July 1759.{MLNJ}

A marriage license was issued to Reuben Swain and ELIZABETH ELDRIDGE, 12 May 1772.{MLNJ}

A marriage license was issued to Ezra Hand and ELIZABETH ELDRIDGE, 2 Jan 1772{MLNJ}

A marriage license was issued to Abraham Hand and ESTHER ELDREDGE, possible dau. of William (3) Eldredge, 18 Aug 1760.{MLNJ}

A marriage license was issued to EZEKIEL ELDRIDGE and Phebe

---

37 Tabernacle Cemetery.

38 Tombstone at Cold Spring Cemetery reads d. 2 Nov 1820, aged 30 years, 1 month.

39 Possibly son of Ezekiel who mentions a son Ezekiel and noting Ezekiel (7) mentioned a brother Elisha, dec., in his will, dated 18 May 1774 and proved 4 Sep 1779. He refers to Elisha, son of brother, Elisha.

Crowell, 18 Oct 1768.{MLNJ}

GEORGIANA ELDREDGE of Cape May Co. d. prior to 9 March 1776, the day Eli Eldredge was appointed admin. Fellowbondsman: Phillip Cresse, both of said county.{NJCW 38:79}

JAMES ELDRIDGE of Evesham Township, Burlington Co., d. leaving a will dated 7 June 1760. Mentioned were wife Esther and children: Abigail, Enoch, William, Isaac, Abram, Levi and James.{NJCW 10:36}

A marriage license was issued to Rynear Hollingshead and JANE ELDRIDGE, 5 June 1772.{MLNJ}

A marriage license was issued to Jonathan Mills and JUDITH ELDREDGE, 30 Dec 1767.{MLNJ}

JUDITH ELDREDGE is buried at Cold Spring Cemetery (b. 8 Aug 1759, d. 26 Aug 1831).{Cold Spring Cemetery}

LEVI ELDREDGE of Cape May Co. d. prior to 7 Jan 1743 when administration was granted to Elizabeth Eldredge, his widow. Fellow bondsman: John Eldredge. Witnesses: Henry Young and James Whilldin.{NJCW Cape May Wills:114E} Inventory of the estate was made on 6 Jan 1743/4 which included cattle and horses; appraised by John Eldredge and James Whillden. On 25 Nov 1748 an account of the estate was made by Elizabeth Skillinger, late Elizabeth Eldridge, admx. Moneys paid to Robert Parsons, Nathan Hand, John Eldridge, James Welding, Ezekiel Mulford, Elisha Hand, Charles Golehar, John Hand, Jacob Spicer, Richard Shaw, Henry Young and Elisha Eldridge.{NJCW}

Levi Eldredge, only son and heir of Levi Eldredge of Cape May petitioned that Lemuel Swaine of Cape May be appointed his guardian. On 18 March 1758 a bond was issued for Lemuel Swain of Cape May Co., yeoman, as guardian.{NJCW Cape May Wills:186E}

A marriage license was issued to LEVI ELDRIDGE and Abigail Crowell, 7 Aug 1766.{MLNJ}

LEVI ELDRIDGE, b. 17 Oct 1776, d. 23 Nov 1822; buried with wife Elizabeth (b. 4 Dec 1780, d. 11 Jan 1868).{Cold Spring Cemetery}

A marriage license was issued to Henry Stites and LYDIA ELDRIDGE

17 Jan 1759.{MLNJ}

A marriage license was issued to Nathaniel Foster* and MARY ELDREDGE, 19 March 1754.{MLNJ}

A marriage license was issued to Edmund Bacon (Cumberland Co) and MARY ELDRIDGE, 28 March 1766.{MLNJ}

A marriage license was issued to John Shaw and MARY ELDREDGE, 4 Jan 1771.{MLNJ}

A marriage license was issued to ROBERT ELDRIDGE and Esther Edwards, 11 Jan 1776.{MLNJ}

A marriage license was issued to Josiah Crowell and SARAH ELDRIDGE, 28 Feb 1764.{MLNJ}

ZEBIAH ELDRIDGE m. Jonathan Nottingham 17 Dec 1797. Of age.{Baptists}

October Term 1795. On application of Philip Godfrey on behalf of Zebiah Eldredge, orphan child, for a division of lands late of Daniel Hildreth, dec., between said Zebiah Eldredge and Daniel Hildreth.{Ltrs&Inv A(Rev):112}

ENGLISH

JAMES ENGLISH of Cape May, Cape May Co., yeoman, d. prior to 2 April 1737 when administration of his estate was granted to William Greer of Cape May, yeoman. Fellow bondsman Peter Boynton of Burlington, merchant. Witness: Joseph Rose.{NJCW Cape May Wills:88E} The estate was inventoried on 13 April 1737 and included 3 hates, 10 silk hancklers, deers skins, furs and articles of merchandise. Appraised by James Statham and John Willits.{NJCW}

JOHN ENGLISH m. Rebecca (N). John had a son: JOHN[40].{Book of Mortgages A: 126, dated 1783}

---

40 The Gloucester Co. Court records show John English, Jr. of Great Eggharbour, Gloucester Co., m. Anne Inskeep of Burlington Co., spinster. {Gloucester Co. Court records dated 30 Sep 1749}

At May Court 1787 Rebecca Inglish complained that John Inglish, her son, had dispossessed her of her dower and asked for relief. The court gave the opinion that the ought to seek her redress by a suit of law.{Ltrs&Inv A(Rev):11}

John d. prior to 25 May 1784 when Rebecca English was appointed admx. Fellowbondsman: John English of Cape May Co. Witnesses: Thomas Scott and Eli Townsend.{NJCW 38:79}

MARY ENGLISH of Eggharbour, Gloucester Co. m. Elias Gandy by license dated 17 June 1737.{MLNJ}

SUSANNAH ENGLISH and Evy Bellangy m. by license dated 22 April 1738.{MLNJ}

WILLIAM ENGLISH m. Jane Lake of Great Eggharbour 18 June 1750.{Baptists}

EVANS

DAVID EVANS of Cape May Co. d. leaving a will dated 14 Nov 1755, proved 5 Feb 1760. Mentioned was cousin Nicholas Stillwell of said county, merchant, sole heir and exec. The will was witnessed by Isaiah Hand and John Leek.{NJCW 9:406} On 20 Nov 1759 an inventory of the estate was filed by John Willets and James Hathorn which included 1/3 of a sloop.{NJCW }

JOHN EVANS of Cape May Co., mariner, d. leaving a will dated 12 Aug 1770, proved 13 Feb 1771. Mentioned were wife Hannah; daus.: Rebecca Evans, Mary Evans, Hannah Evans, Elizabeth Evans and Sarah Evans; sons: William to whom was devised the plantation and the tract that joined Peter Corson between Willits thoroughfare and Tocehow River; two youngest sons: John; David, £130. Execs. were wife, son William Evans and Rebecca Evans and Mary Evans. The will was witnessed by Joseph Ludlam, Azariah Pain and Ananias Pain. On 31 Jan 1771 the estate was inventoried by John Townsend and Joseph Corson, including the sea sloop called the *Two Brothers* (£127); insolvent debts due in North Carolina, £13.14.3.{NJCW 15:268}

John was father of the following children: REBECCA; MARY; HANNAH, probably m. Neri Hand by license dated 15 Sep 1775{MLNJ}; ELIZABETH; SARAH; WILLIAM; JOHN; DAVID.

FISH

JOHN FISH signed on 1 July 1693 an ante nuptial agreement, showing his intentions to marry Mary Curwithy, both of Cape May. Should he survive her, then he was obligated to leave 1/2 of his property to her children. On 1 June 1693 John Fish gave authority of Mary Fish to convey all her land and tenements to her dau. Martha. Martha Curwithen born 16 June 1689.{First Public Rcds:271} On 1 Sep 1693 Mary Fish appointed Thomas Hand and Jacob Dayton, late of East Hamton of Long Island, to receive and manage her estate for her child until she was of age of 18 or day of marriage.{First Public Rcds:271}

At court 21 Sep 1698 John Fish, dec., by his exec. William Shaw, was discharged of his bond to the Justices of the County. "if hee did not pay the inventory of his wife Mary Fish, formerly Mary Curwithen, in defraying her debts, he, the sd. Fish, would pay itt to "her daster." Recorded 10 July 1703.{First Official Rcds}

According to Norman Harvey Vanaman, "The Account Book of John Parsons, With Notes," Cape May County Mag. of Hist. and Gen., p.169, John Parsons died about mid January 1693 and his widow m. John Fish who died in about 6 months and on 1 May 1696 the said widow died. Thus John Fish m. Elizabeth Parsons* between 1 Sep 1693 and 22 April 1695, Elizabeth Parsons, widow of John Parsons (Persons).

On 22 April 1695 was recorded letters of administration to Elisabeth Fish, widow and relict of John Fish.{First Official Rcds}

Elizabeth d. 1695/1696. Letters of administration were granted to William and Lidey Shaw, execs. to and for Elisabeth Fish, dec. on 12 Jan 1696.{First Official Rcds} An inventory of the estate of Elizabeth Fish, was taken by William Whitlock and John Richardson, 28 July 1696.{First Official Rcds}

FLOWER

JOHN FLOWER of Cape May Co., yeoman, d. prior to 16 Jan 1764 when William Flower, Gent. was appointed admin. Fellowbondsman: George Newton, Gent. of Cape May Co. An inventory was filed on 21 Dec 1763 (£909.8.7) by John Eldredge and Timothy Hand.{NJCW 11:504}

WILLIAM FLOWER d. leaving a will dated 31 Dec 1769, proved 20 Jan 1770. Mentioned were wife Mary; son William to whom was devised land on which testator lived and a tract of 22 acres bought of Samuel Jones on the Delaware Bay. Dau. Silvitha Flowers land on which Benjamin Ingram lived. Dau. Judith Flowers, land where Mary Taylor lived. Dau. Mary Flowers, land bought of Daniel Swain, Esqr. Exec. was wife. The will was witnessed by Samuel Eldredge, Edward Church and Jonathan Mills. On 22 Jan 1770 Henry Hand and Downes Edmunds were appointed admins. Fellowbondsmen: Timothy Hand and Christopher Foster, Gent., of Cape May Co. Witnesses: Zeruiah Hughes and Abigail Reeves. On 20 Jan 1770 an inventory (£372.1.11) was filed by Christopher Foster and Timothy Hand.{NJCW 14:270}

On 5 Sep 1774 Judith Flower of the Lower Precinct, Cape May Co., dau. of William Flower was appointed a guardian, Richard Edmunds. Fellowbondsman: Elisha Hand, both of said place, yeoman. Witnessed by John Newton and Isaac Willets.{NJCW 15:530}

On 24 April 1779 Mary Flower of Cape May Co., dau. of William Flower, dec. was appointed a guardian, Richard Edmunds. Fellowbondsman: Aaron Eldredge, both of said county, gent. Witnessed by James Watt and Elijah Hughes.{NJCW 22:63}

On 10 Feb 1772 William Flower of Cape May Co., son of William Flower of said county, dec., was appointed a guardian, Benjamin Ingrum. Fellowbondsman: Abraham Woolson, both of said county, gent. Witnessed by Zeruiah Hughes and Israel Hughes.{NJCW 14:506}

William was father of the following children: WILLIAM; SILVITHA; JUDITH; MARY.

FOREMAN

1. JONATHAN FOREMAN, possible brother of Ezekiel and John of Freehold, Monmouth Co., NJ.{See NJCW, v. 2, p. 183. Ezekial and John Foreman, both mention a brother Jonathan.} Jonathan m. Sarah (N). They were the parents of MARY, d. 6 Jan 1780, age 59 years, 9 mos., 14 days, m. Aaron Leaming*, Jr., by license of 13 Feb 1738.{Baptist Burials; MLNJ}

Jonathan Foreman of Cape May Co. d. prior to 19 Feb 1754 when Patience Foreman had been appointed admx.{NJCW 5:463}

Patience Foreman, possible widow of Jonathan, m. John Foster by license dated 5 Aug 1761.{MLNJ}

2. JONATHAN FOREMAN, son of Jonathan Foreman, was appointed a guardian, Joshua Shaw, on 13 Sep 1766. Fellowbondsman: George Taylor of Lower Precinct in Cape May Co. Witnesses: John Townsend, John

Taylor and Marcy Taylor.{NJCW 12:327}

Jonathan Forman m. Anna Hand on 16 June 1771.{Baptists; MLNJ}

3. MARTHA FOREMAN, dau. of Jonathan Foreman, was appointed a guardian, John Shaw on 19 Oct 1763.{NJCW 11:439}

NATHANIEL FOSTER

1. NATHANIEL FOSTER m. Mary Eldredge by license dated 19 March 1754.{MLNJ}

Nathaniel d. leaving a will dated 17 Feb 1769, proved 20 Feb 1769. Mentioned were wife Mary; sons: Salathaniel and Nathaniel; dau. Esther Hand. Exec. was son Salathaniel. On 22 Feb 1769 an inventory (£90.11.7) was filed by John Eldredge and Aaron Eldredge.{NJCW 14:180}

Nathaniel was the father of the following children: SALATHIEL; NATHANIEL; ESTHER, m. (N) Hand.

2. SALATHIEL FOSTER, son of Nathaniel (1) Foster, m. Mercy Carll 21 Nov 1749.{Year Book of the Church of the Advent, Cape May}

Salathaniel, b. 10 Jan 1725, d. 22 May 1792{Sheppard Papers} leaving a will dated 21 May 1792, proved 6 Aug 1792. Mentioned were wife Marcy [or Mercy]; son Salathaniel; son George; grandchildren: Reuben, Macy, Cornelia and Rachel Foster.{NJCW 34:460} On 5 May 1792 an inventory was filed (£170.2.10 3/4) by Constantine Carll and Robert Parsons.{NJCW 570E}

Based on the will, Salathiel was father of the following children: SALATHIEL, b. 1767; GEORGE. The Charles E. Sheppard Papers also show JAMES, b. 1751; REUBEN, b. 1757; and SARAH, b. 1760.{Sheppard Papers}

3. SALATHANIEL FOSTER, son of Salathiel (2) Foster, m. Judith Hughes by license dated 5 Oct 1787.{MLNJ}

4. GEORGE FOSTER, son of Salathiel (2) Foster, b. 11 Aug 1754, d. 30 Dec 1788, m. Rachel Edmonds*. They were parents of the following children: MARCH; CORNELIUS; RACHEL.{Sheppard Papers}

SAMUEL FOSTER

1. SAMUEL FOSTER, carpenter, of Cape May Co., d. leaving a will

dated 17 Dec 1762, proved 23 July 1764. Mentioned were wife Elizabeth, daus.: Hannah Foster, Elizabeth Stites, Marjery Young, Mary Foster; sons: Jonathan and William; grandson Samuel Foster. Execs. were wife and Jonathan Smith. On 21 July 1764 an inventory was filed (£128.14.8) by John Shaw and Daniel Smith.{NJCW 12:32}

Elizabeth Foster of Cape May Co., probable widow of Samuel Foster, d. prior to 14 Jan 1777 when Daniel Smith, Esq., was appointed admin. of her estate. Fellowbondsman: Benjamin Stites, both of said county. On 14 May 1777 an inventory was made by David Smith and Jotham Townsend.{NJCW 22:40}

Samuel was father of the following children: HANNAH; ELIZABETH, m. (N) Stites; MARJERY, m. (N) Young; MARY; JONATHAN; WILLIAM.

2. JONATHAN FOSTER, probable son of Samuel (1) Foster, m. Hannah Willden by license dated 28 July 1759.{MLNJ}

Jonathan Foster of Cape May Co. d. prior to 30 Jan 1777 when Hannah Foster, widow, was appointed admx. Fellowbondsman: Ezekiel Stevens, yeoman, of Cape May Co. On 30 Jan 1777 an inventory was made by Ezekiel Stevens and Thomas Hand.{NJCW 22:41}f

Unplaced

ABIGAIL FOSTER m. William Jonson by license dated 19 April 1742.{MLNJ}

CHARLES FOSTER m. Abiah Townsend*, by license dated 16 Oct 1764. {MLNJ}

CHRISTOPHER FOSTER m. Lydia Hand by license dated 18 Jan 1732. {MLNJ}

CONSTANTINE FOSTER m. Bathia Eldridge by license dated 1 June 1773.{MLNJ} They were the parents of the following children: JACOB; MARY, m. Richard Cresse{Deeds B:68}; RICHARD.{Ltrs&Inv A (Rev):118, 133}

DAVID FOSTER of Cape May Co. d. prior to 13 Oct 1762 when Samuel Foster was appointed admin. On 26 Oct 1762 an inventory (£121.8.0) was filed by John Shaw and John Smith.{NJCW 11:414}

HENRY FOSTER, brother of Samuel, m. Rhoday Smith by license dated

18 Sep 1777.{MLNJ}

Henry d. leaving a will dated 24 Jan 1781, proved 22 Oct 1781. Mentioned were son Henry, wife Rhoda and brother Samuel Foster. Extx. was wife Rhoda. On 5 July 1781 an inventory was filed (£84.9.6) by John Cresse and Benjamin Taylor.{NJCW 24:76}

Henry was the father of HENRY.

JOHN FOSTER m. Patience Foreman by license dated 5 Aug 1761.{MLNJ}

A marriage license was issued to MARY FOSTER m. Ephraim Stratton 20 July 1763.{MLNJ}

MARY FOSTER m. Isaac Stratton, Jr., 15 Oct 1734. His oldest dau. Hannah, b. 14 March 1734/5.{First Official Recds}

RICHARD FOSTER of Cape May d. prior to 13 Aug 1751 when a bond was issued for Christopher Lupton as admin.{NJCW Cape May Wills:152E}

SAMUEL FOSTER, d. 19 June 1814, age 61 years, 11 mos., 26 days {Baptist Burials}, m. by license dated 25 April 1774, Mary Smith, widow of John Smith* and dau. of Nathaniel Jenkins*.{MLNJ} Mary d. 4 March 1814, in her 76th year.{Baptist Burials}

STEPHEN FOSTER m. Abigail Stevenson by license date 4 Oct 1762.{MLNJ}

STEPHEN FOSTER m. Abigail Fancher 2 March 1773.{Baptists}

GANDY

1. THOMAS GANDY of Cumberland Co. d. in 1748.[41] The name of Thomas Gandy appears in Cape May County land records in the return of survey for Thomas Gandy, 50 acres, called the *Addition*, on seaboard side, adjoining Gandy's Hall, recorded 20 April 1699.{Deeds A:16} He left a will dated 21 May 1748, proved 31 Aug 1748. To son Aaron was devised land in line with Isaac Garrison's land, to mouth of a small creek that puts

41 In the same year died John Gandy and Samuel Gandy, both of Morris River, Cumberland Co. See NJCW 6:19 and NJCW 6:18, respectively.

out of "great tide pond" on the north side. Son David to have otherland and marsh. Daus. Patience (married), Catherine, Sarah (married), Mary, Phebe, Hannah, Priscilla, Rebecca (the last three to be bound out to learn trades) and Naomy. Execs. were son-in-law Nathan Shaw and John Ogden. The will was witnessed by Daniel Ogden, Elizabeth Ogden and Isaac Garrison.{NJCW 6:506} An inventory was filed (£180.12.3) on 31 Aug 1748 which included cattle, horses, swine and books; appraised by Henry Pierson and Daniel Ogden.

Thomas was father of the following children: AARON, DAVID, PATIENCE, m. Nathan Shaw*, son of William and Lydia Shaw; CATHERINE; SARAH; MARY; PHEBE; HANNAH; PRISCILLA; REBECCA; NAOMY(?).

2. AARON GANDY of Cumberland Co., probable son of Thomas (1) Gandy, d. leaving a will dated 24 Jan 1772, proved 10 March 1773. Mentioned were son Abiah Gandy to whom was devised land in Yockwock; son Moses; wife Elizabeth; dau. Elishaba Hult; dau. Hannah Gandy who would be given moveable estate when age 21. Execs. were friends, Joseph Ogden and William Dollis, Jr. The will was witnessed by Dan Lore, Anne Lore and David Shepherd. On 4 March 1773 an inventory was filed (£151.2.3) by David Shepherd and William Dalles.{NJCW 16:82}

Aaron was father of the following children: ABIAH; MOSES; ELISHABA, m. (N) Hult; HANNAH.

3. DAVID GANDY of Cape May Co., probable son of Thomas (1) Gandy, d. prior to 29 Nov 1757 when an inventory of the estate was filed by Joseph Goldin and Joseph Edward which included bonds and book debts. On 13 Dec 1757 a bond was issued for Rebecca Gandy admx.; Joseph Goldin fellowbondsman, both of Cape May Co.{NJCW 8:497}

4. PHEBE GANDY of Fairfield in Cumberland Co., possible dau. of Thomas (1) Gandy, m. David Casto, 17 Aug 1752.{Baptists}

5. ABIJAH GANDY of Cumberland Co., son of Aaron (2) Gandy, d. leaving a will dated 23 April 1776, proved 12 March 1777. Wife Mary to have use of the plantation and the bringing up of the children. Oldest son Henry would have the plantation at his mother's decease. Also mentioned were sons Abijah, Shepherd (minor); dau. Deborah Gandy. Youngest two youngest sons to be bound out to trades, according to an agreement if son-in-law lives with his mother until of age. Execs. were Mary and Nathan Shepherd. The will was witnessed by Gideon Heaton, Anna Lore and

Tabitha Shepherd. On 12 March 1777 an inventory was filed (£151.5.2) by Gideon Heaton and Hosea Shepherd.{NJCW 18:156}

Abijah was father of the following children: HENRY; ABIJAH; SHEPHERD; DEBORAH.

6. MOSES GANDY of Downs Township, Cumberland Co., son of Aaron (2) Gandy, was made a ward of Silas Newcomb on 23 Feb 1774. Fellowbondsman: John Daniel of Fairfield of Cumberland Co., yeoman.{NJCW 15:514}

Moses d. leaving a will dated 26 Dec 1776, proved 12 March 1777. Mentioned were brother Abijah; sister Elishabe Hewet; sister Hannah Gandy and Elishabe Hewet's dau. Mary Hewet; brother Abijah Gandy's 3 sons: Henry, Abijah and Shepherd Gandy. Execs. were Dan Lore and David Lore. The will was witnessed by Ann Shepherd, Anna Lore and George Taylor. On 13 Jan 1777 an inventory was filed (13.6.3) by Alban Davis and Thomas Campbell.{NJCW 18:168, 24:171}

Unplaced

DAVID GANDY of Downs Township, Cumberland Co., yeoman, of unknown relationship to the above persons, d. leaving a will dated 13 Nov 1772, proved 17 Aug 1775. Mentioned were three oldest sons, Thomas David and Ephraim to whom was devised the lands. Three youngest children to have £50. Execs. were James Diament and David Whitecar. On 27 July 1775 an inventory was filed (£132.18.2) by John Daniels and Timothy Elmer. On 5 May 1777 was filed by David Whitecar. Cash had been paid to Rachel Garrison, Naomi Hewit, Dan Lore, Abijah Gandy, Jonathan Lore, Sarah Joslin, Mary Nixcson, Catharine Gandy, John Garrison, James Benson and David Garrison. Paid Nathan Daniels, towards the support of 3 children which testator ordered to be put out, £13.12.6. For bringing up an infant of but 2 years old till it can be put out clear of expense, £24. Paid Mary Davis for support of another child, from 5 years old till the same arrives at age of 18, £12.{NJCW 17:229, 18:469}

David was father of the following children: THOMAS[42]; DAVID; EPHRAIM; others.

A marriage license was issued to ELIAS GANDY and Mary English (Gloucester Co.), 17 June 1737.{MLNJ}

---

42 This may be the Thomas Gandy who d. 4 March 1814 in his 78th year and m. Dorcas Hildreth, widow of Jonathan Hildreth.{Baptist Burials}

A marriage license was issued to Hugh Hathorn and ELIZABETH GANDY, 13 Aug 1761.{MLNJ}

A marriage license was issued to JOHN GANDY and Lydia Williams, 30 Aug 1774.{MLNJ}

John d. by 31 March 1800 when Lydia Gandy was appointed admx. of his estate.{NJCW 39:92, File:733E}

A marriage license was issued to John Bartson and RHODA GANDY, 30 Nov 1763.{MLNJ}

SAMUEL GANDY of Cape May Co. d. leaving a will dated 20 Nov 1771, proved 30 March 1772. Mentioned were wife Mary; eldest son David Gandy to whom was left the home tract when 21; brother Thomas Gandy; second son Aaron to be put apprentice at age 14 to brother John Gandy to learn the trade of shoemaker; youngest son John Gandy; dau. Easter to have 1 1/2 years schooling. On 18 March 1772 an inventory was filed (£147.13.8) by John Townsend and Joseph Corson.{NJCW 16:1}

A marriage license was issued to Gabriel Regain and SUSANNA GANDY, 8 July 1749.{MLNJ}

A marriage license was issued to THOMAS GANDY and Elizabeth Young, 12 Dec 1768.{MLNJ}

A marriage license was issued to URIAH GANDEY and Lydia Baner, 23 Feb 1767.{MLNJ}

GARLICK

The following information is largely based on the article, "The Account Book of John Parsons, With Notes," *The Cape May County Magazine of History and Genealogy*, p. 166. June 1942. By Norman Harvey Vanaman. See also "The Leamings - Some Historical Notes of a Family and the Times," *The Cape May County Magazine of History and Genealogy*, p. 85. June 1956. By Karl A. Dickinson. See this article for more details on the early family history in New England.

According to Mr. Vanaman,

1. JOSHUA GARLICK of New England, m. Elizabeth Hardy, and

they were the parents of the following children: HANNAH, b. 1665, m. Henry Stites on 15 Feb 1693/4{First Public Rcds}; JOHN, d. unmarried; JOSHUA, b. Oct 1672, d. 24 Aug 1677; ELIZABETH, b. 1675; ABIAH, 18 Sep 1677.

Joshua Garlick had an account with John Parsons in 1676.{Parsons Account Bk} Reference is made to Elizabeth Garlick, widow, in 1679.{Parsons Account Bk} Following the death of Joshua Garlick, Elizabeth m. John Parsons* 21 May 1679. As his wife she moved to Cape May Co. in 1691.[43] Following the death of John Persons in January 1693 Elizabeth m. John Fish.

Joshua Garlick, Junr., d. leaving a will dated 24 Aug 1677. He left 12 acres and a mill to his wife Elizabeth until son Joshua arrived at age 21. Also mentioned was son John under age of 21 and daus. Hannah and Elizabeth. An inventory was filed on 31 May 1678. {Suffolk Co. [Long Island] Sessions:78}

2. HANNAH GARLICK, dau. of Joshua (1) and Elizabeth Garlick, b. 1665, d. 1734, m. Henry Stites by license dated 15 Feb 1693/4. They were the parents of HENRY, RICHARD, JOHN, JOSHUA, ISAIAH, MARY and PHEBE.

3. ELIZABETH GARLICK, dau. of Joshua (1) and Elizabeth Garlick, m. (N) Thomson and d. at Long Island.

4. ABIAH GARLICK, dau. of Joshua (1) and Elizabeth Garlick, m. Ceaser Hoskins and settled on the w. side of Morris River. She and her husband were the parents of the following children: CESER; JOHN; MERCY and THOMAS. Ceaser Hoskins later m. Rebecca (N).

5. JOSHUA GARLICK, Sr. of Cape May Co., yeoman, probable son of Joshua (1) Garlick[44], m. Lucy Brookes by license dated 14 Sep 1738.

Joshua d. leaving a will dated 20 April 1746, proved 6 Aug 1746. Mentioned was wife Lucy. {A marriage license was issued to Lucy

---

43 See Dickinson article.

44 On 27 Oct 1693 Joshuah Garlick of East Hampton on Long Island, weaver, signed a release and discharge of all claims to John Parsons [his step-father].

Brookes and Josiah Garlick, dated 14 Sep 1738}. In the will Lucy was to have all wool and leather at Elisha Hand's and all flax if she lived at Cape May. Wife's dau., Sarah Brooks. Son John and grandson Richard Stites, son of dau. Abigail Stites, to have equally testator's right in the plantation belonging to the "Prispeteren Society." Daus.: Abigail Stites, Phebe Smith, Rebecca Johnston (had children), and grandson, Abenor Church (under age). Cattle at Cohansey and bond due from Ebenezer Johnson to dau. Abigail Stites and her son Richard. Execs. were dau. Abigail and grandson Richard Stites. The will was witnessed by David Cresey, Ephraim Edwards and Elijah Hughes.{NJCW 5:313} On 6 Aug 1746 an inventory was taken of the estate by Jeremiah Hand and Ephraim Edwards.{NJCW}

Joshua was father of the following children: JOHN; ABIGAIL, m. Richard Stites*; PHEBE, m. (N) Smith; REBECCA, m. (N) Johnston.

6. JOSHUA GARLICK, Jr., of Cape May Co., yeoman, d. prior to 15 July 1733 when Joshua Garlick, Sr. was appointed admin., of the estate. Fellow bondsman, John Garlick, both of afsd. county. Witnesses: Jacob Spicer and Silvanus Garlick.{NJCW 3:357} On 21 July 1733 an account was made which included cattle and sheep. Sworn before Jacob Spicer, Surrogate.{NJCW}

GARRETSON (GARRISON)

See "Rem and Rebekah Erritsen Cape May County Pioneers," *The Cape May County Magazine of History and Genealogy*, p. 156. June 1958. By Marie E. Garretson. This is a continuation of the story, which was published in the 1955 Magazine, of Rem and Rebekah Hubbard Gerritsen and their many descendants.

First Generation

1. JACOB GARRISON of Cohansy, Salem Co., d. leaving a will dated 4 Sep 1705, with codicil dated 9 June 1708, proved 19 Sep 1709. Mentioned were wife Christiana, son Abraham, grandson Isaac, son of son Isaac Garrison, lately dec., and his wife Lidian. Extx. was wife. The will was witnessed by William Dare, Jr., Petter Garrison and Samuel Alexander. The codicil stated that since the testator had sold to John Garrison some land, bequeathed to son Abraham, he gives him another lot.{NJCW 1:244} On 30 April 1709 an inventory of the personal estate was filed (£111.19.10) which included one Negro, made by Benjamin Seelie and James Paget.{NJCW Salem Wills}

Garret, Peter, Jacob and John Garrison released to their mother Christian all rights or claims they had to the estate of their father - sworn to at Burlington on 19 Sep 1709.

On 13 June 1709 his estate was inventoried by John Townsend.{NJCW Cape May Wills}

Jacob was father of the following children: ABRAHAM; ISAAC; GARRET; PETER; JACOB; JOHN.

2. REM GARRISON/Garson/Garretson was younger brother of Jacob (1) Garrison, according to Marie E. Garretson. Rem d. leaving a will dated 29 April 1715, proved 10 May 1715. Mentioned were wife Rebecker; sons: Jacob, Daniel, Garot, Joab and Noah; daus.: Mary, Elisebeth and Rachel. Wife was extx. The will was witnessed by Robert Townsend (27 years old), Henery Linard and Abraham Benor. The estate was inventoried on 9 May 1715 by John Somers and Robert Townsend. On 18 Sep 1715 Rebeckah Garreson gave oath as extx.{NJCW 2:26}

An indenture was made on 25 March 1693, between George Taylor of Cape May, yeoman, attorney for Thomas Kane, Knt., Edmund Harrison, Doctr. Daniell Cox, Esqr. & the West Jersey Society, & William Golder, and Rem Garison, of Graves End, Long Island, for £101.12 was sold to Golder and Garrison 1016 acres in Cape May Co. on southwest side of Eggharbor.{First Public Rcds}

Rem was the father of the following children: REM; JACOB; DANIEL; GAROT; JOAB; NOAH; MARY[45]; ELIZABETH; RACHEL.

Second Generation

3. JACOB GARRETSON, son of Rem (2) Garretson, d. 27th day, 3rd mo., 1765. On 4th day, 10th mo., Jacob Garritson was charged with frequently taking too much strong drink and attending a disorderly marriage.{GEMM}

Jacob d. leaving a will dated 24 July 1763, proved 8 June 1765. Mentioned were wife Martha; children: Rem, Garret, Rebecca Wilson and Phebe Goldin; granddau. Mercy Daniels. One-half of the plantation of 320 acres was devised to Rem Garrison and 1/2 to Garret Garrison. Wife to be guardian of Garret. Execs. were wife and said Rem Garrison. The will was witnessed by Daniel Garretson, Hannah Eldredge and Jacob Spicer. On 30 April 1765 an inventory was made (£157.2.7) by John Willets and Isaac Baner.{NJCW 12:128}

---

45 This may be the Mary Garretson who m. Benjamin Holdin on 9-11-1715. {Misc. recds}

Children of Jacob Garritson{GEMM}: RACHEL, b. 5th day, 4th mo., 1721, d. 4th day, 11th mo., 1721; REM, b. 26th day, 2nd mo., 1722, d. 7th day, 3rd mo., 1722; RACHEL, b. 26th day, 5th mo., 1728, d. 2nd day, 8th mo., 1757; REBECKAH, b. 2nd day, 7th mo., 1725, m. (N) Wilson; JACOB, b. 22nd day, 3rd mo., 1728, d. 13th day, 2nd mo., 1758; MARCY, b. 9th day, 12th mo., 1731/32, d. 4th day, 7th mo., 1754; PHEBE, b. 4th day, 2nd mo., 1735; d. 4th day, 7th mo., 1735; PHEBE, b. 3rd day, 9th mo., 1736, m. Joseph Golding by license dated 12 Sep 1760{MLNJ}; REM, b. 31st day, 3rd mo., 1739; GARRIT, b. 4th day, 3rd mo., 1742, d. 4th day, 4th mo., 1743; GARRIT, b. 27th day, 10th mo., 1745, d. 23rd day, 8th mo., 1775; MARTHA, b. 19th day, 8th mo., 1748, d. 19th day, 10th mo., 1752.

Martha Garretson, wife of Jacob Garretson, d. 18th day, 8th mo., 1775.{GEMM} Died of "Bloody Flux," May/June 1775, old Martha Garretson and grandson.{Leaming Diaries} Of Upper Precinct, Martha Garretson left a will dated 14 Aug 1774, proved 6 Sep 1775. Mentioned were son Garret Garretson and dau. Phebe Golden to whom she left 1/3 the estate of Jacob Garretson as devised to her. Granddau. Rachel Butler received a heifer. Execs. were son Garret and dau. Phebe. The will was witnessed by Japhet Hand, Jeremiah Perkins and Lovica Terry. On 26 Aug 1775 an inventory was filed by Hugh Hathorn and Samuel Garretson.{NJCW 17:248}

Marcy Daniel, granddaughter of Jacob Garritson, b. 12th day, 8th mo., 1755.

4. DANIEL GARRITSON, son of Rem (2) Garritson, b. 1706 and Hannah Garritson, his wife, b. 1703. Children of Daniel and Hannah Garritson: DANIEL, b. 27th day, 2nd mo., 1738; JOSHUA, b. 28th day, 9th mo., 1739, m. Phebe Scull by license dated 23 Nov 1763{GEMM; MLNJ} and d. by 22 May 1792 when Phebe Garretson, widow, was appointed admx. of his estate{NJCW 34:465}.

5. NOAH GARRETSON, son of Rem (2) Garretson, m. Marey Golden by license dated 1 Nov 1737{MLNJ}.

Noah d. 23rd day, 3rd mo., 1773{GEMM}, leaving a will dated 22 March 1772, proved 16 March 1774. Mentioned were wife Mary, son Elijah to whom the plantation was devised, he to pay son James Garretson, 5 shillings, and to son Samuel £10. Son James to have the care of the plantation that now belongs to Noah Garrison, so far that my son Elijah shall not sell. Execs. were wife Mary and son James. Witnesses: John Baker, Hannah Brandeth, Joshua Garretson and Isaac Willets. On 16 March 1774 Samuel Garretson, yeoman, was appointed admin., with will annexed. Fellowbondsman: John Willets, Sr., both of Cape May Co. Witnesses: John Goldin and Hugh Hathorn. On 9 June 1773 an inventory was made by Isaac Willits and Hugh Hathorn. (£138.11.4 3/4){NJCW 17:172}

Noah was father of the following children: ELIJAH; JAMES; SAMUEL.

6. REM GARRITSON, son of Rem (2) Garretson, m. Esther Hand by license dated 13 Oct 1761.{MLNJ} He was disowned by Great Egg Harbor Monthly Meeting on 1st day, 2nd mo., 1762 for marrying out of Unity.{GEMM}

Rem Garretson of Cape May Co. d. leaving a will dated 10 Dec 1772, proved 30 April 1773. Mentioned were wife Easther, daus. Martha Garretson and Easter Garretson. If wife had a son then the land to go to him. Wife and Eli Eldredge to be guardians of children. Execs. were wife and Eli Eldredge. The will was witnessed by Archibald Hughes, Caleb Aydelott and Hannah Stites. On 22 April 1773 the estate was inventoried by Isaac Willets and John Baker.{NJCW 17:36}

On May Term 1776 the estates of Rem Garretson were ordered to be divided between Martha Oarum, wife of Samuel Oarum and Easter Baker, wife of John Baker, Jr. 1 Aug 1786.{Ltrs&Inv A(Rev):6}

Rem was father of the following daus.: MARTHA, m. 16 Nov 1778 m. Samuel Oarum (Orem){MLNJ} and had children; ESTHER (Easter), m. John Baker, Jr.

Third Generation

7. GARRET GARRETSON, son of Jacob (3) Garretson, b. 27th day, 10th mo., 1745, d. 23rd day, 8th mo., 1775. Garret (of Upper Precinct) d. leaving a will dated 15 Aug 1775, proved 6 Sep 1775. Mentioned were sister Phebe Golden to whom he left all his estate. Extx. was his said sister. The will was witnessed by Samuel Garretson, Japheth Hand and Lovica Terry. On 26 Aug 1775 an inventory was made by Hugh Hathorn and Samuel Garretson.{NJCW 17:250}

8. DANIEL GARRETSON, son of Daniel (4) Garretson, m. Mary Osborn by license issued 19 June 1761.{MLNJ} Mary was the dau. of Ananias Osborne. Daniel and Mary were the parents of SAMUEL (1790).{Deeds A:169}

Daniel d. prior to 19 April 1783 when Mary Garretson was appointed admx. Fellowbondsman: Eli Eldredge of Cape May Co. Witnesses: Philip Godfrey and Judith Hughes. On 4 April 1783 an inventory was filed (£272.5.0) by Philip Godfrey and Eli

Eldredge.{NJCW 24:265}

9. JAMES GARRETSON, yeoman, son of Noah (5) Garretson, m. Sarah Golden* by license dated 28 April 1760.{MLNJ}

James d. 2nd day, 2nd mo., 1774{GEMM}, leaving a will dated 20 April 1773 and proved 16 March 1774. Mentioned were wife Sarah, son not yet named, and his is to pay dau. Elizabeth Garretson, £10. Execs. were wife Sarah and Isaac Townsend; they were to sell that tract of 100 acres on Peck's Beach. The will was witnessed by Joseph Edwards, Isaac Willets and Amos Ireland. On 10 March 1774 the estate was inventoried by John Baker and John Golden (£145.12.7){NJCW 17:174}

James was father of the following children: ELIZABETH; SON unnamed in will.

Unplaced

A marriage license was issued to Daniel Hand and ESTHER GARRISON, 8 Oct 1774.{MLNJ}

DEBORAH GARRISON m. 8 May 1726, John Taylor, after the death of his wife Lydia (Schillinx).{First Official Recds}

William Hand and HANNAH GARRISON (Cumberland Co.), 17 Nov 1775.{MLNJ}

A marriage license was issued to Richard Shaw and JERUSHA GARRITSON, 19 June 1764.{MLNJ}

JOB GARRETSON, d. 30th day, 9th mo., 1763.{GEMM}

William Golden & MARY GARISON, both of Tuckehoo, m. 10 Sep 1766.{Baptists}

Ezekiel Steward and RACHEL GARISON, m. May 4, 1773.{Baptists}

SAMUEL GARRISON and Rhoda Hewet, m. Feb 24, 1773.{Baptists}

STEPHEN GARISON and Sarah Hand, m. Jan 20, 1773.{Baptists}

GODFREY

1. BENJAMIN GODFREY was living on Cape May in 1692. The Acts of Assembly were published publickly at a town meeting at the house of Benjamin Godfrey on Cape May on 10 May 1692.{First Public Rcds} On 2 May 1693 the West Jersey Society conveyed to Benjamin Godfrey, merchant, 210 acres.{Deeds A:322}

2. ANDREW GODFREY of Cape May Co., and possibly related to Benjamin (1) Godfrey, d. leaving a will dated 30 April 1736, proved 15 July 1736. Mentioned were wife Elizabeth to whom was devised the plantation during her widowhood and afterwards to son James. Sons Philip and Andrew to have a tract up Great Egg Harbour River. Legacies to daus. Anne (eldest), Tibitha, Rebecca and Rachel. Execs. were wife Elizabeth and son James. The will was witnessed by Jacob Garretson, Peter Corson and John Leonard. Letters granted 24 Aug (1736).{NJCW 4:63} On 24 May 1736 an inventory was made which included Negro man Dag and another Negro man, 37 cattle, 40 sheep, 3 horses and 23 swine - appraised by Henry Young and John Willets.{NJCW}

Andrew was father of the following children: JAMES; PHILIP; ANDREW; ANNE; TIBITHA; REBECCA; RACHEL.

3. PHILIP GODFREY, probable son of Andrew (2) Godfrey, m. Ruth Osborn*, dau. of Nathan Osborn, by license dated 19 Oct 1748.{MLNJ}

Oct. 2 [1777] Ruth Godfrey aged about 26 died of the Bloody flux.{Leaming diaries} [One would guess that Ruth was the dau. of Philip and Ruth Godfrey.]

Philip Godfrey d. leaving a will dated 4 Dec 1795, proved 24 Oct 1797. Mentioned were wife Ruth; sons: Philip, Nathan, Thomas, John; grandchildren: James Godfrey, son of son Thomas, Richard Campbell, Elizabeth and Mathew, children of dau. Rachel, minors; daus.: Lydia, Sylvia, Elizabeth, Mary, Rachel and Phebe.{NJCW 37:155} An inventory was filed (£1098.71) on 21 Aug 1810 by Elijah Townsend and Shamgar Hewitt.{NJCW File:680E}

Philip was father of the following children: PHILIP; NATHAN; THOMAS; JOHN; LYDIA; SYLVIA[46]; ELIZABETH; MARY; RACHEL; PHEBE; possibly RUTH who d. 1777 at age 26.

---

46 Sylvia sometimes is transcribed for Lydia in the records.

4. RACHEL GODFRE, probable dau. of Andrew (2) Godfrey, m. Samuel Townsend*. On 3rd day, 8th mo., 1752, the marriage of Samuel Townsend and Rachael Godfree was reported as orderly accomplished.{GEMM}

5. JAMES GODFREY, probable son of Andrew (2) Godfrey, d. leaving a will dated 1 June 1795, proved 17 May 1795. Mentioned were wife Elishabea; sons: James, Jacob, Elijah; daus. Elizabeth Corson, Priscilla Smith and Elishabea Godfrey; grandsons: James, Jacob and George Godfrey.{NJCW 36:177} An inventory was filed on 10 Aug 1795 (£642.5) by Abijah Smith and John Swain.{NJCW File:622E}

James was the father of the following children: JAMES; JACOB; ELIJAH; ELIZABETH, m. Peter Corson by license dated 20 July 1763{MLNJ}; PRISCILLA, m. (N) Smith; ELISHABEA.

6. ANDREW GODFREY, probable son of Andrew (2) Godfrey, m. Abigail Smith by license dated 5 Jan 1770.{MLNJ}

7. JAMES GODFREY, probable son of James (5) Godfrey, m. Phebe Townsend by license dated 26 Feb 1765.{MLNJ}

James d. leaving a will dated 1 March 1798, proved 27 Sep 1798. Mentioned were sons: James, Thomas, Matthew and Enoch; sons?: George and Jacob.{NJCW 37:554} On 27 Sep 1798, no extx. having been appointed, Phebe Godfrey was appointed admx.

In February term, 1802, a decree of the Orphan Court was made to divide the lands of the legatees of James Godfrey, dec. and Parmanas Corson, Esqr., between the said legatees and the said Parmanas Corson, one of the legatees being a minor under the age of 21. On 26 May 1802 division was made between Parmanas Corson and Thomas Godfrey, Matthew Godfrey and Enoch Godfrey. (plat shown){Ltrs&Inv A(Rev):159}

James was father of the following children: JAMES; THOMAS; MATTHEW; ENOCH.

8. PHILIP GODFREY, probable son of Philip (3) Godfrey, m. Phebe Smith by license dated 4 Feb 1775.{MLNJ}

9. ELIJAH GODFREY, probable son of James (5) Godfrey, m. Martha Swain by license dated 8 Nov 1769.{MLNJ}

Unplaced

The Bloody Flux prevailed. 26 Sep 1777. ANDREW GODFREY aged

about 4 yrs. & 27th RICHARD GODFREY about 9 years died.{Leaming diaries}

GOFF

See "Early West Creek Settlers," *The Cape May County Magazine of History and Genealogy*, p. 142. June 1958. By Roy Hand.

See "The Goff and Bishop Families," *The Cape May County Magazine of History and Genealogy*, p. 45. June 1964, by Dr. Roy Hand.

According to Dr. Hand,

> Rev. Stephen Goff was born in Cambridge, England, in 1571. He was Rector of Stanmore Parish, Sussex Co., England. Sons: Edward and William. Edward, son of Stephen, m. Joyce (N). In 1634 they sailed from Ipswick, England, and landed in Watertown, MA in 1635. Their son Samuel (d. 15 Jan 1706) m. Ann Bernard (b. 1635-1679) John Goff (b. Nov 1666) sailed from Norwalk, CT, and settled at Tarkill on the Tucahoe River, NJ, ca. 1700. He bought land along East Creek in Cape May Co. ca. 1710. He recorded his ear mark in Cape May Co. 31 Jan 1710-11. John Goff (b. 1702, d. 1761), grandson of Samuel and Ann (Bernard) Goff, moved to Cape May Co. ca. 1750.

1. JOHN GOFF d. on 1 Jan 1761 as mentioned in "Diaries of Aaron Leaming."

John Goff of Upper Precinct, Cape May Co., yeoman, left a will dated 11 April 1754, proved 11 Feb 1761. Mentioned were wife Mary; sons: David and John to whom were left lands in Cape May Co. and sons: William and Thomas to whom were devised lands in Cumberland Co. Exec. was wife Mary and if she remarried then son David. The will was witnessed by Joseph Savage, Clement Daniels and Deborah Daniels.

John was father of the following children: DAVID; JOHN; WILLIAM; THOMAS.

2. JOHN GOFF, son of John (1) and Mary Goff, b. 22 April 1743, d. 15 Oct 1809, m. Sarah Bishop* (b. 22 Feb 1744, d. 3 Aug 1831), 13 July 1766, dau. of Samuel and Mary Bishop{Goff Family Bible}.

John and Sarah (Bishop) Goff were parents of the following children (8 of their 10 children d. before maturity): WILLIAM, b. 20 Dec 1776, d. 10 Dec 1795; SARAH, b. 31 July 1787, d. 14 April 1808, m.

Samuel Bishop, son of John and Rachel Bishop.{See article by Roy Hand.}

3. DAVID GOFF, son of John (1) and Mary Goff, d. leaving a will dated 16 March 1784, proved 5 Feb 1793 in which he mentioned his brothers William and John, and his son David.{NJCW 33:275}

David and Mary Goff were the parents of the following children: JOHN, b. 22 Feb 1781, d. 6 March 1864; LYDIA, b. 22 Feb 1781, d. 5 July 1865; DANIEL, b. 16 Feb 1778, d. 31 Dec 1856, m. Sarah Bishop (b. 26 Jan 1777), dau. of John and Rachel Bishop; DAVID, m. Ellen Corson, dau. of Joseph and Barbara (Bennett) Corson; WILLIAM, d. intestate in 1814.{See article by Roy Hand.}

4. WILLIAM GOFF of Cape May Co., yeoman, son of John (1) Goff, d. leaving a will dated 15 Dec 1765, with codicil dated 16 Dec 1765, proved 18 Jan 1766. Mentioned were wife Margaret and daus.: Mary, Hannah, Prissiller and Rhoda; sons: Silus to whom the plantation where he lived was devised, William to whom was devised the plantation where testator lived and a bond. Execs. were wife Margaret and sons Silus and William Goff. The will was witnessed by Daniel Hildreth, Benjamin Stites and Lydia Foster. The codicil was witnessed by John Leonard, Lydia Foster, Mathas Foster and Anne Leonard. On 18 April 1766 an inventory was filed (£113.3.8) by Levi Crandal and Joseph Lord.{NJCW File No. 28 F}

Margaret Goff d. prior to 31 May 1768 when John Cresse was appointed admin. Fellowbondsman: John Smith of Cape May Co. Witness: Elihu Smith. On 31 May 1768 an inventory was filed (£46.19.2) by John Smith and Elihu Smith.{NJCW 13:442}

William was father of the following children: MARY, probably m. by license dated 12 Dec 1749, Daniel Cresse{Baptists}; HANNAH; PRISSILLER, m. by license dated 2 May 1761, Daniel Hildreth{MLNJ}; RHODA; SILAS; WILLIAM.

5. SILAS GOFF, son of William (4) Goff, m. Rachel Hewet* of Cape May 13 Feb 13 1752.{Baptists}

Silas Goff, weaver of Cape May Co. d. leaving a will dated 12 March 1765, proved 21 Feb 1767 by John Cresse, the other witnesses being dead. Mentioned were wife Rachel; daus.: Hannah and Phebe to whom were devised lands and cedar swamp. Execs. were wife and his father William Goff. The will was witnessed by William Goff, Mary Norton and John Cresse. On 9 Jan 1767 an inventory was filed (£134.6.1 1/2){NJCW 13:137}

Rachel Goff, probable widow of Silas, m. John Cresse 12 Nov

1767.{Baptists}

Silas was father of the following children: HANNAH; PHEBE.

6. HANNAH GOFF, probable dau. of William (4) Goff, m. Israel Cresse by license dated 3 Nov 1761.{MLNJ}

7. RHODA GOFF, probable dau. of William (4) Goff, m. Zebulon Cresse* by license dated 14 Sep 1764.{MLNJ}

8. WILLIAM GOFF, son of William (4) Goff, m. 1st Susannah Dillen by license dated 18 Oct 1764.{MLNJ} and m. 2nd Rebecca Errixson by license dated 3 Oct 1770.{MLNJ}

William Goff of Cape May Co. d. before 3 Aug 1773, the day on which Rebecca Peterson, formerly Rebecca Goff, was appointed admx. Fellowbondsman: Jonathan Jenkins, both of said county. Witnesses: John Cresse and Thomas Smith. On 22 May 1772 an inventory of the estate was made by Thomas Smith and John Cresse.{NJCW 15:529}

Rebecca Goff, widow of William Goff, m. Hance Peterson by license dated 21 July 1773.{MLNJ}

9. HANNAH GOFF, probable dau. of Silas (5) Goff, m. Thomas Shaw 5 July 1770.{Baptists; MLNJ}

Unplaced

JEREMIAH GOFF m. Assinah Wheaton by license dated 14 May 1739. {MLNJ}

See "Early West Creek Settlers," *The Cape May County Magazine of History and Genealogy*, p. 142. June 1958. By Roy Hand.

According to Dr. Hand, Jeremiah and Assinah Goff had four sons who were named in Jeremiah Goff's will, proved 25 Aug 1761. Records show that there were three Goff's from the Tarkiln section who served in the Revolution, namely Nathan, John and Joseph. It may be that these three were three of the four brothers referred to in the above will as the names are identical. Nathan Goff, of Patton's Regiment, Continental Army, was wounded in the Battle of Brandywine, 11 Sep 1777, and received a disability discharge 3 Sep 1783.

The will of Joseph Goff, proved 17 June 1777, son of Jeremiah Goff, gives additional family data and names sister Mary Corson. (John Corson, Jr., m. by license dated 19 Dec 1761, Mary Goff{MLNJ}. John Corson, Jr's. sister, Rhoday, m. 13 Aug 1754, William Robinson. Their oldest son, William Robinson, Jr., m. 20 June 1772, Mary Young. (Both are buried in West Creek Baptist Cemetery.)

GOLDING (GOULDER, GOLDEN, GOULDING)

The following is based partially on the following articles:

(1) H. Clifford Campion, Jr., "William Golding (Gelder, Golden, Goulding) of Cape May County." appearing in *The Cape May County Magazine of History and Genealogy*, p. 239, June 1944. For a great deal of background on the early generations see this article.

(2) Richard W. Cook, "The Goulder Family," appearing in *Genealogies of New Jersey Families*, published by Genealogical Publishing Co. (1996). This was a reprint of a series of articles first appearing in *Genealogical Magazine of New Jersey*, Vol. XXIX (1954), 49-56; Vol. XXX (1955), 73-75; Vol. XL (1965), 82-83.

First Generation

Mr. Campion states,

> 1. WILLIAM GOLDING, Sr., came to New Amsterdam ca. 1640 and eventually settled in Gravesend.[47] He m. 1st (N) by whom he had a dau. ANN. Ann m. prior to 1660 Jan Smith.
>
> William Golding m. 2nd 4 June 1644 (New York Dutch Church Records), Ann Catharyn ---. William and Ann were the parents of the following children: WILLIAM, m. Margaret Lake; MARGRIETTE, bapt. 2 April 1646; JOSEPH[48], d. 1684; possibly JACOB (Yacum), listed in Gravesend in 1679; JOSIAH, aged 28 in 1682, m. Neeltje Klass, left issue; HESTER, m. 2 Nov 1676 at Gravesend, Jon Johnson; possibly others.

---

47 H. Clifford Campion, Jr., notes that there was a William Golding listed in the Barbadoes tax list in 1638.

48 This is the same person which Campion calls Josiah.

Second Generation

2. WILLIAM GOLDING, son of William (1) and Ann Catharyn Golding, m. 1st 7 April 1676 at Gravesend, L.I., Margaret Lake, dau. of John and Ann (Spicer) Lake and m. 2nd 19 June 1689 Deborah Quimby, dau. of John of Westchester Co., NY.

William and Margaret were the parents of the following children: SARAH, b. 2/14/1676, m. Timothy Brandreth*; MARY, b. 25 July 1678, m. Samuel Matthews, Jr.; WILLIAM, b. 10/25/1679, d. intestate at Tuckahoe, Cape May, estate administered by Nathan Golder (a son?) on 26 July 1735; JOHN, b. 11/21/1681; ESTHER (also Hester), b. 3/20/1683; SAMUEL, b. 9/2/1686, m. Sarah (N), d. 1714/15 leaving a will and issue.

William Golding and his second wife, Deborah, were the parents of a son: JOSEPH.

William d. leaving a will dated 15 Jan 1712, proved 18 May 1712.[49]

William Goldin of Tuckaho, Cape May Co., yeoman, d. prior to 26 July 1735 when Nathan Goldin, yeoman, was appointed admin. Fellow bondsman: Joseph Goldin, yeoman. Both of afsd. county. Witnesses: Henry Young, Elias Gandy and Jacob Spicer.{NJCW 4:23} The estate was inventoried on 26 July 1735 and included cattle, lumber in the swamp and pine boards; appraised by Henry Young and Elias Gandy.{NJCW}

3. JOSEPH GOLDING, son of William (1) and Ann Catharyn Golding, m. Eleanor (N). He d. 1684 leaving a will recorded in the Book of Miscellaneous Deeds and Wills, held by the Manuscript Department at Albany, NY; he named his brother William as exec.

4. SAMUEL GOULDING of Cape May Co., son of William (2) and Margaret Golding, yeoman, d. leaving a will dated 6 Feb 1714/5, proved 20 April 1715. Mentioned were wife Sarah; sons: Joseph, Daniel; dau. Margaret. Wife was extx. with Samuel Johnson and John Cresse as overseers. The will was witnessed by James Somers, John Cresse (43 years old) and Catharine Corson. Inventory was made on 9 May 1715 by John Somers and Robert Townsend.{NJCW 2:36}

Samuel was father of the following children: JOSEPH; DANIEL; MARGRET.

---

49 The will was omitted from the New Jersey Archives.

5. JOSEPH GOLDIN of Cape May Co., son of William (2) and Deborah Golding, d. leaving a will dated 24 Aug 1759, proved 11 Feb 1760. Mentioned were children: Jacob, addicted to the excessive use of spirituous liquors; John; Deborah Nicolson, widow; Mary Daniels; Eleazer, now in the service of the Crown. Grandchildren: Dorcas Goldin, Abiah Goldin and Ezekiel Hand, all three under age. Home farm of 200 acres in said county on Great Egg Harbour River; upland and marsh at Tuckahoe, bought of James Hubbert. Execs. were son John and Jeremiah Leaming. The will was witnessed by Jacob Garretson, Jeremiah Hand, David Evans and Jacob Spicer. Jeremiah Leaming refused to act as exec.{NJCW 9:404} On 15 Feb 1760 an inventory was filed by Joseph Corson and Joseph Edwards.{NJCW}

A cattle mark was recorded for Deborah Golden, dau. of Joseph Golden. 24 May 1734.{First Official Rcds}

Joseph was the father of the following children: JACOB; JOHN; DEBORAH, m. (N) Nicolson; MARY, m. Thomas Daniels*, by license dated 2 July 1740{MLNJ}; ELEAZER.[50]

Third Generation

6. JOSEPH GOULDEN, Deerfield, Cumberland Co., probable son of Samuel (4) Goulding, d. leaving a will dated 9 Sep 1765, proved 23 Oct 1765. Mentioned were children: JOHN, JOSEPH, m. Phebe Garretson* by license dated 12 Sep 1760{MLNJ}, SAMUEL, SARAH, probably m. James Garretson* by license dated 28 April 1760{MLNJ}; ABILAL, probably m. John Hayes 30 May 1771.{Baptists; Cumberland Wills}

Unplaced

A marriage license was issued to Ezekiel Hand and DEBORAH GOLDIN, 12 Dec 1737.{MLNJ}

A marriage license was issued to ISAAC GOLDIN and Hannah Mickell, 2 Nov 1772.{MLNJ}

A marriage license was issued to Noah Garritson and MAREY GOLDEN,

---

50 Stevens, p. 127, mentions that a Eleazer Golden of Cape May, aged 34 (a sailor by occupation), was in the company of Pennsylvania Militia under Capt. McClaughan. He enlised 25 April 1758.

1 Nov 1737.{MLNJ}

Jonathan Smith & MARY GOLDEN, m. at Tuckehoo, 15 Aug 1764.{Baptists}

A marriage license was issued to NATHAN GOLDIN and Hannah Lord, 17 Feb 1730.{MLNJ}

WILLIAM GOLDEN & Mary Garison, both of Tuckehoo, m. 10 Sep 1766.{Baptists}

GRIFFING

The following is based on "The Stillwells - A Patriotic Family, And Their Descendants," *The Cape May County Magazine of History and Genealogy*, p. 51. June 1940, by William Evans Price. For details see this article.

According to Mr. Price,

1. MOSES GRIFFING, b. 16 Sep 1745, m. by license dated 17 Oct 1770{MLNJ} Sarah Stillwell*, dau. of Nicholas (4) and Sarah Stillwell. Sarah Griffing died 13 May 1804 in Philadelphia. Sarah and Moses Griffing were the parents of the following children: EXPERIENCE, b. 18 Jan 1771, d. 17 July 1847, m. Nicholas Willets; ELIZABETH, b. 9 April 1772, d. in Georgia in 1851, m. 1st Capt. James Edwards of Philadelphia, m. 2nd Rev. Hopkins; ROXANNA, b. 11 March 1774, m. 1st Samuel Benezet and m. 2nd Parmenas Corson; MOSES, b. 11 Feb 1776, lost at sea between the Cape of Good Hope and St. Helena, on the ship *Star*; ANGELINA, b. 8 Feb 1778, m. 1st Capt. Hastings of Philadelphia, m. 2nd Daniel Hunt of Portland, ME - she was living in 1852; REBECCA, b. 29 Oct 1779 at Philadelphia, probably died young; JOSEPH CORSON, b. 1 Dec 1781 at Philadelphia, d. in Calcutta, m. Abigail Brickley; SAMUEL, b. 10 April 1784 at Philadelphia, d. of yellow fever in West Indies, m. Ann Thompson.

2. EXPERIENCE GRIFFING, dau. of Moses (1) and Sarah Griffing, b. 18 Jan 1771, d. 17 July 1847, m. Nicholas Willets*. They were the parents of the following children: MOSES, m. (N) Young and left 6 children; AMOS, m. Caroline Collins; REUBEN, b. 4 July 1801, m. 20 Nov 1826 Hanna Brick; JAMES of Tuckahoe; JOHN, m. Catherine; SARAH.

3. ELIZABETH GRIFFING, dau. of Moses (1) and Sarah Griffing, b. 9 April 1772, d. in Georgia in 1851, m. 1st Capt. James Edwards of Philadelphia, and left issue: James Carson; and m. 2nd Rev. Hopkins by whom there was no issue.

4. ROXANNA GRIFFING, dau. of Moses (1) and Sarah Griffing, b. 11 March 1774, m. 1st Samuel Benezet and m. 2nd Parmenas Corson and by him had a son ALBERT.

HAMILTON

WILLIAM HAMILTON of Cape May Co. d. prior to 30 May 1743 when Hannah Hamilton (Quaker) was appointed admx. Fellow bondsman, John Paige. Witnesses: Enoch Lewis and Benjamin Houlden. {NJCW 4:380} On 30 April 1743 an inventory of the estate of "Doctor William Hamilton" was made. It included broad cloath coat, black vest, leather breeches, blew coat, double breasted vest and old breeches, old red great coat, old banyan, 13 gloves and old wig, cane and belts, small papers containing some pills, rasins and powders; an amputating knife and saw, 2 saw plates, some other chirurgeon's instruments, case of chirurgion's instruments, case of lancets. Debts due from James Townsend, Silvanus Townsend, estate of John Grandam, estate of John Stites. Appraisers: Aaron Leaming and Elisha Hand. On 29 March 1745 an account was made showing cash paid to Lydia Taylor, Joseph Rose (surrogate), Elisha Hand, Enoch Lewis, Samuel Stevans, Jacob Spicer, David Culver, Henry Young, Benj. Holdin, William Mulford, Aaron Leaming, Henry Stites (Justice of the Peace). {NJCW}

Hannah Hamilton, widow, of Cape May d. prior to 4 Oct 1762 when William Simkins was appointed admin. Fellowbondsman: Ephraim Kent of Cape May Co. Witnesses: Jacob Richardson and Daniel Cresse. On 6 March 1762 an inventory was filed (£28.15.5) by Ephraim Kent and Ephraim Bancroft. {NJCW File No. 231 E}

HAND

Helpful in the reconstruction of this family's lineage was an article in *The Cape May County Magazine of History and Genealogy*, p. 255, June 1944, "Ancestry of Christopher Hand, of Hand's Mill," by H. Clifford Campion, Jr. Also helpful was *Mayflower Descendants in Cape May County*, by Rev. Paul Sturtevant Howe, p. 338. Other sources are indicated. See also *Genealogies of New Jersey Families*, p. 834, "Family Records - Levi Hand," cited hereafter as Levi Hand Records.

According to Rev. Howe in *Mayflower Descendants*,

1. JOHN HAND, b. Lynn in Massachusetts Bay Colony as early as 1636 and moved to the whaling settlement at Southamton, Long Island, before 7 March 1644. He m. Alice Gransden and had the following children: JOHN, b. ca. 1633; STEPHEN, b. ca. 1635; JOSEPH, b. 1638; MARY, m. before 1657, Charles Barnes; SHAMGAR, moved to Cape May, d. there ca. 1727; BENJAMIN, b. ca. 1644; JAMES, b. in Easthampton, d. there 13 March 1733; THOMAS, one of the Cape May whalemen, b. 1646, drowned off Cape May 1714[51], m. Katherine (N); a DAUGHTER.

Second Generation

2. SHAMGAR HAND of Cape May Co., son of John (1) and Alice Hand, d. leaving a will dated 16 March 1727/8, proved 22 April 1728. Mentioned were wife Sarah and children: ZELOPHEHAD and his children unnamed; JOSIAH and his children unnamed; SHAMGAR who had Cornelius, William, Shamgar, Ichabod and Jamamie; MARTHA Hobbard; HESTER Seagrave (who had m. Joseph Huitt and had issue: Thomas Huit, Mary Huit, Ester Huit, Ann Huit, Joseph Huit; and m. (William?) Seagrave and had issue: William Seagrave and Onesimus Seagrave, all under age).{NJCW 2:536} An inventory was taken on 22 April 1728 by Humphrey Hughes and Henry Young. An account was made on 11 April 1729.

3. BENJAMIN HAND, son of John (1), had sons ABRAHAM and BENJAMIN, both of age in 1700.{Deeds B:25}

---

51 The will showed his death to be earlier. [The will was proved in 1713.]

4. THOMAS HAND, son of John (1) and Alice Hand, b. 1646, m. Katherine (N).{See also Deeds B:19} They were the parents of JOHN, b. at East Hampton ca. 1666, d. at Cape May before 27 April 1736, m. Mercy (N) (d. before 19 April 1746).

Thomas Hand recorded his ear mark on 5 Oct 1706 which was later recorded for George Hand, son of Thomas Hand in 1734.{First Official Rcds} Thomas Hand also recorded his ear mark on 16 April 1696, later the mark of David Hand, son of George Hand.{First Public Rcds}

Thomas Hand of Cape May, yeoman, d. leaving a will dated 21 Oct 1707, proved 3 Nov 1713 at Salem. Mentioned were wife Katharine; daus: Deborah, Alce, Prudence Crowel; sons: John, Recompence and two others unnamed. Real and personal estate including slaves. The will was witnessed by Shamgar Hand, John Townsend and Samuel Mathews.{NJCW 1:501} Inventory was made on 9 Oct 1714 by John Paige and John Parsons. On 7 March 1714/5 a letter was submitted from Recompence Hand asking for letters of administration and promising a keg of oysters, if granted. A bond was issued to Recompence Hand as admin. on 1 April 1715; Richard Downes and Christopher Church fellow bondsmen.{NJCW}

Record of deeds in 1700 shows Thomas had sons: Jeremiah, Thomas, Recompense, John and George, all of age.{Deeds B:28-29}

Thomas Hand was the father of the following children: JEREMIAH; THOMAS; RECOMPENSE; JOHN; GEORGE; DEBORAH; ALCE; PRUDENCE, m. (N) Crowell.

Third Generation

5. ZELOFEAD HAND, probable son of Shamgar (2) Hand, recorded his ear mark on 12 Nov 1708; later his son Nathanl. Hand's.{First Official Rcds}

Zelophead Hand of Cape May Co., yeoman, d. leaving a will dated 13 Nov 1732, proved 10 May 1733. Mentioned were wife Sarah to whom was left 1/3 of personal estate and £5 more for maintaining an expected child, and use of all lands and a Negro man until sons Nathaniel and Daniel were age 21. Son Onezemus. Nathaniel to have southwesterly half of plantation next to William Seagraves, Daniel the northeasterly side joining Cornelius Hand's land. Legacies to wife's son Jacob and to testator's daus. Susannah, Jerusha, Deborah (all unmarried) and an expected child. Execs. were wife Sarah and Nathaniel Rusco. The will was witnessed by Thomas Hewet, Shamgar Hand and Elisabeth Hand.{NJCW 3:334} An inventory of the estate was submitted on 28 Nov 1732 which included cattle, sheep, swine and horses; appraised by John Shaw and Jacob Garrison. An account was submitted by the exec. Nathaniel Rusco on 28 Oct 1737 which showed payments to Jeremiah Hand, Thomas Stoneback, Thomas Hand, Joshua Shaw, Thomas Hewett, Benjamin Johnson, Ruth Hand, Ananias Osborn, James Cresse, John Garlick, Peter Hand, Henry Young, Aaron Leaming, Henry Stites, George Crandall, Ebenezer Swaine, Robt. Cresse, John Cresse, Jacob Spicer, Nathan Osborn, William Seagrave, Elizabeth Crowell, Lemual Swaine, Doctor Flood, John Shaw, --- Jones and Jerusha Hand.{NJCW}

On 25 April 1741 an inquest ruled that Jeremiah Hand, son of Zelophead Hand, dec., died from a kick by a mare belonging to John Shaw which mare struck the said Jeremiah Hand near the belly or pit of his stomach from which he died on 24 Aug 1740. (Filed 25 April 1741)

Sary (Sarah) Hand of Cape May Co., widow, d. leaving a will dated 13 Feb 1732, proved 10 May 1733. Mentioned were son Jacob, 1/2 of rights for houses, land, goods, etc. to which testatrix was entitled by her husband's last will; the other half to son Jeremiah. Exec. was friend Nathanel Rusco. The will was witnessed by James Flood, Jeremiah Hand and Hester Hewit.{NJCW3:333}

Zelophead Hand m. Sarah (N) and was father of the following children: JEREMIAH; NATHANIEL; DANIEL; ONEZEMUS; SUSANNAH; JERUSHA; DEBORAH; Expected Child.

6. SHAMGER HAND of Cape May, cooper, son of Shamgar (2), d. leaving a will dated 4 June 1707, proved 16 Nov 1709. Mentioned were wife Abigell and sons: Cornelius and William. Mentioned was land from John Cresse's to Crooked Creek, near brother Zelophehad's field, other real estate and personal property. The wife extx. with father-in-law Petter Corson and brother Cornelius Hand as overseers. The will was witnessed by John Cresse and Elener Lence.{NJCW 1:247} On 19 Oct 1709 the estate was inventoried by John Cresse, George Crafford and Richard Townsend.{NJCW Cape May Wills}

Shamgar m. Abigail, dau. of Peter Corson. Shamgar was father of the following children: CORNELIUS; WILLIAM; SHAMGAR; ICHABOD; JAMAMIE.

7. ABRAHAM HAND, probable son of Benjamin (3) Hand, d. leaving a will dated 25 Feb 1714/5, proved 2 April 1715. Mentioned were children: Abraham, John, a minor, Jeremiah, minor, Sarah, Rachel, Elezabeth, Ezekiel; Martha Corson, nurse of son Ezekiel. Execs. were father-in-law John Gersom and brother Benjamin Hand. The will was witnessed by Nathaniel Jenkins, John Cresse and Hannah Leamyng. On 20 Oct 1715 an account of the estate was made by Benjamin Hand, Jr., admin. The final

account was made in May 1727.{NJCW 1:539}

Abraham Hand recorded his ear mark 9 March 1695/6. Later his son John Hand; later Thomas Leaming's.{First Public Rcds}

Abraham was father of the following children: ABRAHAM; JOHN; JEREMIAH; SARAH; RACHEL, d. 7 Aug 1773, aged 68 years{Baptist Burials}, m. Richard Smith by license dated 1 Dec 1737{MLNJ}; ELIZABETH; EZEKIEL.

8. BENJAMIN HAND, probable son of Benjamin (3) Hand, m. 1st Ann Chue (Chew), of Cape May Co., before Justice of the Peace, 14 Jan 1706/7.{First Official Recds} and m. 2nd Ruth (N). Witnesses to 1st marriage: Jonathan Osborne, Charles Robinson, William Shaw, Robert Townsend, William Smith, Benjamin Stits, Abnah Hand, Henrey Stits, Hannah Stits, Silvenes Townsend, Peter Hand. Their children: ISACK, b. 14 Aug 1709; PACIANC [Patience], b. 19[52] Aug 1711; JACOB, b. 21 April 1714.{First Official Rcds}

Noting that Benjamin left a widow named Ruth we must assume he married at least twice.

Benjamin Hand of Cape May Co. d. leaving a will dated 8 Feb 1732, proved 20 March 1732. Wife to have 1/2 of plantation. Son Isaac has the other half and will take his mother's half at her death. Daus.: Patience and Phebe Hand. Execs. were wife Ruth and son Isaac Hand.{NJCW 3:340} On 19 Feb 1732/3 an inventory was made of the estate which included a yoke of oxen, 12 cows, 35 sheep, rum and 1/2 a shallop -appraised by Nathaniel Resco and Robert Townsend.{NJCW}

9. RECOMPENCE HAND, son of Thomas (4) Hand, had the following children: Deborah, b. 14 Nov 1716; dau. Abiah, b. 5 Nov about half an hour after 3 o'clock in the afternoon [year not given].{First Public Rcds:275}

On 27 Sep 1716 Recompence Hand gave a general release as admin. of his father, Thomas Hand, dec. of his brothers, John Hand, George Hand, Jeremiah Hand and Thomas Hand, yeomen.{First Public Rcds}

Recompence was the father of the following children: DEBORAH; ABIAH.

10. JOHN HAND, son of Thomas (4) and Katherine Hand, b. at East Hampton ca. 1666, d. at Cape May before 27 April 1736, m. Mercy (N),

52 Stevens gives the date as 9 Aug 1711.

who d. before 19 April 1746. They were the parents of SILAS, b. ca. 1722, d. May 1770, m. 1751 Sarah Crowell*; ELISHA (youngest son), b. 1706, d. 1753; JOHN; ABIGAIL, m. (N) Buck; MARY, m. (N) Paige; JANE, m. James Whilldin*; ISAIAH; (N), m. Richard Smith; ELIHU.

John Hand of Cape May Co., d. prior to 27 April 1736 when Elisha Hand was appointed admin. Fellow bondsman: Ebenezer Newton, both of county afsd. Witnesses: Thomas Hand, William Simkins and Jacob Spicer, Jr.{NJCW 4:65} An inventory of the estate was submitted on 24 April 1736 which included cattle, hogs and geese; appraised by Ebenezer Newton and Thomas Hand. An account was submitted on 7 June 1738 showing payments to Nathl. Norton, Thos. Hand, James Page, John Crandall, Thos. Ross, John Hand, Ebenezer Newton, Mercy Hand (widow), Jane Hand, Rachel Hand (daus.), Thos. Buck, etc.{NJCW Cape May Wills:86E}

Mercy Hand of Cape May Co. d. leaving a will dated 9 Feb 1744/5, proved 5 Feb 1745/6. Mentioned were sons Elisha and John Hand; daus.: Abigail Buck, Mary Paige and Jane Whilldin; son-in-law Richard Smith. Son Isaiah Hand to have Negro man Will. Elihu Hand, youngest son (not of age). Residue to sons Silas, Isaiah and Elihu. Execs. were Elisha Hand and Richard Smith. The will was witnessed by Barnabas Crowell, Jr., Ezekiel Mulford, Sr., Samuel Eldredge and Jacob Spicer.{NJCW 5:244} An inventory of the estate was made by Elijah Hughes and Barnabas Crowell, Jr. on 3 Dec 1745.{NJCW}

11. GEORGE HAND, son of Thomas (4), b. ca. 1675, d. July 1758. He was the father of the following children: GEORGE, b. ca. 1700, d. before 21 June 1758; THOMAS; JEREMIAH; DANIEL; SARAH, m. Richard Stillwell* by license dated 1 Jan 1736{MLNJ}; EUNICE, m. Nathaniel Norton* by license dated 20 Nov 1733; NATHAN, d. before 21 June 1758.

George Hand, Sr. of Cape May Co., yeoman, d. leaving a will dated 21 June 1758, proved 1 Aug 1758. Mentioned were children: Thomas, Jeremiah, Daniel and Sarah Stillwell. Grandchildren: Thomas, son of Jeremiah; issue of dau. Eunice Norton, to wit: Hannah (wife of David Smith), George and Mary (wife of Job Young); children of dec. son George, viz.: Elias, George, Sarah, Rhoda and Lois; children of dec. son Nathan, viz.: Japhet, Nathan, Stephen and Hannah. Legacy to Presbyterian Meeting House at Cold Spring. Home farm at Cape Island; land at the Thicket; land called the Five Mile Beach. Execs. were the three sons. The will was witnessed by James Whilldin, John Foster and John Coulon.{NJCW 9:18} On 29 July 1758 an inventory was filed by John

Eldredge and James Whilldin.{NJCW}

12. JEREMIAH HAND of Cape May Co., yeoman, son of Thomas (4) Hand, and brother of George, Recompense and Thomas, d. leaving a will dated 4 Oct 1732, proved 26 Feb 1732/3. Mentioned were wife, cousin George Hand, former son of brother George Hand, 1/2 of the "home stall land" whereon the testator lived, next to brother Recompence. John Hand, son of John Hand, the remainder of said land. They to possess the five mile beach with 90 acres of land near Green Creek branches, with 15 acres of marsh near the "Seader Homakes." Brother Recompense and his children, 2/3 of moveable estate. Legacies to cousin Mary Hand, brother Thomas and his children. Exec. George Hand, Sr. The will was witnessed by John Hiatt, James Flood and Richard Downes.{NJCW 3:260} An inventory was made on 7 Oct 1732 by Nathaniel Rusco and William Mathews. An account of the estate was submitted on 27 May 1733 showing moneys paid to Eliza. Hand (widow), Recompence Hand, John Jones, Saml. Bustill, Rebecca Garlick, Peter Hand, James Flood, Richard Downes, Jeremiah Hand, Jacob Spicer, Nathaniel Rusco, William Mathew, George Crandal, John Crandal, Trustam Hedges, Christopher Foster, Ebenezer Swaine, George Hand and Mary Hand.{NJCW}

13. THOMAS Hand, son of Thomas (4) Hand had a son JACOB.{Deeds E:331}

THOMAS Hand of Cape May Co., yeoman, son of Thomas, d. leaving a will dated 16 Feb 1731/2, proved 27 May 1732. Mentioned were wife and sons: Thomas, the home lands at Fishing Creek; Jacob, all lands and meadow at Goshen; Jeremiah, £10; Aaron, £10; son Leuey, £5. Legacies to daus.: Leusey, Mary, Lidey and Jerusey. Execs. were wife and George Hand. The will was witnessed by Richard Downes, Jeremiah Hand and Jeremiah Church. Letters to George Hand, the surviving exec. on 27 May 1733.{NJCW 3:311} An inventory of the estate was submitted on 26 April 1733 which included cattle; appraised by John Flower and John Hughes. An account was submitted on 27 July 1738 showing payments to Jacob Spicer, Samuel Bustill, Francis Bevis, Christopher Foster, Richd. Downs, Jon. Hughs, Mary Hand, Ruth Crowell, Joseph Lord, Nathaniel Foster, George Crandall, Nathan Osborne, Nicholas Stillwell, Andrew McFarland, Recompense Hand, William Smith, Tristam Hedges, Christopher Foster and Jeremiah Hand, etc.{NJCW}

Thomas was father of the following children: THOMAS; JACOB; JEREMIAH; AARON; LEUEY; LEUSEY; MARY; LIDEY; JERUSEY.

Fourth Generation

14. NATHANIEL HAND, weaver, probable son of Zelophead (5) Hand, m. by license dated 23 March 1742 Hannah Eldridge.{MLNJ}

Nathaniel d. leaving a will dated 4 Jan 1752, proved 19 May 1752. Mentioned were wife Hannah and sons: Timothy, Ezekial, Eleazer and Henry. Home farm; another farm of 120 acres; 52 acres bought of Isaac Whildine; Bud's Island; and 26 acres bought of Joseph Whildine. Execs. were son Ezekiel and Elijah Hughes.{NJCW Cape May Wills:159E} On 24 June 1752 an inventory was filed by Elisha Hand and Ebenezer Johnson. An account was filed by the execs. on 30 May 1754.{NJCW}

Nathaniel was the father of the following children: TIMOTHY; EZEKIEL; ELEAZER; HENRY.

15. WILLIAM HAND of Cape May Co., possible son of Shamgar (6), d. prior to 31 March 1733 when Shamgar Hand was appointed admin of the estate. Fellow bondsman Nathaniel Rusco, both of county afsd. Witnesses: William Mathews, Jacob Spicer and Jacob Spicer, Jr.{NJCW Cape May Wills:70E} An inventory of the estate was submitted on 18 Nov 1732 which included cattle; appraised by Nathaniel Rusco and Jacob Garrison.{NJCW}

16. SHAMGAR HAND, probable son of Shamgar (6) Hand, d. leaving a will dated 10 Dec 1760, proved 11 March 1761. Mentioned were son Stephen to whom was devised 100 acres of the homestead, next to James Cresse. To son Shamgar the rest of the homestead and 25 acres of back land. Son William received the rest of the back lands. Youngest son Cornelius to be allowed to cut timber off the land. Eldest dau. Abigail, wife of Gideon Hand, 5 shillings. Referred to "small children." Execs. were wife Ann and son Shamgar. The will was witnessed by Nathan Stites, Nathaniel Jenkins and Daniel Hewet. On 3 March 1761 an inventory was filed (£154.5.4} by Lewis Cresse and Joshua Hildreth. An account was filed in 1771 by Shamgar Hand and Anne Hand, the execs.{NJCW 10:162; 14:408}

In "Diaries of Aaron Leaming," is mentioned the death of Shamgar Hand in 1760.

Shamgar was father of the following children: STEPHEN; SHAMGAR; WILLIAM; CORNELIUS; ABIGAIL, m. Gideon Hand*.

17. SILAS HAND, son of John (10) and Mercy Hand, b. ca. 1722, d. May 1770, m. 1751 Sarah Crowell. They were the parents of ELISHA, b. Jan

1752, d. 18 Nov 1814,[53] m. 25 March 1783, Esther Teal (b. 10 Nov 1762, d. 4 June 1802).

Silas apparently m. 2nd Mary (N).

Silas d. leaving a will dated 1 May 1770, proved 16 May 1770. Mentioned was wife Mary. Son Silas was devised 200 acres, bought of Thomas Hand. Sons, Elisha and Jonathan, the rest of lands belonging to the plantation where testator lived. Son Isaiah, two tracts at Nummies of 179 acres and 8 acres of cedar swamp bought of Jeremiah Ludlam. To all of his children: Elisha Hand, Silas Hand, Jonathan Hand, Patience Hand, Sarah Hand, Mary Hand, Isaiah Hand, Jane Hand and Rhoda Hand, 2/3 of the moveable estate. Exec. was wife Mary and his two sons, Elisha and Silas. The will was witnessed by Constantine Hughes, Elisheba Hughes and Constantine Foster. On 30 May 1770 an inventory (£316.11.2) was filed by Robert Parson and Henry Hand. On 22 March 1774 an account was filed by Mary Edmunds (late Mary Hand), exec. of Silas Hand.{NJCW 14:339; 15:531}

Mary Hand m. Dounes Edmunds by license dated 18 Jan 1774.{MLNJ}

Silas Hand was the father of the following children: ELISHA; SILAS; JONATHAN; PATIENCE; SARAH; MARY; ISAIAH; JANE; RHODA[54].

18. ELISHA HAND of Cape May Co., son of John (10) and Mercy Hand,[55] and brother of Silas and Elihu Hand, m. 1st by license dated 22 Jan 1731 Experience Smith; he m. 2nd, Lydia, dau. of Ezekiel Eldredge. Elisha d. leaving a will dated 5 June 1749, proved 8 Aug 1753. Mentioned were wife Lydia, dau. Experience and brothers Silas and Elihu Hand. Home farm, 500 acres of upland and marsh at Nummies. Execs. were wife and brother-in-law, John Eldredge. Trustees: brother Silas Hand and brother-in-law, Jacob Spicer [half-brother of wife]. The will was witnessed by Nathaniel Foster, Thomas Bancroft and Ebenzer Johnson.{NJCW Cape May Wills:164E} On 20 July 1753 an inventory was filed by Elijah Hughes and Jacob Spicer which included a silver watch, books, household goods, plantation utensils, shoemakers' tools, Negro man and

---

53 Cold Spring Cemetery.

54 This may be Rhoda Hand, b. 1763, d. 27 June 1820. {Cold Spring Cemetery}

55 Lydia, widow of Elisha, mentions her father-in-law, John Hand.

Negro woman. On 22 Jan 1755 Experience, dau., petitioned that Jacob Spicer be confirmed as her guardian. On 29 Jan 1755 a bond was issued to Jacob Spicer of Cape May Co. as her guardian; Gabriel Blond fellowbondsman.{NJCW}

Elisha m. 2nd by license of 30 Aug 1736, Lydia Eldredge* (b. 1695, d. 1755), dau. of Ezekiel (1) and Sarah Eldredge.

Elisha Hand and Lydia Eldridge are both buried in a private burial ground on what was known as the Bishop Farm on the west side of the Bay Shore Road, south of Fishing Creek. In addition to the stones of Elisha and Lydia is the tombstone of Experience Robinson, dau. of Elisha Hand. While Lydia calls Experience her dau, the tomb stone shows she d. 3 Dec 1760, aged 24 years, making her birth prior to 3 Dec 1736. Elisha m. 1st by license dated 22 Jan 1731, Experience Smith, b. 24 Oct 1712 (according to her father's Bible), dau. of William. Mr. Campion expresses the belief that Experience Hand was her child.

Lydia Hand of Cape May Co. d. leaving a will dated 19 Nov 1754, proved 31 March 1755. Mentioned were dau. [probably step-dau.] Experience, sole heiress, under guardianship of Jacob Spicer, and in case of her death without issue, the estate to be divided between Hannah, dau. of William Eldredge; Elisha Hughes; Lydia, dau. of John Eldredge; Hannah, dau. of Nathan Hand; Jeremiah, son of Ezekiel Eldredge, dec.; Nancy, dau. of Rev. Daniel Lawrence. Legacy to Presbyterian Meetinghouse, "now erecting in the Lower Prescinct of this County." Exec. was Jacob Spicer. The will was witnessed by Samuel Eldredge, Mary Eldredge and Isaac Whildin. Inventories were filed by Elijah Hughes and James Whilldin in Dec 1754, Jan 1755 and Feb 1756. The appraisers included a turkey, apparel for John Hughes and Judith Brooks, apprentices, open accounts against Thomas Johnson, Edward Saunders and Josena Schillinks (all absconded), James Taylor, Elizabeth Nicoles and Richard Forster (all insolvent), and a pair of family spoon moulds belonging to John Hand, father-in-law of dec. In 1759 an account was filed by the exec., Jacob Spicer, who reported the rents of the plantations at Coxe Hall and at Nummies, left by her husband, Elisha Hand, in his will.

EXPERIENCE, dau. of Elisha Hand, m. John Robertson (or

Robinson) by license dated 23 Nov 1756, d. without issue (as of 1789).{Deeds A:129}

19. ISAIAH HAND, probable son of John (10) Hand, b. 1723, d. 28 Feb 1765.{Cold Spring Cemetery}

Susannah Hand, widow of Isaiah, was appointed admx. on 20 May 1765. Fellowbondsman: Daniel Crowell of Cape May Co. Witnesses: Henry Young and Henry Hand. On 16 May 1765 an inventory (£290.15.0) was filed by Henry Hand and Daniel Crowell.{NJCW 12:128}

Susannah Hand m. James Whildin by license dated 13 Jan 1766.{MLNJ}

20. ELIHU HAND, son of John (10) Hand, d. prior to 8 March 1768 when Lydia Hand, spinsters, and Silas Hand were appointed admins. Fellowbondsman: Isaac Matthews of Cape May Co. Witnesses: Zeruiah Hughes and Henry Hand. On 29 Feb 1768 an inventory (£82.16.7) was filed by Cornelius Schellenger and Henry Hand.{NJCW 13:332}

21. GEORGE HAND, son of George (11) Hand, b. ca. 1700, may have m. Mary Stratt [Stratton?].

From John Townsend's Journal (the original of which is in the Cape May County Historical Society):

> "On November 25, 1748 George Hand went deer hunting and wounded a deer which escaped. The next day with a neighbor he went as soon as daylight was clear enough to trace the deer to find and kill it. He was accidentally shot and died from the wounds four days afterwards."

George Hand, Jr., of Cape May Co., d. leaving a will dated 30 Nov 1748, proved 16 May 1749. Mentioned were wife Mary who received use of plantation and mill, during widowhood, to bring up the children. Son Jeremiah Hand, the homestead house and land and a piece of marsh at Fishing Crick and 1/2 piece of land at head of Green Creek. Son Elias, land at Ash Swamp, the mill and 4 acres of marsh between William Mathews and Recompense Hand, and 1/2 of land at head of Green Creek and 5 miles of beach. Daus.: Sarah, Ahrhoda and Naome. An expected child, if a boy to have £20, to be paid by son Jeremiah Hand. Execs. were brother Thomas Hand and wife Mary. The will was witnessed by Daniel

Hand, Edward Church and Nathan Hand.{NJCW 6:367} An inventory of the estate was made on 10 April 1749 which included cattle, sheep, horses and swine - appraised by Richard Crafford and Elisha Hand.{NJCW}

George Hand was the father of the following children: JEREMIAH; ELIAS; SARAH; AHROADA (Rhoda); NAOMI; GEORGE; LOIS. (The latter two are twins, mentioned in the will of their grandfather, George Hand, apparently born after the death of their father.)

22. THOMAS HAND, probable son of George (11) Hand.
In "Diaries of Aaron Leaming," he mentioned the death of Thomas Hand of Gravelly Run, on 2 Oct 1760 and his wife Elizabeth on 30 Sep 1760, both of the bloody fever.

Thomas Hand of Middle Precinct, Cape May Co., yeoman, d. leaving a will dated 3 Oct 1758, proved 25 Nov 1760. Mentioned were wife Elisabeth and children: Gidion, Neri, David and Thomas, some of them under age. Other children? Land at Mores on the Bayside of the county between brother Nathan Hand, Pond Creek and the Bay; land at Tuckahoe; land at Gravity Run on the seaside. Execs. were wife with sons Gideon and David. The will was witnessed by Thomas Hewet, Thomas Stites and Nathaniel Jenkins.{NJCW 10:224} On 21 Nov 1760 an inventory was filed by Lewis Cresse and Nathaniel Jenkins.{NJCW}

Thomas was father of the following children: GIDEON; NERI; DAVID; THOMAS.

23. NATHAN HAND of Cape May, son of George (11), d. leaving a will dated 30 April 1755, proved 31 Oct 1755. Mentioned were wife Lydia and children: Japheth, Nathan, Stephen and Hannah, all under age. Execs. were wife, Ezekiel Mulford and Isaiah Hand. The will was witnessed by John Eldridge, John Leek and Jacob Crowell.{NJCW 8:226} An inventory was filed by John Eldredge and James Whilldin on 11 May 1756 which included a servant man.{NJCW}

Nathan m. Lydia (N).

Nathan was the father of the following children: JAPHETH, d. by 14 April 1792 when Rachel Hand was appointed admx. of his estate{NJCW 34:466}; NATHAN; STEPHEN; HANNAH.

24. EUNICE HAND, dau. of George (11) Hand, m. Nathaniel Norton by license issued 20 Nov 1733.{MLNJ} They were the parents of HANNAH,

m. David Smith by license issued 11 Aug 1752; GEORGE; MARY, wife of Job Young.{See will of her father, George Hand, dated 21 June 1758.}

25. CORNELIUS HAND of Cape May Co., yeoman, possible son of Shamgar (6) Hand, d. leaving a will dated 7 Nov 1732, proved 31 March 1733. Mentioned were wife Deborah, to have the use of all land during widowhood. Son Cornelius (under age 21) to ultimately possess the same. Dau.-in-law [step-dau.] Deborah Taylor, 1/3 of 1/3 of moveable estate. Execs. were wife and father-in-law, Henry Young. The will was witnessed by Nathaniel Rusco, Jacob Garrison and Shamgar Hand.{NJCW 3:338} An inventory of the estate was taken on 18 Nov 1732 which included a Negro boy, cattle, sheep and horses.{NJCW}

Cornelius m. Deborah Taylor*. widow of John (4) Taylor. Following the death of Cornelius she m. Jeremiah Hand.

Cornelius was father of CORNELIUS.

26. JACOB HAND, son of Thomas (13) Hand, m. Experience Crowell, by license dated 8 June 1748.{MLNJ}

Thomas Hand had son Thomas (of age in 1711) who had son Jacob (dec.) whose two sons were Jacob (wife Patience) and Thomas (dec.), as mentioned in deeds dated 1779.{Deeds E: 331}

Jacob Hand had sons Jacob and Thomas. The latter died intestate without issue. {Book of Mortgages A:99, dated 1777}

Jacob Hand of Middle Precinct, Cape May Co., d. leaving a will dated 26 Dec 1771, proved June 1772. Mentioned were wife Experience, son Jacob to whom he left his gun and son Thomas to whom he left a steel trap and youngest son Jeremiah. Daus. mentioned were Mary, Silvia, Jerusha, Elizabeth, Experience and Lydia. To son Jacob 1/2 of plantation, being the south part from Delaware Bay to the head, joining the old 400 acre line purchased by Thomas Hand, Sr. of Jeremiah Bass, agent for the New Jersey Society. Son Thomas the north side of the plantation by a line formerly of Christopher Church, and now by George Taylor. Sons, Jacob, Thomas and Jeremiah and six daus. (above named) all his right in Five Mile Beach. Execs. were son Jacob, Elijah Hand and Jonathan Hand. The will was witnessed by Benjamin Stites, Jedidiah Hughes and William Stites.

Jacob was father of the following children: JACOB[56]; THOMAS;

---

56 This may be Jacob Hand who m. Patience Foreman by license dated 2-22-1774. {MLNJ}

JEREMIAH; MARY; SILVIA; JERUSHA; ELIZABETH; EXPERIENCE; LYDIA.

Fifth Generation

27. TIMOTHY HAND, probable son of Nathaniel (14) Hand, m. Mary (N).

Timothy Hand and wife Mary were mentioned in 1774 deeds.{Deeds D:86}

28. EZEKIEL HAND of Lower Precinct, Cape May Co., of Nathaniel (14) Hand, d. leaving a will dated 17 June 1780, proved 27 Sep 1780. Mentioned were wife Esther; daus. Lidia and Mary, each a bed. Three youngest boys to have schooling. Daus. Elishaba, Lydia and Mary, rest of personal estate. Land to be sold and money to be given to sons, Ezra, Aaron, Lewes and Ezekele when age 21. Exec. was brother Henry Hand. The will was witnessed by Elijah Shaw, Abner Bennett and Lydia Conger. On 27 Oct 780 an inventory was made by Silas Swain and Jeremiah Eldredge. (£9,245.16.3){NJCW 24:82}

Ezekiel was father of the following children: LYDIA; MARY; ELISHABA; EZRA; AARON; LEWES; EZEKIEL.

29. ELEAZER HAND, son of Nathaniel (14) Hand, had a son Ellis whose wife was Zylpah (1778).{Deeds A:152}

In "Diaries of Aaron Leaming" he mentioned the death of Eleazer Hand, sometime after 28 Oct 1760.

He left a will dated 2 Oct 1760, proved 26 March 1761. Mentioned was wife Jerusha, eldest son Ellis to whom land was devised where his father lived and to youngest son James, lands on Fishing Creek. Daus.: Elizabeth and Johanah received the moveable estate. Execs. were wife Jerusha and brother Henry Hand. Youngest children, Johana and James were to have learning. Brother Timothy was to take the oldest boy and keep him until 21. Oldest girl to live with her uncle Henry until 18. The will was witnessed by Ebenezer Johnson, Hance Woolson and Elizabeth Hand. On 2 Jan 1761 an inventory was filed (£153.2.4) by John Eldredge and Ebenezer Johnson.{NJCW 10:166}

Eleazer was father of the following children: ELLIS; JAMES; ELIZABETH; JOHANAH.

30. HENRY HAND, probable son of Nathaniel (14) Hand, d. 26 Sep 1787, age 59.{Cold Spring Cemetery}

Henry m. Elizabeth Page, by license dated 26 Dec 1759.{MLNJ}

Henry d. leaving a will dated 21 Aug 1787, proved 20 Oct 1787.

Mentioned were son Eleazaar to whom he devised the home plantation bought of Cornelous Schellenger at Cold Spring. Wife Elizabeth to have use of 1/2 the lands. Dau. Hannah to have use of part of the house while single.{NJCW 29:232}

Elizabeth Hand, widow, b. 31 April 1740, d. 31 Dec 1788, age 48 years, 8 mos.{Cold Spring Cemetery}, left a will dated 2 Feb 1788, proved 27 Jan 1789. Mentioned were son Eleazar and his sister Hannah.{NJCW 31:362}

Henry was father of ELEAZAR and HANNAH.

31. ELISHA HAND, son of Silas (17) and Sarah Hand, b. Jan 1752, d. 18 Nov 1814, m. 25 March 1783, Esther Teal who was b. 10 Nov 1762, d. 4 June 1802.[57] They were the parents of AARON B., b. 5 May 1791, d. 23 Dec 1861, m. 18 Feb 1818 Jane Hand Bancroft (b. 20 Aug 1793, d. 14 Jan 1864[58]).

32. SILAS HAND, son of Silas (17) Hand was assigned a guardian, James Whilldin, Esq. on 16 May 1770. Fellowbondsman: Daniel Swain of Cape May Co. Witnesses: Mary Hand and Zeruiah Hughes.{NJCW 15:68}

33. GEORGE HAND, son of George (25) and Mary Hand, b. 9 April 1749, d. 24 March 1824[59], m. 1st on 4 June 1771[60], Sarah Ingram and m. 2nd 7 May 1773 Sylvia Mills and m. 3rd 1 Aug 1774 Naomi Smith, dau. of Uriah and Mary (Somers) Smith. He m. 4th Lois (N) 1792 or earlier. He m. 5th 18 March 1804 Experience Smith (b. Jan 1760, d. Jan 1826), sister to his 3rd wife.

George and Naomi (Smith) Hand were the parents of the following children: GEORGE, b. 1775; URIAH, b. 5 Nov 1777[61]; JUDITH, d. 1870.

George and Lois Hand were the parents of the following children:

---

57 Tombstone at Cold Spring Cemetery shows Esther Hand, b. 10 Nov 1766, d. 4 June 1802.

58 Cold Spring Cemetery.

59 From the family Bible of Thomas and Levice Hand, held by the Cape May County Historical Society.

60 First Baptist Church records of Cape May Co.

61 See tombstone of Uriah Hand, b. 25 Nov 1777, d. 16 Dec 1829. {Cold Spring Cemetery}

ISRAEL, d. prior to 24 March 1824; LEVICE, b. 24 1782; CHRISTOPHER, b. 25 April 1792.

34. ELIAS HAND, probable son of George (21) Hand, m. Mary Page, 3 May 1762.{MLNJ}

Elias Hand d. by 27 July 1773 when Mary Hand, widow, was appointed admx. of his estate. On 23 July 1773 an inventory was filed (£124.3.11) by Henry Hand and Daniel Crowell.{NJCW 15:529}

At August Term 1785 a division of the lands of Elias Hand, dec., was made to determine each of his children's share of the lands. First division beginning on the old mill dam for the share of Sarah, wife of George Taylor, Jr., eldest dau. of Elias Hand. The second division to Elizabeth Hand, second dau. of said Elias Hand and wife of Thomas Hand. The third and last division or share to Mary Hand, third and youngest dau. of said Elias Hand. 19-22 Aug 1785.{Ltrs&Inv A(Rev):1}

Elias was father of the following children: SARAH, m. George Taylor, Jr.; ELIZABETH, m. Thomas Hand; MARY.

35. CORNELIUS HAND, possible son of Cornelius (25) and Deborah Hand, m. Deborah Ludlam of Cape May, 11 June 1750.{Baptists}

Recorded in the deed book: Ruhumah, wife of Nicholas Stillwell, dau. of Cornelius Hand, (b. 22 Sep 1755) Amelia Hand, wife of Christopher Hand, both granddaus. of Jeremiah Ludlam, as of 1785.{Deeds A:18} These facts suggest that RUHAMAH and AMELIA were daus. of Cornelius and Deborah Hand, and that Deborah was dau. of Jeremiah Ludlam. The deed book shows the following children of Cornelius Hand who d. intestate: LUDLAM, d. a minor; RUHAMAH, m. Nicholas Stillwell; AMELIA, m. Chistopher Ludlam.{Deeds A:60}

Cornelius d. prior to 27 1767 when his widow, Deborah Hand, was appointed admx. Fellowbondsman: Jeremiah Ludlam of Cape May Co. Witnesses: Benjamin Stites and Eli Eldredge. On 27 Aug 1767 an inventory was filed (£530.9.8) by Eli Eldredge and Benjamin Stites. On 30 April 1770 an account was made by Jonathan Jenkins who m. Deborah Hand, widow of Cornelius Hand.{NJCW 13:146; 15:15}

36. GIDEON HAND, probable son of Thomas (22) Hand, m. Abigail Hand* 5 Jan 1757.{Baptists} Gideon d. leaving a will dated 5 Feb 1762, proved 14 June 1762. Mentioned were wife Abigail, son Absalam and child wife is big with. Execs. were wife Abigail and Lewis Cresse. On 10 June 1762 an inventory was filed (£360.9.11) by John Shaw and Elijah Hand. On 7 Aug 1769 an account was filed by Lewis Cresse, admin of

Abigail Hand, relict of Gideon Hand.

Abigail Hand d. prior to 26 Aug 1762 when Lewis Cresse was appointed as admin. Fellowbondsman: John Shaw of Cape May Co. Witness: George Norton. On 27 Aug 1762 an inventory was filed (£17.9.9) John Shaw and Elijah Hand. On 7 Aug 1769 an account of Lewis Cresse and Abigail Hand, execs. of Gideon Hand. "David Hand, as a legacy, £106.12.3 3/4."{NJCW 11:224; 15:10}

On 7 March 1774 Absalom Hand of Cape May Co., son of Gideon Hand, dec., was appointed a guardian, Shamgar Hand, yeoman. Fellowbondsman: Philip Cresse, yeoman, both of said company. Witnesses: Humphrey Hughes and Elijah Hughes.{NJCW 15:530}

Gideon Hand was father of ABSALOM, d. 1826, age 67, m. Martha (N) (d. 1824, age 67).{Baptist Burials}; GIDEON. [See will of Thomas Hand in which he refers to sons of Gideon Hand: Absolam and Gideon Hand. Apparently Gideon is the child who wife "was big with," and thus b. 1762. On 8 Feb 1777 Gideon was appointed a guardian, Elijah Matthews and on 13 Jan 1780 he was appointed another guardian, George Hand.{NJCW 38:80, 22:63}

37. NERI HAND, son of Thomas (22) Hand, was appointed a guardian, David Hand, on 17 Dec 1764. Fellowbondsman: John Shaw of Cape May Co. Witnesses: Henry Young and George Norton.{NJCW 12:128} Neri Hand m. Hannah Evans by license dated 15 Sep 1775.{MLNJ} On 24 Feb 1777 Neri Hand died of pleurisy.{Leaming Diaries}

38. THOMAS HAND, son of Thomas (22) Hand, d. leaving a will dated 22 March 1783, proved 13 May 1783. The land, according to the will of his father, Thomas Hand, to be sold, and said land was in Joseph Mores Neck, below the road leading from Absolam Hand's house to the causeway and bank by Thomas Smith's, and said land begins at the line of Absolam Hand and Gideon Hand, left to them by their father, Gideon Hand, and runs down their land till it strikes the Bay, then among the Bay till it strikes the mouth of Wills Creek, on line of John and Josiah Hand, left them by their brother, David Hand, dec., and then up said line till it comes to said road. Wife Jerusha, 1/3 of moveable estate and £20, and a bed taken out of the estate in lieu of £20 left to dau. Elizabeth by her grandmother, Martha Lore. Dau. Elizabeth, a bed. Son Thomas was devised lands in said Neck above lie above the road and 1/4 of the moveable estate, after the legacy of his mother; and the rest of the moveable estate to dau. Elizabeth Hand and younger dau. Easther Hand. Execs. were Benjamin Taylor and Richard Edmonds. The will was

witnessed by Benjamin Stites, Lewis Cresse and Absolam Hand.{NJCW 38:71}

Thomas m. Jerusha Johnson by license dated 19 May 1773.{MLNJ}

Thomas was father of the following children: ELIZABETH; THOMAS, b. ca. 1780, d. 26 Sep 1815, m. Levice Hand, dau. of George and Lois Hand; EASTHER.

At May Term 1795 Carman Smith applied to the court on behalf of himself and wife late Abigail Johnson for a division of land late Gideon Johnson's between the said Abigail and the heirs of Jerusha Hand and the child of William Fox. The court ordered a division of said land.{Ltrs&Inv A(Rev):99}

39. NATHAN HAND, probable son of Nathan (21) Hand, d. prior to 27 Dec 1784 when Stephen Hand was appointed admin. of his estate. Fellowbondsman: Aaron Eldredge of Cape May Co. Witnesses: Constantine Foster and Job Thomas.{NJCW 38:79}

On 8 March 1789 a bond was taken of Shamgar Huet to take care of the person and estate of Elizabeth Hand, dau. of Nathan Hand, dec., infant under 14.{Ltrs&Inv A:18}

At February Court 1789 on application for a guardian to be appointed to Elizabeth Hand a minor, and dau. of Nathan Hand, dec, until age 14, Shamgar Huet and Rachel his wife, mother of sd. infant, were appointed guardians.{Ltrs&Inv A(Rev):31}

Nathan had a dau. ELIZABETH.

Sixth Generation

40. GEORGE HAND, son of George (33) and Naomi (Smith) Hand, b. 1775, d. 31 July 1813 in New Castle, DE, m. 5 July 1801 Judith Parsons (b. 8 March 1780), d. 20 Sep 1803 in Philadelphia, dau. of John and Louisa (Edmunds) Parsons. He m. 2nd 27 Jan 1805 Hannah Chew, dau. of Aaron.[62]

41. URIAH HAND, son of George (33) and Naomi (Smith) Hand, b. 5 Nov 1777, d. 18 Dec 1829, bur. Cold Spring Presb. Church Yard, m. Martha Swain (b. 24 Feb 1780, d. 22 Nov 1845), dau. of Reuben.

42. JUDITH HAND, dau. of George (33) and Naomi (Smith) Hand, d. 1870, m. 30 Aug 1797, Anthony Cresse (b. 4 Jan 1773, d. 23 Jan 1834).

---

62 *Pulson's Daily Advertiser*, 12 Feb 1805.

43. ISRAEL HAND, son of George (33) and Lois Hand, d. prior to 24 March 1824, m. Mary Hand. She m. 2nd 24 March 1824 Levi Corson.

44. LEVICE HAND, dau. of George (33) and Lois Hand, b. 24 Oct 1782, d. 4 May 1862,[63] m. 4 Nov 1804 Thomas Hand (b. ca. 1780, d. 26 Sep 1815), son of Thomas and Jerusha (Johnson) Hand. She m. 2nd 6 Sep 1822, William Manuell (b. 4 Sep 1794).

45. CHRISTOPHER HAND, son of George (33) and Lois Hand, b. 25 April 1792, d. 14 June 1871, m. 5 March 1815, Isabella Holmes (b. 20 Sep 1796, d. 14 Feb 1872), dau. of Nathaniel and Hannah (Hand) Holmes.

46. SHAMGAR HAND, probable son of Shamgar (14) Hand, m. Priscilla Hildreth [probably widow of Daniel Hildreth*], 28 Feb 1772.{Baptists} The license was issued on 27 Feb 1772.{MLNJ}

Shamgar d. leaving a will dated 8 Sep 1784, proved 21 July 1785. Mentioned were sons Jonathan, Stephen and Cornelius to whom was devised the old tract of land where their father lived. Jonathan was to have the north side, Stephen the south side and Cornelius the middle. Wife Priscilla to have a horse, saddle and her right according to law. Dau. Sarah's children, £3. Son Cornelius to be bound to a trade at age 14. Execs. were son Jonathan and David Hildreth. The will was witnessed by Daniel Smith, Philip Cresse and Christian Corson. On inventory was filed on 15 June 1785 by Joshua Hildreth and Philip Cresse.{NJCW 38:66}

Shamgar was father of the following children: JONATHAN; STEPHEN; CORNELIUS, chose Stephen Hand as his guardian on 12 Oct 1793{NJCW 33:280, File 587E}; SARAH.

47. LUDLAM HAND, son of Cornelius (34) and Deborah (Ludlam) Hand, m. Elizabeth Jenkins, dau. of Nathaniel Jenkins, Jr., by license dated 5 July 1768.{MLNJ}

Ludlam Hand d. prior to 8 Aug 1770 when Jesse Hand was appointed admin. Fellowbondsman: Nathaniel Hand of Cape May Co. Witnesses: Benjamin Stites and Jonathan Leaming. On 2 Aug 1770 an inventory was filed (£229.12.11) by Benjamin Stites and Nathaniel Hand. An account was filed in 1779.{NJCW 15:70; 22:360}

---

63 From the family Bible of Thomas and Levice Hand, held by the Cape May County Historical Society.

DANIEL HAND

1. DANIEL HAND of Cape May Co., yeoman, d. leaving a will dated 2 June 1768, proved 6 Aug 1768. Mentioned were wife Judah; sons: John to whom was devised the west part of the homestead, Eli, the next part, Daniel the east part. To his three sons was devised his right on Five Mile Beach. Dau. Judah was to have movables when 18. Execs. were wife Judah and Aaron Eldredge. The will was witnessed by Daniel Crowell, Hannah Crowell and Mercy Hughes. On 5 Aug 768 an inventory (£213.13.3} was filed by Richard Stites and Daniel Crowell.{NJCW 13:470}

Daniel was father of the following children: JOHN; ELI; DANIEL; JUDAH.

2. ELI HAND, son of the above Daniel (1) Hand, d. leaving a will dated 9 June 1773. He mentioned a tract between the lands of his brother John Hand on the west and brother Daniel Hand on the east which was a part of the tract left by his father Daniel Hand, dec. - the land to be given to his brother Daniel when age 14. Brother John Hand to have rest of estate. On 12 Aug 1773 an inventory was filed (£59.15.11) by Jeremiah Eldredge and Thomas Ewing.{NJCW 17:26}

3. On 27 Sep 1780 Daniel Hand of Cape May Co., son of Daniel (1) Hand, dec., was made a ward of John Hand, Sr.{NJCW 24:87}

Unplaced

A marriage license was issued to ABIAH HAND and James Townsend, 7 Jan 1740.{MLNJ}

ABRAHAM HAND, son of John Hand, m. Esther Eldredge by license dated 18 Aug 1760.{MLNJ}

In "Diaries of Aaron Leaming," he mentioned the death of Abraham Hand, son of John Hand, on 15 Dec 1760.

Abraham left a will dated 12 Dec 1760, proved 3 April 1761. Mentioned was wife Esther to whom was left all his estate. If he had no children then his estate was to fall to his cousin, Jesse Hand. Execs. were wife and cousin Jesse Hand. The will was witnessed by Silvanus Townsend, Jr., Jacob Smith and Levi Eldredge. On 16 Jan 1761 an inventory was filed (£104.5.5) by John Leonard and Silvanus Townsend.{NJCW 11:74}

A marriage license was issued to AMELIA HAND and Christopher Ludlam, 26 March 1776.{MLNJ}

A marriage license was issued to ANNA HAND and Jonathan Foreman, 15 June 1771.{MLNJ} Jonathan Forman and ANNA HAND m. 16 June 1771. {Baptists}

ANNE HAND d. prior to 25 May 1765 when Shamgar Hand was appointed admin. Fellowbondsman: Lewis Cresse, Gent. of Cape May Co. Witnesses: John Shaw and George Norton. On 26 April 1765 an inventory (£138.8.11 1/2) was filed by John Shaw and Lewis Cresse. An account was filed by Shamgar Hand, admin., in 1771.{NJCW 12:249; 14:110}

CABEL HAND, b. 1760, d. 20 Dec 1772.{Cold Spring Cemetery}

DANIEL HAND & Hannah Page of Cape May, m. 10 April 1751{Baptists}

A marriage license was issued to DANIEL HAND and Esther Garrison, 8 Oct 1774.{MLNJ}

A marriage license was issued to DAVID HAND and MARY HAND, 2 July 1764.{MLNJ}

A marriage license was issued to DAVID HAND and Martha Yeates, 16 May 1769.{MLNJ}

Josiah Giffer & DEBORAH HAND, both of Cape May, m. Jan 4, 1752.{Baptists}

A marriage license was issued to Jonathan Jenkins and DEBORAH HAND, 13 April 1768.{MLNJ}

A marriage license was issued to ELIJAH HAND and RACHEL HAND, 24 Jan 1758.{MLNJ}

Elijah d. by 31 Aug 1790 when Rachel Hand was appointed admx. Fellowbondsmen: Nathan Hand and Sarah Leamyng of Cape May and Cumberland Co. Witnesses: Elijah Hand and Philip Stites.{32:106}

A marriage license was issued to ELISHA HAND and Lydia Mathews, 16 Aug 1766.{MLNJ}

A marriage license was issued to ELISHA HAND and Ruth Taylor, 26 Jan 1774.{MLNJ}

A marriage license was issued to ELISHEBA HAND and Constantine Hughes, 1 Feb 1769.{MLNJ}

A marriage license was issued to Dounes Edmunds and EXPERIENCE HAND, 10 Aug 1752.{MLNJ}

A marriage license was issued to ESTHER HAND and James Willets, 1740.{MLNJ}

A marriage license was issued to ESTHER HAND and Rem Garritson, m. 13 Oct 1761.{MLNJ}

A marriage license was issued to EUNAS HAND and Francis Irons, 5 Oct 1774.{MLNJ}

A marriage license was issued to EZEKIEL HAND and Deborah Goldin, 12 Dec 1737. {MLNJ}

A marriage license was issued to EZRA HAND and Elizabeth Eldridge, 2 Jan 1772{MLNJ}

EZRA HAND and MARY HAND m. 20 Dec 1774.{Baptists, MLNJ}

Ezra d. by 2 Dec 1786 when Mary Hand was appointed admx. by his estate. Fellowbondsmen: Timothy Hand and Ellis Hughes, Jr. Witnesses: Henry Hand and Elizabeth Richardson. On 27 Oct 1786 an inventory was filed (£194.17.1) by Henry Hand and Ellis Hughes, Jr.{NJCW 28:249}

GEORGE HAND, b. 1758, d. 1822.{Cold Spring Cemetery}

GEORGE HAND and Sarah Ingram, m. 9 June 1771.{Baptists}; the marriage license was dated 3 June 1771.{MLNJ}

GEORGE HAND and Silvia Mills, m. 7 May 1773.{Baptists}; The marriage license was dated 7 May 1773.{MLNJ}

A marriage license was issued to GEORGE HAND and Naomi Smith, 1 Aug 1774.{MLNJ}

A marriage license was issued to William Bennet and HANNAH HAND, 8 Sep 1752.{MLNJ}

A marriage license was issued to HANNAH HAND and Thomas Hewit, Jr., 4 Dec 1764.{MLNJ}

A marriage license was issued to ISAAC HAND and Marsey Thompson, 3 April 1730.{MLNJ}

A marriage license was issued to JACOB HAND and Patience Foreman, 22 Feb 1774.{MLNJ}

A marriage license was JANE HAND and Nathaniel Ogden (Cumberland Co.), 24 April 1761.{MLNJ}

JEMIMA HAND and Elijah Shaw, m. 12 April 1768.{MLNJ}

JEREMIAH HAND of the Lower Precinct, Cape May Co., possible son of George Hand or Thomas Hand, m. Rachel Crawford*, 17 March 1739{MLNJ} and d. leaving a will dated 26 Dec 1759, proved 5 Feb 1760. Mentioned were wife Rachel, extx. Children: David, Sarah, Jane, Deborah, Rachel, dau. Douesalah(?) and Emily. The will was witnessed by Daniel Lawrence and Thomas Hand.{NJCW 9:407} An inventory was filed on 25 Jan 1760 by Richard Stites and Isaiah Hand.{NJCW}

JEREMIAH HAND and Deborah Hand, m. by license dated 27 March 1734.{MLNJ}

In the deed books of 1800 is noted Jeremiah Hand, wife Deborah.{Deeds 29-35}

Jeremiah of Middle Parish, Cape May Co., d. leaving a will dated

5 Aug 1760, proved 3 April 1761. Mentioned were wife Deborah[64]; dau. Experience Edmonds, wife of Downs Edmonds to whom he devised lands adjoining James Miller in the Lower Parish. Daus. Jane and Judith were to receive £100 when 21. Son Jesse was to receive the rest of the real estate. Exec. was son Jesse. The will was witnessed by John Leonard, Abraham Hand, Jonathan Hildreth and Joseph Norbury. On 29 Jan 1762 an inventory (£331.17.6) was filed by Jacob Spicer and James Godfrey.{NJCW 11:78}

JEREMIAH HAND and Martha Townsend, m. by license dated 12 July 1763.{MLNJ}

Jeremiah d. prior to 27 June 1767 when his widow Martha was appointed admx. Fellowbondsman: Daniel Swain, Esq. of Cape May Co. Witnesses: John Eldredge and Zeruiah Hughes. On 23 June 1767 an inventory (£224.19.6) was filed by John Eldredge and Daniel Swain. An account was filed in 1771 by Martha Hand.{NJCW 13:146; 14:410}

A marriage license was issued to JERUSHA HAND and William Shaw, on 8 March 1762.{MLNJ}

A marriage license was issued to JESSE HAND and Mary Smith, 7 Nov 1759.{MLNJ}

JESSE HAND, b. 15 Jan 1738{Jesse Hand Bible} and Sarah Leaming* (b. 21 Feb 1744{Jesse Hand Bible}, m. 27 Jan 1763{Jesse Hand Bible} by license dated 26 Jan 1763.{MLNJ} Sarah d. 21 Feb 1826, aged 82.{Jesse Hand Bible} Jesse d. of consumption 29 Jan 1791, aged 53 years, 14 days.{Jesse Hand Bible} Sarah was the dau. of Aaron Leaming, Jr.

Jesse d. leaving a will dated 16 Sep 1790, proved 22 March 1791. Mentioned were wife Sarah; sons: Jeremiah, Enoch, Aaron, Jesse, Louis; daus.: Mary Bowan, Sarah Sommen [Somers], Lydia Hand, Deborah Hand.{NJCW 32:298} An inventory was filed (£1003.9.3) on 7 June 1791 by Thomas Shaw and Henry Stites.{NJCW File:551E}

Jesse and Sarah were the parents of MARY, b. 24 Oct 1763, d. of influenza 10 Feb 1791, m. (N) Bowen; JEREMIAH, b. 16 Dec 1765, d. 2 June 1813; AARON, b. 8 June 1768, d. of influenza 3 Feb 1791; SARAH, b. 27 Aug 1770, d. 22 Feb 1796, m. Constant Somers*, son of Richard Somers; JESSE, b. 28 Oct 1772, d. 7 Dec 1772; LYDIA, b. 24

64 Probable the widow of Cornelius (25) Hand.

Feb 1774, d. 15 Feb 1813; JESSE, b. 10 Oct 1776, d. 9 Feb 1808; LEWIS W., b. 9 May 1779, d. 20 Feb 1802; ENOCH, b. 13 July 1782, d. 27 May 1810; DEBORAH, b. 23 March 1787, d. 7 Oct 1830, m. (N) Diverty.{Only Mary, Jeremiah, Sarah, Lydia and Aaron were mentioned in the will of their grandfather, Aaron Leaming, Jr. NJCW}

A marriage license was issued to JOHN HAND and Sarah Buck, 17 April 17--.{MLNJ}

JOHN HAND and Elinor Peterson, m. by license dated 29 Oct 1737.{MLNJ}

John d. prior to 1 June 1743 when Elener Hand was appointed admx. Fellow bondsman: Robert Townsend of county afsd. Witnesses: Clement Conicle and Jeremiah Hand.{NJCW Cape May Wills:111E} On 28 Jan 1742 an inventory of the estate was submitted by Moses Crosly and John Ireland. An account was submitted in 1744 showing payments to William Morceland and Elener his wife, loan office, Joseph Roas, Henry Stits, Esqr., Joseph Maps, Richard Smith, Silvanes Townsend, Robert Townsend, George Holenshead, John Ireland, Henry Young, Esqr., "Colnor and Jury to vew the dead body," Moses Crosle.{NJCW}

JOHN HAND of Cape May Co. d. prior to 20 May 1747 when Silas Hand was appointed admin. James Whildin fellow bondsman, both of county afsd., gent. Witnesses: Elijah Hughes and Jeremiah Hand.{NJCW 5:457} Inventory of the estate was submitted on 1 Aug 1747 by Elijah Hughes and Barnabas Crowell, Jr.{NJCW}

A marriage license was issued to JOHN HAND and Mary Buck, 28 July 1769.{MLNJ}

JOHN HAND of Cape May Co. d. by 1 June 1790 when Mary Hand and Jacocks Swain were appointed admins. Fellowbondsman: Richard Townsend. Witnesses: Judith Smith and Jesse Hand. On 12 June 1790 an inventory was filed (£155.12.8)

A marriage license was issued to JOHN HAND Jr., and Sarah Newton, 5 May 1774.{MLNJ}

A marriage license was issued to JONATHAN HAND and Rebecca Yates, 25 March 1776.{MLNJ}

August Term 1790. Recompence Hand prayed for an order to the division of the land and real estate of Jonathan Hand, dec. between his two minor children: Achsa Hand and Jonathan Hand. Ordered.{Ltrs&Inv A(Rev):51, 57} (plats shown)

JUDITH HAND and Jonathan Leaming, 14 Aug 1766.{MLNJ}

A marriage license was issued to John Bateman of Cumberland Co. and JUDITH HAND, 27 July 1771.{MLNJ}

LEVI HAND, b. 4 March 1728.{Levi Hand Records}

LEVI HAND of Cape May d. prior to 18 Nov 1756 when an inventory was filed by Edward Church and Jacob Richardson. On 1 Dec 1756 a bond was issued for Mary Hand as admx.; Jacob Richardson and Edward Church, fellow bondsmen, all of Cape May Co.{NJCW Cape May Wills:177E}

LEVI HAND, b. 3 June 1751. {Levi Hand Records}

He m. 1st Zabriah Scull by license dated 10 May 1772.{MLNJ} which appears to conflict with the Baptist church record: Levi Hand and Zibiah Scull m. 10 May 1773.{Baptists}

Zebiah, wife of Levi Hand, b. 11 Feb 1752, d. 19 Feb 1774.{Levi Hand Records}

Levi m. 2nd Esther Hewet 8 Nov 1775{Baptists; MLNJ}. They were parents of the following children: ZIBIAH, b. 12 July 1775; LEVI, b. 2 March 1778; THOMAS, b. 10 Feb 1783; AARON, b. 5 July 1785.{Levi Hand Records} Esther, wife of Levi, d. 13 June 1791, aged 46 years.

Levi m. 3rd Priscilla (N). She d. 19 Dec 1793, aged 49 years.

Levi Hand d. 15 Oct 1820, aged 69 years, 4 mos., 12 days.{Levi Hand Records}

A marriage license was issued to LYDIA HAND and Christopher Foster, 18 Jan 1732.{MLNJ}

Joseph Hewet, son of Thomas Hewet, m. LYDIAH HAND, both of Cape May, April 14, 1751.{Baptists}

A marriage license was issued to LYDIA HAND and Benoni Mills (Cumberland Co.), 10 April 1769.{MLNJ}

A marriage license was issued to Levi Corson and MARGARET HAND, 23 Dec 1766.{MLNJ}

A marriage license was issued to Amos Townsand and MARTHA HAND, 10 Oct 1745.{MLNJ}

A marriage license was issued to MARTHA HAND and Abraham Van Gilder, 22 Aug 1757.{MLNJ}

A marriage license was issued to MARY HAND and Dounes Edmunds, 18 Jan 1774.{MLNJ}

A marriage license was issued to MARY HAND and Isaac Matthews, 17 Dec 1774.{MLNJ}

MATTHEW HAND, b. 7 Oct 1754.{Levi Hand Records}

A marriage license was issued to MATTHEW HAND and ELIZABETH HAND, 31 Jan 1775.{MLNJ}

MERCY HAND, b. 1727, d. 31 Jan 1775.{Cold Spring Cemetery}

NATHAN HAND of Cape May, Gent., probable son of Nathan Hand, d. leaving a will dated 17 Oct 1758, proved 13 Nov 1758. Mentioned were wife Rachel and children: Nathan, Johannah and Rachel. Execs. were wife and son-in-law, Elijah Hand. The will was witnessed by Thomas Smith, Elihu Smith and Edward Foster.{NJCW 9:151} 16-18 Nov 1758 an inventory was filed by Jeremiah Hand and Thomas Smith including Negroes, cattle, horses, sheep, hogs and geese. An account of the estate was filed on 18 May 1762.

Jonathan Cresse and NAOMI HAND, both of Cape May, 1 July 1763.{MLNJ}

PATIANS HAND, b. 14 Feb 1726, d. 20 Nov 1746.{Cold Spring Cemetery}

A marriage license was issued to Richard Smith and RACHEL HAND, 1 Dec 1737.{MLNJ}

Jacob Smith and RACHEL HAND, m. 29 --- 1758.{Baptists}

RACHEL HAND and William Smith, 2 Aug 1762.{MLNJ}

A marriage license was issued to RACHEL HAND and James Watt, 22 Oct 1770.{MLNJ}

A marriage license was issued to REBECCA HAND and John Swain, 6 June 1760.{MLNJ}

A marriage license was issued to RECOMPENCE HAND and Martha Church, 15 Nov 1762{MLNJ}

Recompence Hand of Fairfield, Cumberland Co. d. prior to 22 March 1769 when Martha Hand was appointed admx. Fellowbondsman: Jonathan Hand of Middle Precinct, Cape May Co. On 21 Feb 1769 an inventory was filed (£255.0.6) by David Shepherd and William Dalles. On 20 March 1771 an account was filed Martha Sheppard, late Martha Hand, admx.{NJCW 13:530; 15:103}

RECOMPENCE HAND of Cape May Co. d. prior to 8 Feb 1766 when Jonathan Hand was appointed admin. Fellowbondsman: Thomas Smith, Gent., of Cape May Co. Witness: John Eldredge. On 2 Jan 1765 an inventory was filed (£312.8.9 1/2) by John Eldredge and Thomas Smith.{NJCW 12:357}

A marriage license was issued to William Billings and RHODA HAND, 20 Feb 1763.{MLNJ}

RICHARD HAND d. before 31 Jan 1726/7 when a bond was issued to John Anderson of Burlington Co. as admin of the estate. Nathaniel Leonard, exec. of the will dated 21 Sep 1726 having declined to act. John Dagworthy and Jepththa Smith of Burlington Co., fellow bondsmen.{NJCW Cape May Wills}

A marriage license was issued to ROHANNAH HAND and Henry Ludlam, 8 Jan 1772.{MLNJ}

A marriage license was issued to SARAH HAND and Benjamin Ingram, 29 Oct 1759.{MLNJ}

A marriage license was issued to Ira Buck and SARAH HAND, 14 Jan 1760.{MLNJ}

Stephen Garison and SARAH HAND, m. 20 Jan 1773.{Baptists}

A marriage license was issued to SHAMGAR HAND and Lydia Smith, 5 Sep 1761.{MLNJ}

A marriage license was issued to SILAS HAND and Patience Church, 28 March 1746.{MLNJ}

A marriage license was issued to SILAS HAND and Sarah Crowell, 22 April 1751.{MLNJ}

A marriage license was issued to WILLIAM HAND and Catharine Mackey, 28 Jan 1731.{MLNJ}

A marriage license was issued to WILLIAM HAND and Hannah Garrison (Cumberland Co.), 17 Nov 1775.{MLNJ}

HATHORN

1. JAMES HATHORN of Cape May Co. d. leaving a will dated 30 May 1766, proved 15 Jan 1767. Mentioned were son Hugh to whom he devised the home plantation and 10 acres of cedar swamp in the Old Bridge Neck. To dau. Anne Godfrey was devised part of a tract in Cumberland Co. at Tuckaho. Dau. Sarah Plumer received the other part of the land give to Ann. Grandchildren: James Godfrey, land; Joseph Plummer, James Plumer and Samuel Plumer the land after the death of Sarah. Wife Cattron to receive 1/3 of the land. Grandchildren: Sarah Covenover and James Covenover, £50 each. Exec. was son Hugh. The will was witnessed by Francis Taylor, Japheth Hand and Elihugh Hand.{NJCW13:139} On 14 Jan 1767 an inventory was filed (£218.0.9) by John Willets and Joseph Corson. On 17 Dec 1767 an account was filed by the exec.

James was the father of the following children: HUGH; ANNE; SARAH.

2. HUGH HATHORN, probable son of James (1) Hathorn, m. Elizabeth Gandy by license dated 13 Aug 1761.{MLNJ}

Three of Hugh Hathorn's children died of the "Bloody Flux" in

May/June 1775.{Leaming Diaries}

Hugh Hathorn d. leaving a will dated 6 Feb 1786, proved 9 May 1799. Mentioned were wife Elizabeth; son HUGH; daus.: SILVIA, BETTY, PHEBE and SOPHICH Hathorn, minors.{NJCW 38:418, File 725E}

HEDGES

1. JAMES HEDGES of Cape May Co. d. leaving a will dated 29 Sep 1765, proved 11 Nov 1765. Mentioned were wife Marey; sons: James, David; daus.: Zeruiah Hedges, Margaret Rodgers. Exec. was Joshua Shaw, Sr. The will was witnessed by Robert Parsons, Sarah Parsons and James Whilldin.{NJCW 12:334}

James was father of the following children: JAMES; DAVID; ZERUIAH; MARGARET, m. (N) Rodgers.

Mary Hedges, possible widow of James, m. John Taylor by license dated 26 March 1777.{MLNJ}

2. DAVID HEDGES, probable son of James (1) Hedges, d. prior to 1 June 1785, when James Ross was appointed admin. Fellowbondsman: Henry Y. Townsend of Cape May Co. Witnesses: John Musentine and David Townsend.{NJCW 38:79}

Unplaced

A marriage license was issued to THOMAS HEDGES m. Mary Lupton 16 Feb 1762. {MLNJ}

HEWETT/HUITT

First Generation

1. RANDALL HUIT m. Dorothy (N).

On 22 Feb 1694/5 was recorded the inventory of Randall Huit, appraised by Samuell Crowell and Tim. Brandreth. In his will dated 22 Dec 1694 he mentioned his son Randel and wife Doritey to whom he left his house and improvements on Cape the Cape Island.{First Official Rcds}

An inventory of the estate of Dority Huitt was appraised by Samll. Crowell and Samll. Crowell and Timothy Brandreth on 3 March 1695/6 filed by her son Randall Huitt on 19 March 1695.{First Official

Rcds}

Randall was the father of RANDEL.

Second Generation

2. RANDALL HEWETT of Cape May Co., yeoman, son of Randall (1) Hewett, d. leaving a will dated 12 Feb 1732/3. Mentioned were wife, 1/3 of estate, Negro man Tom and mulatto boy Jonah. To son Randall was devised 140 acres out of the tract where testator lived next to Thomas Hewet on the north and 40 acres at the head of the same land. To son Reuben was devised 60 acres on the north side of Thomas Hewet's, formerly William Whitlock's and 20 acres of back land. Son Joseph was devised 180 acres on south side of tract whereon the testator lived and 60 acres of back land. Moveable estate to sons Jacob, Nathaniel and Ebenezer. The will was witnessed by John Hughs, Lewis Crese and Nathaniel Rusco.{NJCW} On 27 June 1733 Randal Hewett, son of dec., was granted letters of administration as will of father did not name an exec.{NJCW 3:345} An inventory of the estate was submitted on 26 April 1733 which included weaver's loom, cattle, sheep, swine, Negro man, a mulatto and 1/2 of small shallop. The estate was appraised by Richard Downes and John Hughes.{NJCW}

Randall Hewett was the father of the following sons: RANDALL; REUBEN; JOSEPH; JACOB; NATHANIEL; EBENEZER.

3. JOSEPH HUITT of Cape May, possible son of Randall (1) Huit, d. prior to 10 Dec 1714 when the estate was inventoried by Richard Downes and Nathaniel Jenkins. On 13 Feb 1714/5 a petition was submitted by Esther [Hester], widow of Joseph Huitt, stating that as she was left with 5 children, one born after her husband's death, she was unable to travel; she asked that Jeremiah Basse grant her letters of administration, to be sent by Richard Downes.{NJCW}

Joseph Huitt m. Ester Hand*, dau. of Shamgar Hand. Following his death Ester m. (William?) Seagrave.[65]

Ages of Joseph Huitt's children: Thomas, b. 31 Aug 1707; Mary, b. 18 Dec 1708; Hester, b. 4 Feb 1711/10; Anne, b. 10 Oct 1712; Joseph, b. 26 Jan 1715/14.{First Official Rcds}

Joseph Huit recorded his ear mark on 20 Nov 1708; later recorded to his son Thomas Huet.{First Official Rcds}

Joseph was father of the following children: THOMAS; MARY;

---

65 There is a reference to William Segrave's son, William, b. 14 Oct 1716. {First Court Rcds:328}

HESTER; ANNE; JOSEPH.

Third Generation

4. THOMAS HUITT, son of Joseph (3) Hewitt, b. 31 Aug 1707.

Joseph Hewit had eldest son Thomas as mentioned in deeds dated 1754.{Deeds E:92}

Thomas Hewitt says that he was married 48 years ago last July (1776). If so, he was married in 1728.{Leaming Diaries}

Thomas Hewet of Cape May Co., Gent., d. leaving a will dated 27 Jan 1775, with codicil dated 15 Jan 1776. The Will was proved 18 Aug 1780, codicil not proved. Mentioned were wife Abigaill; sons: Jonathan, Azariah, Daniel, Thomas (dec.), Aaron, Joseph; daus.: Ester, Abigail and Jane. Sons Jonathan and Azariah were devised the tract where testator lived and the back land. Son Azariah, part of same tract, the south part. Jonathan and Azariah to have the cedar swamp. Son Daniel and grandson Aaron Hewet (son of son Thomas dec.), the lands on the branches or head of Dyers Creek. Daus. Ester, Abigail and Jane to have the land left to Aaron, if he die without issue. Son Joseph's two daus., Rhoda and Rachel Hewet, lands. The execs. were wife Abigail and sons Daniel and Azariah. The will and codicil were witnessed by Richard Teail, Elihu Smith and Thomas Smith. The estate was inventoried on 17 Aug 1780 by Thomas Smith and Philip Cresse. (£10.353.2.2){NJCW 24:80}

Thomas was the father of the following children: JONATHAN; AZARIAH; DANIEL; THOMAS, d. before 27 Jan 1775; AARON; JOSEPH; ESTER; ABIGAIL; JANE.

5. JOSEPH HEWET, son of Randol (2) Hewet, m. Hannah Leonard (both of Cape May), March 26, 1751.{Baptists}

6. JOSEPH HEWET, probable son of Joseph (3) Hewet, d. leaving a will dated 25 Feb 1762, proved 26 May 1762. Mentioned were sons: Elijah, Shamgar and Benaiah; daus.: Phebe, Zeruel. Youngest [younger] children: Zeruel, Shamgar and Benaiah, to be bound out to trades. His wife [unnamed] to receive 1/3 personal estate. Exec. was son Elijah. The will was witnessed by Nathaniel Jenkins, Nathan Shaw and Henry Hewit. On 25 May 1762 an inventory (£130.11.2) was filed by Thomas Smith and Daniel Smith.{NJCW 11:228}

Joseph was father of the following children: ELIJAH; SHAMGAR, m. 1st Elizabeth Smith* 24 April 1778{MLNJ} and m. 2nd her sister, Rachel Smith*; BENAIAH; PHEBE; ZERUEL.

Fourth Generation

7. DANIEL HEWITT, probable son of Thomas (4) Hewitt, m. Mary Holden by license dated 1 Feb 1764.{MLNJ}

Daniel d. leaving a will dated 22 Jan 1784, proved 6 Feb 1786. Mentioned were wife Mary, son Thomas to whom was devised land south of Fishing Creek road and 5 acres of swamp over the road to the southwest of testator's house, joining Aron Hewet's line. Son Daniel was devised the land below the Washway, joining Aron Leaming's line. Son Isaac was given the rest of lands. Daus.: Rebecca, Philethetta and Abigal were left moveable estate. Sons were all under 21. Execs. were wife Mary and Jonathan Hildreth. The will was witnessed by Daniel Holden, Samuel Foster and Jean Holden.{NJCW 38:65}

Daniel was father of the following children: THOMAS; DANIEL; ISAAC; REBECCA; PHILETHETTA; ABIGAL.

8. THOMAS HEWIT, son of Thomas (4) Hewet, m. Hannah Hand by license dated 4 Dec 1764.{MLNJ}

Thomas d. prior to 2 Aug 1769 when his widow, Hannah, and Thomas Hewet, Sr., of Cape May Co. were appointed admins. In July 1769 an inventory (£42.2.1) was filed by Benjamin Stites and Joshua Hildreth.{NJCW 15:5}

9. JOSEPH HEWET, son of Thomas (4) Hewet, m. Lydiah Hand, both of Cape May, 14 April 1751.{Baptists}

In "Diaries of Aaron Leaming," he mentioned the death of Joseph Hewitt, son of Thomas, in March 1761.

On 23 Aug 1761 Lydia Hewit was appointed admx. Fellowbondsman: Joshua Hildreth of Cape May Co. Witnesses: Nathaniel Hand and Thomas Hewit. On 28 July 1761 an inventory (£68.16.0 was filed by John Shaw and Lewis Cresse.{NJCW 11:73}

Lydia Hewit of Cape May Co. d. leaving a will dated 23 Feb 1772, proved 27 May 1772. Mentioned were daus. Rhoda Hewit and Rachel Hewet, to whom were left the personal estate when age 18. Execs. were Jacob Smith and Joshua Hildreth. The will was witnessed by Daniel Cresse, John Crowell and Lewis Cresse. The inventory of the estate was filed on 20 March 1772 (£101.3.0) by Nathaniel Hand and Jonathan Jenkins.{NJCW 16:27}

Joseph was father of the following children: RHODA, m. Samuel Garrison 24 Feb 1773{Baptists}; RACHEL, m. 1st 13 Feb 1752, Silas Goff* {Baptists} and probably m. 2nd John Cresse on 12 Nov 1767.{Baptists}

10. AZARIAH HEWET, son of Thomas (4) Hewet, m. Lydia Buck, by license issued 12 June 1775.{MLNJ}

At October Court 1788 Lydia Stites asked that Philip Hand, Esqr., be appointed to the guardianship of her three children: Esther, age about 13; Humphry, age 11 and Azariah Huett, age 9, children of Azariah Huet, dec. It was approved.{Ltrs&Inv A(Rev):28}

On 7 March 1789 a bond was taken of Philip Hand to take care of the person and estate of Humphry Huet, son of Azariah Huet, dec. an infant under age of 14.{Ltrs&Inv A:18}

On 7 March 1789 a bond was taken of Philip Hand to take care of the person and estate of Azariah Huet, son of Azariah Huet, dec. an infant under 14.{Ltrs&Inv A:18}

At August Term 1797 it was noted that Azariah Hewit was seized of one undivided moiety of a tract of Cedar Swamp in the upper precinct of the county and Jonathan Hewit likewise stood seized of the other moiety which tract was purchased by Thomas Hewit of Jeremiah Ludlam and devised by his last will to his two sons, above named. And whereas the said Azariah Hewit by his last will dated 19 June 1783 devised all his part of said Cedar Swamp known by the name of the Old Lot joining the long cedar Swamp bridge to be equally divided betwixt his two sons, Humphry and Azariah Hewit. (plat shown){Ltrs&Inv A(Rev):148}

Azariah was the father of sons: ESTHER, b. ca. 1775; HUMPHRY, b. ca. 1777; AZARIAH, b. ca. 1779. Humphry and Azariah were both wards of Philip Hand in 1789.{NJCW 31:372, 33:280, File 589E}

11. HUMPHRY HEWET, son of Azariah (1) Hewet, b. ca. 1777, probably m. Polly Smith 4 June 1800.{Co. Clerk Rcds - Book A}

Unplaced

ELIJAH HEWITT and Naomi Young, 14 June 1763.{MLNJ}

Levi Hand m. ESTHER HEWET, 8 Nov 1774.{Baptists}

A marriage license was issued to Levi Hand and Esther Hewitt, 8 Nov 1774.{MLNJ}

JACOB HEWET m. Elizabeth Steward, Jan 26, 1773.{Baptists}

A marriage license was issued to RACHEL HEWETT and Francis Taylor, 1 June 1770.{MLNJ}

Jonathan Mills m. ZERRUEL HEWET on 8 March 1773.{Baptists}

HILDRETH

For additional records of the family of Jonathan Hildreth, son of Jonathan (2) see "Records of The Hildreth Family," *The Cape May County Magazine of History and Genealogy*, p. 82. By Alice G. Stathem (Mrs. Paul Woodson Stathem). This article transcribes the records copied 20 March 1956 by Alice G. Stathem from the Bible then owned by Paul Woodson Stathem. Cited hereafter as Hildreth Bible.

1. DAVID HILDRETH, Sr. of Cape May Co., yeoman, d. leaving a will dated 31 Dec 1731, proved 20 March 1732/3. Mentioned were wife Elizabeth to whom was devised that home plantation (186 acres, mortgaged in the Loan Office) during widowhood or until son Joshua reached age 21. Land lately surveyed joining Indian Neck to be paid for at Loan Office, and divided equally among four sons: Jonathan, Joseph, James and David. Son Noah to have £5 when 21 and dau. Mercy the same at 18 or married. Wife Elizabeth, extx. Henry Young, Esq., assistant. The will was witnessed by Aaron Leaming, Nathaniel Jenkins, Jr. and Elizabeth Ludlim.{NJCW 3:312} An inventory of the estate was submitted on 2 Nov 1732 and included cows, calves and sheep; appraised by Nathaniel Rusco and John Shaw.{NJCW}

David Hildreth recorded his ear mark for sheep on 6 June 1722; later recorded for his son Joshwa Hildreth.{First Official Rcds}

David Hildreth m. Elizabeth (N) and was the father of the following children: JOSHUA; JONATHAN; JOSEPH; JAMES; DAVID; NOAH; MERCY; DANIEL.

Second Generation

2. JOSHUA HILDRETH, probable son of David (1) Hildreth, had a son JOSEPH, mentioned in the will of Joseph (4) Hildreth. [See below.]

3. JONATHAN HILDRETH, probable son of David (1) Hildreth, had sons Jonathan and Ephraim, dec.; also a dau., Hannah who m. Silas Eldredge as mentioned in deeds dated 1794.{Deeds E: 273}

Jonathan Hildreth had dau. Silva, wife of Stillwell Shaw, as mentioned in deeds dated 1796.{Deeds E: 278}

Sarah, dau. of Jonathan Hildreth, mentioned in deeds dated 1796.{Deeds E: 272}

George Munyan and wife Hannah Hildreth, dau. of Jonathan

Hildreth, mentioned in deeds dated 1797.{Deeds E: 270}

Jonathan Hildreth had a dau. Martha who m. Solathiel Townsend, as mentioned in deeds dated 1797.{Deeds E: 276}

Jonathan was the father of the following children: JONATHAN, b. 15 Dec 1740, m. Dorcas Mills; EPHRAIM; HANNAH; probably WILLIAM{see will of William below in which he mentions brother Jonathan and Jonathan's son, William}.

4. JOSEPH HILDRETH, son of David (1) Hildreth, m. Zabiah Corson*, dau. of Peter Corson, by license dated 16 Feb 1748.{MLNJ}

Joseph d. leaving a will dated 1 Sep 1781, proved 28 May 1785. Mentioned were wife Zibiah; nephews: James and Joseph Hildreth, son of James, dec., to whom were devised lands after the death of the widow; and if they died under age then to the two sons of Daniel Hildreth, dec., namely, Aaron and Daniel. To Joseph Hildreth, son of Joshua, land in Cumberland Co., near West Creek. To Annabaptist Church of Cape May Co., £40, to be possessed in the hands of Thomas Smith, Elder, and Daniel Smith, Deacon. To James Hildreth and Joseph Hildreth, sons of James, dec.; Proseilla Hildreth, dau. of Daniel Hildreth, dec., and Phebe Whillden, wife of Matthew Whillden, rest of moveable estate. Execs. were wife Zibiah and James Hildreth and Joseph Hildreth, sons of James, dec. The will was witnessed by Thomas Pretten, Mary Stevens and Joanna Pratten. On 5 Oct 1784 an inventory was filed (£667.16.11) by James Godfrey and John Cresse.{NJCW 27:520}

Zibiah Hildreth d. leaving a will dated 16 Nov 1789, proved 4 May 1790. Mentioned were her two sisters: Rebecca Townsend, wife of Daniel Townsend and Rachel Dole, wife of Isaac Dole; brothers: Rem and Peter Corson; nephew, Levi Corson, son of brother Levi Corson; youngest brother Jesse Corson; Rachel Scull and Jesse Scull, dau. and son of John and Deborah Scull.{NJCW 32:287, File 554E}

5. JAMES HILDRETH, carpenter, son of David (1) Hildreth, d. leaving a will dated 1 Aug 1766, proved 28 May 1767. Mentioned were dau. Phebe Hildreth to whom was devised land bought of Daniel Hildreth, when she is 20; son James to whom was left 1/2 of other lands; and son Joseph, the other 1/2 when 21. Wife Lydia was to have use of all estate. Execs. were wife Lydia and brother Joseph Hildreth. The will was witnessed by John Cresse, Daniel Hildreth and Zibiah Hildreth. Letters were granted to Joseph Hildreth, the surviving exec. On 29 May 1767 an inventory (£47.1.3) was filed by Thomas Smith and Elihu Smith.{NJCW 12:492}

James may have m. Lydia Johnson, dau. Benjamin and Penelope Johnson*. [Based on the will of Penelope Johnson which mentions dau. Lydia Hildreth and granddau. Prisciller Heldreth.]

James was father of the following children: PHEBE, m. Matthew, son of James Whillden*; JAMES; JOSEPH.

6. DAVID HILDRETH, probably son of David (1) Hildreth, m. Jane Edwards by license dated 21 April 1769.{MLNJ}

7. DANIEL HILDRETH, son of David (1) Hildreth, d. leaving a will dated 18 May 1769, proved 6 Feb 1770. Cedar swamp to be sold and 1/2 of 56 acres on the head of William Goff's land. Brother Joseph Hildreth to have the other 1/2 of the 56 acres. Wife Prissilla to have use of the other lands to bring up the children. His children: Elizabeth Hildreth and Aaron and Daniel to have lands when of age. Execs. were wife Priscella and brother Joseph. On 12 Jan 1770 an inventory (£163.5.1/2) was filed by Joshua Hildreth and Thomas Smith.{NJCW 15:79}

Daniel m. Prisila Goff by license dated 2 May 1761.{MLNJ} Priscilla Hildreth, probable widow of Daniel, m. Shamgar Hand* on 28 Feb 1772.{Baptists} A marriage license was issued to them on 27 Feb 1772.{MLNJ}

In "Diaries of Aaron Leaming," he mentioned on 2 April 1750, "Daniel Hildreth, which is David Hildreth's youngest son."

Daniel was father of the following children: ELIZABETH; AARON; DANIEL; PRISCILLA who was mentioned in the will of Joseph [above].

Third Generation

8. JONATHAN HILDRETH, son of Jonathan (3) Hildreth, was b. 15 Dec 1740. He m. 1 Aug 1764, Dorcas Mills (b. 13 Sep 1747). Jonathan d. 31 Oct 1787. An inventory of his estate was filed (£254) on 9 Jan 1788 by Philip Cresse and Eli Eldredge.{NJCW 31:93} Dorcas m. 2nd Thomas Gandy; she d. 27 Nov 1809, in her 63rd year.{Baptist Burials}

At August Court Term 1790 Dorkas Hildreth laid before the court an account for maintaining her three children: George, William and Rachel, children of Jonathan Hildreth, dec.{Ltrs&Inv A(Rev):50}

At February Court Term 1790 Silas Eldredge complained that Dorkas Hildreth, admx., retained a legacy due his wife and dau. of said Jonathan Hildreth, dec.{Ltrs&Inv A(Rev):45}

At February Term 1794 and August Term 1795 Salathiel Townsend on the part of his wife Martha requested division of the lands of Jonathan Hildreth, dec., between his surviving children, viz., Hannah wife of Silas Eldredge; Sarah; Martha, wife of the applicant; Silva; Rachel; William and George Hildreth. The court so ordered. The record shows Jonathan Hildrith d. intestate and division of the lands between his nine surviving children at the time of his death, viz., Hannah, Sarah, Silvia, Rachel, George, Ephraim, Jonathan, William and Martha. Division was made to William Hildreth, George Hildreth, Rachel Hildreth, Sarah Hildreth, Stillwell Shaw in right of his wife, Hannah Eldredge, Salathiel Townsend in right of his wife, James Thompson in right of Ephraim Hildreth, dec, by purchase. (plats shown) The plats show the additional names of Silvia Shaw, Martha Townsend, Samuel Foster and Enoch Gandy.{Ltrs&Inv A(Rev):89, 93, 106}

Jonathan and Dorcas were the parents of the following children: HANNAH, b. 20 July 1765, d. 1825, m. Silas Eldredge; EPHRAIM, b. 21 Dec 1767, d. 24 Feb 1793; SARAH, b. 9 Sep 1769, d. 4 April 1816; JONATHAN, b. 25 Sep 1771, d. 12 Dec 1792; SILVIA, b. 15 Dec 1773, d. 20 March 1798, m. Stillwell Shaw* 2 Jan 1793{Baptists}; MARTHA, b. 28 Feb 1776, d. 24 March 1803, m. Salathiel Townsend; RACHEL, b. 2 Nov 1778, d. May 1867; WILLIAM, b. 29 Dec 1780, d. Feb 1867; GEORGE, b. 13 May 1783, d. 24 May 1839; JACOB, b. 18 Aug 1785, d. 1 March 1786.{All dates from Hildreth Bible}

9. JOSEPH HILDRETH, probable son of James (5) Hildreth, d. 10 April 1815 in his 53rd year{Baptist Burials}, m. by license dated 28 Jan 1789{MLNJ} Martha Stillwell*, dau. of Enoch Stillwell, dec.{MLNJ} Martha was b. 28 April 1770, d. 17 March 1791. They were the parents of the following children: SARAH, b. 31 Aug 1788; LYDIA, b. 6 April 1790. Both daus. d. young.

At February Court 1789 Mr. Van Leuveneigh in behalf of Joseph Hildreth who m. Martha Stillwell, dau. of Enoch Stillwell, dec. and one of the heirs of Joseph Savage, dec. the court appointed Elijah Hudges, Persons Leaming and Philip Hand as auditors to make division of the real estate of said Joseph Savage.{Ltrs&Inv A(Rev):30}

Joseph m. 2nd 1 April 1793, Ann Stillwell (b. 28 July 1778, d. 10 Nov 1820{Baptist Burials}), dau. of Enoch and Sarah Stillwell. Ann was the sister of his dec. wife, Martha. Joseph and Ann had the following children: ROXANNA, b. 18 Jan 1795, m. Aaron Edmunds* and d. 26 Sep 1876; STILLWELL, b. 10 Sep 1797; JOSEPH, b. 14 May 1802; SOPHIA STILLWELL SOMERS, 10 Dec 1805, m. Samuel Compton; JULIAN; LYDIA, m. Thomas Holmes who d. soon after their marriage.

10. WILLIAM HILDRETH, probable son of Jonathan (3) Hildreth, d. prior to 24 Feb 1783 leaving a will dated 24 Feb 1783, proved 26 April 1783. Mentioned were brother Jonathan Hildreth, wife Martha, nephew William Hildreth, son of brother Jonathan. Extx. was wife Martha. The will was witnessed by Alice Hildreth, Absalom Hand and Archibald Campbell.{NJCW 38:75}

11. JAMES HILDRETH, possible son of James (5) Hildreth.

On 10 Feb 1789 Joseph Hildreth was appointed admin. of the estate of James Hildreth. On 13 Feb 1790 an inventory was filed (£393.5.3) by Thomas Shaw and Jotham Townsend.{NJCW 31:370}

On 10 Feb 1789 a bond was taken of Joseph Hildreth on the guardianship of James Hildreth, minor son of James and Martha Hildreth, dec.{Ltrs&Inv A:18}

On 10 Feb 1789 a bond was taken of Joseph Hildreth to take care of the person and estate of Martha Hildreth, minor dau. of James and Martha Hildreth.{Ltrs&Inv A:18}

February Court 1789. On application of Mr. Van Leuvenigh that the court appoint Joseph Hildreth guardian of James and Martha Hildreth minor children of James Hildreth dec. until age 14. Approved.{Ltrs&Inv A(Rev):30}

James and Martha were parents of the following children: MARTHA; JAMES.

12. PHEBE HILDRETH, dau. of James (5) Hildreth, m. Matthew Whilldin on 23 April 1771.{Baptists} A marriage license was issued to Matthew Whildin and Phebe Hildreth, on 22 April 1771.{MLNJ}

Unplaced

JOSHUA HILDRETH, son of David Hildreth, d. by 9 Jan 1790 when his sons, James and Joshua, were made wards of David Hildreth. James was under the age of 14.{NJCW 32:107}

JOSEPH HOLDEN

1. JOSEPH HOLDEN m. Hannah Jonson, dau. of William Johnson, by license dated 11 Oct 1690.

Joseph d. before 1 May 1696 when an inventory of his estate of was appraised by John Jervis, Shamger Hand and Jacob Dayton.

Reference was made to his widow's bed and furniture.{First Official Rcds}

Letters of administration were granted to Hanah Holdin, widow and relict of Joseph Holdin, dec. 15 Dec 1696.{First Official Rcds}

Hannah later m. Henry Leonard of Cape May. On 29 Jan 1697/8 was recorded the affadavit of Hannah concerning the will of her father William Johnson who d. 14 May 1689. She mentioned her mother Elizabeth and her brother William.{East Jersey Deeds, Liber G:18} William Johnson of Elizabeth Town left a will dated 14 Nov 1688, proved 12 Oct 1699. Mentioned were sons: John, Daniel, Samuel, Benjamin, William, Henry and daus.: Kathren, Hannah [above], and Abigail.{East Jersey Deeds, G:17}

2. BENJAMIN HOLDIN, probable son of Joseph (1) Holden, m. Mary Garretson (Garetson), 11 Sep 1715. Witnesses: Hanah Cosson, Martha Cosson, John Corson, Hanah Lenard, Henry Lenard, Jacob Gareson, Elizabeth Gareson, Christian Corson, Thomas Gandy, John Hubord, Benja. Martino. Entered 14 Sep 1715.{First Official Rcds}

Benjamin Houldin of Cape May Co., yeoman, d. leaving a will dated 29 May 1717, proved 6 May 1718. Mentioned were wife Mary, extx. and son Benjamin as heirs. Reference was made to 200 acres of land between John Huebard and William Goldin, for which brother Joseph Houldin was to pay. Wit: Henry Leonard, Jonathan Swain and John Taylor.{NJCW 2:87} On 10 June 1717 inventory was made of the estate by Joseph Houldin and John Taylor.{NJCW}

Benjamin was father of BENJAMIN, probably b. ca. 1716.

3. JOSEPH HOLDEN, probable son of Joseph (1) Holden, was mentioned in the will of his brother, Benjamin (2) Houldin. He may have m. Jane (N)? for whom the following entries pertain.

Jane Holding of Cape May d. before 7 Dec 1730 when her estate was inventoried including her husband's coat, 7 bushels of wheat, and 6 barrels of corn, by William Johnson and George Taylor. On 2 Aug 1731 a bond was issued to Joseph Holden (Holding) admin of the estate. William Johnson fellow bondsman - both of Cape May Co.

On 2 Aug 1731 Joseph Holding was appointed admin. Fellow bondsman, William Johnston, both of afsd. county. Witnesses: Henry Noden, Jacob Spicer and Jacob Garrison.{NJCW 3:139} On 7 Dec 1730 an inventory was submitted by William Johnson and George Taylor.{NJCW}

4. BENJAMIN HOLLDEN, probable son of Benjamin (2) Holdin, m. Elizabeth Briggs* by license dated 18 Dec 1739.{MLNJ}

Benjamin Holden and Abigail Leonard, m. 5 April 1746.{MLNJ}

DANIEL HOLDEN [HOLDER]

1. DANIEL HOLDER (Holden) m. Sarah Iszard, by license dated 4 Sep 1754{MLNJ}, widow of Michael Iszard.

Sarah Holden of Cape May Co. d. leaving a will dated 10 Dec 1755, proved 2 Jan 1758. Mentioned were children: Reeves Iszard, John Iszard, Simeon Iszard (under age), whose father Michael Iszard is named. Exec. was Jacob Spicer. The will was witnessed by Deborah Spicer, Christopher Leamyng, Sylvia Spicer and Sarah Spicer.{NJCW 8:520}

2. JEREMIAH HOLDEN of Cape May Co., probable son of Daniel (1) Holden, Gent., d. leaving a will dated 28 Feb 1774, proved 16 May 1778. Mentioned was a plantation on Maurice River in Cumberland Co. of 260 acres which descended to him from his father, Daniel Holden and which he now gave to his nephews, Jeremiah Johnson and James Lyon. Also mentioned were nieces Martha Johnson and Phebe Lyon. If Jeremiah Johnson should die under age, then Imla Johnson was to enjoy his part and if James Lyon should die under age then Jonathan Ludlam Lyon was to enjoy his part. Execs. were David Johnson and Rev. James Lyon. The will was witnessed by Jeremiah Ludlam and Anna Ludlam.{NJCW 38:78}

Unplaced

Benjamin Taylor and HANNAH HOLDEN, 3 Oct 1768.{MLNJ}

A marriage license was issued to Josiah Cresse and MARY HOLDING, 26 Sep 1737.{MLNJ}

Daniel Hewitt and MARY HOLDEN, 1 Feb 1764.{MLNJ}

HUGHES

See Hughes Family of Cape May County, New Jersey 1650-1950. A Genealogy of descendants of Humphrey Hugghes of Long Island 1650 and later of Cape May County, New Jersey. Privately printed (1950) for Raymond Finley Hughes, 3561 Monteith Ave., Cincinnati, 8, Ohio. Copies are held at Cape May County Library and Cape May County Historical Society. This book details the descendants of Humphrey (1) Hughes. It is referenced below in some entries by the citation,{HUGHES}.

There are two articles of special importance. See "Origin of the Hughes Family in Cape May County, N.J. - and the Seven Humphreys," *The Cape May County Magazine of History and Genealogy*, p. 143. June 1942; and see also "Concerning Ellis Hughes, Son of Uriah," *The Cape May County Magazine of History and Genealogy*, p. 78. June 1949.

1. Humphrey Hughes, may have come from England. According to Raymond Finley Hughes:

> "The earliest record of him on Long Island refers to him as an Englishman and mentions his being with John Griggs whose name never reappears in Long Island records. A full account of the episode referred to in this record of Humphrey Hughes, appears on page 187 of the first edition of Thompson's History of Long Island ... .
>
> "In 1666 Humphrey Hughes received a whaling grant from Peter Carteret: 'to license the said Huse and Company to enjoy the privilege to make use of all the whales that shall be cast up or that they can use anysways to kill or destroy, between the inlet Roanoak and the inlet of Caretuck.' This grant was shared with Nicholas Stevens of Boston and John Cooper of Southampton, each receiving 1/3 interest in transactions recorded at Southampton in 1667.
>
> "On 5 Nov 1679 the town of Southampton by major vote gave Humphrey Hughes 10 acres of land. On 30 July 1669 Humphrey Hughes' son Humphrey was born. Lists of townsmen in 1694 show his wife's name as Martha and mentions his five sons by name. In 1689 Humphrey Hughes purchased from Simon Charles, 243 acres on Cape Island later Cape May.{Deeds A:155} Humphrey Hughes sold his Southampton property in 1699; the deed was signed by him and his wife Martha. He d. between 1699 and 1705. (Court records of Cape May Co. 1705 refer to his wife as widow Hughes.)"

Humphrey was the father of the following children: CONSTANT; HUMPHREY; JOHN; ABNER; URIAH; JEDEDIAH, d. a bachelor in New York City in 1714.

Second Generation

2. CONSTANT HUGHES, son of Humphrey (1) and Martha Hughes, was probably b. in Southampton ca. 1684,

d. 10 June 1746 in Cape May, m. (N) Matthews, dau. of Samuel Matthews of Jamaica, L.I. and late of Cape May, NJ. He was the father of the following children: CONSTANT, d. a widower without issue in 1746; ELLIS, m. Hannah, dau. of Joseph and Mary Whilldin*; JACOB.

Raymond Hughes writes regarding Constant Hughes, "He is established as a son of Humphrey Hughes 1st by the will of Jedidiah Hughes which names Humphrey and Constant as his brothers. He is established as the father of Ellis Hughes and the grandfather of Memucan Hughes by the record of earmarks. In Cape May Courthouse, Deed Book A Miscellaneous, page 6, is recorded "Constant Hughes this earmark being a hal penny on the upper side of the right ear." Recorded 27 day of Jan 1707. In Deed Book A Miscellaneous, Page 43, is recorded "The earmark of Memucan Hughes beig the uper side of the right ear. Entered this 20th day of August 1760 it being the mark of my grandfather, Constant Hughes."{Hughes}

Constant was the father of the following children{Hughes}: CONSTANT, JR., d. a widower in 1746; ELLIS, b. 1708; JACOB, b. 1711.

3. HUMPHREY HUGHES, son of Humphrey (1) and Martha Hughes, was b. 30 July 1669 in Southampton, Long Island, d. 1745 in Cape May. He m. 1st in Cape May, Mary Brandriff (Brandreth), dau. of Timothy and Sarah Brandriff and m. 2nd Elizabeth, widow of Daniel Wells.

Humphrey Hughes of Cape May Co., yeoman, d. leaving a will dated 13 Feb 1744/5, proved 4 Feb 1745/6. Mentioned was wife Elizabeth, to whom he left an annuity. Son Elijah was devised 3 tracts in Cape May Co. between lands of Ebenezear Swain and Cornelius Schilinks joining land of Zebulon Swain at the northwest part, and 1/3 of right in the five-mile beach. Son Uriah, 3 tracts at Nummes near George Stites and Jonathan Forman and 1/3 of right in five-mile beach. Grandson Humphrey Hughes, all land on Cape Island, the tract between Joseph Whillden and Robert Parsons, a tract at the northernmost part of the land of Zebulon Swaine and 1/3 of right in five-mile beach upon condition he pay £20 to his brothers, John and Elisha when they arrived at age 21. In case of failure to pay the £20 the lands to be divided among grandsons, Humphrey, John and Elisha Hughes. 1/2 of rents of these lands shall be used to bring them up to learning; the other half given to Humphrey.

Daus.: Martha Fithian and Judith Spicer. Exec. son Elijah Hughes. Overseers: Jacob Spicer and Elisha Hand. The will was witnessed by George Hand, George Sharwood and Abiel Caril.{NJCW 5:240} An inventory of the estate was submitted on 27 May 1746 by Elisha Hand and James Whilldin. On 14 Oct 1755 an account was submitted showing payments to James Willden, Elisha Hand, Charles Dennis, Nathaniel Hand, Mary Schillinks, Joseph Willden, Phebe Foster, Benjamin Laughton, James Hedges, Henry Whitefield, Isaac Nuton, David Whillden, Levi Hand, Jacob Spicer, Mathias Fithian, Richd. Stillwell, John Kinsey, etc.{NJCW}

By his first wife Humphrey was father of the following children: HUMPHREY; ELIJAH, b. 1708, d. 19 Feb 1762{Cold Spring Cemetery}; URIAH, b. 1709; JUDITH, d. 1747, age 33, m. Jacob Spicer* by license dated 10 June 1738*; MARTHA, m. Mathias Fithian.

4. JEDIDIAH HUGHES, son of Humphrey (1) Hughes, recorded his ear mark on 12 Oct 1706; later recorded for Humphry Hughes, Esqr.{First Official Rcds}

Jedidiah Hughes d. in New York City, leaving a will dated 21 Jan 1714/5, proved 18 Feb 1714/5. Mentioned were brothers: Humphrey, Constant and John Hughes and cousin Martha Hughes. Brother John exec. The will was witnessed by John Hand, Benjamin Crafford and Sarah Hand.{NJCW 1:504} The estate was inventoried on 31 Jan 1714/5 by Samuel Fostar and John Hand.{NJCW}

Third Generation

5. CONSTANTINE HUGHES of Cape May, son of Constant (2), d. leaving a will dated 4 Sep 1747, proved 19 Oct 1747 before Deputy Secretary of the Province of New York. Mentioned were brothers Jacob Hughes and Ellis Hughes. They were instructed to convey all real estate in houses or land in New Jersey or elsewhere with personal estate (except two Negroes); brother Jacob to have Jack and brother Ellis to have London. Apparel of dec. wife to Precila Holliday. The will was witnessed by Benjamin Kiersted, Jno. Alsop, W. Blake. On 28 Nov 1747 letters granted to Jacob Hughes and Ellis Hughes as execs.{NJCW 5:377}

6. HUMPHREY HUGHES, son of Humphrey (3) and Mary (Brandriff) Hughes was b. 1702 in Cape May, d. 1744. He m. Bethia Crowell, dau. of Samuel Crowell, Jr. They had the following children: HUMPHREY; ELISHA; JOHN.

Humphrey Hughes, Jr., of Cape May Co., d. prior to 4 Feb 1741/2 when Bethia Hughes was appointed admx. Fellow bondsman

Elisha Hand, both of Cape May. Witnesses: George Hand and Nathaniel Hand.{NJCW Cape May Wills:106E} Inventory of the estate submitted 4 Feb 1741/2 and included cattle, sheep and leather; appraisers: George Hand and Nathaniel Hand.{NJCW} An account of the estate was submitted on 28 Sep 1745 by Ezekiel Mulford of Cape May Co. who m. Bethia Hughes, late dec. widow and admx. of Humphrey Hughes, Jr. Payments were made to Joseph Whilldin, Eliza. Eldridge, Abigail Stites, George Hand, William Hamilton, John Flower, Samuel Emlen, Henry Young, Elisha Hand, Richard Crawford, Joseph Whilldin, Elijah Hughes and Benjamin Crawford, etc.{NJCW}

7. ELIJAH HUGHES, son of Humphrey (3) Hughes, b. Cape May, 1708, probably m. 28 Oct 1740 by license{MLNJ} Hannah Stites, dau. of Richard Stites*.[66] Elijah was the father of the following children: ELIJAH, JR., b. 15 Feb 1744; ARCHIBALD, d. in Gloucester Co., NJ, 1784; ZERUIAH, m. by license dated 11 Nov 1775{MLNJ}, David Bowen of Cumberland Co.

Elijah Hughes, b. 1708, d. 19 Feb 1762.{Cold Spring Cemetery} On 19 Aug 1762 Hannah Hughes and Elijah Hughes were appointed admins. to his estate Fellowbondsman: Richard Stites of Cape May Co. Witness: Daniel Crowell. On 29 June 1762 an inventory was filed (£238.15.9) by Richard Stites and Daniel Crowell. On 21 April 1768 an account was filed by Elijah Hughes and Hannah Hughes, the admins.

8. URIAH HUGHES, son of Humphrey (3) Hughes, b. 1709. He m. Mary Whilldin*, dau. of Joseph Whilldin, Jr., and Mary Whilldin. Uriah was the father of the following children: ELLIS, d. in Northumberland Co., PA, 1800; JUDITH, m. by license dated 10 July 1772{MLNJ}, Richard Matthews; MARY, m. 14 June 1763, her cousin Jesse Hughes, son of Ellis and Hannah (Whilldin) Hughes.

9. MARTHA HUGHES, dau. of Humphrey (3) Hughes, m. Mathias Fithian, son of Samuel and Priscilla (Burnett) Fithian, born Easthampton, Long Island, 3 Feb 1694, d. Greenwich, NJ, in 1749.{Hughes; see also Craig, Cumberland County NJ Gen. Data:215}

Matthias Fithian of Cumberland Co., carpenter, d. leaving a will dated 29 May 1749, proved 24 Oct 174; mentioned son HUMPHRY and "rest of 9 children ... son DANIEL, dec. ... sons WILLIAM and

---

66 Raymond Finley Hughes has her as probably dau. of dau. of Henry and Hannah (Garlick) Stites.

EPHRAIM."{NJCW 6:340}

10. ELLIS HUGHES, b. ca. 1719, son of Constant (2) Hughes, m. before 1739, Hannah Whilldin (b. ca. 1719, d. 1752), dau. of Joseph Whilldin, Jr., and Mary Whilldin*.

Hannah and Ellis Hughes were the parents of the following children: MEMUCAN, b. 12 April 1739, 8 Jan 1812,[67] m. 1st on 10 March 1761, Martha Hughes and m. 2nd, Rhoda Allen{Hughes}; ELLIS, b. d. 16 April 1817, age 71 years, 8 mos.{Cold Spring Cemtery}; JESSE, b. before 1745{Hughes}; CONSTANTINE, m. Elisheba Hand by license dated 1 Feb 1769{MLNJ}; DAVID, b. 19 Sep 1749{Cold Spring Cemtery}.

Ellis Hughes of Cape May Co. d. leaving a will dated 9 May 1751, proved 4 Feb 1752. Mentioned were sons Memucan, Jesse, Ellis, Constant and David, the last three under age. Home farm, bought of John Page and lying near New England in the Lower Precinct of the county; 40 acres of wood land adjoining George Hand, James Hedges, Samuel Crowell and others.; 40 acres of upland bought at auction out of the estate of Levi Eldredge adjoining James Whillden. Execs. were wife and Richard Crawford. The will was witnessed by Marcy Ross, Elihu Hand, Jacob Spicer and Nathan Eldredge. On 30 July 1752 an inventory was filed by John Eldredge and James Whillden.{NJCW Cape May Wills:160E}

11. JACOB HUGHES, son of Constant (2) Hughes, ca. 1711, d. 28 Sep 1772{Cold Spring Cemetery}, m. 1744, Priscilla (Leaming) Stites (b. 15 June 1710, d. 21 Sep 1758), dau. of Thomas and Hannah (Whilldin) Leaming* and widow of John Stites*. Both are bur. in Cold Spring Cemetery. Jacob was father of the following children: JACOB, b. 9 Aug 1746, d. 22 March 1796[68] who m. by license issued in PA 24 Nov 1773, Ann Lawrence (b. 1753, d. 27 Nov 1817); HANNAH, b. 7 Dec 1756, d. 24 April 1787, m. as his second wife, Rev. James Watt (b. 12 March 1743, d. 19 Nov 1789), son of Robert Watt.{Hughes}

On 16 Jan 1773 Jacob Hughes was appointed admin. of the estate of Jacob Hughes of Cape May Co. On 13 Jan 1773 an inventory was filed (£1,276.4.0 by Aaron Eldredge and Jeremiah Eldredge.{NJCW 14:520}

---

67 Tombstone at Tabernacle Cemetery.

68 Cold Spring Cemetery.

Fourth Generation

12. HUMPHREY HUGHES, son of Humphrey (6) and Bethia (Crowell) Hughes, was b. 1724 in Cape May, d. 25 May 1755, bur. at Cold Spring. He was father of the following sons: HUMPHREY, b. 1752{Hughes}; JOHN[69].

Humphrey d. prior to 29 May 1755 when Zebulon Swaine of the same county was appointed admin. Bondsman, Joseph Corson, Gent., of the same place. Witnesses: Henry Young and Elizabeth Mackey.{NJCW 8:198} On 23 July 1757 an inventory of the estate was made by John Townsend and Jacob Spicer and accounted for by Elijah Hughes.{NJCW}

John Hughes, son of Humphrey Hughes of Cape May was on 21 Aug 1755 an orphan when a bond was issued for Elijah Hughes as guardian; Jacob Spicer fellow bondsman, both of Cape May Co.{NJCW Cape May Wills:173E}

In the Books of Deeds D:46 dated 1797 is mentioned John Hughes, brother of Humphrey, dec., and grandson of Humphrey.{Deeds D:46}

13. JOHN HUGHES, son of Humphrey (6) and Bethia (Crowell) Hughes, b. ca. 1725, d. 1763, m. Rebecca (N).{Hughes}

John was father of the following children: WILLIAM, b. 30 July 1752; MARY, b. 24 April 1754; JOHN, b. 8 June 1756, d. 6 June 1821; RICHARD; JAMES; JOSEPH, b. 28 Dec 1763; REBECCA, b. 19 April 1756; MARGARET, b. 5 April 1770.{Hughes}

14. ELIJAH HUGHES, son of Elijah (7) Hughes, b. 13 Feb 1744, d. 26 Nov 1797.{Cold Spring Cemetery}

Elijah m. 27 Oct 1773 Judith Spicer*, dau. of Jacob and Judith (Hughes) Spicer. She d. at age 69. Elijah was father of the following children: NANCY, b. 1774, d. 1838, m. John Bennett; SARAH, b. 1775, d. 1840, m. 1796, James Mulford; SPICER, b. 1777, d. 1849 unmarried.{Hughes, Cold Spring Cemetery}

15. WILLIAM FITHIAN, son of Mathias and Martha (9) (Hughes) Fithian, b. in Greenwich, NJ, 21 Jan 1733, d. in Greenwich, 25 Nov 1786. He m. in Greenwich, 8 May 1754, Deliverance Caruthers (b. 24 Sep 1735, d. Greenwich 29 Jan 1786). William was father of the following children: HOPE, b. 9 March 1766; WILLIAM, b. 22 Nov 1757; DELIVERENCE, b. 6 June 1759; GEORGE, b. 24 March 1761; PRISCILLA, b. 5 Jan 1765, d. 7 June 1767; JAMES, b. Greenwich, NJ, 25 Nov 1766; JEREMIAH, b.

---

69 Omitted by Raymond Hughes.

18 June 1772; ESTHER, b. 26 Nov 1774; HANNAH, b. 26 Feb 1776, m. Isaac Coffee of Salem.{Hughes}

16. EPHRIAM FITHIAN, son of Mathias and Martha (9) (Hughes) Fithian, b. Greenwich, NJ, 28 Feb 1739, d. Greenwich, 1773. He m. at Greenwich, 4 Feb 1761, Temperance (N) (b. 24 Oct 1740). Ephraim was father of the following children: MATHIAS, b. 20 Dec 1761; IRA, b. 23 July 1766, d. 1812, m. Elizabeth (N); PHOEBE.{Hughes}

17. JESSE HUGHES, son of Ellis (10) Hughes, b. before 1745, d. leaving a will proved 17 Nov 1798. Mentioned were wife Mary, son JESSE, daus.: MARY Smith, LOUISA Hughes, VASHTE Hughes.{NJCW 38:154} An inventory was filed on 28 Nov 1798 by Robert Edmunds and Eleazer Hand.{NJCW File:703E}

Jesse m. 14 June 1763, Mary Hughes.

Jesse was father of the following son: Jesse, Jr., b. 1770, d. 14 Jan 1845[70].

Jesse Hughes, son of Ellis Hughes of Cape May Co., between 14 and 21 years old declared on 15 Oct 1759 that he chose James Whilldin of said county as his guardian. On 2 Nov 1759 a bond was issued for James Whilldin as guardian; Jacob Spicer fellowbondsman.{NJCW 10:602}

18. ELLIS HUGHES,[71] son of Ellis (10) Hughes, d. 16 April 1817, age 71 years, 8 mos., bur. Cold Spring Cemetery, m. by license of 21 Sep 1768, Elinor Hurst (b. 23 Feb 1747, d. 11 April 1786), widow of Wilmon Whilldin and dau. of William and Martha Hurst. Ellis m. 2nd 7 Dec 1786, Judith (N) (d. 8 Nov 1789, age 29){Cold Spring Cemetery}. Ellis m. 3rd 7 Dec 1795, Abigal (Collins) Williams (b. 10 Feb 1759, d. 24 Feb 1847), widow of Col. Williams and dau. of Richard Collins and Hetty (Zane) Collins of Burlington Co., NJ. Ellis and Elinor (Hurst) Hughes had the following children: THOMAS HURST, b. 10 Jan 1769, d. 10 Nov 1839, m. 3 Dec 1788, Lydia Paige (b. 13 May 1767, d. 3 May 1828{Cold Spring Cemetery}); ELLIS, b. 10 Nov 1770, d. 1 Nov 1793, unmarried; JOSEPH BUCK, b. 17 Nov 1772, d. 13 March 1813, m. Judith Bennett; MARTHA,

70 Cold Spring Cemetery.

71 The records of Charles Welsh Edmunds deposited at the Historical Society of Pennsylvania gives a list of the descendants of this family.

b. 27 Oct 1774, d. 21 Oct 1798, m. in Christ Church, Philadelphia, 12 Dec 1792, James Pritchard; HANNAH, b. 23 Sep 1776, m. Dr. Philip Ford; ELEANOR, b. 7 Aug 1776, d. 5 Oct 1818, m. 20 Dec 1798, Silas Matthews (b. Fishing Creek, NJ, 17 Sep 1777, d. Cape May 8 Sep 1830); SARAH, b. 14 Aug 1780, d. 14 Jan 1785; ELIZABETH; WILLIAM. Ellis Hughes and Judith, his 2nd wife, had a son: RICHARD.{Hughes}

19. DAVID HUGHES, son of Ellis (10) Hughes, b. 19 Sep 1749, d. 23 Nov 1815, m. 8 Aug 1778, Rachel Hand who d. 13 Dec 1818, age 62 years, 1 month, 14 days.{Cold Spring Cemetery} They were the parents of the following children{Crawford-Hughes Bible}: AARON, b. 30 Oct 1779, d. 17 Oct 1842; DAVID, b. 10 Sep 1781, d. 13 April 1805; JEREMIAH, b. 7 April 1783, d. 23 Feb 1815; RACHEL, b. 28 Jan 1785, d. 6 Jan 1841; JAMES, b. 13 Jan 1791, d. 9 June 1820; SARAH, b. 14 Jan 1791, d. 26 Aug 1832; ALLEN, b. 9 Jan 1793, d. 29 Oct 1824; LEMUEL, b. 12 Jan 1798, d. 12 March 1841[72]; LEVI, b. 31 Oct 1800, d. 27 Oct 1814.[73]

20. JACOB HUGHES, son of Jacob (11) and Priscilla Hughes, b. 9 Aug 1746, d. 22 March 1796, m. by license issued in Pennsylvania on 24 Nov 1773, Ann Lawrence (b. 1753, d. 27 Nov 1817). Jacob and Ann Hughes were parents of the following children: MARY, b. 18 Aug 1776, d. 22 Sep 1779; JACOB, b ca. 1777, d. ca. 1830, m. 28 July 1800, Sophia Stillwell; Dr. DANIEL b. 1779, d. 3 July 1815{Cold Spring Cemetery}, m. 12 Nov 1804, Charlotte Bennett; MARY, b. 1780, m. 17 Feb 1800, John Bennett; JEREMIAH, b. 1783, d. 23 Feb 1815,[74] m. Rhoda Taylor (b. 11 April 1778, d. 11 Sep 1843, m. 2nd 11 May 1820, Edward Price); ELIZABETH, m. 29 Jan 1806, John Church; JAMES RAINY, b. at New England, Lower Township, Cape May Co., 6 July 1791, d. 13 March 1865,[75] m. 9 Jan 1815, Eliza Eldredge (d. 6 Jan 1876, age 79, dau. of Aaron Eldredge[76].{Hughes, Cold Spring Cemtery}

---

72 Tombstone at Cold Spring Cemetery reads b. 14 Jan 1798, d. 13 March 1841.

73 Raymond Finley Hughes gives name as Levis Ingram Hughes.

74 Cold Spring Cemetery.

75 Cold Spring Cemetery.

76 See The Eldredge Family.

Jacob d. leaving a will dated 27 April 1795, proved 30 May 1796. Mentioned were wife Ann; children: Jeremiah and James R., under age 16, Jacob, Daniel, Mary Hughes, Elizabeth Hughes.{NJCW 36:267} On 30 May 1796 an inventory was filed (£1944.0.9) by Aaron Eldredge and Matthew Whilldin.{NJCW File:737E} Ann Hughes later m. Jeremiah Edmunds*.

21. HUMPHREY HUGHES, son of Humphrey (4) and Bethia Hughes was in Cape May 1752, lost at sea after Oct 1778 while Master of the privateer sloop, *New Comet.* He m. 1774 Jane Whilldin, dau. of James Whilldin and Jane (Hand) Whilldin. She was born 15 June 1756, d. 26 Dec 1790. They had a son: HUMPHREY.{Hughes}

22. WILLIAM HUGHES, son of John (13) Hughes, b. 30 July 1752, d. 24 March 1824, m. Mary (N). William was father of the following children: JOHN; WILLIAM; ISAAC; MARY JANE; REBECCA; MARY.{Hughes}

23. RICHARD HUGHES, son of John (13) Hughes, b. 19 Sep 1758 had the following children: JOHN; RICHARD; JAMES; REBECCA; JOHN; SAMUEL; BEULAH ANN, m. (N) Cubberly.{Hughes}

24. JAMES HUGHES, son of John (13) Hughes, b. 15 Sep 1760, had a son RANDALL.

25. THOMAS HURST HUGHES, son of Ellis (18) and Elinor (Hurst) Hughes, b. 10 Jan 1769, d. 10 Nov 1839,[77] m. 3 Dec 1788, Lydia Paige (b. 13 May 1767, d. 3 May 1828). They were the parents of the following children: THOMAS PAIGE, b. 19 Jan 1790, d. 8 Sep 1863,[78] m. in Cumberland Co., NJ, 25 Sep 1810, Mary Boone; ELLIS, b. 2 July 1793, d. 1 June 1863, m. 1st Sarah Higgins who d. 15 Oct 1821, m. 2nd Nancy Teal; LYDIA, b. 4 Dec 1795; ELEANOR, b. 12 May 1798, m. Smith Ludlam; SARAH, b. 31 May 1800, m. Eli B. Wales; LOUISE.{Hughes; Cold Spring Cemetery}

26. JOSEPH BUCK HUGHES, son of Ellis (18) and Elinor (Hurst) Hughes, b. 17 Nov 1772, d. 13 March 1813, m. Judith Bennett. They were the parents of the following children: JUDITH, m. Isaac Whilldin* (b.

77 Cold Spring Cemetery.

78 Cold Spring Cemetery.

15Feb 1784); THOMAS BUCK, m. Jane Kennedy Schellenger.

27. ELEANOR HUGHES, dau. of Ellis (18) and Elinor (Hurst) Hughes, b. 7 Aug 1776, d. 5 Oct 1818, m. 20 Dec 1798, Silas Matthews (b. Fishing Creek, NJ, 17 Sep 1777, d. Cape May 8 Sep 1830). They were the parents of the following children: WILLIAM, b. 9 March 1800, m. 1st Elizabeth Isard, m. 2nd Sarah Izard; THOMAS, b. 19 Dec 1801, d. early; ELEANOR, b. 26 June 1804, m. Mathias Lee; HANNAH, b. 24 Sep 1806, m. Thomas Page Crowell; THOMAS, b. 4 Oct 1808; SILAS, b. 1 Aug 1811, m. Charlotte Leaming, d. without issue; ISABELLA, b. 9 Oct 1813, m. Andrew H. Reeves; CHARLOTTE, b. 21 Nov 1816, d. 14 Nov 1847, unmarried.{Hughes}

28. HUMPHREY HUGHES, son of Humphrey (21) and Jane (Whilldin) Hughes, was b. 20 Nov 1775, d. 21 Aug 1858, m. 9 March 1800, Hetty Williams, dau. of Col. William Williams and Abigail (Collins) Williams. She was b. 14 Dec 1781, d. 4 Feb 1870.[79] Capt. Humphrey Hughes, b. 1775, d. 21 Aug 1858.{Cold Spring Cemetery}

29. DANIEL HUGHES, b. 1780, son of Jacob (20) Hughes, appears in the article "Medical Men of Early Times in Cape May," *The Cape May County Magazine of History and Genealogy*, p. 133, June 1934, by Dr. Julius Way, describes Daniel Hughes, son of Jacob Hughes and Ann (Lawrence) Hughes, born at Cape May in 1779, d. 3 July 1815. m. Charlotte Bennett of Cape May 12 Nov 1804. Practiced in lower part of the county.

Dr. Daniel Hughes, b. 1779, d. 3 July 1815.{Cold Spring Cemetery}

Unplaced

ELIZABETH HUGHES of Cape May Co. d. prior to 13 May 1746 when Elijah Hughes was appointed admin. Fellow bondsman Elisha Hand, both of Cape May Co. Witnesses: James Whilldin and Cornelius Schillinks.{NJCW 5:248} On 27 May 1746 the inventory of the estate was submitted by Elisha Hand and James Whilldin.{NJCW}

ELLIS
HUGHES m. Mary Willdin by license dated 2 Oct 1761.{MLNJ}

---

79 Cold Spring Cemetery.

EXPERIENCE HUGHES m. John Crowell by license dated 13 Feb 1770.{MLNJ}

HUMPHREY HUGHES, b. 1734, d. 20 Feb 1754.{Cold Spring Cemetery}

JOHN HUGHES, possible son of Humphrey (12) Hughes, m. Martha Iszard by license dated 24 Dec 1760.{MLNJ}

He d. prior to 15 Jan 1763 when Martha Hughes was appointed admx. Fellowbondsman: Davis Corson of Cape May Co. Witnesses: Mary Young and Henry Young.{NJCW 11:414}

A marriage was issued to Martha Hughes and Reuben Swain 3 Nov 1766.{MLNJ}

JOHN HUGHES d. prior to 24 April 1764 when Jedidiah Hughes was appointed admin. Fellowbondsman: John Eldredge of Cape May Co. Witnesses: William Mathews and Phebe Young. On 6 April 1761 an inventory was filed (£299.8.5) by William Mathews and John Eldredge.{NJCW 11:504}

JOHN HUGHES of Lower Penns Neck, Salem Co., d. by 29 July 1775 when Martha Hughes was appointed admx. of his estate. On 13 Jan 1773 an inventory was filed (£296.2.2) by Allen Congleton and Francis Philpot.{NJCW 15:551}

On 1 Sep 1777 JOHN HUGHES son of John Hughes of Cape May, dec. above the age of 14 was made a ward of Abraham Bennit. Witnessed by Ellis Hughes, Sr. and James Whilldin.{NJCW File No. 389E}

JUDITH HUGHES, b. 1760, d. 8 Nov 1789.{Cold Spring Cemetery}

MARY HUGHES, b. 1752, d. 24 April 1773.{Cold Spring Cemetery}

MARY HUGHES, b. 22 Aug 1776, d. 22 Sep 1779.{Cold Spring Cemetery}

PRUDENCE HUGHES, b. 26 Aug 1776, d. 7 Aug 1841.{Cold Spring Cemetery}

SUSANNAH HUGHES m. Elisha Bancroft on 7 April 1773.{Baptists}

A marriage license was issued to Elisha Bancroft and Susannah Hughes, 7 April 1773.{MLNJ}

INGERSUL

JOHN INGERSUL, son of Daniel Ingersul, b. 16th day, 11th mo., 1713/14 m. Sarah, dau. of Joseph Dole. She was b. 16th day, 11th mo., 1718, d. 16th day, 12th mo., 1758.

They were the parents of the following children: SARAH, b. 30th day, 9th mo., 1737; JANE, b. 1st day, Nov, 1740; JOHN, b. 29th day, 11th mo., (Jan), 1743; HANNAH, b. 26th day, 11th mo., (Jan) 1746; ISAAC, b. 19th day, 3rd mo., (March) 1751; ELIZABETH, b. 5th day, 5th mo., 1755, d. 21st day, 7th mo., 1755; MARY, b. 2nd day, 4th mo., 1757.{GEMM}

This may be the same John Ingersul, Sr. of Gloucester Co. who d. by 6 March 1775 when Isaac Ingersul was appointed admin. of his estate. Fellowbondsman: Amos Ireland. On 2 March 1775 an inventory was filed (£148.9.2) by Amos Ireland and Samuel Risley.{NJCW 15:535}

Joseph Edwards and SUSANNAH INGERSOL m. by license dated 9 Dec 1776.{MLNJ}

Joseph Edwards and ELIZABETH INGERSOL (Gloucester Co.) m. by license dated 1 Aug 1752.{MLNJ}

EBENEZER INGERSOLL and Mary Scull, 24 April 1761.{MLNJ}

Ebenezer Ingersul of Great Egg Harbor, husbandman, d. leaving a will dated 21 May 1773, proved 30 June 1773 with codicil of 23 May 1773. Mentioned were eldest dau. Elizabeth Townsand, dau. Rachel French, dau. Susana Ingersul and wife Mary. Reference was made to 5 youngest children when they come of age. Son Daniel to have no part of personal estate, but his share to be divided among his 4 youngest daus.: Catherine, Rebicah, Jemime and Mary Ingersul. Execs. were wife Mary and brother John Ingersul. The will was witnessed by Noah Smith, Daniel Ingersul and Robert P. Tyrrill. On 17 June 1773 an inventory was filed (£227.12.0) by Noah Smith and Samuel Risley.{NJCW 16:123}

Ebenezer was father of the following children: ELIZABETH, m. (N) Townsend; RACHEL, m. (N) French; SUSANA; DANIEL.

Hannah Ingersoll, dau. of John Somers and widow of Joseph Dole, m.

BENJAMIN INGERSOLL. Hannah b. ca. 1691, d. 24th da., 2nd mo., 1737.

IRELAND

1. DANIEL IRELAND[80], b. 1688, d. 25th day, 4th mo., 1762 and Ruth Ireland, his wife b. 1699, d. 25th day, 2nd mo., 1757 were the parents of the following children{GEMM}: MARCY, 10th mo., 1711; ELIZABETH, b. 8th mo., 1713; DANIEL, b. 13th day, 5th mo., 1715; MARY, b. 27th day, 11th mo., 1716/17; REUBEN, b. 1st day, 6th mo., 1718; THOMAS, b. 1st day, 5th mo., 1721; JOHN, b. 26th day, 8th mo., 1723; JOB, b. 3rd day, 9th mo., 1725; RUTH, b. 28th day, 11th mo., 1728, d. 15th day, 6th mo., 1761, m. Henry Woodward; JAMES, b. 10th day, 1st mo., 1730; SILAS, b. 4th day, 8th mo., 1733; DANIEL, b. 22nd day, 5th mo., 1738; HAZEKIAH, b. 15th day, 5th mo., 1741.

On 6th day, 11th mo., 1758, it was reported that Job Ireland had removed without a certificate.{GEMM}

In 1758 it was reported that James, Silas, Daniel (Jr.) and Hezakiah Ireland had married out.{GEMM}

On 19 April 1762 Daniel Ireland was appointed admin. of the estate of Daniel Ireland of Great Egg Harbor. Fellowbondsman: William Mapes. Witnesses: Job Young and Phebe Young. On 12 April 1762 an inventory was filed (£109.16.5) by James Somers and William Mapes.{NJCW 11:71}

2. DANIEL IRELAND of Great Egg Harbor, son of Daniel (1) and Ruth Ireland, b. 13th day, 5th mo., 1715, d. leaving a will dated 11 April 1764, proved 17 Feb 1768. Mentioned were wife (unnamed) and daus. (minors): Ruth, Pheby and Rhody. Execs. were his brothers, Reuben and Thomas Ireland. On 30 Nov 1767 an inventory was filed (£85.1.4) by William Mapes and Noah Smith. On 14 April 1774 an account was filed by Mary Ireland, widow of Thomas Ireland, extx. of said Thomas Ireland, who was the acting exec. of Daniel Ireland.{NJCW 13:312, 15:521}

Daniel was the father of the following children: RUTH; PHEBY;

---

80 Daniel is probably the brother of Amos, James and Joseph Ireland. In the will of James Ireland of Great Egg Harbour, Daniel and Amos Ireland petitioned on 19 June 1732 that their brother Joseph be given power to administer the very small estate of their brother James. {Burlington Wills:2301-6 C} Amos Ireland of Egg Harbor d. leaving a will dated 6 Jan 1740/1, proved 14 Jan 1745. {NJCW 5:214} Mentioned were son Amos and daus. Katherine and Sarah Ireland.

RHODY.

3. REUBEN IRELAND, son of Daniel (1) and Ruth Ireland, b. 1st day, 6th mo., 1719, m. by license dated 15 Dec 1744{MLNJ}, Deborah Gandy (b. 1st day, 6th mo., 1725). They were the parents of the following children: RUTH, b. 24th day, 4th mo., 1747; REUBEN, b. 25th day, 2nd mo., 1750; JONATHAN, b. 16th day, 10th mo., 1752; DEBORAH, b. 13th day, 9th mo., 1755; HANNAH, b. 27th day, 11th mo., 1757, d. 14th day, 8th mo., 1759; HANNAH, b. 7th day, 10th mo., 1760; ELIZABETH, b. 4th day, 4th mo., 1763; RACHEL, b. 17th day, 4th mo., 1767.

Probably pertaining to Reuben (3) Ireland is the following item: On 6th day, 1st day, 1755, Reubin Ireland acknowledged his marrying out.{GEMM}

4. THOMAS IRELAND, son of Daniel (1) and Ruth Ireland, b. 1st day, 5th mo., 1721. On 25th day, 5th mo., 1761, members of the monthly meeting reported speaking with him concerning the marriage of his dau. out of unity.{GEMM} The estate records of Thomas' brother Daniel (2) [above] show that Thomas m. Mary (N).

Thomas of Great Egg Harbor Township, d. leaving a will dated 11 Jan 1773, proved 16 Feb 1773. Mentioned was his son George to whom he left the home plantation with 100 acres adjoining, bought of Gideon Scull. To son Amos he left 1/2 the tract belonging to the sawmill and 1/2 of the partnership with Elias Smith and 1/2 the meadow on west side of Great Egg Harbor River, the meadow which Daniel Ireland bought of Charles Dingly. To son Thomas was left 1/2 of the sawmill on Great Run and 1/2 of the cedar swamp in partnership with Thomas Champion, when of age. Dau. Abigail to receive one bed more than the other girls and moveable estate to be divided between her and the 4 younger daus.: Sophia, Jemima, Mary and Silvy. Wife Mary to have use of the home place. Five shillings to be given to Sarah, Japheth and Hannah if demanded. Execs. were wife and John Sommers, son of James Sommers. On 12 Feb 1773 an inventory was filed. On 16 April 1774 Mary Ireland reported in the account a balance remaining due from the estate of Thomas Ireland to the estate of Daniel Ireland, £6.10.1.{NJCW 15:521, 16:110}

Thomas was father of the following children: GEORGE; AMOS; THOMAS; ABIGAIL; SOPHIA; JAMIMA; MARY; SILVY; SARAH; JAPHETH; HANNAH.

5. RUTH IRELAND, dau. of Daniel (1) and Ruth Ireland, b. 28th day,

11th mo., 1728, d. 15th day, 6th mo., 1761, m. Henry Woodward. They were parents of the following children{GEMM}: MARY, b. 2nd da, 3rd mo., 1747; REBECKAH, b. 3rd da., 4th mo, 1749, d. 1st da, 8th mo, 1751; JERUSAH, b. 1st da, 7th mo, 1751; REBECKAH, b. 15th da, 1st mo, 1754; ANNE, b. 16th da, 8th mo, 1756; RHODA, b. 3rd da, 10th mo., 1759.

Unplaced

JOHN IRELAND & Elisabeth Croslee of Cape May m. 10 July 1750.{Baptists}

On 5th day, 11th mo., 1746 the marriage of JOHN IRELAND and Rebekah Addams was reported orderly accomplished.{GEMM}

JOHN IRELAND of Cape May Co. d. prior to 28 April 1760 when an inventory of the estate was filed by James Hathorn and John van Gelder. On 3 May 1760 a bond was issued for Mary Ireland admx.{NJCW 9:422}

JOHN IRELAND d. prior to 5 Aug 1768 when Thomas Ludlam and William Robinson of Cape May Co. were appointed admins of his estate. Fellowbondsman: Daniel Crowell. Witnesses: Archibald Hughes and Zeruiah Hughes. On 8 Aug 1768 an inventory (£83.8.6) was filed by Reuben Ludlam and Nathan Young. On 5 Aug 1769 an account was filed by admins.{NJCW 13:442; 14:23}

ISZARD

For earlier history of the family see "Izard Family," *The Cape May County Magazine of History and Genealogy*, p. 301. June 1954. By Margaret Irwin McVickar. Some of the following information was taken from Michael Izard, III, Bible, on p. 68 of Cape May Co., N.J. Genealogical Data, Sarah Stillwell Chapter, D.A.R. Also see "Bible Records, *The Cape May County Magazine of History and Genealogy*, p. 111. June 1957. By Margret Irwin McVickar.

1. MICHAEL ISZARD of Cape May Co. d. prior to 15 Jan 1757 when an account of the estate was filed by Daniel Holding (Holden) in behalf of his wife Sarah, late Sarah Issard, admx. of Michael. After debts were paid 1/3 to the widow and the remainder to be divided among 8.{NJCW Cape May Wills:182E}

Michael Iszard m. Sarah, dau. of John Reaves*.{Deeds C:24} Sarah Iszard, widow of Michael, m. Daniel Holden* by license issued 4 Sep 1754.{MLNJ}

Sarah Holden of Cape May Co. d. leaving a will dated 10 Dec 1755, proved 2 Jan 1758. Mentioned were children: Reeves Iszard, John Iszard, Simeon Iszard (under age), whose father Michael Iszard is named. Exec. was Jacob Spicer. The will was witnessed by Deborah Spicer, Christopher Leamyng, Sylvia Spicer and Sarah Spicer.{NJCW 8:520}

Michael was the father of the following children: REEVES, m. by license issued 12 Jan 1761, Mary Cresse{MLNJ}; JAMES, d. ca. 1754; SIMEON, m. Margaret Tompson 26 Jan 26 1774{Baptists}{MLNJ}, d. 1829; MARTHA, m. John Hughes by license issued 24 Dec 1760{MLNJ}; SARAH, b. 23 Aug 1735, m. William Yates (b. 30 Aug 1732) by license issued 24 Aug 1762{MLNJ}; JOHN, m. Mary Smith by license dated 11 Nov 1770 {MLNJ}.

Michael Iszard (living 1745) and sons Reaves and John. Jonathan Smith, wife Rebecca. (1801){Deeds B:71}

2. JAMES ISZARD, son of Michael (1) Iszard, d. prior to 1 Aug 1754 when an inventory was filed by William Mathews and William Stites. On 7 Aug 1754 a bond was issued for Jane Isard admx.; Ephraim Edwards, fellow bondsman, both of Cape May Co.{NJCW 8:66}

3. JOHN ISZARD, son of Michael (1) Iszard, m. Mary Smith by license dated 11 Dec 1770.

[In the diaries of Aaron Leaming he mentioned the death of JOHN ISARD's wife in 1760.]

John Iszard of Cumberland Co., d. leaving a will dated 28 March 1769, proved 7 June 1769. Mentioned was wife to whom he left £1 and what the law gives her. To his eldest son Mical he devised his lands at Morris River and Dividing Creek. To his youngest sons, James, Gabriel and Johnis, movables. Execs. were wife and son Michael. The will was witnessed by John Terry, Christopher Foster and Elizabeth Foster. On 2 May 1769 an inventory was filed (£144.14.8) by John Terry and Christopher Foster.{NJCW 14:10}

John was father of the following children: MICHAEL; JAMES; GABRIEL; JOHNIS.

4. MICHAEL IZARD of Cumberland Co., son of John (3) Iszard of Cumberland Co., d. by 8 April 1777, when Ephraim Fithian was appointed admin. Fellowbondsman: Lot Fithian of Cumberland Co. Witness: Rachel

Clunn. On 23 June 1777 an inventory was filed (£67.16.1} by Jacob Miller and Oliver Russell.{NJCW 16:523, 18:213}

Unplaced

A marriage license was issued to Harris, William and ELIZABETH ISZARD (Cumberland Co.), dated 27 Oct 1750.{MLNJ}

HENRY ISARD, d. 9 March 1845, age 79 years, 2 mos., 11 days. His wife Deborah d. 16 Nov 1856, age 59 years, 3 mos., 6 days.{Cold Spring Cemetery}

A marriage license was issued to James Whildin* and JANE ISZARD, 20 July 1761.{MLNJ}

Levi Hand m. MARGRET ISARD, June 10, 1798. Virtue of consent. {Baptists; Co. Clerk Rcds - Book A}

Possibly connected to this family was MICHAEL ISARD of Greenwich, Salem Co., yeoman, who d. by 14 day, 10th mo., 1694, when an inventory of his estate was filed (£80.8). On 17 Dec 1694 administration was granted to his widow, Mary Isard.{Salem Wills, A:128}

NICHOLAS ISZARD of Cape May Co. d. by 21 March 1776 when Derick Peterson was appointed as admin. of his estate. On 19 March 1776 an inventory was filed (£115.9.3).{NJCW 16:492}

David Corson & PHEBE ISARD, both of this county of Cape May, m. 13 Oct 1751.{Baptists}

JEACOCKS

See "Swain Family," *The Cape May County Magazine of History and Genealogy*, p. 251. June 1953. By Margaret Irwin McVickar. For more details on this family and the Ashmans, see this article.

First Generation

According to McVickar,

> 1. FRANCIS JACOCKS, son of Francis Jacocks of Stratford-on-Avon came first to Hampstead, Long Island, NY where he is listed in the town records in 1673. He lived with his dau. Frances

(Jacocks) Champion, and d. after 16 Jan 1672. He was the father of the following children: THOMAS, bapt. Stratford-on-Avon 20 March 1619, d. at Passayunk, later Philadelphia Co., PA, before 11 Sep 1677; WILLIAM, bapt. Stratford-on-Avon, 12 Aug 1627, d. before 24 Dec 1694; FRANCES, m. Thomas Champion, Sr., ca. 1640.

Second Generation

2. THOMAS JACOCKS, son of Francis (1) Jacocks, bapt. 20 March 1619 at Stratford-on-Avon, d. at Passayunk, m. Ruth Ashman (b. 1656), dau. of Robert Ashman. They had a son William, b. 1656, who came to Cape May County. He was unmarried when listed in the tax records of New Castle Co., DE, tax records in 1677. He made a court deposition in Cape May County at the age of 42 in 1698. He was in Upland, PA in 1681, where he was granted 200 acres. He purchased land from the West Jersey Company on 16 July 1689, 340 acres at Cape May City. He d. shortly after 1708.

Thomas Jacocks m. Sarah (N), widow of Richard Swain. She d. leaving a will dated Feb 1714, at that time the wife of William Mason. She named her following children: Ruth Jacocks, wife of Jonathan Swain and Mary Jacocks, wife of Ebenezer Swain; sons: Joshua and James Jacocks.{NJCW 2:56}. Jonathan Swain and Ebenezer Swain were sons of Richard Swain*.

Thomas and Sarah were parents of the following children: WILLIAM, b. 1656; RUTH; MARY, m. Ebenezer Swain*; JOSHUA; JAMES.

3. WILLIAM JACOKS, son of Thomas (2) Jacocks, b. ca. 1656. On 16 July 1689 a return of survey was made for William Jacocks for 340 acres on seaside.{Deeds A:16 reverse}

On 20 Feb 1694/5 William Jacox recorded his earmark.{First Public Rcds} On 11 of 8br 1698 William Jacoks, aged about 42 years complained that on 6 instant October he was compelled by Benjamin Godfory, merchant, to move his sloop called *The Joseph* out of a safe harbor called the Greene Creek into the town Creek at Cape May where he haith received much damage both in the sloop and goods; that belonging to the said Benjamen Godfroy by reason of stress of weather we received there.{First Official Rcds}

4. JAMES JACOCKS, mariner of Cape May, son of Thomas (2) Jacocks,[81] mariner, d. leaving a will dated 18 July 1732, proved 18 Aug 1732. Mentioned were cousins: James Swaine (when 21, the plantation I live on at Cape May), Mary, Sarah, Daniel, Nezer, Ruth (one sheep running at Samuel Swaine's), Silas (my Bible); they all being the children of my sister Mary Swaine. Friend, Judah Swaine (a gun); brother Jonathan Swaine right to a tract of land at Cape Fear, to dispose of to which son he thinks best, after Swaine or Liffelet Swaine. Cousin Jemima Beal, a cow and calf running at her father's at Cape Fear. Cousin Jonathan Swaine, at Cape Fear, an old gun; and all the cattle to be divided among his brothers that are left, he having his equal part. Exec. brother Ebenezer Swaine. The will was witnessed by Samuwell Swaine, Jarusha Swaine and Reuben Swaine.{NJCW 3:314} Inventory of the estate was submitted on 5 Aug 1732 and included a mare, other living creatures, two guns, whaling craft, tuls [tools] and all sundries of old iron. Appraised by Nathaniel Foster and Samuwell Swaine. "This is an inventory of James Jacock's estate, deceased at Cape May on July the 21th, 1732."

JENKINS

See "The Jenkins Family of Cape May County, New Jersey," *The Cape May County Magazine of History and Genealogy*, p. 369. June 1963. By Grace C. Gallaher.

First Generation

According to Ms. Gallaher,

> 1. NATHANIEL JENKINS, Sr. was a Welshman, born in Caerdicanshire, March 25, 1678, came to America 1710, and settled at the Cape in 1712. He became pastor of the First Baptist Church of Cape May at Cape May Court House, which was constituted a church June 24, 1712, and remained with them until 1730.
>
> He removed to Salem County, that part of which is now Cumberland County, and became the fourth pastor of Cohansey Baptist Church in Hopewell Township in 1730, remaining with them until his death the 2d of 6th month, 1754, in the 77th year of his age.

---

81 Noting that he referred in his will to "my sister Mary Swaine," and noting that Mary Jacocks, dau. of Thomas, was wife of Ebenezer Swain as shown in the will of Sarah Jacocks.

He m. 1st Esther Jones in Wales 1703, and m. 2nd Ruth Sayre, widow, Salem Co., on 21 April 1743 (N.J.A.:22:215).

In his will Nathaniel Jenkins of Cohansey, Cumberland Co., written 5 March 1754 and proved 20 June 1754 he named wife Ruth who had children of her own: dau. Esther, with legacies to John Brick and Samuel Fithian; son Abinadab, sold exec. Inv. 151, including books - 14.6, made by Joh Remention and Isaac Wheaten (N.J.A:32:176).

In a letter from American Baptist Historical Society, Rochester, NY, dated 3 April 1861 the children were listed. Nathaniel and Esther (Jones) Jenkins were parents of the following children: HANNAH, m. Capt. William Shaw*; PHEBE; NATHANIEL; TABITHA, m. John Dowdney; DAVID, moved to Cumberland Co.; JONATHAN; ESTHER, m. (N) Poole or (N) Pooler; ABINADAB; JONADAB.

Second Generation

2. NATHANIEL JENKINS, son of Nathaniel (1), " ... [was] born in Wales, April 11, 1710, and brought in arms to this country: called to the ministry in 1744; ordained in 1747, when he took on the care of this church; but he continued not long therein, but fell into the power of hurtful spirits, which brought on fits and a premature dotage; he d. in 1769. His wife was Elizabeth Selley, by whom he had children, Phebe, Mary, Rhody, Hannah, Nathaniel, Jonathan, and Ephraim."{The article continues with excerpts from Morgan Edward's History of the Baptist in New Jersey re Nathaniel Jenkins, Jr.}

He was pastor of the First Baptist Church of Cape May at Cape May Court House, 1747 to 1753.

He m. 1st ca. 1732, Elizabeth Seeley, and m. 2nd, Esther Stites by license dated 15 May 1755 (N.J.A.:22:215). Elizabeth Seeley, born about 1714, was dau. of Ephraim and Mary Seeley of Fairfield, Salem Co., now Cumberland Co. Esther was the dau. of Benjamin Stites; apparently dec. by 1791.

Nathaniel Jenkins d. leaving a will dated 21 Nov 1755, proved 3 May 1770. Mentioned were wife Esther; sons: Nathaniel and Jonathan to whom he devised lands where he lived which he bought of his father on 12 April 1737. Son Ephraim the land back of the above. Marsh and oyster ground to be given to sons Nathaniel, Jonathan and Ephraim. Personal estate to be given to daus.: Phebe Smith, widow; Hannah Stites, wife of

Thomas Stites; Mary Smith, wife of John Smith; Rhoda Jenkins and Ansis Jenkins. Execs. were dau. Mary and her husband John, until son Nathaniel is 17 years old and then he is to be exec. with them until son Jonathan is 17 and then he is to be exec with them until son Ephraim is 17 and then sons Nathaniel, Jonathan and Ephraim shall be the execs. The will was witnessed by Jonathan Stites, Jonadab Jenkins and Deborah Jenkins. On 5 Aug 1771 an inventory was filed (£21.11.6) by Daniel Smith and Joshua Hildreth.{NJCW 15:185}

Nathaniel was father of the following children: PHEBE m. 1st 19 Aug 1750, William Smith and m. 2nd 7 Nov 1759 Samuel Crowell and m. 3rd 18 Oct 1768 Ezekiel Eldredge; MARY, m. 1st 2 Oct 1753, John Smith and m. 2nd 25 April 1774 Samuel Foster; HANNAH, m. 19 June 1756, Thomas Stites; RHODA; ANNIS, named in his father's will 21 Nov 1755; NATHANIEL, m. 15 Aug 1764, Willeramina Stites; JONATHAN, m. 13 April 1768, Deborah (Ludlam) Hand; EPHRAIM; ELIZABETH, m. 5 July 1768, Ludlam Hand.

3. TABITHA JENKINS, dau. of Nathaniel (1) Jenkins, b. ca. 1712, m. ca. 1730, John Dowdney and resided in Cumberland Co., NJ. John Dowdney was b. ca. 1700. In his will dated 17 Feb 1758 and proved 22 March 1858, he named wife Tabitha and children. Execs. were wife and son Nicholas. Children named in will: NICHOLAS, m. 18 Dec 1771, Sarah Warrell; MARY, m. Abner Sheppard; GEORGE; BURROWS; JOHN, m. 20 Nov 1773, Sarah Howell. John d. prior to 18 April 1782 in Gloucester Co.; NATHANIEL.

4. DAVID JENKINS of Hopewell, Cumberland Co., son of Nathaniel (1) Jenkins, d. leaving a will dated 26 March 1775, proved 29 July 1778. Mentioned were sons Daniel to whom he left 1/3 of the home plantation to be taken at the north end by the lands of Nicholas Dowdney and Andrew Jenkins; Nathaniel who was to bring up son Thomas; THOMAS (under age 14); HANNAH; AMY (under age of 18). Execs. were sons Daniel and Nathaniel.{NJCW 20:211, 22:64} In 29 July 1778 Elisha Swinney was appointed admin. in place of the sons, "who are said to have gone over to the enemy." Children: DANIEL; NATHANIEL; HANNAH, m. Joel Sheppard, son of Ephraim and Sarah Dennis Sheppard (b. 9 Sep

1748, d. 19 Jan 1820)[82] David was a member of Cohansey Baptist Church, 1757.

5. ABINADAB JENKINS, son of Nathaniel (1) and Esther Jenkins, resided in Salem Co., NJ.

6. PHEBE JENKINS, dau. of Nathaniel (1) and Esther Jenkins, b. ca. 1734, m. 19 Aug 1750{Baptists}, William Smith, son of William Smith and Phebe Garlick, b. ca. 1726, d. 1755. Phebe m. 2nd 7 Nov 1759, Samuel Crowell. She m. 3rd 18 Oct 1768, Ezekiel Eldredge.

Third Generation

7. MARY JENKINS, dau. of Nathaniel (2) and Elizabeth (Seeley) Jenkins, b. 1738, d. 4 May 1814, m. 1st John Smith* on 2 Oct 1753{Baptists}, son of John and Martha Smith (b. ca. 1720, d. 1771. (Hook Book, "Smith, Iron and Gates Families," pp. 27-29) In his will written 10 Dec 1770, proved 29 May 1777 he named wife Mary and children.

Children of Mary Smith by her first marriage: ABIJAH, b. 9 Jan 1764, d. 18 July 1834, m. Rhoda Ludlam, dau. of Anthony, 3rd, and Elizabeth Cresse Ludlam (b. 1768, d. 11 June 1848); ELIZABETH, b. ca. 1758, d. 15 June 1786, m. by license dated 24 April 1778{MLNJ} Shamgar Hewitt* (b. 29 Jan 1750, d. 3 Nov 1840, bur. Calvary Baptist Church Cemetery in Ocean View, Cape May Co.; RACHEL, b. 10 March 1765, d. 19 May 1830, m. as his 2nd wife after the death of her sister Elizabeth, Shamgar Hewitt*, 20 Nov 1788.

Mary (Jenkins) Smith m. 2nd on 25 April 1774, Samuel Foster (N.J.A:22:378) He was b. 24 June 1752, d. 19 June 1814. Children: THOMAS, b. 1775/80, d. 1826; LAVI (LEVY), b. 12 Dec 1782, d. 31 July 1831, m. 27 March 1802, Elizabeth Hand.

8. HANNAH JENKINS, dau. of Nathaniel (2) and Elizabeth (Seeley) Jenkins, b. ca. 1736, m. Thomas Stites* 19 June 1756, son of George and Esther Stites. Hannah m. 2nd (N) Young.[83]

---

82 See *The Vineland Historical Magazine*, Oct. 1942, p. 411 and *Cape May County Magazine of History and Genealogy*, p. 369, June 1963, "The Jenkins Family of Cape May County, New Jersey," by Grace C. Gallaher.

83 For marriage to Thomas Stites see "A True Copy of the Complete List of Marriages from the 'First Writings' of the First Baptist Church of Cape May Cape May Court House, New Jersey," *The Cape May County Magazine of History and Genealogy*, p. 23. June 1955. Transcribed by M. Catharine Stauffer.

9. RHODA JENKINS, dau.of Nathaniel (2) Jenkins is named in the will of her aunt Hannah (Jenkins) Shaw.

10. NATHANIEL JENKINS, son of Nathaniel (2) and Elizabeth (Seeley) Jenkins, m. 15 Aug 1765, Willeramina Stites (NJA:22:215), dau. of Benjamin and Rhoda (Church) Stites, b. 1745, d. 4 June 1770. Their children: SILSBY(Silba); ELI; EVAN.{Deeds A:137}

11. JONATHAN JENKINS, son of Nathaniel (2) and Elizabeth (Seeley) Jenkins, b. 9 June 1745, d. 16 Sep 1779, m. by license dated 13 April 1768, Deborah (Ludlam) Hand, dau. of Jeremiah and Martha (Stites) Ludlam, b. 1730, d. Nov 1779.

Jonathan Jenkins of Cape May Co., Gent., d. leaving a will dated 31 Aug 1779, proved 27 Sep 1779. Mentioned were wife Deborah; nephew Abijah Smith, son of John Smith, his plantation in the Middle Precinct at Goshen, which testator bought of David Smith. Nephew, Silsba Jenkins, son of brother Nathaniel, the cedar swamp in Upper Precinct at the Long Bridge. Nephew Evan Jenkins, son of brother Nathaniel, the meadow, fishing and oyster ground in Middle Precinct which was left to testator by his father. Brother Ephraim Jenkins, his apparel. Sister Rhoda Jenkins, £200. Rest of personal estate to said nephew, Silba Jenkins and Evan Jenkins and niece, Hanah Jenkins, dau. of brother Ephraim. Execs. were wife Deborah and Jesse Hand. The will was witnessed by Joshua Hildreth, Elihu Smith, Robert Harris and Joseph Sanders. On 27 Sep 1779 an inventory was made by John Holmes and Eli Eldredge (£17,153.18.7).{NJCW 21:260}

12. EPHRAIM JENKINS, son of Nathaniel (2) and Elizabeth (Seeley) Jenkins, had a child HANNAH.

13. ELIZABETH JENKINS, dau. of Nathaniel Jr., m. Ludlam Hand by license dated 5 July 1768{MLNJ}, son of Cornelius and Deborah (Ludlam) Hand, b. 1749, d. intestate and under the age of 21 years. (Hand Genealogy, p. 173)

Unplaced

Fulkit Bennet and PHEBE JENKINS, March 31, 1771.{Baptists}

WILLIAM JOHNSON

1. WILLIAM JOHNSON testified, as recorded in Cape May records on 10 May 1692, against John Jarvis for helping the Indians to rum.{First Public Rcds} William Johnson/Johnston of Cape May Co., yeoman, d. leaving a will dated 13 Dec 1713, proved 6 May 1718. Mentioned were children: Benjamin, Thomas, Catren, Elizabeth, William. Land between John Cresse and Benjamin Hand, Jr. at the lower side of Cape May. Son William was exec. with brother Benjamin Leonard and John Taylor as overseers. The will was witnessed by Jonathan Swaine, Benjamin Holdin, Ebenezer Swaine.{NJCW 2:88} On 6 May 1718 William Johnston gave an oath as exec. On the same day inventory of the estate was made by John Taylor and Samuel Johnson.{NJCW}

William Johnson recorded his ear mark, later his son William, on 5 Dec 1693.{First Public Rcds}

William Johnson was father of the following children: BENJAMIN LEONARD; THOMAS; CATREN; ELIZABETH; WILLIAM.

2. BENJAMIN JOHNSON of Cape May Co., yeoman, probable son of William (1), probably m. Penelope Brandreth*, dau. of Timothy and Sarah Brandreth. Benjamin d. leaving a will dated 13 July 1757, proved 19 Oct 1757. Mentioned were wife (unnamed) and children: Amos, Milicent, Lydia Hildreth and Temperance Mathews. Grandchildren: Hannah Newton, Mary Mathews, Phebe and Priscilla Hildreth. Execs. were son Amos and dau. Milicent. The will was witnessed by Robert Cress, Jonathan Cresse and Nathaniel Jenkins.{NJCW 8:494}

Penelope Johnson, widow of Benjamin, d. leaving a will dated 18 April 1759, proved 21 April 1759 (in Cape May Co). Mentioned were children: Lidia Eldreth [Hildreth], Milicent Young, Amos and Temperance. Grandchildren: Mary, dau. of Samuel Mathues; Hanah Nuton; Prisaler Heldreth. Exec. was Samuel Mathues. The will was witnessed by Robert Cresse, Mary Cresse and Jeremiah Hand.{NJCW 9:314} On 25 April 1759 an inventory was filed by Richard Smith and Jeremiah Hand.{NJCW}

Benjamin was the father of the following children: AMOS; MILICENT, m. (N) Young; LYDIA, probably m. James Hildreth*; TEMPERANCE, m. Samuel Mathews*.

3. THOMAS JOHNSON, possible son of Benjamin (2) Johnson, m. Rebecca Church by license dated 30 Dec 1741.{MLNJ}

4. WILLIAM JOHNSON of Cape May, probable son of William (1), d.

leaving a will dated 8 March 1748/9, proved 16 May 1749. Mentioned were wife Abigail, extx. to have all the estate during her lifetime, after which the same to be given to testator's nephew, Amos Johnson. The will was witnessed by Timothy Hand, Ezekiel Hand and Elijah Hughes.{NJCW 6:73} On 29 April 1749 an inventory of the estate was filed by George Stites and Joshua Shaw.{NJCW} William Jonson m. Abigail Foster by license dated 19 April 1742.{MLNJ}

SAMUEL JOHNSON

1. SAMUEL JOHNSON of Cape May Co., yeoman, d. leaving a will dated 12 Feb 1725/6, proved 20 Sep 1726. Mentioned were wife Abigail and children: Ebenezer (under age), Josiah, Phebe, Abigail. Homestead land in Cape May Co. and in Darby Township, New Haven Co., CT. The wife was extx. with John Persons and Nathaniel Rusco as overseers. The will was witnessed by Richard Downes, John Stillwell, William Mulford.{NJCW 3:83} Inventory of the estate was taken on 25 April 1726 by John Taylor and Christopher Church.{NJCW}

Abigail, widow of Samuel Johnson, later m. Thomas Smith*. She d. prior to 11 Dec 1732 when Aaron Leaming was appointed admin. Witnesses: Saml. Bustil and Robert Davis. On 17 Nov 1732 Ebenezer Johnson, Phebe Johnson and Abigail Johnson, children of the said dec. by her former husband, Samuel Johnson, renounced their right in favor of Aaron Leaming.{NJCW 3:227}

Samuel and Abigail Johnson were the parents of the following children: EBENEZER; PHEBE; SAMUEL.

Samuel Johnson was also the father of JOSIAH.

2. EBENEZER JOHNSON, son of Samuel (1), was the father of the following children: NAOMI; ABIGAIL; GIDEON, d. without issue; JERUSHA, m. Thomas Hand by whom she had issue: Thomas and Esther who m. Philip Nickoson by 1801{Deeds B:148} and probably Samuel who d. prior to 19 Nov 1766.

Ebenezer d. leaving a will dated 2 Sep 1766, proved 11 Oct 1766. Mentioned were wife Amey; sister Phebe Johnson; daus.: Jerusha, Abigail and Neomy; son Gideon. Execs. were wife and son Gideon and Downes Edmunds. The will was witnessed by Mary Hand, Enos Buck and Mary Hoffman. On 23 Oct 1766 an inventory was filed (£189.11.4) by Isaac Newton and Henry Hand. On 11 April 1774 an account was filed by Downes Edmunds, surviving exec.{NJCW 12:354; 15:531}

3. SAMUEL JOHNSON of Cape May Co., yeoman, son of Samuel (1) Johnson, d. leaving a will dated 21 Nov 1728, proved 2 May 1732; codicil proved 13 and 27 May 1732. Mentioned were wife Charity, extx., to use all lands until she remarried or until son, Samuel arrived at age 21. Land at Goshen alias Mackrel Neck in Cape May Co. where testator lived was devised to son Samuel Johnson. Daus.: Sarah, Hannah, Phebe, Charity and Susannah were to be paid as they arrived at age 18 or marriage. The will was witnessed by Daniel Walker, Benjamin Mareus and Henry Stites, Jr. Codicil dated 8 April 1729 mentioned dau. Phebe being dead, her share to go to the other four daus. The codicil witnessed by Arn. Leaming and Cornelius Schillinks, Jr.{NJCW 3:201} An inventory was submitted on 9 Feb 1732 and included cattle, sheep and swine, etc.; appraised by Benjamin Hand and Henry Stites, Jr.{NJCW}

Samuel Johnson was the father of the following children: SAMUEL; SARAH; HANNAH; PHEBE, d. prior to 8 April 1729; CHARITY; SUSANAH.

4. AMY JOHNSON, probably Neomi, dau. of Ebenezer (2) Johnson, m. Jonathan Mills by license dated 9 June 1768.{MLNJ}

5. GIDEON JOHNSON/JOHNSTON, probable son of Ebenezer (2) Johnson, m. Lydda Shaw by license dated 24 April 1767.{MLNJ}

He d. prior to 5 July 1770 when his widow Lydia was appointed admx. Fellowbondsman: Downs Edmunds, yeoman of Cape May Co. Witnesses: Abraham Woolson and Jonathan Leaming. On 4 July 1770 an inventory was filed (£109.14.1 1/2) by Jonathan Leaming and Abraham Woolson.{NJCW 14:400}

Lydia Johnson m. Joseph Hayes 16 Dec 1771.{Baptists; MLNJ}

6. SAMUEL JOHNSON, waterman, brother of Gideon and probable son of Ebenezer (2) Johnson, d. prior to 19 Nov 1766 when Gideon Johnson, his brother was appointed admin of his estate. Fellowbondsman: Abraham Woolson of Cape May Co. On 24 July 1767 an inventory was filed (£36.17.0 was filed by Benjamin Ingrum and Hance Woolson.{NJCW 12:358}

7. JERUSHA JOHNSON, probable dau. of Ebenezer (2) Johnson m. Thomas Hand, son of Thomas Hand, by license dated 19 May 1773.{MLNJ}

BENJAMIN JOHNSON

1. BENJAMIN JOHNSON, Gent., d. leaving a will dated 1 Jan 1770, proved 24 May 1770. Mentioned were wife Anna; sons: Daniel and David; dau. Sarah Stephenson; grandson Aaron Stephenson. Execs. were sons Daniel and David. The will was witnessed by Thomas Smith, Eli Eldredge and Aner Eldredge. On 27 Feb 1770 an inventory was filed (£147.16.4) by Thomas Smith and Eli Eldredge.{NJCW 15:75}

The deed book shows Imlay Johnson, son of David and his wife Sarah; David being son of Benjamin, who was living in 1768 but now (1790) dec.{Deeds A:77}

Benjamin was father of the following children: DANIEL; DAVID; SARAH, m. Richard Stephenson.

2. DANIEL JOHNSON, dec., was son of Benjamin (will 1770) and had brother David and brother-in-law Richard Stephenson as shown in deeds dated 1794.{Deeds E: 76}

This may be the Daniel Johnson who m. Temperance Billings by license dated 5 March 1765.{MLNJ}

3. DAVID JOHNSON, son of Benjamin (1) Johnson, m. 1st Sarah (N) and m. 2nd Hannah More. He d. leaving a will dated 24 Sep 1784, proved 18 Nov 1785. Mentioned were children by first wife: Jonathan, Martha, Loammy [Imlay?] and Hamor. Hannah Johnson received £3, for her dower and to each of her children, Jacob and Sarah, £10. Execs. were brother David Johnson and brother-in-law, Richard Stevenson. An inventory was filed on 15 Nov 1785 by John Cresse and Eli Eldredge.{NJCW 36:187}

At August Court 1787 Hannah More stated that she was mother of two infants, Jacob Johnson aged 9 years and Sarah Johnson, aged 5 years, children of David Johnson, dec. who needed support. The court ordered the children to be delivered to execs. of estate, David Johnson and Richard Stevenson, and placed under their care.{Ltrs&Inv A(Rev):14}

David was father of the following children: JONATHAN; MARTHA, probably m. James Ludlam, son of Anthony, by license of 5 Jan 1790{MLNJ}; IMLAY; HAMOR; (by Hannah): JACOB, b. ca. 1778; SARAH, b. ca. 1782.

4. MARTHA JOHNSON, possible dau. of David (3) Johnson, m. James Ludlam by license dated 5 Jan 1790.{MLNJ}

5. IMLAY JOHNSON, son of David, d. by 7 Jan 1796 when Phebe

Johnson was appointed admx. On 9 April 1797 an inventory was filed (£1463.19.3) by Jacocks Swain and Reuben Townsend.{NJCW File:655E}

OLIVER JOHNSON

1. OLIVER JOHNSON entered an action against John Carman on 10 May 1692.{First Public Rcds:269}

On 21 Dec 1698 a letter of administration was granted to William Segrave on the effects of Olever Johnson, dec. {First Official Recds}

John Johnson, shown as son of Oliver in 1711.{Deeds B:123}

Daniel Johnson, shown as son of Oliver, cooper, in 1719.{Deeds B:145, 155}

Oliver was father of JOHN and DANIEL.

Unplaced

DANIEL JOHNSON recorded his ear mark 4 April 1694; later Nathaniell Hand and later Ezekiel Hand.{First Public Rcds:272}

A marriage license was issued to Joseph Houldin and HANNAH JONSON, 11 Oct 1690.{MLNJ}

On 28th day, 5th mo., 1753 JOSEPH JOHNSON requested a certificate in order for marriage.{GEMM}

SARAH S. JOHNSON, b. 1776, d. 7 Sep 1839.{Cold Spring Cemetery}

The WIDOW JOHNSON's estate was appraised by John Richardson and John Stilwell, 13 Oct 1698.{First Official Rcds}

KENT

Following are several persons named Kent living in Cape May County in the colonial period of no known relationship.

EPHRAIM KENT of Cape May Co. d. before 23 Jan 1777, the day on which Gideon Kent was appointed admin. of the estate. Fellowbondsman: Richard Edmunds, both of said county, yeomen. Witnesses: Downes Edmunds and Richard Stites. Ephraim Kent left a will by word of mouth, hence the appointment of an admin.{NJCW 38:79}

GIDEON KENT d. leaving a will dated 8 Aug 1785, proved 10 Oct 1788. Mentioned were wife Mercy; children: EPHRAIM; MARTHA; DEBORAH; LIDYA; HANNAH. Execs. were wife Mercy, son Ephraim and dau. Martha Kent. The will was witnessed by Rachel Woodruff, Jeremiah Edmunds and Constantine Carll. An inventory was filed on 8 Dec 1787 by Jeremiah Edmunds and Constantine Carll. It included part of a vessel, £9.{NJCW 31:80}

EPHRAIM KENT, d. 1 April 1821, age 56 years, 1 month, 6 days.{Cold Spring Cemetery} Ephraim m. Rachel (N) who d. 20 Sep 1822, age 64 years, 6 mos., 15 days.{Cold Spring Cemetery}

SUSANNAH KENT m. James Miller by license dated 3 June 1755.{MLNJ}

ESTHER KENT m. William Seagrave, by license dated 3 Oct 1737.{MLNJ}

LAUGHTON

Benjamin Laughton of Cape May Co., tailor, d. leaving a will dated 24 Dec 1744, proved 23 Aug 1760. Mentioned were wife Elisabeth and sons-in-law, John Bancroft and Nathan Newton. Legacy to William Laughton of Salem Co. Home farm; land bought of Henry Young as trustee of Messrs. Latouch & Haines of New York City, agents of the West New Jersey Society in England. Execs. were wife and her son John Bancroft. The will was witnessed by Thomas Bancroft, John Foster, John Chester and Jacob Spicer.{NJCW 11:66} An inventory was filed on 27 Aug 1760 by John Eldredge and Ebenezer Johnson.{NJCW}

Benjamin m. Elizabeth Huton by license dated 23 Feb 1739/40.{MLNJ} [This could be Elizabeth Nuton in which case she was probably widow of Ebenezer Newton who d. testate in 1739. Evidently Elizabeth m. 1st (N) Bancroft, 2nd Ebenezer Newton and 3rd Benjamin Laughton.]

LAWRENCE

Rev. Daniel Lawrence was b. on Long Island in 1718, d. at Cape May 13 April 1766.{Cold Spring Cemtery} He m. 1st Elizabeth (N) (d. 1 Dec

1754, age 30) and m. 2nd Sarah (N) (d. 20 Jan 1768, aged 45 years{Cold Spring Cemetery}). Daniel Lawrence of Lower Precinct of Cape May Co., clerk, d. leaving a will dated 12 March 1766, proved 8 Dec 1766. Mentioned were dau. Nancy Lawrence to whom was given all cloth that was her mother's. To son Benjamin, books; to son Daniel, 16 acres of land joining Daniel Hand on the west, Elijah Hughes on the south and southwest. Wife Sarah and my children, Nancy Lawrence, Benjamin Lawrence, Deborah Lawrence and Daniel Lawrence, household goods and 2 Negroes. Execs. were wife and friends, Rev. Andrew Hunter, Rev. William Ramsey, James Whilldin, Esq. and Thomas Hand. The will was witnessed by Henry Stevens, Mary Hughes, Elenor Whilldin and Elijah Hughes. On 17 March 1766 a codicil was added (Sarah Lawrence qualified as extx. same date and Andrew Hunter as exec.) On 23 July 1766 an inventory was filed (£455.14.10) by John Eldredge and Henry Hand. On 9 Oct 1775 an account was filed by Amy Hunter, extx. to Rev. Andrew Hunter, one of the execs. of Rev. Daniel Lawrence which included costs of "keeping 4 small children for 2 years, £39.1.10."{NJCW 12:338; 15:547}

Sarah Lawrence d. leaving a will dated 17 Jan 1768, proved 9 Feb 1768. She left all her possessions to her two youngest children, Deborah and Daniel. Exec. was James Whillden, Esq. The will was witnessed by Daniel Crowell, Elenor Whillden and Henry Hand. On 9 Feb 1768 an inventory was filed (£416.13.0) by John Eldredge and Henry Hand. On 17 May 1774 an account was filed by exec. which included legacies paid to Ann Lawrence, Jacob Hughes and wife and Nancy Lawrence.{NJCW 13:525; 15:518}

Rev. Daniel Lawrence was father of MERCY[84]; ANN (Nancy), m. Jacob Hughes[85]; DANIEL; BENJAMIN; DEBORAH.

2. BENJAMIN LAWRENCE, d. 17 Oct 1854, age 30.{Cold Spring Cemetery}

Unplaced

Jonathan Stites and ELIZABETH LAWRENCE, 10 Feb 1774.{Baptists}

---

84 Mentioned in the will of Lydia (Eldredge) Hand dated 1754, as Mercy, dau. of Rev. Daniel Lawrence. However p. 337 of *Mayflower Descendants in Cape May County* omits Mercy and names only the dau. Ann Lawrence and a son Daniel.

85 Raymond Hughes stated Ann Laurence m. 24 Nov 1733 Jacob Hughes, son of Jacob Hughes. He also gave her birth as 17 Aug 1753, d. 17 Nov 1817. {Hughes}

LEAMING

See the following articles:

"Descendants of Esther Leaming," *The Cape May County Magazine of History and Genealogy*, p. 59. June 1932. By Rev. Paul Sturtevant Howe, Ph.D.

"Diaries of Aaron Leaming," *The Cape May County Magazine of History and Genealogy*, p. 69. June 1932. Copied by Lewis T. Stevens.{Leaming Diaries}

"The Leamings - Some Historical Notes of a Family and the Times," *The Cape May County Magazine of History and Genealogy*, p. 85. June 1956. By Karl A. Dickinson. In this article the author refers to the "Visitations of York" in tracing the origins of the family, beginning with Christopher Lemyng of Burneston of the county of York who m. Margaret Metcalf and had a son John who lived in London and in 1634 m. Joanna Polly, dau. of Giles Polly of Essex, England. Their son Christopher went to America with his brother Jeremiah ca. 1670. Jeremiah d. en route. [See this article for more details on this family.]

First Generation

According to Karl Dickinson,

1. CHRISTOPHER LEAMING m. Esther Burnet, dau. of Aaron Burnet of Sag Harbor, East Hampton, L.I., in 1674. According to Dickinson, Christopher left his family to come to Cape May County ca. 1691 and Thomas his son came to Cape May County ca. 1705. The name of Christopher Leaman appears on a return of survey for 204 acres, dated 4 April 1694, since conveyed to Thomas Leaman, his son. Christopher d. ca. 1697.

In his diary, Aaron Leaming, son of Aaron, stated,

"My father's father, Christopher Leaming, was an Englishman, and came to America in 1670, and landed near or at Boston; thence to East Hampton. There he lived till about the year 1691, and then leaving his family at Long Island, he came himself to Cape May, which, at that time, was a new county, and beginning to settle very fast, and seemed to promise good advantages to the adventurers. Here he went whaling in the proper season, and at other times worked at the cooper's trade, which was hisoccupation, and good at the time by reason of the great number of whales caught in those days, made the demand and pay for casks certain. He died of a pleurisie in 1696."

Second Generation

2. THOMAS LEAMING, son of Christopher, b. Southampton, Long Island, 9 July 1674, d. Cape May 31 Dec 1723, m. at Cape May 18 June 1701, Hannah Whilldin* (b. at Yarmouth 1683, d. Cape May ca. 1728), dau. of Joseph and Hannah (Gorham) Whilldin. Hannah m. 2nd Philip Syng of Philadelphia, by whom she had no issue. Hannah and Thomas Leaming were the parents of the following children: ESTHER, b. 3 July 1702, d. 5/8/1773, m. William Eldredge, son of Ezekiel Eldredge*; MERCY, b. 10 Dec 1704, d. 1769, m. Samuel Eldredge, son of Ezekiel Eldredge*; JANE, b. 15 Oct 1706, m. William Doubleday; PHEBE, b. 4 Nov 1708, m. John Garlick; PRISCILLA, b. 15 July 1710, d. 21 Sep 1758, m. 1st John Stites* and m. 2nd Jacob Hughes*; CHRISTOPHER, b. 1714, m. Deborah Hand; THOMAS, b. 31 March 1718, m. Elizabeth Leaming, dau. of Aaron (3) Leaming.

Thomas Leaming recorded in a manuscript,

> "In July, 1674, I was born in Southampton, on Long Island. When I was eighteen years of age I came to Cape May, and that winter had a sore of the fever and flux. The next summer I went to Philadelphia with my father, Christopher, who was lame with a withered hand, which held him till his death. The winter following I went a whaling, and we got eight whales, and and five of them we drove to the Hoarkills, and we went there to cut them up, and stayed a month. The 1st day of May we came home to Cape May, and my father was very sick, and the third day, 1695, departed this life at the house of Shamgar Hand. ... I was married in 1701, and 1703 went to Cohansie and fetched brother Aaron. In 1706 I built my house." {Leaming manuscript}

In April 1694 was recorded a return of survey for Christopher Leaman of 204 acres of the Society's land in Cape May Co. ... and since conveyed to Thomas Leaman his son. {Revels Book of Surveys:11}

Thomas Leamyng recorded his ear mark on 11 June 1722; he later recorded as the mark for his son, Christopher Leamyng.

Thomas Leamyng of Cape May Co. d. leaving a will dated 7 Feb 1721/2, proved 23 July 1724. Mentioned were wife Hannah and children: Christopher (eldest son, under 14), Jane, Easther, Mercy, Phebe, Prissillah,

Thomas. Included in the estate were a Negro man and Negro woman and 6 children who were to be disposed of. Execs. were wife and brother Aaron Leamyng. The will was witnessed by Andrew Godfrey, Daniel Mackey, Hannah Leonard. Codicil of 7 March 1722/3 made unimportant changes and was witnessed by William Doubleday, Henry Paine and Daniel Mackey.{NJCW 2:275} The estate was inventoried on 1 Feb 1723/4 by Richard Townsend and William Segrave.{NJCW}

3. AARON LEAMING, son of Christopher, was mentioned in the will of his brother, Thomas, dated 7 Feb 1721/2. According to Dickinson, Aaron first settled at Goshen. He became justice of the peace, county clerk and a member of the state legislature. In 1723 he purchased Seven Mile Beach, now Avalon and Stone Harbor, for a long time known as Leaming's Beach.

Aaron Leaming m. 12 Oct 1714, Lydia Shaw, dau. of John and Elizabeth Person [Parsons]* and widow of Capt. William Shaw*.{Deeds B:128}

In the diary of Aaron Leaming, son of the above Aaron, he states,

> "Aaron Leaming (the first) of the County of Cape May, depared this life at Philadelphia, of a pleurisie, on the 20th of June, 1746, about five o'clock in the afternoon. He was born at Sag, near East Hampton, on Long Island, Oct. 12th, 1687, being the son of Christopher Leamyeng (as he spelt his name), an Englishman, and Hester, his wife, whose maiden name was Burnet, and was born in New England. Christopher Leamyeng owned a lot at Easthampton, but he came to Cape May, being a cooper, and stayed several years and worked at his trade; and about 1695-6 he died at Cape May, and his land fell to Thomas Leamyeng, his eldest son; the rest was left poor."

In his diary (p. 79) Aaron Leaming, Jr., stated on 17 July 1775 that he was the only child of his mother that was now left behind.

> "She died 2d October, 1762 and left 8 children alive, the youngest of them being 41 years of age. Six of them lived to be above 60 years of age each. Richard when he died was near 74; Lydia 63; John almost 67; Joshua 66; Nathan 62; Jeremiah near 57 [b. ca. 1718]; Elizabeth 47 & now I am 60 years old. Lydia Leaming, she herself died at above 82 years."{Leaming Diaries}

Aaron Leaming, d. 20 June 1746, aged 58 years, 8 months; buried in Old Christ Church, Philadelphia. He left a will dated 15 Oct 1743, proved 20 April 1747. Mentioned were wife Lydia and son Jeremiah Leaming, to have all the land whereon I live between the land of David

Cresse and John Shaw's Creek. Son Aaron Leaming, Jr. all lands at the Bay side and other. To sons, Jeremiah and Aaron, the saw mill on Manatico at Prince Maurice's River, Salem Co. and lands near the said river in Salem Co. Dau. Elizabeth Leaming, all land and marsh at Goshen and other land. [Other parcels of land to the three children, described.] Execs. were the three children, Aaron, Jr., Jeremiah and Elizabeth. The will was witnessed by Thomas Eldrige, William Eldridge and Esther Eldridge.{NJCW 6:266} On 16, 17, 18 April 1747 an inventory of the personal estate was submitted; it included 12 Negroes, a set of the Statutes at Large, other law books, 19 horses and mares, 8 pair of oxen, 192 cows, steers and other cattle, 83 sheep, a gun, 5 pistols, 2 cutlasses and a sword, and other items. Appraised by Elisha Hand and Richard Crafford.{NJCW}

Lydia, b. 10 April 1686, Easthampton, d. 2 Oct 1762.{Leaming diary; Baptist Burials}. She left a will dated 12 Oct 1759, proved 8 Oct 1762. Mentioned was the plantation where she formerly lived between James Edwards and Jeremiah Leaming which she gave to her son Jeremiah Leaming a part. He was to pay her son Richard Shaw £65; dau. Lydia Taylor, £65; son John Shaw, £65; son Joshua Shaw, £65; and son Nathan Shaw, £40. Son Aaron Leaming was to have the rest of the lands. Son, Richard Shaw, £50. The residue of the estate was to go to children: Lydia Taylor, John Shaw, Joshua Shaw, Nathan Shaw; Aaron Leaming, Jeremiah Leaming and Elizabeth Leaming. Execs. were sons John Shaw and Aaron Leaming. The will was witnessed by Samuel Foster, Ephraim Edwards and Lewis Cresse. On 2 Oct 1762 the inventory was filed (£863.14.4 1/2) by Jacob Richardson and Lewis Cresse. On 13 Feb 1773 an account was filed by execs.{NJCW 11:236; 14:514}

Aaron and Lydia were the parents of the following children: AARON, b. 6 July 1715, d. 28 Aug 1780[86]; JEREMIAH, b. 23 Feb 1716; MATTHIAS, d. 20 March 1732/3 of a pleuresy; ELIZABETH, b. 14(18?) Sep 1721, d. 26 Jan 1769, m. 29 April 1740, Thomas Leaming*, son of Thomas (2){Baptist Burials}; LYDIA; JOHN; JOSHUA; NATHAN; RICHARD.

Third Generation

4. JANE LEAMING, dau. of Thomas (2) and Hannah Leaming, b. Cape

86 Inscription on his monument reads died Aug. 28th, 1780, age of 65 years, 1 mo., 11 days.; buried in the old Leaming burying-ground. {Historical Collections of the State of New Jersey...}

May, 15 Oct 1706, m. William Doubleday, who d. intestate 1740.[87]

5. CHRISTOPHER LEAMING[88], son of Thomas (2) and Hannah Leaming, b. 18 April 1712, d. Cape May, 31 Dec 1751, m. Deborah Hand who was b. 14 Nov 1716, d. Cape May, 27 Feb 1794. They were the parents of the following children: HANNAH, b. 30 Sep, 1735; ESTHER, b. 16 Sep 1737; CHRISTOPHER, b. 2 Oct 1739 and d. Cape May 1788, m. by license of 8 Aug 1761, Sarah Spicer; PRISCILLA, b. 8 Nov 1742, m. Eli Eldredge*, son of William and Esther Eldredge by license dated 20 June 1761.

Deborah, widow of Christopher, m. 16 Dec 1752, Jacob Spicer*.

6. THOMAS LEAMING, son of Thomas (2) and Hannah Leaming, b. Cape May, 31 March 1718, d. at Cape May, 19 Dec 1795,{Baptist Burials}, m. at Cape May, 29 April 1740{License dated 25 April 1740 - MLNJ}, Elizabeth Leaming, b. at Cape May, 18 Sep 1721, d. at Cape May, 26 Jan 1769,[89] dau. of Aaron (2) Leaming.

Thomas Leaming (the Elder) d. leaving a will dated 14 July 1794, proved 31 Dec 1795. Mentioned were dau., Lydia Eldredge, wife of Jeremiah Eldredge; son Thomas; grandson Thomas Leaming; granddaus.: Elizabeth and Lydia; Esther Williams, dau. of Abigail Williams; Hannah Eldredge, wife of Aaron Eldredge.{NJCW 36:179} On 27 July 1796 an inventory was filed (£4164.6.11 1/2) by Philip Godfrey and Nathaniel Holmes.{NJCW File:1626E}

Thomas and Elizabeth were parents of the following children: THOMAS, b. in Cape May, 20 Aug 1748, d. Philadelphia, 29 Oct 1797, m. at Philadelphia, 19 Aug 1779, Rebecca Fisher; LYDIA, b. 22 Aug

---

87 The article assumed that Lydia Doubleday, wife of Joseph Norbury was undoubtedly the dau. of Jane and William Doubleday.

88 A great amount of the information on the descendants of Christopher Leaming comes from an article in *The Cape May County Magazine of History and Genealogy*, "The Ohio Leaming Bibles: A New Record of Pilgrim Descendants of Cape May County." Note the differing dates of birth for Christopher taken from this article (1712) and that from Dickinson on p. 158 (1714).

89 Records also show Eliz. Leaming d. 26 Jan 1760.{Baptist Burials}

1751, m. 1st Jeremiah Eldredge* by license dated 8 Sep 1775{MLNJ}, son of Samuel, and m. 2nd Anthony Van Mannerick.

7. AARON LEAMING, son of Aaron (3) and Lydia Leaming, was b. 6 July 1715, d. 28 Aug 1780. He represented Cape May County in the Colonial Assembly, 1740-1773.

Aaron Leaming, Jr. m. Mary Foreman*, dau. of Jonathan and Sarah Foreman, by license issued on 13 Feb 1738.{Baptist Burials; MLNJ}

In his diary between 26 May 1761 and 31 May 1761 Aaron Leaming makes the following entries: Matthias is 12 years of age next September and is 4 feet 9 inch and 1/2 high. Stephen 8 years old last October and 4 feet and 1/2 inch high. Parson will be 5 years old next July 7 is 3 feet 5 inches and 1/2 high. Philip Stevens was 5 years old last April and is the same height. Derick is 9 years old this May and is 4 feet 5 inches high. (See "Diaries of Aaron Leaming," in *The Cape May County Magazine of History and Genealogy*, p. 69, June 1932.)

Aaron Leaming, yeoman, d. leaving a will dated 16 June 1774 with codicil dated 17 Aug 1780, proved 8 Sep 1780. In his will Aaron gave the dates of birth, and some deaths, of his children: Jonathan, b. 5 July 1738; Aaron, b. 28 Aug 1740; dau. Sarah, b. 21 Feb 1743/4[90], m. Jesse Hand* by license, 26 Jan 1763{MLNJ}; Mathias, b. 19 Sep 1749 (all old style to here); dau. Mary, b. 19 Oct 1753; son Persons, b. 23 July 1756, named for his grandfather John Persons. Mathias d. 27 Sep 1763; Aaron d. 31 Aug 1764.{NJCW}

Mentioned in the will (several pages long) was wife Mary, the above named children and grandchildren, Mary, Jeremiah, Sarah and Lydia, Aaron, children of Jesse Hand.

Mary, widow of Aaron Leaming, Jr., d. 6 Jan 1780, aged 59 years, 9 months, 14 days.{Baptist Burials}

Aaron and Mary Leaming were the parents of the following children: JONATHAN, b. 5 July 1738; AARON, b. 28 Aug 1740, d. 31 Aug 1764; SARAH, b. 21 Feb 1743/4, m. Jesse Hand*; MATHIAS, b. 19 Sep 1749, d. 27 Sep 1763{Baptist Burials}; MARY, b. 19 Oct 1753; PERSONS, b. 23 July 1756.

8. JEREMIAH LEAMING, son of Aaron (3) Leaming, b. 23 Feb 1716, d. 18 Jan 1774.{Baptist Burials} He left a will dated 1 Dec 1769, proved 25 Jan 1774. Mentioned were cousin Jonathan Leaming's dau. Priscilla Leaming to whom he devised land in the Middle Precinct, 400 acres.

---

90 See The Hand Family.

Cousin, Lydia Leaming, dau. of sister Elizabeth Leaming, dec., a tract in said precinct, bound by brother Aaron Leaming of 1000 acres. Cousin Thomas Leaming, son of sister, Elizabeth Leaming, dec., right to 1/2 part of the Seven Mile Beach. Cousin, Lydia Leaming, dau. of sister Elizabeth Leaming, dec., his right to Five Mile Beach and other land. Cousin Thomas Leaming, son of sister Elizabeth Leaming, dec., 1/2 the land owned in the Upper Precinct. To Priscilla Raney, widow, living in Cape May Co., the use of land in Lower Precinct during her lifetime. To Enoch Raney, son of said Priscilla, a tract south of Jacob Eldridge in Lower Precinct. Brother Nathan Shaw, £5. To Jedediah Hughes' wife, Elizabeth, £5. To Aaron Eldridge, £10. To William Ewing's wife, Sarah, £5. To Jeremiah Eldridge, £5. Rest of estate to brother, Aaron Leaming and sister Elizabeth Leaming's children, to wit, Thomas Leaming, Jr. and Lydia Leaming. Execs. were cousin Thomas Leaming, Jr. and cousin Lydia Leaming, his sister. The will was witnessed by Mary Mulford, Elizabeth Edwards and Esther Edwards. The estate was inventoried 14 Oct 1774 by Jedidiah Hughes and Joshua Hildreth. On 3 May 1775 an account was filed by Thomas Leaming and Lydia Leaming, execs. The following legacies paid: To Priscilla Raney, £200; to Aaron Eldridge, £10; to Elizabeth Hughes, as per receipt of Jedediah Hughes, £5; to Jeremiah Eldredge, £5; to the children of Nathan Shaw, dec., £5; to Sarah Ewing, as per receipt of William Ewing, £5.{NJCW 15:534; 17:40}

Fourth Generation

9. CHRISTOPHER LEAMING, son of Christopher (5) and Deborah Leaming, was b. before 1739, d. 1788, m. by license of 8 Aug 1761, Sarah Spicer*, who d. at Cape May ca. 1797.

Christopher d. leaving a will dated 10 Dec 1787, proved 10 Sep 1788. Mentioned were wife Sarah who received use of 1/2 the lands. Sons Jacob Leamyng was devised those tracts bought of Abraham Bennet and Samuel Jones and wife Sylvia at the Neck and 1/2 of Two Mile Beach. Son Christopher received 1/2 of the home plantation, next to Jesse Hand. He gave cedar swamp to sons Spicer, Jacob, Christopher and Humphrey. Son Allinson Leamyng was to be kept at school until age 14. Son Spicer to have all lands devised to him by wife, he to pay £60 as legacies to daus.; he was also to be given land adjoining land of Aaron Eldredge, dec. Son Jacob to pay £60 when age 22 to execs. Son Christopher Leaming to pay £60. Son Humphrey Leaming to pay £60. If sons do not make payments then the lands to be divided among daus., Deborah Leaming, Hannah Leaming and Esther Leaming. Execs. were wife Sarah and son Spicer and friend Elijah Hughes. The will was witnessed by Elisha Hughes, Reeves

Iszard and John Swain. An inventory was filed (£341.6.8) by Eli Townsend and Henry Y. Townsend.{NJCW 31:82}

They had the following children: SPICER, b. 14 April 1762, m. Hannah Swain*, dau. of Zebulon Swain; DEBORAH, b. 11 Sep 1764; HANNAH, b. 23 Feb 1768, m. 1st Edward Rice, m. 2nd Amos C. Moore; JACOB, b. 31 Oct 1771; CHRISTOPHER, b. 5 July 1775, m. Ann Mecray and had a child Edwin Leaming; ESTHER, b. 9 Feb 1778, d. at Lebanon, Ohio, m. Eli Foster, moved to Ohio in 1806; HUMPHREY, b. 6 Dec 1780, m. Mary Stites; ALLISON, b. 25 Sep 1784.

10. THOMAS LEAMING, son of Thomas (6) and Elizabeth (Leaming) Leaming, b. 20 Aug 1748 (old style), d. 29 Oct 1797 at Philadelphia, m. at Philadelphia, 19 Aug 1779, Rebecca Fisher (b. 31 Oct 1757 [old style], d. at Philadelphia, 9 Sep 1833). They were parents of the following children: ELIZA, b. 13 Aug 1780, d. 1835, m. 3 Jan 1799, Charles Caldwell, M.D.; THOMAS FISHER, b. 14 July 1786 at Philadelphia, m. 23 June 1839 Susan Murgatroyde; LYDIA, b. 28 Aug 1789, m. J. Somers Smith; JEREMIAH FISHER, b. 8 Oct 1795 at Philadelphia, m. Rebecca Waln. [For more details on this family see *Mayflower Pilgrim Descendants In Cape May County New Jersey*.]

Thomas Leaming, wife Rebecca, mentioned in the deeds dated 1797.{Deeds E: 87}

Fifth Generation

11. JONATHAN LEAMING, son of Aaron (7) Leaming, d. leaving a will dated 24 Oct 1794. He stated that his dau. Priscilla Stites, now wife of Humphrey, b. of wife Margaret Leaming on 9 Oct 1764; son Jonathan, Jr. b. of wife Judith Leaming on 21 June 1770. To his present wife Sarah he gave use of home plantation. Son Jonathan received all lands in the county and in Cumberland Co.{NJCW 35:103} An inventory was filed (£1739.13.6) by Nathaniel Holmes and Philip Cresse on 3 Dec 1794.{NJCW File:607E}

Jonathan m. 1st Margaret (N) and by her had a dau. PRISCILLA, b. 9 Oct 1764 who m. Humphrey Stites.

Jonathan m. 2nd Judith Hand by license dated 14 Aug 1766. Judith Leaming was b. 26 April 1747 (old style), d. 9 Nov 1779 (N.S.).{Baptist Burials} They were the parents of JONATHAN, Jr., b. 21 June 1770 and AARON, b. 9 July 1776, d. 9 Feb 1779{Baptist Burials}.

Jonathan m. 3rd. Sarah (N).

12. SPICER LEAMING, son of Christopher (9) and Sarah (Spicer)

Leaming, b. 14 April 1762, d. 1 Oct 1838{Cold Spring Cemetery}, m. Hannah Swain*, dau. of Zebulon. They were the parents of the following children: SWAIN, b. 22 June 1787, d. 1850, m. Sarah Dixon; JAMES, b. 19 Feb 1789, d. 12 Aug 1870, m. 1st Mrs. Lydia Schellenger (d. 13 Feb 1856, age 66 years, 24 days), m. 2nd Sarah Bennett; MARIA, b. 4 Aug 1806, m. David Cresse; ISRAEL, b. 14 Feb 1808, m. Judith E. Hughes; LEMUEL, b. 2 Oct 1809, d. 3 May 1879, m. Lydia Leaming; JACOB, b. 16 Jan 1812, m. Melvina Eldredge; SPICER, d. 8 Oct 1814, age 22 years, 6 mos., 28 days. {Cold Spring Cemetery}

Hannah Leaming, widow of Spicer, b. 3 March 1767, d. 11 Sep 1857.{Cold Spring Cemetery}

LEE

See "The Mills of East and West Creek," Part II, "The Hoffmans," *The Cape May County Magazine of History and Genealogy*. p. 273. June 1961. By Dr. Roy Hand.

According to Mr. Hand,

1. ABEL LEE, Sr. m. Mary Scull Wood, by license dated 7 March 1733. She was the widow of Jonas Wood of Great Egg Harbor, Gloucester Co.

2. ABEL LEE, (b. ca.. 1735), son of Abel (1) Lee, m. Mary Doughty, by license dated 7 Feb 1761{MLNJ}, dau. of Edward and Margaret. See will of Edward Doughty, proved, 28 March 1770. He m. 2nd Susannah Snell by license dated 24 July 1783.{MLNJ}

Susannah Lee, widow of Abel Lee, m. Archibald Stewart, 13 June 1795, of Cumberland Co. Abel Lee, Jr., d. 1792.

Abel Lee, Jr. had: JOHN, b. 1769, d. 1840, m. 30 Oct 1798, Jemima Crandal, dau. of Levi and Dorothy Hollingshead Crandal.

Unplaced

RACHEL LEE of Great Egg Harbor m. Jesse Freeman by license dated 27 Feb 1760.{MLNJ}

LUDLAM

According to Dr. Beesley (1857) as quoted by Lewis Townsend Stevens in his *The History of Cape May County* ... (1897), "Joseph Ludlam was here in 1692, and made purchases of land on the seaside, at Ludlam's Run, upon which he afterwards resided; and likewise purchased, in 1720, of Jacob Spicer, a large tract in Dennis' Neck. He left four sons: Anthony who settled upon the South Dennis property, Joseph, Isaac and Samuel, from whom all the Ludlams of the county have descended. He died in 1761, aged 86 years."

On page 46 of *History of Cape May County* Stevens says Anthony Ludlam, came from England in the early days and by 1640 had become a member of the whaling colony in Southampton, Long Island. Joseph, son of the New England settler, came to Cape May about 1692.

See p. 379 of *Genealogies of New Jersey Families* in which is stated Samuel Andrews sold to Joseph Ludlum on 15 Nov 1687 all his Oyster Bay land.

1. JOSEPH LUDLAM, d. aged near 86 in Feb 1761.{Diaries of Aaron Leaming}

According to the land records of Cape May County, Joseph Ludlam (of age in 1733) had a son Anthony who had two sons, Reuben and Anthony 2nd. Reuben had a son Christopher and a grandson Richard Townsend[91]. Anthony 2nd had a son James, whose wife was Martha (1783-7).{Deeds A:98-107}

Joseph Ludlam left a will dated 3 Jan 1760, proved 12 Feb 1761. Mentioned were grandson Joseph Ludlam (elder son of my son Joseph, dec.), to whom he devised his right in the beach called Ludlam's Beach with the plantation whereon he dwelled and all other lands when age 30. Carmon Smith, who was married to one of testator's relations - he gives to his wife Lydia Smith, an ox. To son Isaac, 5 shillings. Personal estate to be given to son Jeremiah and daus.: Abigail Scull and Elizabeth Cresse, 1/6 of personal estate to each and 1/6 part to grandchildren, children of son Anthony, dec. and 1/6 to grandchildren, children of son Joseph, and 1/6 to Phebe Young, wife of Henry Young, Esq. Execs. were Providence Ludlam, Abigail Scull and Elizabeth Cresse. On 12 Feb 1761 an inventory

91 Perhaps the name Reuben was intended.

was filed by Jesse Hand and Silvanus Townsend. Some tobacco and one "cain" was all owed to John Scull and his wife.{NJCW 11:80} On 30 Aug 1765 an account was filed by Providence Ludlam, as one of the execs. Abigail Scull, being aged and infirm, could not appear.

Joseph Ludlam was father of the following children: JOSEPH; ISAAC, had a dau. Phebe{will of Isaac's sister Phebe Young, proved 1760}; JEREMIAH, had a dau. Deborah who m. Cornelius (35) Hand; ABIGAIL, m. (N) Scull; ELIZABETH, m. Lewis Cresse by license dated 1 Sep 1740{MLNJ}; ANTHONY; PHEBE, b. 1710, d. 23 Aug 1766, m. 1st Elisha Eldredge, m. 2nd Daniel Norton and m. 3rd Henry Young[92].

2. ANTHONY LUDLUM, son of Joseph (1), of Cape May, Cape May Co., d. leaving a will dated 15 Jan 1736/7, proved 21 July 1737. Mentioned were wife Presela.[93] Daus.: Elizabeth, a pair of curtains that were her aunt Sarah's; Jude and Elizabeth to have £7.10 in gold and 1/2 of right of land surveyed by Henry Young. Son, Providence, land at Popler Island, Cape May, with mills, houses, etc., at age 20 and other land. Son Reuben, at age 20, 1/2 the plantation. Son Anthony, at age 20, the other half of the plantation and other land. Rent of the mills, house and plantation to be applied to the schooling of sons Providence, Anthony, Reuben and Joseph. Whomsoever has the mill shall grind toll free for testator's father and wife. Execs. were wife, Presela and his father, Joseph Ludlam. The will was witnessed by Joseph Ludlam, Deborah Young and Henry Young.{NJCW 4:111} An inventory of the estate was submitted on 13 July 1737 by Henry Young and Jeremiah Hand.{NJCW}

Anthony m. Priscilla (N). They were the parents of the following children: ELIZABETH; JUDE; PROVIDENCE, living in 1764[94]; REUBEN; ANTHONY; JOSEPH.

3. JOSEPH LUDLAM, Jr., of Cape May Co., yeoman, son of Joseph (1),

---

92 It appears she m. 1st Daniel Norton* and after his death (ca. 1755) she m. 2nd Daniel Norton* (d. ca. 1755) and m. 3rd Henry Young by license dated 28 Dec 1764. {MLNJ} Phebe Young, wife of Henry Young, mentioned her Ludlam siblings in her will dated 1 Sep 1761.

93 Noting that Charles Dennis, husband of Priscilla, had at the time of his death in 1747-49, sons-in-law [probably step-sons] John Cresse (minor) and Joseph Ludlam, it is likely that Priscilla was the Priscilla Ludlam, widow of Anthony Ludlam who d. 1736/7 and Priscilla Cresse, the widow of John Cresse who d. in 1745.

94 Deeds B:64.

d. leaving a will dated 6 Feb 1753, proved 2 March 1753. mentioned were wife Abigail and children: Joseph, Henry Thomas and daus. (unnamed), all under age. Farm now occupied by the father on the seaside; marsh called the Great Flat; right to the beach called Ludlam's; land bought of the Society in England adj. Moses Crosley; land on east side of Jarret's Gut in Upper Precinct between Barnabas Crowell, Lewis Cresey and Thomas Smith on the west side of Dudecan's Branch; Thomas or Daniel Eldredge and William Goff; home farm in said Upper Precinct. Execs. were Daniel Norton, John Mackey and Providence Ludlam. The will was witnessed by John Goff, William Bond and Joseph Savage. In 2-5 May 1753 an inventory was filed by Jeremiah Hand and Jacob Spicer, with a long explanation by appraisers giving reasons why they have not included in the inventory goods given by the will to the widow, Joseph (Tertius, the eldest son), Phebe (the eldest dau.), Thomas (second son), Alathear (second dau.) and Esther (third dau.).{NJCW Cape May Wills:165E}

Joseph Ludlam m. Abigail Young by license in 1747. {MLNJ}

Joseph was father of the following children: JOSEPH; HENRY; THOMAS (2nd son); PHEBE (eldest dau.); ALATHEAR (2nd dau.); ESTHER (Hester) (3rd dau.).

Third Generation

4. REUBEN LUDLAM, son of Anthony (2) and Priscilla Ludlam.

On 8 March 1789 a bond was taken of Christopher Ludlam to take care of the estate of Deborah Ludlam, dau. of Ruben Ludlam, minor above age of 14.{Ltrs&Inv A:18}

Christopher Ludlam, son of Reuben Ludlam at May Court 1787, applied for the appointment of auditors to divide the plantation, late of his father Ruben Ludlam, according to the will, between said Christopher and Ruben Townsend, a minor and son of Henry Townsend.{Ltrs&Inv A(Rev):11}

Reuben was the father of CHRISTOPHER and DEBORAH, b. prior to 1775, who chose as her guardian, Christopher Ludlam of Middle Precinct, on 20 April 1789.{NJCW 31:373}

5. ANTHONY LUDLAM, probable son of Anthony (2) and Priscilla Ludlam, d. on 29 or 30 Sep 1777 of the "Bloody Flux."{Leaming Diaries} He left a will dated 8 June 1776, proved 21 May 1778. Mentioned were wife Phebe; oldest dau. Rachel, 2nd dau. Lovicea; son Jeams when 21; other children: Rhodea and Elizabeth. The four daus. to have plantation bought of Norton Ludlam and 1/2 of cedar swamp which Providence Ludlam bought of Michal Iszard at the Long Bridge; also 60 acres bought

of Joseph Ludlam's execs. and Jacob Spicer, joining Reuben Ludlam's Rag Wheal tract. Son Jeams, the rest of the lands. Execs.: Joseph Hildreth and brother Providence Ludlam. The will was witnessed by Isaac Townsend, Eli Townsend, James Townsend and Amos Ireland. On 21 April 1778 an inventory was made by David Smith and Thomas Smith.{NJCW 21:248}

On 11 May 1786 it was recorded that the land which Anthony Ludlam left to his daus. had been divided by auditors. The land was located in the middle precinct of the county of Cape May, bound to the southward by land late of Thomas Smith, dec., to the westward by Goshen Creek, northerly by a small creek called Cedar Swamp Creek and to the northeastward by land late the property of John Shaw, dec. The daus. were Rachel, wife of Levi Smith; Lovisa, wife of Philip Hand; Rodah Ludlam and Elizabeth (now to her heirs). 11 May 1786.{Ltrs&Inv A(Rev):4}

Anthony was the father of the following children: PHEBE; RACHEL, m. Levi Smith; LOVICEA, m. Philip Hand who may have been the son of Nathaniel Hand*; JAMES, m. Martha Johnson by license dated 5 Jan 1790 who may have been the dau. of David Johnson*{MLNJ}; RHODEA; ELIZABETH.

6. JOSEPH LUDLAM, son of Anthony (2), of Cape May Co. d. prior to 22 Jan 1757 when a bond was issued to Providence Ludlam as admin; John Mackey, fellow bondsman, both of said county.{NJCW 8:496} On 23 Jan 1757 an inventory was filed by Henry Young and John Mackey.{NJCW}

This is probably the Joseph Ludlam who m. Alathan Smith by license dated 23 Jan 1732.{MLNJ} Alathan Ludlam m. Jonathan Smith by license dated 26 Dec 1761.{MLNJ}

7. PROVIDENCE LUDLAM, of Greenwich, Cumberland Co., son of Anthony (2) Ludlam, d. 5 July 1792, in his 67th year. He m. Sarah Vickers by license dated 6 Sep 1760.{MLNJ} Saley [Sally/Sarah] d. 11 March 1782, age 49.{Old Cohansey Bur. Ground} Providence left a will dated 1 June 1792, proved 27 Aug 1792. Mentioned were children: NORTON, d. 5 Nov 1791 in his 39th year{Old Cohansey Bur. Ground}; JACOB, JUDITH Wheaton, RACHEL Sayres, PHEBE Sheppard, SALLY Watson, PRISCILLA S. and LYDIA; grandchildren: Sarah Remington, Ephraim and Reuben Ludlam; Providence, son of Norton Ludlam.{Cumberland Wills}

8. JOSEPH LUDLAM, Jr., probable son of Joseph (3) Ludlam, m. Abigail Scull by license dated 18 Jan 1757.{MLNJ}

9. THOMAS LUDLAM, son of Joseph (3) Ludlam, d. leaving a will dated 29 July 1781, proved 15 Feb 1782. Mentioned were sons: THOMAS; HENRY, to whom was devised 150 acres of cedar swamp on east side of lands adjoining brother Henry Ludlam and Philip Cresse; PHEBE; MARGARATE; ELIZABETH; MARY. Execs. were Thomas Smith and Eli Eldredge. The will was witnessed by Richard Stephenson, Sarah Stephenson and Phebe Ludlam. On 20 Dec 1793 Henry Stites was appointed admin. Fellowbondsman: Henry Ludlam of Cape May Co. The execs both died leaving part of the estate unadministered. On 15 June 1782 the estate was inventoried (£573.7.1) by John Cresse and Archabald Campbell. On 5 Feb 1794 another inventory was filed (£149.6.8) by William Hawkins and Eli Townsend.{NJCW 24:260; 33:279}

Fourth Generation

10. CHRISTOPHER LUDLAM, son of Reuben (4) Ludlam at May Court 1787, applied for the appointment of auditors to divide the plantation, late of his father Ruben Ludlam, according to the will, between said Christopher and Ruben Townsend, a minor and son of Henry Townsend.{Ltrs&Inv A(Rev):11}

On 8 March 1789 a bond was taken of Christopher Ludlam to take care of the estate of Deborah Ludlam, dau. of Ruben Ludlam, minor above age of 14.{Ltrs&Inv A:18} Settled the accounts of Hannah Summers, Henry Young Townsend and Christopher Ludlam, execs - to estate of Ruben Ludlam.{Ltrs&Inv A:18}

11. JAMES LUDLAM, son of Anthony (5) Ludlam, m. Martha Johnson, 5 Jan 1790{MLNJ} Reuben Ludlam was assigned guardian of James Ludlam on 19 April 1779.{NJCW 22:63}

12. JACOB LUDLAM, son of Providence (7) Ludlam, b. 1752, d. 14 Jan 1795. He m. by license 21 Jan 1784, Rachel Worthington (d. 30 July 1793 in her 36th year.{Old Cohansey Bur. Ground, Cumberland Co. Gen. Data}

13. THOMAS LUDLAM, son of Thomas (9) Ludlam, chose as his guardian, Joseph Ludlam on 16 June 1782. Witnesses: Samuel Orum and Daniel Townsend.{NJCW 38:80}

Unplaced

A marriage license was issued to BEULAH LUDLAM and John Cresse 18

May 1739.{MLNJ}

DEBORAH LUDLAM m. Cornelius Hand 11 June 1750.{Baptists}

A marriage license was issued to CHRISTOPHER LUDLAM and Amelia Hand dated 25 March 1776.{MLNJ}

HENRY LUDLAM m. Hannah Smith, 30 June 1772.{Baptists; MLNJ}
In the land records are shown Henry Ludlam and wife Hannah (1800).{Deeds B:43}

A marriage license was issued to HENRY LUDLAM and Rohannah Hand 8 Jan 1772.{MLNJ}

A marriage license was issued to JEREMIAH LUDLAM and Anna Whildin 16 Feb 1774. {MLNJ}

A marriage license was issued to PHEBE LUDLAM and Elisha Eldridge 20 Sep 1729.{MLNJ}

A marriage license was issued to PHEBE LUDLAM and Henry Reed of Fairfield 31 Oct 1765.{MLNJ}

SARAH LUDLAM m. Richard Townsend*. On 6th day, 7th mo., 1731 the marriage of Richard Townsend, Jr., and Sarah Ludlam, both of Cape May Monthly Meeting, was reported orderly accomplished.{GEMM}

LUPTON

Following are persons named Lupton for which relationships have not been determined.

CHRISTOPHER LUPTON of Cape May Co. d. prior to 20 March 1732/3 when Abigail Lupton was appointed admx. Fellow bondsman: Richard Downes, Esq. Witnesses: John Eldridge, Jacob Spicer, Jr. and Francis Bevis.{NJCW Cape May Wills:75E} An inventory of the estate was submitted 19 March 1732/3 by Benjamin Crafford and Elisha Hand. On 23 July 1733 an account was submitted showing payments to Richard Downes, John Hand, Francis Bevis, Isaac Flood, Elisha Hand, John Scull, Benjamin Crafford, Jacob Spicer, Nathaniel Foster and George Crandall.{NJCW}

CHRISTOPHER LUPTON d. in 1760. In "Diaries of Aaron Leaming," is mentioned the death of Christopher Lupton in 1760.

Christopher Lupton d. prior to 26 March 1761 when Marcy Lupton was appointed admx. Fellowbondsman: Benjamin Ingrum of Cape May Co. Witnesses: Henry Hand and John Eldredge. On 28 Jan 1761 an inventory was filed (£97.16.0) by Benjamin Ingrum and Henry Hand.{NJCW 10:163}

SILAS LUPTON m. Mary Stites by license dated 11 May 1756.{MLNJ}

MARY LUPTON m. Thomas Hedges by license dated 16 Feb 1762.{MLNJ}

MACKEY

JOHN MACKEY of Cape May Co. d. prior to 16 May 1733 when Jeames Hathorn was appointed admin. Fellow bondsman, William Johnson, both of Cape May. Witnesses: Humphrey Hughes, Samuwell Swaine and Jacob Spicer.{NJCW Cape May Wills:76E} On 10 April 1733 an inventory of the estate was filed which included a linen wheel and a woolen wheel. Appraised by Samuwell Swaine and William Johnson. On 29 May 1741 an account was filed by James Hathorne, admin., showing payments to Jacob Spicer, John Flower, John Jones, Ezekiel Eldridge, Wm. McGowen, Robert Swaine, John Roberts, John Jones, Wm. Seagrave, Jas. Flood, Elias Taylor, Benjamin Richison, Lemual Swaine, Corns. Schillinger, Joshua Shaw and Wm. Johnson, etc.{NJCW}

JOHN MACKEY m. Elizabeth Young by license dated 25 April 1746.{MLNJ}

In the land records are shown John Mackay and wife Elizabeth in 1800.{Deeds B:39}

JOHN MACKEY d. leaving a will dated 25 April 1784. Mentioned were son JOHN; daus.: ABIGAL, m. Jacob Willets, by license dated 27 April 1777{MLNJ}; MARTHA, m. Darius Corson by license dated 4 June 1778{MLNJ}; TOBITHA, m. (N) Willets; PHEBE, m. Joseph Badcock by license dated 1 Feb 1780{MLNJ}; ELIZABETH, m. (N) Young.

CATHARINE MACKEY m. William Hand by license dated 28 Jan 1731.{MLNJ}

MASON

WILLIAM MASON, yeoman, appears in the land records of Cape May Co. as owing quit rent on 150 acres on 22 April 1695.{Deeds A:452}

William Mason of Cape May d. leaving a will dated 22 Feb 1714/5, proved 5 April 1715. Son-in-law James Jacox is principal heir. Legacies to Daniel Brandreth, Debberah Russell, Epherem Carman and dau.-in-law Mary Ranor. Execs. were John Townsend, John Page and Timothy Brandreth. The will was witnessed by Thomas Gandy, William Lines and Mary Townsend.{NJCW 1:525 and Cape May Wills} An inventory was taken of the estate on 28 March 1715 by Joseph Whilldon and John Parsons.{NJCW}

William m. Sarah, who had previously m. Richard Swain* who d. prior to 22 May 1707, then m. Thomas Jaccocks* who d. sometime after 1708 and she then m. William Mason. Sarah d. leaving a will dated 16 Feb 1714/5. Mentioned were sons: Jonathan Swain, Ebenezer Swain, Joshua Jacocks and James Jacocks, granddau. Joanna Swain, and "my own daughter." A legacy to Nathaniel Jencens. Son-in-law Jonathan Swain and Elizabeth [Ebenezer?] Swain to be "overseers of my own sons and executors." The will was witnessed by Humphrey Hughes, Joseph Welden, Debrow Russell.{NJCW 2:56}

JOSEPH MASON m. Esther Lozer by license dated 7 Jan 1763.{MLNJ}

WILLIAM MASON m. Judith Brooks by license dated 10 Nov 1776.{MLNJ}

MATHEWS

The name Mathews appears recorded on 22 April 1695, as Samuel Matthews, whaler, owning 175 acres.{Deeds A:451} Thomas Mathews recorded his ear mark on 2 June 1696.{First Public Rcds:273}

1. (N) MATHEWS, father of John and Samuel Mathews.

2. JOHN MATHEW of Cape May Co., son of (1), yeoman, d. leaving a will dated 25 Jan 1714/5, proved 9 May 1715. Mentioned were wife Charity, dau. Lishabe, sister Elizabeth Mathews, cousin William Mathews. Brother Samuel Mathews was exec. The will was witnessed by George Crafford, Henry Stevens and John Taylor.{NJCW 1:506} The estate was inventoried on 3 Feb 1714/5 by John Paige and John Taylor. A bond was issued to Charity Mathews as admx. on 9 May 1715. John Taylor of Cape

May and George Willis of Burlington fellow bondsmen.{NJCW}

John Mathew m. Charity (N). They were parents of the following child: LISHABE.

3. SAMUEL MATHEWS of Cape May Co., yeoman, son of (1), d. leaving a will dated 4 Feb 1714/5. Mentioned were wife Mary and children: William, John, Samuel, Margaret, Elizabeth. Reference was made to land at Long Neck, at Henry Steephens. His wife was extx. The will was witnessed by David Wells, Eekiell Eldridge and John Taylor.{NJCW 2:27 and Cape May Wills} Inventory of the estate was made on 18 Feb 1714/5 by John Paige and John Taylor.{NJCW}

Samuel Mathews m. Mary (N). They were the parents of the following children: WILLIAM; JOHN; SAMUEL; MARGARET; ELIZABETH.

4. SAMUEL MATHEWS, son of Samuel (3) Mathews, was living in 1697.{Deeds B:16} He d. leaving a will dated 26 March 1765, codicil dated 2 July 1765, proved 25 May 1768. Mentioned were son Samuel to whom was devised the plantation bought of Amos Johnson, of 196 acres, in Middle Precinct which was part of that plantation that formerly belonged to Benjamin Johnson (last wife's father) and where he lived. Son Elijah was devised land where testator lived in the Middle Precinct. Dau. Mary Matthews was bequeathed £300; she would be age 18 on 19 June 1774. And whereas Benjamin Johnson gave Samuel's dau. Mary, £5, and her grandmother, Penelope Johnson, gave her a bed which bequests are to be paid and she is to have the clothing that was her mother's. Son Samuel to be guardian of dau. Mary. Execs. were sons Samuel and Elijah. The will was witnessed by Jeremiah Ludlam, Mary Leaming, Aaron Leaming and Jonathan Leaming. On 8 June 1768 an inventory was filed (£741.2.0 1/4) by John Townsend and James Godfrey.{NJCW 15:463}

Samuel m. Temperance Johnson*, dau. of Benjamin Johnson. Samuel was the father of the following children: SAMUEL; ELIJAH; MARY, b. 19 June 1756. Mary Matthews (probably Mary, dau. of Samuel) m. Stephen Stephens 8 Sep 1774.{Baptists} The marriage license was dated 5 Sep 1774.{MLNJ}

5. WILLIAM MATHEWS, probable son of Samuel (3) Mathews, m. Bethia Mills of Salem Co. by license issued 12 Dec 1740.{MLNJ}

William d. leaving a will dated 9 Aug 1766, proved 19 March 1767. Mentioned was oldest son John, to whom was devised the northwest side of the home plantation (80 acres). Son Isaac to received 100 acres where the dwelling house stood. Son Richard was devised the remainder of the land. The 1/4 part owned by William in partnership with Richard Shaw and Lewis Cresse of certain islands in Middle Precinct, on the northwest side of Five Mile Beach, he gave to his son Thomas. Sons John and Isaac to support and care for unfortunate dau. Martha, for 4 years after William's death, and after that time to be supported by John, Isaac and Richard to the end of her life. Wife Bathia, to receive the best bed and 1/3 of moveable estate. The remainder to go to daus. Lydia, Elizabeth, Elishaba and Bathia Matthews and to granddaus. Jane and Esther Edwards. Execs. were wife and son Isaac. The will was witnessed by Ephraim Edwards, Aaron Leaming, James Edwards and Samuel Matthews. On 24 March 1767 an inventory was filed (£133.12.4} by John Eldredge and Samuel Matthews.{NJCW 13:141}

William was the father of the following children: JOHN; ISAAC; RICHARD; THOMAS; MARTHA; LYDIA; ELIZABETH; ELISHABA; BATHIA.

6. SAMUEL MATTHEWS, possible son of Samuel (4) Matthews, m. Temperance Stites 10 Aug 1771.{Baptists; MLNJ} She appears to be Temperance Bowen who m. Eli Stites* by license dated 22 July 1769.{MLNJ} Eli d. prior to 2 June 1770.

Samuel d. prior to 5 Aug 1778 when Temperance Norton was appointed as admx. of his estate. Fellowbondsman was Benjamin Stites, Sr. On 21 March 1778 an inventory was filed (£524.2.11) by Benjamin Stites and Jonathan Jenkins.{NJCW 22:39}

At October Court 1788 Landal Bowen of Cumberland Co. applied to take on himself the guardianship of his sister's two children: Martha and Temperence Marthews, daus. of Samuel Marthews, dec. Approved.{Ltrs&Inv A(Rev):27}

On 31 Oct 1788 was given by Land Bowen of Cumberland Co., two guardianship bonds, to take charge of the persons and estate of Martha Marthews and Temperance Marthews, two minors and daus. of Samuel Marthews, dec.{Ltrs&Inv A:15, NJCW 31:94}

Samuel and Temperance were parents of the following children: MARTHA; TEMPERANCE.

7. ELIJAH MATTHEWS, probable son of Samuel (4) Matthews, m. Martha Smith, 10 Oct 1770.{Baptists; MLNJ}

He d. by 25 May 1780 when Martha Matthews was appointed admx. of his estate. Fellowbondsman was Isaac Matthews. On 9 Dec 1779 an inventory was filed (£3,644.9.3) by Isaac Mathews and Daniel

Gerretsen.{NJCW 24:86}

8. JOHN MATHEWS, son of William (5) Mathews, and wife Phebe sold 11 acres on 24 Aug 1767 to Aaron Leaming, being part of the plantation formerly belonging to William Mathews.

9. THOMAS MATTHEWS, probable son of William (5) Mathews, m. Hannah Creese by license dated 8 Jan 1768.{MLNJ}

Thomas d. before 10 Aug 1778 when Hannah Mathews was appointed admx. Fellowbondsman: Isaac Matthews, both of said county. Witnesses: Thomas Smith and John Cresse. On 14 July 1778 an inventory was made by Thomas Smith and John Cresse.{NJCW 22:42}

The will of Isaac Matthews (below) indicates that Thomas had a son, SILAS. Silas m. Eleanor Hughes by license dated 20 Dec 1798.{County Clerk Rcds Book A}

10. ISAAC MATTHEWS of Cape May Co., probable son of William (5) Matthews, d. leaving a will dated 16 Nov 1790, proved 18 June 1791. Mentioned were wife Priscilla; dau. Deborah Matthews when 18; Hannah Hand, dau. of Shamgar Hand, dec; Jacob Hand, son of Elishab Conner; Richard Matthews, son of Richard Matthews, to whom was devised 20 acres adjoining lands of Richard Matthews, dec.; Silas Matthews, son of Thomas Matthews, dec. Friend Stephen Hand to be guardian of dau. Deborah until age 21. Execs. were wife Priscilla and Stephen Hand. The will was witnessed by Philip Cresse, Hannah Cresse and Abigail Hand.{NJCW 32:296} On 16 June 1791 Priscilla Matthews renounced the will. On 19 April 1791 an inventory was filed (£167.14.7 1/2) by Constantine Carll and Philip Cresse.{NJCW File:556E}

Isaac was father of DEBORAH.

11. RICHARD MATTHEWS, probable son of William (5) Matthews, m. Judith Hughes by license dated 10 July 1772.{MLNJ}

Richard Matthews of Cape May Co., weaver, d. leaving a will dated 24 Aug 1789, proved 4 Jan 1790. Mentioned were son Richard to whom was devised land when 21 and daus. Elizabeth, Judith, Bethiah, Sarah and Charlotte to whom was left 20 shillings each, when age 18. Wife Judith received the rest of the moveable estate and use of land until son was age 21. He was to be put to a trade when age 14. Extx. was wife Judith. The will was witnessed by Thomas Hand, Elizabeth Hand and Constantine Carll. On 23 Sep 1789 an inventory was filed (£182.54) by Isaac Matthews and Constantine Carll.{NJCW 31:50}

Richard was father of the following children: RICHARD; ELIZABETH; JUDITH; BETHIAH; SARAH; CHARLOTTE.

Unplaced

A marriage license was issued to Nathaniel Norton and ELESHA MATHEWS [Lishabe?, dau. of John (1)?], 19 April 1731.{MLNJ}

Thomas Bancroft m. ELIZABETH MATTHEWS, 6 April 1715.{First Official Rcds}

A marriage license was issued to ISAAC MATTHEWS and Mary Hand, 17 Dec 1774.{MLNJ}

A marriage license was issued for Elisha Hand and LYDIA MATHEWS, 16 Aug 1766.{MLNJ}

EZEKIEL MULFORD

Ca. 1730 John DeCamp and Ezekiel Mulford settled on a tract of 110 acres, part of a large tract north of the Passaic River at present-day Myersville.{*Genealogies of New Jersey Families*, Vol. 1, p. 632}

1. EZEKIL MULFORD of Cape May Co., son of Thomas Mulford and Mary Conkling, m. at East Hampton 14 July 1714, Biah Osborne, dau. of Benjamin.{*Genealogies of New Jersey Families*, Vol. 1, p. 632}[95] Ezekil d. leaving a will dated 15 March 1720/1, proved 2 Jan 1721/2. Mentioned were wife Abiah and children: Jonathan, Ezekiel, Mary. The wife was extx. The will was witnessed by Ebenezer Norcott, William Mulford, John Bradner. Martha Carman of Cape May Co., spinster, 17 years old, though not a subscribing witness, also swears to the execution of the will.{NJCW 2:204} The estate was inventoried in April 1721 by Humphrey Hughes and Nathaniel Hand.{NJCW}

Ezekiel was the father of the following children: JONATHAN; EZEKIEL; MARY.

2. EZEKIEL MULFORD, son of Ezekiel (1) Mulford, m. Mary Edwards

---

95 For more on the Osborn family see this article.

by license issued 4 May 1762.{MLNJ} Mary, dau. of James Edwards, is also mentioned in Book of Mortgages A: 56, dated 1767.

Ezekiel Mulford d. prior to 13 May 1782 when Mary Mulford, widow, was appointed admx. Fellowbondsman: Ellis Hughes, Jr. of Cape May Co. Witnesses: Henry Hand and Isaac Matthews. On 11 May 1782 an inventory was filed (£273.0.6) by Henry Hand and Isaac Matthews.{NJCW 24:85}

WILLIAM MULFORD

1. WILLIAM MULFORD of Cape May Co. d. leaving a will dated 28 Nov 1751, proved 22 March 1755. Mentioned were wife Charity and children: Ezekiel, Thomas, Lewis, Daniel (exec) and Mary. The will was witnessed by James Whilldin, Jane Whilldin and John Leek.{NJCW 8:141} On 24 March 1755 an inventory was filed by Samuel Clark and Jeremiah Fithian which included bonds, bridle, saddle, divinity books and apparel.{NJCW} William m. Charity (N) by 1726.{Deeds B:196}

William was the father of the following children: EZEKIEL; THOMAS; LEWIS; DANIEL; MARY.

2. DANIEL MULFORD, probable son of William (1) Mulford, m. Ruth Swain*, dau. of Ebenezer Swain, by 21 Sep 1733.{See will of Ebenezer Swain, Cape May Wills:179E.} Ruth m. 2nd Richard Stites* by license dated 28 Nov 1779.{MLNJ}

3. EZEKIEL MULFORD, probable son of William (1) Mulford, m. Jemima Nicholson, by license dated 15 Jan 1770.{MLNJ}

Ezekiel Mulford of Cumberland Co. d. prior by 1786 when Jemima Mulford, widow, was appointed admx. On 6 Jan 1787 Jemima, now married to Henry Sharp, living in Cape May, gave her account.{NJCW File No. 6055F}

Unplaced

SARAH MULFORD, b. 1775, d. 1840.{Cold Spring Cemetery}

A marriage license was issued to James Whildin and RHODA MULFORD, dated 8 Dec 1774.{MLNJ}

EBENEZAR NEWTON

1. EBENEZAR NEWTON of Cape May Co. d. leaving a will dated 18 May 1739, proved 18 July 1739. Mentioned were wife Elizabeth and sons Caleb, Isaac, Ebenezer and Nathan. Daus.: Sarah and Martha. The will was witnessed by Peter Johnson, Joseph Johnson and Israel Johnson.{NJCW Cape May Wills:93E} At Derby in the county of New Haven, CT, on 9 July 1739 appeared Petter Johnson, Joseph Johnson and Israel Johnson to take the deposition of the last will of Ebenezer Newton, late dec. in Derby. On 10 Aug 1739 an inventory of the estate was submitted which included 44 head of cattle and 12 calves, 3 horses, 60 sheep, 12 hogs, 13 pigs, 39 geese, 2 turkeys, wheat, corn, rye, flax, barley, oats, a Negro woman, whale boat and craft, leather, books, yarn and indigo. Appraised by Ezekiel Eldredge and Thomas Ross.{NJCW}

Ebenezer Nuton recorded his ear mark 10 July 1731 for his son Caleb Nuton.{First Official Rcds}

Ebenezar was father of the following children: CALEB; ISAAC; EBENEZER; NATHAN, listed with "youngmen" in the 1751 tax list; SARAH; MARTHA.

2. CALEB NEWTON, probable son of Ebenezar (1) Newton, d. on 7 Feb 1761 as mentioned in "Diaries of Aaron Leaming." On 28 Feb 1761 John Newton was appointed admin. of his estate. Fellowbondsman: Christopher Foster of Cape May Co. Witnesses: Ebenezer Johnson and Mehetabel Godfrey. On 24 Feb 1761 an inventory was filed by Christopher Foster and Ebenezer Johnson.{NJCW 10:162}

3. ISAAC NEWTON, probable son of Ebenezar (1) Newton, is probably the father of ISAAC Newton, Jr., b. 1741, d. 30 Jan 1777 and perhaps of TRYPHOSE NEWTON, b. 1751, d. 15 April 1770.{Cold Spring Cemtery}

4. EBENEZER NEWTON of Cape May, probable son of Ebenezar (1) Newton, d. prior to 21 Jan 1754 when the estate was inventoried by Isaac Newton and Daniel Stillwell. On 26 Jan 1754 a bond was issued for Rachel Newton as admx.; Christopher Foster fellow bondsman, both of Cape May Co.{NJCW Cape May Wills:194E}

5. ISAAC NEWTON, probable son of Isaac (3) Newton, d. by 18 March 1780 when Tryphena Newton and Ebenezer Newton were appointed admins. of his estate.{NJCW 24:87}

6. NATHAN NEWTON of Downs, Cumberland Co., probable son of Ebenezar (1) Newton, d. by 17 June 1777 when Benjamin Newton was appointed admin. of his estate.{NJCW 24:87}

JOHN NEWTON

1. JOHN NEWTON m. Elizabeth Leaming by license issued 25 June 1761.{MLNJ} He d. leaving a will dated 20 Feb 1781, proved 3 July 1783. Mentioned were wife Elizabeth; son Caleb to whom was devised land to the east and south of a certain line which runs from a corner of land that William Simkins, dec., bought of Ephraim Bancraft and bounding by land late of Daniel Skellinger, dec., to the Delaware Bay. Son John was devised land to north and west of said line. Dau. Margaret Newton was bequeathed moveable estate. Execs. were wife Elizabeth and Jonathan Hand. The will was witnessed by Silvanus Church, Richard Shaw and Alice Newton. On 3 July 1773 an inventory was filed (£570 by Levi Eldredge and Matthew Whilldin.{NJCW 27:500}

Elizabeth Newton of Cape May Co. d. leaving a will dated 7 Nov 1789, proved 16 Nov 1789. Mentioned were sons John Newton to whom was devised land bought by his mother of Jacob Spicer. Dau. Margaret Ware to receive her apparel. The execs. were son John Newton and dau. Margret Ware. The will was witnessed by Ebenezer Newton, Elihu Hand and John Bridges. On 14 Nov 1789 an inventory was filed (294.9.9) by Ebenezer Newton and Robert Parsons.{NJCW 31:365}

John was father of the following children: CALEB; JOHN; MARGARET, m. (N) Ware.

2. CALEB NEWTON, son of John (1) and Elizabeth Newton, d. leaving a will dated 13 June 1785, proved 27 Jan 1789. Mentioned were mother, Elizabeth Newton; father John Newton; brother, John. Execs. were mother Elizabeth and brother John. The will was witnessed by Judith Hughes, James Hughes and Ebenezer Newton. An inventory was filed on 27 Jan 1789 by Richard Shaw and Ebenezer Newton.{NJCW 31:366}

3. JOHN NEWTON, probable son of John (1) Newton, m. Hannah Hand by license dated 22 Aug 1789.{MLNJ}

John Newton of Cape May Co. d. leaving a will dated 24 Jan 1792, proved 20 Aug 1794. Mentioned were wife Hannah to whom was left 1/3 of the estate. Should child that wife was carrying be a boy he was to have the home plantation with plantation Henry Stevens lived on, when of age. If child was a girl then the land to be divided with the other dau., Elizabeth. Elizabeth to have plantation in Cumberland Co. Extx. was wife Hannah. The will was witnessed by Eleazar Hand, David Hughes, Judith Hand and Rachel Hughes.{NJCW 35:106} On 31 July 1797 Hannah Hand, extx. being dec., Eleazar Hand was appointed admin. Fellowbondsmen: Joseph Hughes and Jacob Hughes of Cape May Co.{NJCW File:609E}

Based on the above it appears that Hannah m. 2nd Eleazar Hand and d. prior to 31 July 1797.

At court, August Term 1797, Eleazer Hand, guardian of Elizabeth and Maria Newton applied by petition for a guardian for Elizabeth Newton and Maria Newton infants under the age of 14 years and daus. of John and Hannah Newton, dec. ...{Orphans Courts minutes, loose papers}

Hannah Newton of Cape May Co. d. by 31 July 1797 when Eleazer Hand was appointed admin.{NJCW 37:164} On 13 June 1800 Eleazer Hand, admin, being dec., Joseph Hughes was appointed admin.{NJCW 39:93}

On 3 Aug 1797 Maria Newton, dau. of John and Hannah Newton, dec., being an infant under age 14. On petition of Eleazar Hand for a guardian to Elizabeth and Maria Newton; however Elizabeth d. before Mr. Hand gave bond.{NJCW 37:436, File:707E}

John was father of the following children: ELIZABETH; MARIA.

Unplaced

A marriage license was issued to Cornelius Kuyper, Jr., Philadelphia and HANNAH NEWTON, on 20 June 1769.{MLNJ}

A marriage license was issued to Jacob Richardson and PRISCILLA NEWTON on 31 Aug 1761.{MLNJ}

A marriage license was issued to John Hand, Jr. and SARAH NEWTON, on 5 May 1774.{MLNJ}

NORTON

1. NATHANIEL NORTON of Cape May Co., yeoman, d. leaving a will dated 27 Dec 1721, proved 6 Jan 1721/2. Mentioned were wife Mehitabel and children: Daniel, Nathaniel, Hannah and Mary. The execs. were father-in-law John Parsons and Christopher Church. The will was witnessed by Ebenezer Nuton, John Taylor, Abiah Mulford.{NJCW 2:207} The estate was inventoried on 30 Dec 1721 by John Taylor and

Joseph Ludlam.{NJCW}

Nathaniell Norton's ear mark was recorded on 2 Jan 1717/16; later his son Daniel Norton's.{First Official Rcds}

Nathaniel Norton was the father of DANIEL; NATHANIEL; HANNAH; MARY.

2. NATHANIEL NORTON, son of Nathaniel (1), probably m. 1st Elesha [Elishaba? or Lishabe, dau. of John Mathew?] Mathews by license dated 19 April 1731; m. 2nd by license dated 20 Nov 1733 Eunice Hand*{MLNJ}, dau. of George Hand[96] and m. 3rd Elizabeth, widow of Ezekiel Eldridge*.

Nathaniel Norton of Cape May Co., Gent. d. leaving a will dated 24 Oct 1749, proved 4 April 1750. Mentioned were wife Elizabeth, to whom he bequeathed 1/3 of the personal estate and all the interest arising from the money of the children of Ezekiel Eldredge, dec., "on account of my becoming executor of his estate by marrying his widow." Dau. Elishaba Norton, the house where testator lived. 2/3 of sale of house to be given to son George Norton and he to have an equal part of the personal estate with daus. Hannah and Mary Norton. Execs. were wife and brother Daniel Norton. The will was witnessed by Ellis Hughes, Nathan Eldredge and John Leek.{NJCW 6:363} On 24 April 1750 an inventory of the estate was filed which included a house and 5 acres of land, cattle, sheep and horses; appraised by John Shaw and John Eldredge.{NJCW}

Nathaniel was the father of ELISHABA; GEORGE; HANNAH, m. David Smith, Aug 11, 1752{Baptists}; MARY, m. Job Young by license dated 26 April 1757.{MLNJ}

3. DANIEL NORTON of Cape May Co., son of Nathaniel (1), d. leaving a will dated 26 March 1754, proved 21 May 1755. Mentioned were wife Phebe, Abigail (wife of Jonathan Laurance), David, Nathaniel and Hannah, children of David Ogden of Cumberland Co.; Hannah (wife of David Smith), Mary, dau. of brother Nathaniel Norton; sister Mary Norton; nephew George Norton, son of brother Nathaniel. Execs. were wife and George Norton. The will was witnessed by Richard Swain, Joseph Ludlam and Nathaniel Jenkins, Jr.{NJCW 8:175} On 28 May 1755 an inventory was filed including merchandize, two Negroes, a shallop and

96 See will of George Hand, Sr. who d. 1758. Mentioned was issue of dau. Eunice Norton, to wit: Hannah (wife of David Smith), George and Mary (wife of Job Young). {NJCW}

two canoes, made by John Shaw and Jeremiah Hand.{NJCW}

Daniel Norton m. Phebe Ludlam, dau. of Joseph Ludlam* who, following the death of Daniel, m. Henry Young* by license dated 28 Dec 1757.{MLNJ}

4. GEORGE NORTON, probable son of Nathaniel (2) Norton, m. Deborah Fox by license dated 26 March 1764.{MLNJ}

20 Feb 1777. Deborah Norton died of quinsye.{Leaming Diaries}

5. MARY NORTON, spinstress, probable dau. of Nathaniel (1) Norton, d. leaving a will dated 31 Aug 1758, proved 26 Sep 1766. Mentioned were brother Isaac Reevs and his wife Mercy; Mrs. Phebe Young; Lydia Smith, wife of Carman Smith; Nathaniel Ogden, son of David Ogden; Martha Smith, dau. of Carman Smith; Mary Hoskins, dau. of said Lydia Smith. Execs. were Carman Smith and Lewis Cresse. The will was witnessed by Jonadab Jenkins, Joseph Hildreth, James Hildreth and Nathaniel Jenkins. On 22 Sep 1766 an inventory was filed (£60.16.5 1/2 by Benjamin Stites and Joshua Hildreth.{NJCW 12:336}

OSBORNE

See "The Other Osborne Family," by Richard W. Cook and Donald Lines Jacobus, Vol. XXXVI (1961) 3-7, *Genealogical Magazine of New Jersey*. Published by Genealogical Publishing Co. as *Genealogies of New Jersey Families* (1995). Cited here as{Other Osborne Family}. Researchers should note the entry in Suffolk Co. Sessions:244 which reveals Bazeliell Osborne who d. leaving a will dated 11 Feb 1686/7 at the house of Joseph Osborne. He mentioned his brother Johnathan Osborne and his wife Elizabeth and and his brother Joseph Osborne.

1. WILLIAM OSBORN, d. 30 Sep 1661, m. Friswith (N). She m. 2nd in May 1663 at New Haven as 2nd wife of John Mulford of East Hampton, Long Island.{Other Osborn Family} They were parents of the following children: RECOMPENCE, b. in Dorchester; HANNAH, b. 24 Aug 1646 in Braintree, d. after 1693, m. as 3rd wife, 1663-4, Arthur Howell and m. 2nd 2 June 1685, as 2nd wife, Job Sayre, son of Thomas and Elizabeth Sayre, d. 6 April 1694; BEZALEEL, b. 8 May 1650, d. Feb 1686/7 at East Hampton, m. Elizabeth (N); JOSEPH, b. 6 April 1652 in Boston, d. 20 Feb 1740/1 in Easthampton; JONATHAN, b. 1656 in Boston, d. 1713/14 in Cape May, m. Mary (N).

2. JONATHAN OSBORNE, b. 1656 in Boston, d. 1713/14, son of William (1) Osborn, m. Mary (N). Jonathan was the father of the following children: ABIAH, b. 9 Sep 1692, about 10 o'clock; RUTH, b. 20 Feb 1698/7 at 6 at night; BEZALEELL, b. 21 Jan 1704/3 at 6 at night; NATHAN, b. 2 Feb 1706/5 at noon, m. Ann Smith; ANANIAS, b. 5 Feb 1708/7 at 10 at night{First Official Rcds}; ABIAH{see will below}; ELIZABETH{see will of Elizabeth Pratten}.{Other Osborn Family}

Jonathan Osborn recorded his ear mark on 20 Aug 1694. It later belonged to Bazaleel Osborne; in 1734 the marks were registered to Nathan Osborn.{First Public Rcds:272}

The name, Jonathan Osborne, appears in the land records of 20 April 1695 as owing quit rent on 110 acres.{Deeds A:447}

Jonathan Osborne of Cape May Co., cordwainer, d. leaving a will dated 28 Sep 1713, proved 11 May 1714. Mentioned were wife Mary and sons: Bezelial, Nathan, Ananias; daus.: Abiah and Ruth. The wife was extx. The will was witnessed by Henry Young, Charles Robinson and George Taylor.{NJCW}

Mary, widow of Jonathan Osborne, m. James Savage*.

3. BEZALIEL OSBORNE of Cape May Co., son of Jonathan (2) Osborne, d. leaving a will dated 28 Nov 1729, proved 28 June 1734. Mentioned were brother Ananias Osborne, exec. Movables to sister Ruth and to brother Nathan Osborne. The will was witnessed by Jeremiah Hand, John Robinson, Henry Stites, Jr. On 28 1734 Ananias Osborne the exec., desired that his brother Nathan Osborne administer the estate in his stead, "provided that he shall not at any time contrive to disanulle or make void the sd. will." Witnessed by Jacob Spicer.{NJCW 3:444} On 28 March 1734 an inventory was filed (£45.16.0) by Moses Cross and Henry Leonard.{NJCW 3:444}

4. NATHAN OSBORNE, son of Jonathan (2) Osborne, b. 2 Feb 1706, d. 1745/6, m. Ann Smith. She m. 2nd Walter Milton of Cape May by license dated 19 April 1746.

Nathan Osborne d. leaving a will dated 14 Dec 1745, proved 31 Jan 1745/6. Mentioned were wife Ann, eldest son Richard Osborne to whom was devised all lands except a part devised to wife, he to pay son Nathaniel £20 at age 21. Sons Nathan and John and dau. Ruth to receive residue of the personal estate. Execs. were wife Ann, son Richard and brother-in-law, Daniel Smith. Brother-in-law Jonathan Smith to take son Richard in his care and brother-in-law Daniel to take son Nathan until they arrive at age 20. The will was witnessed by George Jeares, Ann Osborne and Robert Wakely. On 25 April 1746 letters were granted to Ann Osborne and Daniel Smith.{NJCW 5:246} An inventory (£120.16.8) was filed on 1 March 1745/6 which included cattle, horses, sheep and swine; the estate was appraised by Jeremiah Hand and John Leonard.

Nathan was father of the following children: RUTH, m. Philip Godfrey* by license dated 19 Oct 1748; RICHARD, b. 173-, d. Sep-Nov 1765, m. Hannah Smith by license dated 3 May 1762 who m. 2nd David Townsend* by license dated 26 March 1767; NATHANIEL, b. probably 173-; JOHN, d. ca. 1740.{Other Osborn Family}

5. ANANIAS OSBORNE, son of Jonathan (2) and Mary Osborne, b. 5 Feb 1708, d. Jan-Feb 1772, m. Lydia Buck* by license dated 9 June 1738.{MLNJ} who d. prior to 1772.{Other Osborn Family}

Ananias d. leaving a will dated 22 Jan 1772, proved 8 Feb 1772. Mentioned was dau. Mary Garritson, wife of Daniel Garritson, Jr. to whom he left his entire estate, but she to pay dau. Phebe £90 and granddau. Hannah Stites, £30 when 18, grandson Stephen Smith, £30 when 21; grandson Annanias Smith, £30 when 21. The execs were dau. Mary Gerretson and her husband, Daniel Gerretson, Jr. and Thomas Leaming or if he refuses Jesse Hand. The will was witnessed by Jonathan Cresse, Elijah Smith and Aaron Leaming. On 7 Feb 1772 an inventory was filed by Philip Godfrey and Eli Eldredge (£104.14.4}

Ananias Osborne had the following daus.: A dau., d. prior to 1772, m. (N) Stites; MARY, m. Daniel Garretson*{Deeds A:169} by license issued 19 June 1761{MLNJ}; NAOMI, b. 174-, m. Joshua Smith by license date 16 Feb 1762; PHEBE, m. Jonathan Edwards by license dated 31 May 1766{MLNJ}.

6. MARY OSBORN, dau. of Ananias (5) Osborne, m. Daniel Garretson by license issued 19 June 1761. They had a son SAMUEL.{MLNJ, Deeds A:169}

PAGE

1. JOHN PAGE of Cape May Co., yeoman, d. leaving a will dated 27 May 1729, proved 4 July 1729. Mentioned were wife Elizabeth and children: Joseph, James, John, Hannah, Mary, Lydia, Elizabeth and Hulda. Land in Cape May Co., 125 acres bought of Jeremiah Basse, 10 acres bought of Caleb Carman, 10 acres bought of John Parson, 24 acres bought of Colonel Morris, 100 acres on s. side of Timothy's Branch, part of the tract bought of John Stilwell, 600 acres on the north side of said branch, bought

of several persons. Execs. were sons James and John with Richard Townsend of Cape May as overseer and adviser of James during the minority of John, whose guardian said Townsend is to be. The will was witnessed by Joseph Whilldin, Andrew Erickson, Rice Peters, Joseph Breintnall.{NJCW 3:88} The estate was inventoried on 3 July 1729 by George Hand and John Parsons.{NJCW}

John was father of the following children: JOSEPH; JAMES; JOHN; HANNAH; MARY; LYDIA; ELIZABETH; HULDA.

Second Generation

2. JOSEPH PAGE, possible son of John (1) Page, recorded his ear mark on 26 April 1726.{First Public Rcds:276}

Joseph Page of Fairfield, Cumberland Co. d. leaving a will dated 1 Feb 1766, proved 12 June 1767. Mentioned were children: Jonathan, David, Martha and Hannah; grandchildren: David, Ambrose and John Page when 21; son's widow, Mary Page.{Cumberland Wills}

Joseph was father of the following children: JONATHAN; DAVID; MARTHA; HANNAH.

3. JAMES PAGE of Cape May Co. d. prior to 22 May 1745 when Mary Page was appointed admx. Fellow bondsmen: Joseph Page and Elisha Hand of the afsd. county. Witnesses: John Eldredge and James Whilldin.{NJCW 5:121} An inventory was filed on 12 April 1745 and included cattle, horses, sheep and swine, appraised by John Eldredge and James Whilldin.{NJCW}

4. JOHN PAGE, possible son of John (1) Page.

On 5th day, 9th mo., 1750, a certificate was requested for John Page.{GEMM}

Third Generation

5. JONATHAN PAGE, of Cumberland Co., New Jersey, son of Joseph (2) Page (above), m. Bathier Nixon by license dated 15 Jan 1773.{MLNJ}

He d. leaving a will dated 22 March 1777, proved 24 June 1777. Mentioned were wife Bethiah and children: Jonathan, James, Hannah and Elizabeth; brother David Page.{Cumberland Wills}

Jonathan was father of the following children: JONATHAN; JAMES; HANNAH; ELIZABETH.

Unplaced

A marriage license was issued to Henry Hand and ELIZABETH PAGE, dated 26 Dec 1759.{MLNJ}

HANNAH PAGE m. Daniel Hand by license dated 10 April 1751{Baptists}

On 26 April 1726 Peter Paige recorded his ear mark; later JAMES PAIGE's on 18 May 1736.{First Public Rcds:277}

A marriage license was issued to Elias Hand and MARY PAGE, 3 May 1762.{MLNJ}

A marriage license was issued to THOMAS PAIGE and Lydia Church, 7 Aug 1766.{MLNJ}

A marriage license was issued to THOMAS PAIGE and Rachel Parsons, 12 April 1773.{MLNJ}

Thomas Paige [Page] of Cape May Co. d. by 1 Feb 1777 when Rachel Paige was appointed admx. of his estate. Fellowbondsman: Robert Parsons of Cape May Co. On 1 Feb 1777 an inventory was filed (£299.10.8) by Daniel Stillwell and Downes Edmunds.{NJCW 22:41}

PARSONS/PERSONS

Some of the following information on the early Parsons came from "The Account Book of John Parsons, With Notes," *The Cape May County Magazine of History and Genealogy*, p. 166. June 1942. By Norman Harvey Vanaman.

According to Lewis Townsend Stevens in *The History of Cape May County* ... Dr. Beesley gave the following information (1857): John Parsons, 1st, was an Englishman. He came to America and settled at East Hampton, Long Island. He married Mrs. Elizabeth Garlick. Her maiden name was Hardie. As Mrs. Garlick, she was charged in 1657 with witchcraft, was tried at East Hampton on Long Island, and acquitted. John and Elizabeth Persons had a dau. named Lydia, born at East Hampton, L.I., April 10, 1680. In July, 1691, they all came to Cape May County, and Mr. Persons bought a plantation about 4 miles below the present Court House, and settled on it in September, 1691. He died and was buried there in January 1695.

John Persons, 2d, of Lower Cold Spring settlement, an Englishman, and probably a nephew of John Persons, 1st, came also from Long Island to Cape May about 1691. The earliest notice had of him is in reference to ear marks that he had publicly recorded... in 1693. He wrote a will dated 4 Dec 1732 leaving his wife Elizabeth her share and dividing the real estate between his two sons, John Parsons, 3d, and Robert Parsons, 1st ...

1. JOHN PARSONS, weaver, of Easthampton was b. at Winsor in New England ca. 1650, m. 21 May 1679, Elizabeth, widow of Joshua Garlick*. They moved to Cape May 13 July 1691, a few miles below Cape May Court House. They were parents of LYDIA, b. 10 April 1680, d. 2 Oct 1762, m. 1st Captain William Shaw* and m. 2nd Aaron Leaming*. {Baptist Burials} John Parsons d. Jan 1693. Widow Elizabeth m. 3rd John Fish* who d. about 6 months later. Elizabeth d. 1 May 1696.

On 10 May 1692 John (1) Parsons complained against William Stillwell for nonpayment of £1.11.0. Judgment was awarded for Parsons.{First Public Rcds:269}

An inventory of the estate of John Parson was taken on 13 March 1693/4 and presented by his widow Elizabeth.{First Public Rcds:273}

2. JOHN PARSON, Sr. of Cape May Co., possibly related to John (1), d. leaving a will dated 4 Dec 1732, proved 22 June 1732. Mentioned were wife, 1/3 of the moveable estate, rest to children. Real estate to sons John and Robert, excepting the place John bought. "So far my land on Long Island, I give it to my son John, and if he can get it in order he is to give his brother Robert his part." Execs. were wife and son John. On 22 June 1732/3 were made deposition of witnesses, William Mulford and Ebenezer Johnson.{NJCW Cape May Wills:61E} An inventory was filed on 25 Dec 1732 which included cooper's tools, etc., cattle and horses. Appraised by Richard Stites and Thomas Ross. On 3 March 1732/3 Elizabeth Parsons was appointed admx. Fellow bondsman: Joshua Stites. Witnesses: George Stites, Jacob Spicer, Jr. and Jacob Spicer.{NJCW}

It seems likely that John m. Elizabeth who was admx. of his estate and who d. leaving a will dated 16 Oct 1742, proved 7 March

1742/3.[97] Mentioned were daus.: Elizabeth Hand, Charity Mulford [probably wife of William Mulford], Abigail Stites [probably wife of Joshua Stites]; granddau. Mary Edwards. Son Jonathan Forman and son Robert Parsons to have 10 shillings each. Son Joshua Stites, exec. The will was witnessed by John Stites, Elijah Hughes and Cornelius Schillinks, Jr.{NJCW 5:9} On 30 May 1743 an inventory was filed by Elijah Hughes and Robert Parsons.{NJCW}

John Parsons was father of the following children: SARAH, b. 14 Nov 1702; JOHN, b. 7 March 1705/6; ABIGALL, b. 3 Feb 1708/9, probably m. Joshua Stites*; ROBERT, b. 9 June 1710.{First Official Rcds} [The transcriber indicated uncertainty regarding the last name of all but the first child.] Note in the will of John [below] he was brother to: ROBERT; LYDIA; BETHIA; SARAH; JACOB.

3. JOHN PARSONS, son of John (2), of Cape May Co., yeoman, d. leaving a will dated 4th day, --- month, 1732, proved 5 Jan 1732/3. Mentioned were wife Bethia. Brother Robert Parsons was devised the real estate provided he pay to dau. Sarah Parsons, £150 upon her marriage or when she is of age. In case brother Robert died without issue, all shall return to dau. If that money upon Long Island is recovered or received according to the will of my father, my brother Robert should have his equal part. William Mathews to have a cow and calf. Exec. was Ezekiel Eldredge. The will was witnessed by Huson Huse, John Shaw and Mary Crowell.{NJCW 3:237} An inventory was filed on 25 Dec 1732 which included shoemaker's tools; appraised by Richard Stites and Thomas Ross. An account was submitted on 19 March 1732/3 which showed oxen given to sister Lydia, 2 cows to sister Bethia Parsons, cow and calf to sister Sarah Parsons, and same to brother Jacob Parsons. Letter signed Ezekeill Eldredge and dated at Cape May 23 April 1733.{NJCW}

John m. Bethia Eldredge*.

John was the father of SARAH.

4. ROBERT PARSONS, yeoman, probable son of John (2) Parsons, d. leaving a will dated 15 Aug 1782, proved 15 April 1786. Mentioned were wife Sarah; son John to whom was devised land south of a line that was run; son Robert to have land north of said line; daus.: Elizabeth Yates,

97 If this assumption is true, one could explain daus. Elizabeth Hand and Charity Mulford and son Jonathan Forman as children of an earlier marriage.

Mary Edmunds[98] and Rachel Crowell, to whom was left personal estate after wife's death. Exec. was wife Sarah. The will was witnessed by Ellis Hughes, Levi Eldredge and Eli Taylor. On 20 April 1785 an inventory was filed (£159.4.11) by John Parsons and Robert Parsons.{NJCW 28:185}

Robert was father of the following children: JOHN; ROBERT; ELIZABETH, m. (N) Yates; MARY, m. (N) Edmunds; RACHEL, m. (N) Crowell.

Unplaced

A marriage license was issued to JOHN PARSONS and Lovisa Edmunds, dated 30 May 1775.{MLNJ}

John Parsons of Cape May Co. d. leaving a will dated 12 April 1790, proved 16 April 1791. Mentioned were wife Lovice and son Jeremiah Parsons and daus.: Sarah, Judith and Abigail.{NJCW 32:292} An inventory was filed (£182.8.2) by Ebenezer Newton and Robert Edmunds on 12 April 1791.{NJCW File 560E}

A marriage license was issued to Thomas Paige and RACHEL PARSONS, 12 April 1773.{MLNJ}

PIERSON

See "The Pierson Family," *The Cape May County Magazine of History and Genealogy*, p. 6. June 1955. By Margaret Irwin McVickar. See this article which covers the history of this family from 1635 to 1800s. See also H. Stanley Craig, *Cumberland County New Jersey Genealogical Data* (1930s), reprinted by Gloucester County Historical Society in 1981. Also see "The Pierson Family," *The Cape May County Magazine of History and Genealogy*, p. 423. June 1963. By Roy Hand.

Following is a summary based on the McVickar's article mentioned above. Only the direct line to Cape May County descendants is repeated here. See her article for other branches of the family.

---

98 Perhaps this is the Mary <u>Edwards</u> [and not Edmunds] mentioned in the will of Elizabeth Parsons.

According to Ms. McVickar,

1. HENRY PIERSON migrated from England to Boston, MA in 1635 and then settled in Southampton, Long Island, NY, ca. 1640.
2. JOSEPH PIERSON, son of Henry (1) and Mary Pierson, m. Amy Barnes, dau. of Charles and Mary Hand Barnes. She d. 3 Oct 1692 and Joseph m. 2nd Joannah, widow of Thomas Cooper. They had six children of whom was HENRY, the oldest son, b. 17 April 1676, d. at Cohansey, NJ, in 1747.

3. HENRY PIERSON, son of Joseph (2) and Mary Pierson, b. Southampton 17 April 1676, m. Abigail Ludlam, dau. of Henry and Rachel Ludlam. Of the eight children of Henry and Abigail was HENRY, b. 1 Feb 1704.

4. HENRY PIERSON, son of Henry (3) and Abigail Pierson, b. 1 Feb 1704, d. 1776, m. Hannah (N) by whom he had Stephen, b. 21 Feb 1746.

5. STEPHEN PIERSON, son of Henry (4) and Hannah Pierson, m. Mary (N) and moved from Cumberland Co. to Cape May Co. Stephen and Mary were the parents of the following children: RUTH, b. 13 April 1765, d. 10 Dec 1776; LUDLAM, b. 13 June 1767, d. 1 Feb 1781; HENRY, b. 1 Jan 1770; WILLIAM, b. 16 April 1773; MARY, b. 14 Feb 1775, m. Jeremiah Swain*, son of Silas and Judith Swain; STEPHEN, b. 2 Sep 1777, d. 30 May 1851{Cold Spring Cemetery}; THOMAS, b. 21 Nov 1779; NANCY, b. 7 Sep 1782, d. 4 May 1783; JOHN BOWEN, b. 25 Feb 1784, d. 4 Sep 1784; ANN, b. 30 Aug 1786, m. Zaccheus Ray.{Old book of Stephen Pierson as transcribed in Pierson Article}

6. WILLIAM PIERSON, son of Stephen (5) and Mary Pierson, b. 16 April 1773, m. Prudence Stites, by license dated 12 Nov 1799.{Co. Clerk Rcds - Book A}

JONATHAN PINE

JONATHAN PINE of Cape May d. leaving a will dated 14 Dec 1694 and recorded 2 March 1694/5. Mentioned were son Jonathan, wife Abegall and her two children and dau. Abigall. Execs. were Joseph Holden and brother-in-law Jonathan Forman.{First Official Rcds}

Abigail, widow of Jonathan Pine, m. Wm. Sharwood (as of 1700).{Deeds B:53}

PRATTEN (PRATT)

1. JONATHAN PRATT d. prior to 11 Feb 1739/40 when an inventory of the estate was made by Barnabas Crowell and Elisha Hand. On 23 Feb 1739/40 Benjamin Laughton of Cape May Co. was appointed admin. John Eldredge of same county, fellow bondsman.{NJCW Cape May Wills:99E}

2. (N) PRATTEN m. Elizabeth Osborne, sister of Lydia and Annios Osborne. They were parents of THOMAS; HULDA, m. (N) Hand. Apparently (N) Pratten was father of JAMES by an earlier marriage.

Elizabeth Praten of Cape May d. leaving a will dated 9 Oct 1757, proved 7 Jan 1758. Mentioned were son-in-law (step-son?) James Praten; son Thomas Praten; dau. Hulda Hand; sister Lydia Osborn; brother Annios Osborne. Execs. were Annias Osborne and James Pretten. The will was witnessed by John Leonard and William Smith. In 1758 the inventory of the estate was filed by William Smith and John Leonard.{NJCW Cape May Wills:191E}

3. JAMES PRATTEN, son of (N) (2) Pratten, d. leaving a will dated 20 Nov 1760, proved 23 Dec 1760. Mentioned were brother Thomas Pratton, sole heir, but if he died under age, to go to cousin, Judith, dau. of Abner Corsen. Exec. was Daniel Hand of the Middle Precinct. The will was witnessed by Jeremiah Hand, Jonathan Cresse and Jesse Hand.{NJCW 11:71} In 1760 an inventory of the estate was filed by Jonathan Cresse and Jesse Hand.{NJCW}

4. THOMAS PRATTEN, probable son of (N) (2) Pratten, m. Hannah Simpkins 28 Aug 1766.{Baptists} A marriage license was issued on 27 Aug 1766.{MLNJ}

Thomas Pratten m. Hannah Cresse by license dated 21 June 1769.{MLNJ}

Thomas Pratten d. by 22 June 1792 when Philip Hand was appointed admin. On 27 June 1792 an inventory was filed (£107.0.6) by Philip Cresse and Jeremiah Richardson.{NJCW File 578E}

RANEY

1. JAMES RENEY m. Presila Eldridge*, dau. of Samuel and Mercy Eldredge, by license on 12 April 1751.{MLNJ} They were the parents of the following children: JAMES; LETTY[99], m. Thomas Ewing and had a dau. Lydia; ENOCH[100]. Priscilla Raney later m. John B. McCormick by license issued 11 Aug 1775.{MLNJ}

2. JAMES RANEY, of Cape May Co., son of James (1) and Priscilla Bertholama Raney, d. leaving a will dated 8 Dec 1778, proved 23 Aug 1780. Mentioned were mother Priscilla Bertholama McCormick, to whom he left his house and lot which descended to him from his father, lying in the Lower Precinct and joins lands of his uncle, Jeremiah Eldredge, and after her death to his brother, Enoch. Sister Lettice Seany, his mare and silver buckles. Exec. was uncle, Jeremiah Eldridge. The will was witnessed by Joseph Bloomfield, Jonathan Bowen, Jr., James Ewing, Richard Townsend and Jonathan Jenkins. On 23 Aug 1780 an inventory was made by Thomas Ewing and Thomas Buck (£3,431.11.8).{NJCW 24:78}

REAVES/REEVES

Of no known relationships are the following entries:

JOHN REEVE, cooper, bought 200 acres in Cape May on the sound side for the sum of £20 and "under the yearly rent of two fat capons or henes payable," on 23 April 1695.{First Official Recds}

JOHN REAVES of Cape May, yeoman, d. leaving a will dated 29 Dec 1714, proved 22 April 1715. Mentioned were wife Sarah, extx. and dau. Sary. Legacy to John Ingrum when his time is up. The will was witnessed by Daniel Wells, Henry Leonard (56 years old) and Hannah Lenord. The estate was inventoried on 10 Jan 1714/5 by Daniel Wells and John Taylor. On 7 Aug 1731 final account was rendered by John Ingram and his wife Sarah, the extx.{NJCW Cape May Wills}

---

99 Mentioned in the will of her uncle Jeremiah Eldredge.

100 Mentioned in the will of Jeremiah Leaming (written 1 Dec 1769, proved 25 Jan 1774) as Enoch Raney, son of Priscilla Raney, widow.

John was the father of SARY [SARAH].[101]

JOHN REEVE of Philadelphia, mariner, d. leaving a will dated 12th month (Feb), 23rd day, 1736/7, proved 5 Sep 1743. Mentioned were children: Peter, Hannah, Mary and Rachel. Execs. were friend Israel Pemberton and brother Matthias Aspden, both of Philadelphia, merchants. Witnesses: Wm. Hill, Evan Bevan, Abr. Mitchel. {NJCW Cape May Wills, 5:2}

John was father of the following children: PETER; HANNAH; MARY; RACHEL.

A marriage license was issued to ABRAHAM REEVES and Ruth Crowell on 22 Oct 1765. {MLNJ}

A marriage license was issued to ABRAHAM REEVES and Margaret Burch, on 25 Nov 1769. {MLNJ}

RICHARDSON

In the 1704 inventory of the estate of John Stubbs were listed as debtors, John Richardson, Jr. and John Richardson, Sr.

1. JOHN RICHARDSON of Cape May Co., yeoman, d. leaving a will dated 10 Dec 1727, proved 2 Oct 1728. Mentioned were children: Rachel, Benjamin, John (absent from home), Jacob, Samuel (exec.), dau.-in-law (step-dau.?) Mercy Stratton. The will was witnessed by Lydia Leaming, Hannah Jenkins, Gabriel Le Blond. {NJCW 2:559} On 31 Sep 1728 the estate was inventoried by Joseph Holding. {NJCW}

The name John Richardson appears on the land records of Cape May Co. in 19 April 1695, owing quit rent on 124 acres. {Deeds A:447}

John was the father of the following children: RACHEL; BENJAMIN; JOHN; JACOB; SAMUEL.

2. BENJAMIN RICHARDSON, son of John (1) Richardson, of Cape May, yeoman, m. Elizabeth Richardson by license dated 27 Sep 1733. {MLNJ}

He d. leaving a will dated 9 Feb 1738, proved 26 Nov 1739. Mentioned were wife Elizabeth to whom was devised all lands until son

---

101 This is probably the Sarah Reaves who m. Michael Iszard*.

Samuel was age 21; she to bring up and maintain the two children unless she remarried in which case brother Jacob Richardson to take lands and have use of other estate. Son Samuel to have all lands I live on and to pay £20 to his brother John. Wife to maintain the children until each is 14 years old. Execs. were wife Elizabeth and brother Jacob Richardson. The will was witnessed by Ephraim Edwards, James Edwards and An. Leaming, Jr.{NJCW 4:222} On 3 Nov 1739 an inventory was filed which included horse, cattle, sheep, swine and fowls; appraised by Nathl. Jenkins and Ephraim Edwards.{NJCW}

Benjamin was father of the following children: SAMUEL; JOHN, m. Elizabeth Craford*, probable dau. of Benjamin (3) Crawford (Crafford), by license dated 17 Dec 1756.{MLNJ}

3. SAMUEL RICHARDSON of Cape May Co., son of John (1) Richardson, m. Elizabeth Carman by license dated 4 June 1731.{MLNJ}

Samuel d. leaving a will dated 3 Dec 1732, proved 20 March 1732/3. Mentioned were brother Benjamin Richardson to whom was devised all land unless his wife be with child and it comes to age, then said land to belong to the child. Mentioned were brother John Richardson, brother Jacob Richardson, when 21. Wife Elizabeth to have all chattels except best hat which brother Jacob was to have. Execs. were wife Elizabeth and brother Benjamin. The will was witnessed by John Jones, James Flood and Ephraim Edwards. On 17 Jan 1732/3 an inventory was filed by Nathaniel Rusco and Ephraim Edwards.{NJCW Cape May Wills:78E}

4. JACOB RICHARDSON of Cape May Co., son of John (1) Richardson, m. Temperance Scull, 1740.{MLNJ}

Jacob died leaving a will dated 6 May 1777, proved 4 June 1777. Mentioned were son: Jeremiah and Jacob, to whom was left the plantation. Dau. Temperance Crowell, wife of Josiah, 20 shillings. Granddau. Ruth Crowell, £20. Dau. Violeta Richardson, curtains that were her mother's. Daus. Violeta Richardson, Lovisa Richardson, Rachel Richardson and Judith Richardson, rest of personal estate. Execs. were sons Jeremiah and Jacob. The will was witnessed by David Hildreth, Jonathan Leaming, Jane Hildreth and Benjamin Richardson. On 9 June 1777 the inventory was filed (£476.18.8) by Jonathan Leaming and Josiah Crowell.{NJCW 21:236}

Jacob was father of the following children: TEMPERANCE, m. Josiah Crowell* by whom she had a dau. Ruth; VIOLETA; LOVISA; RACHEL; JUDITH; JEREMIAH, probably m. Susannah Church, by license dated 8 Sep 1764{MLNJ}; JACOB.

Unplaced

A marriage license was issued to JACOB RICHARDSON and Priscilla Newton, 31 Aug 1761.{MLNJ}

A marriage license was issued to JACOB RICHARDSON and Mary Marsh, 26 July 1771.{MLNJ}

A marriage license was issued to Robert Townsend and REBECCA RICHARDSON, 1 June 1767.{MLNJ}

ROBINSON

See "The Mills of East and West Creek," Part II, *The Cape May County Magazine of History and Genealogy*. p. 273. June 1961. By Dr. Roy Hand. The Robinsons (p. 276).

According to Dr. Hand,

1. WILLIAM ROBINSON, of Upper Precinct Cape May County, m. Phoebe Young by license dated 20 June 1738. He m. 2nd Rhoda Corson by license dated 13 Aug 1754, dau. of John and Mary (Goff) Corson, and they moved to West Creek.

William Robinson of Cumberland Co. d. leaving a will dated 11 Jan 1777, proved 15 April 1777. Mentioned were oldest son William to whom he devised the home plantation, he to bring up youngest son Enos until age 16. Dau. Rhody would be allowed to live in the room in the west end of the house while single and to have the 3 cows she claims. Children, William, Rhody and Enos to have the rest of the estate. The execs. were James Hollinshead and son William. The will was witnessed by Joseph Corson, Levi Crandol and William Aulls. On 2 April 1772 an inventory was filed (£438.6.11) by William Aulls and Nathan Youngs.{NJCW 18:204}

William was father of the following children: ENOS, b. 1761 or later; RHODY; WILLIAM.

2. WILLIAM ROBINSON, Jr. (b. 1750, d. 4 June 1803), son of William (1) and Phoebe Robinson, m. by license dated 20 June 1772{MLNJ}, Mary Youngs (b. 1755, d. 16 Nov 1822). Both bur. West Creek Baptist Cemetery.

3. DANIEL ROBINSON (b. 1777, d. 19 Feb 1856), son of William (2) and Mary Robinson, m. Judith Steelman (b. 31 Jan 1777, d. 26 Aug 1862), dau. of James and Jemimah Steelman.

Unplaced

CHARLES ROBINSON of Cape May Co., cordwainer, d. prior to 16 April 1719 when his estate was inventoried by William Smith and Nath'll Jenkins. On 21 1719 a bond was issued to Elizabeth Robinson, widow of Charles, as admin. of Wm. Smith of Cape May and Charles Angelo of Salem Co., fellowbondsmen. On 26 July 1724 an account of the estate was made by the admx., now called Elizabeth Crowell.

WILLIAM ROBINSON of Cape May Co., yeoman, d. prior to 3 April 1733 when Dinah Robinson was appointed admx. Fellow bondsman, John Smith, of same county. Witnesses: Daniel Norton, Jacob Spicer and Jacob Spicer, Jr. An inventory was filed on 10 Jan 1732/3 by Daniel Norton and John Smith.{NJCW Cape May Wills:79E}

ROSS

1. THOMAS ROSS, an unworthy member of the Church of Scotland, d. leaving a will dated 8 Aug 1751, proved 1 Oct 1751. Mentioned were wife Masey (signed as Marcy) and children: William, Christopher, Hannah, Lydia and Thomas. Execs. were wife and son Thomas. The will was witnessed by William Bowness, James Hedges and Peter Toullard.{NJCW Cape May Wills:155E} On 4 Oct 1751 an inventory was filed by Elisha Hand and Elijah Hughes.{NJCW}

Thomas was father of the following children: WILLIAM; CHRISTOPHER; HANNAH; LYDIA; THOMAS.

2. WILLIAM ROSS, probable son of Thomas (1) Ross, d. in 1761 as mentioned in "Diaries of Aaron Leaming." On 25 June 1761 Margaret Ross was appointed admx. of his estate. Fellowbondsman: James Hedges of Cape May Co. Witnesses: John Eldredge and Christopher Foster. On 25 May 1761 an inventory was filed (£51.1.7) by James Hedges and John Eldredge.{NJCW 11:71}

3. THOMAS ROSS, probable son of Thomas (1) Ross, d. prior to 5 March 1755 when an inventory was made by John Eldredge and Samuel Crowell.

A bond was issued by 6 March 1755 for William Ross as admin; Samuel Crowell fellow bondsman, both of said county.{NJCW 8:158}

Unplaced

RACHEL ROSS, b. 20 June 1771, d. 16 March 1824.{Cold Spring Cemetery}

SAVAGE

See "Family Records" in *Genealogical Magazine of New Jersey*, Vol. 65 (1990) and published by Genealogical Publishing Co. in *Genealogies of New Jersey Families* (1996). Cited in this section as{Family Records}.

1. JAMES SAVAGE of Cape May Co. d. leaving a will dated 29 Dec 1729, proved 3 Jan 1729/30. Mentioned were sons: John and Joseph, both under age, the first under the care of Benjamin Hand, the other of Henry Stites, and both made execs. Legacy to Ruth, wife of Benjamin Hand. The will was witnessed by Richard Downes, Will'm. Evans and John Bond.{NJCW 3:65} The estate was inventoried on 1 Jan 1729/30 by Richard Downes and Nathaniel Foster. On 1 Dec 1730 a letter from Sam'l. Bustill of Burlington to the execs. concerning the payment of a legacy to children of [Jonathan] Osborn, whose exec. said Savage apparently had been. On 5 July 1732 an account of the estate was made by the execs.{NJCW}

James Savage m. Mary Osborne*, widow of Jonathan Osborne.

James was father of the following children: JOHN; JOSEPH, b. 16 April 1721, d. June 1763{Family Records}.

2. JOSEPH SAVAGE, son of James (1) Savage, m. 18 Sep 1742, Martha Daniels (b. 24 Aug 1721).{Family Records}

Joseph d. leaving a will dated 6 June 1783, proved 17 July 1783. Mentioned were wife Martha to whom was left 1/3 of the plantation, bought of Nathan Hand. Land was devised to grandchildren: Savage, Martha, Sarah, Anna and Sophia Stillwell. Execs. were wife Martha and son-in-law Enoch Stillwill. The will was witnessed by Jonathan Leaming, Samuel Orom, Anne Orom and Rachel Taylor.{NJCW 38:70}

Joseph and Martha were parents of the following children: JOSEPH, b. 6 Oct 1745, d. 11 Jan 1749; SARAH, b. 9 May 1750, d. 19 March 1782, m. 30 Aug 1768, Enoch Stillwell*; JAMES, b. 1 Jan 1755, d. 7 Nov 1773; SILVIA, b. 23 Aug 1758, d. 22 Oct 1760.{Family Records}

SAYRE

The early portion of this entry (down to Jonathan (6)) is based entirely on H. Stanley Craig, *Cumberland County New Jersey Genealogical Data* (1930s), reprinted by Gloucester County Historical Society (1981). Only the direct line to Jonathan is reprinted here. For the descendancy of other lines see this source.

Also see *History And Genealogy Of Fenwick's Colony.* By Thomas Shrouds. Originally published Bridgetown, NJ, 1876. Reprinted by Genealogical Publishing Co., Inc., Baltimore, 1976. See p 227.

According to Mr. Craig,

1. THOMAS SAYRE, son of Francis and Elizabeth (Atkins) Sayre, was born in Leighton Buzzard, England, in 1579. He was the father of the following children: FRANCIS; DAVIS; JOSEPH; JOB; DAMARIS; MARY; HANNAH; DAUGHTER, m. Edmund Howell.[102]

2. FRANCIS SAYRE, son of Thomas (1) Sayre, probably b. in Bedfordshire, England, m. Sarah Wheeler. He lived at Northsea, Southampton, Long Island in 1665 where he d. 20 Jan 1698. Francis and Sarah were the parents of the following children: JOSHUA; JOHN; THOMAS; FRANCIS; JONATHAN; DAMARIS; CALEB; ICHABOD.

3. JOHN SAYRE, son of Francis (2) and Sarah, was b. in Southampton, Long Island in 1665. He m. Sarah (N) and had the following children: JOHN; SARAH; THOMAS; DENNIS; ELIZABETH; JONATHAN, b. 18 Jan 1705; SARAH; HANNAH, d. in infancy; HANNAH, 2d.

4. THOMAS SAYRE, son of John (3) and Sarah, was b. in Southampton in 1696. He m. Rachel Abbott and moved to Cohansey. They had the following children: THOMAS; JAMES; LEONARD;

---

102 Note the entry in Suffolk Co., NY, Sessions:21 to Thomas Sayre of Southampton, Long Island, who d. leaving a will dated 16 Sep 1669, proved 1 March 1670. Mentioned were children: Francis, Daniel, Joseph, Damaris Atwater, Mary Price, Hannah Sayre and Jobe.

JOB[103], m. (N) Warner; RUTH, m. 9th day, 6th mo., 1763, James Daniell of Alloways Creek{Salem Monthly Meeting}.

5. JONATHAN SAYRE of Cape May Co., cordwainer, son of John (3) and Sarah, b. 18 Jan 1705, m. Sarah Percy. He moved to Cohansey and after 1762 moved to Cape May Co. He d. in 1779, leaving a will dated 4 Jan 1777, proved 12 July 1779. Mentioned were wife Sarah, to whom he left wood land and cleared land; son Christopher, 50 acres of woodland; son Jonathan, 50 acres of woodland; son John, 1/2 of home plantation and 1/2 the Sedge Island and 1/2 cedar swamp; son Aaron, 1/2 the home plantation and 1/2 the Sedge Island and 1/2 the cedar swamp. Dau. Sarah Sayre, £10. son Jeremiah, £10. Execs. were wife Sarah and son Jeremiah. The will was witnessed by John Hand and Reuben Kimsey. On 13 July 1779 the inventory (£853.14.8) was filed by Eli Townsend and Jacob Cresse.{NJCW 21:253}

According to a deed, Jonathan Sayres (will 1777) had children Jeremiah, John, Aaron, Christopher, Jonathan and Sarah who m. (N) Daniels. (1799){Deeds B:237}

Jonathan was the father of the following children: CHRISTOPHER, m. 16 July 1771, Catharine MacDouglas{The Sayre Family -Banta}; JONATHAN; JOHN, m. Catharine Teel in 20 Aug 1792{The Sayre Family - Banta}; AARON; SARAH, m. (N) Daniels[104]; JEREMIAH, b. 1740, d. 1811; CATHARINE[105], m. (N) McDouglas(?).

6. THOMAS SAYRE, son of Thomas (4) and Rachel of Cohansey, resided in Lower Aloways Creek Township, Salem Co., NJ. Thomas was the father of the following children: ABBOTT, m. Elizabeth Bacon; REUBEN, m. Hannah Stretch; HANNAH, m. Wade Barker, by license dated 18 Aug 1768{MLNJ}; DAVID, m. Prudence Keasby by license dated 18 Oct 1774{MLNJ}; REUEL, m. Rachel Ludlam, 28 Jan 1779 and Hope Sheppard, dau. of Ephraim and Sarah, 4 Jan

---

103 The name was given as Lot vice Job in *History And Genealogy Of Fenwick's Colony*.

104 Perhaps Jeremiah Daniels. See Book of Mortgages A:172, dated 1788.

105 Craig lists her as a dau. of Jonathan, no source given.

1794{The Sayre Family - Banta}; JOSEPH, moved to Western PA; DENNIS, m. Esther Donelson; RACHEL, m. 1st (N) Sheppard, m. 2nd (N) Lord, moved to a western state; THOMAS, b. 1763, m. Rebecca Moore, 1798; DORCAS; WILLIAM, m. Mary Evans, 1796.

7. JONATHAN SAYER, son of Jonathan (5) Sayre, is shown in the book of Mortgages.{Book of Mortgages A: 101, dated 1775}

8. JOHN SAYRE, son of Jonathan (5) Sayre, was shown in Leaming's diaries. "1777. The Bloody Flux prevailed. John Sayre about 19th [Sep] died of it."{Leaming diaries}

9. JEREMIAH SAYRE, son of Jonathan (5) Sayre, m. Mary Smith by license dated 14 June 1798.{Co. Clerk Rcds - Book A}

10. AARON SAYRE, son of Jonathan (5) Sayre, d. by 1 Aug 1797, when Jeremiah Sayres was appointed admin.{NJCW 37:164, File:691E}

SCHELLENGER (SCILLINGER, SCHILLINX, SCHILLINKS)

The name Skellenger is derived from the Dutch Schillinx or Schillings.

1. CORNELIUS STELINGER (SCHELLENGER) appears in the land records on 22 April 1695 as owning 134 acres.{Deeds A:449}

On Cornelius Schilinx of Cape May Co., yeoman, d. leaving a will dated 4 March 1742, proved 30 May 1743. Mentioned were wife Abigail, extx. and sons: Cornelius, Abraham and William. William to have all lands within the county adjoining land of son Cornelius on one side and lands of Barnabas Crowell, Joshua Stites and John Bradner on the other side and the privilege of having grain ground toll free at the grist mill on Cold Spring Creek. The will was witnessed by Aaron Leaming, William Barlow and Elisha Crowell.{NJCW Cape May Wills:112E} On 3 March 1743 an inventory was filed by Ebenr. Swaine and Elijah Hughes.{NJCW}

Cornelius Schilinx m. Abigail (N) and had the following sons: CORNELIUS; ABRAHAM; WILLIAM.

2. CORNELIUS SCILLINGER, Jr., probable son of Cornelius (1) Schilinx, m. Mary Stites*, dau. of Henry Stites, on 10 June 1715, before

John Townsend, Justice, 10 June 1715. Witnesses: Cornelius Schillinger, Lead daey [Lydia] Schillinger, Henry Stites, Elizabeth Taylor, Henry Stites, Jr., Richard Stites, John Taylor, Daniell Wiggins, John Williss, Richard Forteskue, Isack Brooks, Jr., Benjamin Hand, Jr., Edmund Shaw, Abiah ... Hoskins. Entered 13 June 1715.{First Official Rcds}

Cornelius Schillinks of Cape May Co., yeoman, d. leaving a will dated 14 April 1746, proved 21 May 1746. Mentioned were wife Mary, 1/2 of moveable estate, 1/4 of mill and privilege of 1/2 of the home plantation (it being the half which was given to son Henry Schillinks), during widowhood. Sons: Cornelius, 1/2 of plantation where testator lived, it being the west side joining William Schelink's and 1/4 of the mill; son Henry the eastern most half joining Elijah Hughes; son Enos the 1/2 of plantation at Dividing Creek, Salem Co., it being the western most half joining Nicholas Crosen; son Daniel the other half, it being the eastern most joining Charles Fox. Daus.: Mary Stillwell, Lydia and Hannah Schillinks, 1/2 of moveable estate. Execs. were wife Mary and son Cornelius. The will was witnessed by William Schillinks, Abraham Schillinks, Mary Taylor and Elijah Hughes.{NJCW Cape May Wills:127E} On 29 May 1746 an inventory was filed by Elisha Hand and Elisha Crowell.{NJCW}

Cornelius Schillinks m. Mary (N) and had the following children: CORNELIUS; HENRY; ENOS; DANIEL; MARY, m. (N) Stillwell; LYDIA, b. 1726, d. 14 Jan 1748.{Cold Spring Cemetery}; HANNAH.

3. ABRAHAM SCHELLINKS of Cape May Co., probable son of Cornelius (1), d. prior to 8 Oct 1759 when an inventory of the estate was filed by William Readey and George Taylor. On 9 Feb 1760 a bond was issued for Jane Schellinks admx.; George Taylor fellow bondsman, both of Cape May Co.{NJCW 9:409}

4. WILLIAM SCHILLINKS of Cape May Co., yeoman, probable son of Cornelius (1), d. leaving a will dated 2 March 1744, proved 30 March 1748. Mentioned were wife Josena, extx. to whom was devised the entire estate. If a son was born by wife and he lived to be 20 then he was to have all lands and tenements; if a dau. she was to have all at 18. If no issue, or none to attain majority, all land to go to brother Abraham Schillinks. The will was witnessed by Joshua Stites, Nathan Hand, Daniel Foster and Jacob Spicer.{NJCW Cape May Wills:139E} On 8 Jan 1747/8 an inventory was filed by Ebenezer Swane and Elisha Crowell.{NJCW}

5. HENRY SCHELLENGER (wife Rebecca), pilot, son of Cornelius (2)

who d. 1746 (date of source - 1789).{Deeds B:174}

A marriage license was issued to Henry Schellinger and Rebecca Scull, 30 Nov 1775.{MLNJ}

Rebecca Schellenger, b. 4 June 1742, d. 21 July 1828.{Cold Spring Cemetery}

6. CORNELIUS SCHELLINGER, probable son of Cornelius (2) m. Lydia Tayler*, dau. of George Taylor, by license dated 14 Dec 1756.{MLNJ}

Lydia Schellinger, wife of Cornelius Schelinger, received £6, as niece of Aaron Leaming, Jr. in his will written in 1774{Will of Aaron Leaming, NJCW 22:99}

Cornelius Schellinger of Cape May Co. d. before 21 March 1780 when Lydia Skellinger, widow, and Jacob Skellinger were appointed admins. Fellow bondsman: Nezer Swain, all of said county. Witnesses: Judith Hughes and Elijah Hughes. On 23 March 1780 an inventory of the estate (£4,163.16.0 was filed by Henry Hand and Arn. Eldredge.{NJCW 24:86}

Lydia Schellenger of Cape May Co., widow, d. leaving a will dated 18 Jan 1791, proved 26 May 1792. Mentioned were Mercy Curry, Judith Taylor and Daniel Taylor, children of her brother John Taylor, to whom she bequeathed £6 each when of age. Negroe slaves: Sally Frederick, Wanton Frederick, Prince Frederick, Amy Frederick, Thomas Frederick and Ishmal Frederick, to be set free. To Cornelius Bennett and Judith Mills, the residue. Execs. were friends: Elijah Hughes and Nezer Swain. The will was witnessed by John Clunk, Patience Clark and Nezer Swain.{NJCW 34:463} In May 1792 an inventory was filed (£64.8.9 1/2) by Jacocks Swain and Eleazar Hand.{NJCW File 579E}

7. DANIEL SCHELLINGER, probable son of Cornelius (2) m. Joan Doubleday by license dated 4 July 1758.{MLNJ}

Unplaced

ENOS (SCHELLENGER), b. 1752, d. 16 Jan 1809{Cold Spring Cemetery}

A marriage license was issued to HENRY SCHELLINGER and Prudence Church, 21 Jan 1760.{MLNJ}

A marriage license was issued to JACOB SCHELLINGER and Martha Furman, 22 Jan 1772.{MLNJ}

Jacob Schillenger of Cape May Co. d. by 4 June 1791 when Richard Shaw was appointed admin.{NJCW 32:301} On 4 June 1791

Martha Schillenger, the widow, renounced the administration of the estate. An inventory was filed (£30.9.10) by Robert Corgie and Jacob Richardson on 8 June 1791.{NJCW File:561E}

JAMES SCHELLENGER, b. 1751, d. 25 June 1846.

LYDIA SHILLINX m. John Taylor* on 14 Oct 1722.{First Official Rcds}

PHILOMELIA SCHELLENGER, b. 1752, d. 8 Feb 1793.{Cold Spring Cemetery}

A marriage license was issued to Thomas Crowell and SARAH SHILLINKS, 15 Jan 1771.{MLNJ}

WILLIAM SCHELLENGER, b. 1746, d. 15 June 1827.{Cold Spring Cemetery}

SCULL

See *History And Genealogy Of Fenwick's Colony*. By Thomas Shrouds. Originally published Bridgetown, NJ, 1876. Reprinted by Genealogical Publishing Co., Inc., Baltimore, 1976. See p. 218. According to the author John Scull emigrated from Long Island about 1690. He was owner of a large tract near Great Egg Harbor. He states that John and his wife had 13 children. John d. 1745. See this section for more details.

1. JOHN SCULL m. Mary (N). They were the parents of GIDEON, b. 16th day, 4th mo., 1722, d. 8th day, 12th mo., 1776.{GEMM}

2. GIDEON SCULL, son of John and Mary Scull, b. 16th day, 4th mo., 1722, d. 8th day, 12th mo., 1776 m. 1750, Judith Belangee [Bellanger] (b. 26th day, 1st mo., 1729).[106]

---

106 Gideon Scull, on 1st da., 8th mo., 1750, requested a certificate in order to marry a wife within the verge of Little Egg Harbor Monthly Meeting. At the meeting of 5th da, 9th mo, 1750, the marriage was reported as orderly accomplished. {GEMM} On 8th da, 9th mo, 1750, Giddien Schull and Judith Bellangee announced their intentions to marry. {LEMM}

Gideon Scull of Great Egg Harbor d. leaving a will dated 17 June 1776, proved 21 March 1777. Mentioned were his wife Judith and the small children; eldest son James to whom he devised 70 acres bought of Robert and Rebeckah Smith and other land; sons Gideon, Paul and Mark. Dau. Mary Bassett to receive £5. Daus.: Judith, Hannah, Ruth, Mergery and Rachel Scull who were given each £100 when age 21. Son Mark, £20. Execs. were sons James and Gideon and wife Judith. The will was witnessed by Joseph Mapes, Isaac Steelman and Mary Andrews.{NJCW 18:253}

Gideon and Judith were the parents of the following children: JAMES, b. 2nd day, 10th mo., 1751, d. 25th day, 8th mo., 1812, 61 years of age; MARY, b. 17th day, 11th mo., 1753, m. Daniel Bassett; GIDEON[107], b. 27th day, 4th mo., 1756; PAUL, b. 10th day, 12th mo., 1758, d. 11th day, 12th mo., 1779; HANNAH, b. 23rd day, 12th mo., 1762; JUDITH, b. 13th day, 1st mo., 1763; RUTH, b. 23rd day, 12th mo., 1764; MERGEREY, b. 24th day, 2nd mo., 1767; RACHEL, b. 11th day, 10th mo., 1769; MARK, b. 20th day, 9th mo., 1773, d. 16th day, 10th mo., 1808.{GEMM}

3. JAMES SCULL m. Susanna Leeds.{GEMM} They were the parents of the following children{GEMM}: DANIEL, b. 3rd day, 6th mo., 1775; GIDEON, b. 30th day, 10th mo., 1777; DARIS, b. 7th day, 10th mo., 1780; PAUL, b. 2nd day, 4th mo., 1783; JAMES, b. 11th day, 3rd mo., 1786; SUSANNAH, b. 25th day, 1st mo., 1789; HANNAH, b. 20th day, 6th mo., 1792; JACOB, b. 2nd day, 3rd day, 1796.

4. MARK SCULL m. 1794, Mary Braning, probable dau. of Cornelius and Amelia Branning of Evesham Monthly Meeting.{GEMM} Mark and Mary were parents of the following children: HANNAH, b. 7th day, 4th mo., 1795; EBENEZER, b. 17th day, 11th mo., 1796; AMELIA, b. 25th day, 2nd mo., 1800.

5. MARY SCULL, dau. of Gideon (2) and Judith Scull, m. Daniel Bassett, son of Daniel and Mary Lippincott Bassett. They were parents of the following children: GIDEON, d. 1779, aged 2 1/2 years; DANIEL; MARY.{This entry based on *History of Fenwick's Colony*.}

---

107 *See History And Genealogy of Fenwick's Colony* for more information on him and his family.

Unplaced

A marriage license was issued to John Van Gilder and HANNAH SCULL on 21 July 1757.{MLNJ}

"Diaries of Aaron Leaming," refer to death of HEZEKIAH SCULL, in 1760.

Reference was made to Hezekiah Scull and his brother Isaac on 16 Jan 1758, in "Memorandum book of Jacob Spicer, 1757-1764," *The Cape May County Magazine of History and Genealogy*, p. 112. June 1933.

A marriage license was issued to JOHN SCULL and Sarah Smith on 22 Nov 1776.{MLNJ}

A marriage license was issued to Ebenezer Ingersoll and MARY SCULL, on 24 April 1761.{MLNJ}

PETER SCULL of Turkey Hoe, Cape May Co. d. prior to 12 Jan 1751 prior to an inventory filed by James Hathorn and James Godfrey. On 23 Feb 1751 a bond was issued for John Scull as admin; James Hathorn fellow bondsman, both of Cape May Co., Gent.{NJCW Cape May Wills:156E}

A marriage license was issued to Joshua Garretson and PHEBE SCULL, 23 Nov 1763.{MLNJ}

A marriage license was issued to Israel Stites and PHEBE SCULL (Great Egg Harbor), 11 April 1775.{MLNJ}

A marriage license was issued to Henry Schellinger and REBECCA SCULL on 30 Nov 1775.{MLNJ}

On 5th day, 3rd mo., 1764, RECOMPENCE SCULL and ISAIAH SCULL were visited concerning their going out in marriage and disowned.{GEMM}

John McDaniels m. SARAH SKULL of Cape May 17 Jan 1750/1.{Baptists}

A marriage license was issued to Jacob Richardson and TEMPERANCE SCULL in 1740.{MLNJ}

Levi Hand m. ZIBIAH SCULL, May 10, 1773.{Baptists} A marriage license was issued to Levi Hand and Zabrish Scull, on 10 May 1772.{MLNJ}

SEARLE

John Searle of Cape May Co., labourer, d. prior to 17 June 1724 when a bond was issued to Robert Perryman of Cape May Co., yeoman, as admin. of the estate. Joseph Welch (Welsh) of Burlington fellow bondsman. Endorsed by statement of Joana, widow of John Searle, that she refused to act as admx.{NJCW 2:264 and Cape May Wills} Inventory of the estate was made by John Taylor and Samuel Johnson on 26 Aug 1724. In Sep 1724 an account of the estate was made by the admin. Robert Perryman who credited himself for keeping the wife and two children of dec. with victuals for 6 months when he had gone to East Jersey and for going himself to East Jersey to look for John Searle in 1723.{NJCW}

Constantine Cerl was listed in the 1751 tax for Cape May County.

SHARP

1. JOHN SHARP m. Sarah Reddy by license dated 27 April 1767.{MLNJ}

John d. leaving a will dated 25 Sep 1774, proved 28 Oct 1774. Mentioned were wife Sarah; dau. Isbel; son Solomon, his great-grandfather's little gun; John Sharp, Mary Sharp, Rachel Sharp, Sarah Sharp, Isbel Sharp, Henry Sharp, Peter Sharp, Sophia Sharp, Solomon Sharp (all children by first wife); Sylvia Sharp, Hannah Sharp, Patient Sharp, William Sharp (all children by last wife). Exec. Reuben Ludlam. The will was witnessed by John Goff, Samuel Bishop and John Nickison. An inventory was made on 28 Oct 1774 by John Goff and Eli Eldredge.{NJCW 17:165}

John was father of the following children by his first wife: ISBEL; SOLOMON; JOHN; MARY; RACHEL; SARAH; HENRY; PETER; SOPHIA; SOLOMON. John was father of the following children by Sarah: SYLVIA; HANNAH; PATIENT; WILLIAM.

Sarah Sharp of Cape May Co. d. prior to 16 March 1775 when John Baker was appointed admin. of her estate. Fellowbondsman: Daniel Crowell, both of said county, yeomen. Witnesses: Zeruiah Hughes and Thomas Church. On 21 March 1775 an inventory was made by Reuben Ludlam and Anthony Ludlam.{NJCW 15:539}

2. SOLOMON SHARP, son of John (1) Sharp, on 6 March 1787 complained that Ruben Ludlam was admin. to the estate of his father, John Sharp and execs. of afsd. Ludlam refuse to pay a legacy due from the

estate.{Ltrs&Inv A(Rev):10}

3. SYLVIA SHARP, probable dau. of John (1) Sharp, m. Joseph Scull, noting that on 16 May 1789 a bond was taken of Joseph Scull for a marriage license to Sylvia Sharp.{Ltrs&Inv A:19}

4. WILLIAM SHARP, probable son of John (1) Sharp, m. Abigail Champion, 24 Jan 1798.{Co. Clerk Rcds - Book A}

SHAW

Some of the following information was taken from two articles in *The Cape May County Magazine of History and Genealogy*, "First Official Records of Cape May County," p. 316 and "The Account Book of John Parsons, With Notes," p. 166, June 1942, and other sources as indicated.

Of probable relevance is the entry from Suffolk Co. Sessions, p. 66, which revealed the following:

> Edmond Shaw, Senr., d. leaving a will dated 3 May 1675, proved 6 June 1676. Mentioned were sons: Thomas Shaw and Richard Shaw; daus.: wife of Richard Ludlam and wife of John Foster.

Another entry from Suffolk Co. Sessions, p. 141, is obviously connected to the following family of Cape May Co. The following information is revealed in this entry:

> Richard Shaw, Senr., d. leaving a will dated 7 Sep 1680, proved June 1683 in Suffolk Co., NY. Mentioned were wife Remember and children: Richard (eldest), Edmond (2d son), Edmond, William, Joshua and Benjamin, and Elizabeth. Reference was made to son John's grandfather and grandmother, Garlick.

1. RICHARD SHAW, m. Rembrance Garlick. They were the parents of the following children: RICHARD, b. ca. 1661, d. 1709, m. Rebecca (N); WILLIAM; JOSHUA, b. 1667; EDMUND, b. ca. 1663, d. 1719; EDMUND alias Benjamin, b. ca. 1669; ELIZABETH.

2. Captain WILLIAM SHAW, son of Richard (1) and Rembrance Garlick Shaw, m. Lidia Parsons (b. 10 April 1680), dau. of John and Elizabeth Parsons*, on 8 April 1695 by Samuel Crowell in the presence of Henry

Stites, Hanah Stites, Abram Smith and several more.{Baptist Burials}

Capt. William Shaw d. 17 May 1712. Lydia, his widow m. 12 Oct 1714, Aaron Leaming*. Witnesses were John Richardson and wife Rachel; Joshua Garlick and wife Abigail; Arthur Cresse and wife Mercy; and others.{Deeds B:128}

William and Lydia Shaw were the parents of the following children born: WILLIAM, b. 24 Aug 1697, d. 13 Dec 1714; RICHARD, b. 29 Oct 1699, d. 22 Oct 1773; LIDIA, b. 14 Sep 1703, d. 13 Nov 1766, m. 8 May 720, George Taylor*; JOHN, b. 4 Feb 1705, d. 14 Jan 1773; JOSHUA, b. 26 March 1707; HANNAH, b. 26 March 1708, d. 28 Nov 1774; NATHAN, b. 23 Dec 1710, d. 11 June 1772.{First Official Rcds}

3. BENJAMIN SHAW of Cape May Co., probable son of Richard (1), d. leaving a will dated 1 April 1744, proved 4 Feb 1746/7. mentioned were wife Margatt; sons: Benjamin, Obidiah, Joshua, William; daus.: Sarah and Mary. Execs. were wife Margatt and John Shaw. The will was witnessed by Elisha Hand, Robert Edmonds and Marah Edmons.{NJCW5:360} On 24 Aug 1747 letters were granted to Margaret Shaw in absence of John Shaw. On 29 Jan 1746/7 an inventory was filed which included smith's tools; appraised by Elisha Hand and Richard Crawford.{NJCW}

Benjamin Shaw was the father of the following children: BENJAMIN; OBIDIAH; JOSHUA; WILLIAM; SARAH; MARY.

4. RICHARD SHAW, son of William (2) and Lydia Shaw, b. 29 Oct 1699, d. 22 Oct 1773, m. Patience Stillwell*, dau. of John and Elizabeth Perrine Stillwell.

Richard Shaw left a will dated 10 Sep 1772, proved 28 Oct 1773. Mentioned were wife Patience; sons: William and Richard to whom he devised cedar swamp and the island called Dog Island and his right on Five Mile Beach. Son William received land in the Middle Precinct where testator lived. He was to pay dau. Elizabeth Hughes, £10, dau. Patience Foster, £7 and 10 shillings, son-in-law Jedediah Hughes in trust for use of dau. Lydia Church, £7 and 10 shillings, granddau. Esther Shaw, £7 and 10 shillings. After the death of son William, grandsons Hosea Shaw and Stillwell Shaw to receive the land where testator lied and 50 acres of woodland joining it. Son Richard to receive land in the Lower Precinct bought of John Eldredge. Daus. Elizabeth Hughes, Lydia Church and

Patience Foster were to receive the rest of moveable estate. Execs. were son Richard and sons-in-law, Jedediah Hughes and John Foster. The will was witnessed by Benjamin Ingrum, Rynear Hollinshead, Jane Hollinghead and James Hays. On 28 Oct 1773 an inventory (£119.15.5 1/2) was filed by Aaron Eldredge and Abraham Woolson.{NJCW 17:176}

Richard Shaw was father of the following children: WILLIAM; RICHARD; ELIZABETH, m. Jedediah Hughes; LYDIA, m. (N) Church; PATIENCE, probably m. 1st Jonathan Foreman* and m. 2nd John Foster by license dated 5 Aug 1761.{MLNJ}

Probably pertaining to the above children are dates of birth given in Parsons Account Book: Lydia Shaw, b. 25 Oct 1723; Elizabeth Shaw b. 1725; Patience Shaw b. May 1727; Judith Shaw b. 25 Feb 1730/1; Hannah Shaw b. 26 Sep 1732; William Shaw, b. 13 May 1735.

5. JOHN SHAW, son of William (2) and Lydia Shaw, b. 4 Feb 1705/6, d. 14 Jan 1773, m. Hannah Jenkins, dau. of Nathaniel and Hannah Jenkins*.

An agreement was made by John Shaw to maintain the fence on the south east side of his land between him and his brother Willm. down tourdes [toward] the marsh, said John Shaw having purchased his land from his brother William. Executed 7 Aug 1697. Recorded 3 Dec 1697.{First Official Rcds}

John d. leaving a will dated 18 April 1772, proved 26 Jan 1773. Mentioned were wife Hannah; William Taylor, son of John Taylor; William Shaw; Joshua Shaw, son of brother Joshua Shaw to whom he left the slave Prince; nephew John Shaw, son of brother Nathan Shaw, £10; Joshua Shaw, son of brother Joshua Shaw, to whom he left his home plantation; Thomas Shaw, son of brother Nathan Shaw. Naomy Cresse, wife of Jonathan Cresse, £10; Rhodea Billings, wife of William Billings, £5. to Jacob Teal, son of Richard Teal, land including his broken island of sedge marsh. Execs. were wife and nephews, Joshua Shaw and Thomas Shaw. The will was witnessed by Francis Taylor, Daniel Hewet and John Cresse. On 4 Feb 1773 the inventory (£549.6.7 was filed by Thomas Smith and Henry Hand.{NJCW 16:132}

6. JOSHUA SHAW, son of William (2) and Lydia Shaw, b. 26 March 1707, had three children: JOSHUA, b. 1735{Parsons Account Bk}; ELIJAH; MARY, b. 26 March 1737, m. (N) Gandy.

Joshua (of Lower Precinct), d. leaving a will dated 4 Aug 1770, proved 8 Sep 1775. Son Elijah Shaw was devised land which was bought of William Johnson, lying between lands of George Taylor and Henry

Hand, and 1/2 the land bought of Mark Hewlin at Cold Spring and other land [described]. Son Joshua received Negro boy Job. Dau. Mary Gandy received a Negro wench Nancy. Execs. were sons Joshua and Elijah. The will was witnessed by Jonathan Forman, Racey Parsons and Henry Hand. An inventory was filed on 20 Dec 1775 by Henry Hand and John Taylor.{NJCW 17:251}

7. NATHAN SHAW, son of William (2) and Lydia Shaw, b. 23 Dec 1710, d. 11 June 1772, m. Patience Gandy, dau. of Thomas Gandy. Nathan and Patience Shaw were the parents of the following children: JOHN; THOMAS; NATHAN; MATTHIAS; HANNAH; MARY; PRISCILLA; LYDIA.

In "Diaries of Aaron Leaming," he mentions delivering Jeremiah Leaming's wearing apparel to Nathan Shaw's children ["Priscilla Raney" and Sarah Ewing appeared.]

Nathan Shaw d. leaving a will dated 1 March 1770, proved 7 July 1772. Mentioned were wife Patience; daus.: Hannah and Mary (not yet 21), £2 each; rest of moveable estate to Priscilla, Lydia, Hannah and Mary. To son John land where testator lived and a lot of back land that lies at the head of plantation and joining land of Jacob Hewit, bought of John Leonard, Esq., by a power from this brother, Henry Leonard. Son Thomas lands that formerly belonged to Joseph Hewit, son of Randle Hewit, dec. and 10 acres of woodland bought of Jacob Hewit. Son Matthias to receive lands at Dividing Creeks between the land that was formerly Joseph Page's and Joseph Goff's. Execs. were sons, John and Thomas Shaw. On 26 June 1772 an inventory was filed by Jedidiah Hughes and Abraham Woolson. An account was filed on 6 Jan 1774 by both execs. Joseph Hayes was paid for keeping a child in consequence of an agreement of the testator, £10.{NJCW 15:531; 16:3}

8. OBIDIAH SHAW, son of Benjamin (3) Shaw, probably m. Deborah (N) and had a son named OBEDIAH.

Obadiah d. by 19 April 1787 when Deborah Shaw was appointed admx. of his estate. On 18 April 1787 an inventory was filed by Abraham Woolson and Gideon Kent.{NJCW 29:241}

Deborah d. by 17 March 1791 when Carman Richardson was appointed admin. of her estate. Fellowbondsman: Thomas Shaw.{NJCW 32:301} On 16 March 1791 an inventory was filed (£35.16.3) by David Cresse and Thomas Shaw.{NJCW File:562E}

Obediah Shaw, son of Obediah Shaw, dec., was made a ward of Carman Richardson on 29 May 1792.

At the February and August Terms of 1796 Thomas Church on behalf of his wife, late Theoda Shaw, applied for a division of lands, late the property of Obadiah Shaw of the Lower Precinct, who d. intestate - between the said Theoda and Obadiah Shaw, a minor, who are the only surviving children of said dec. (plat shown){Ltrs&Inv A(Rev):114, 123}

Obediah Shaw was father of the following children: THEODA; OBADIAH.

9. JOSHUA SHAW, son of Joshua Shaw, m. 18 May 1773 Anne Furman{Baptists}, by license dated 17 May 1773.{MLNJ}

Joshua d. by 22 July 1790 when Rachel Shaw and Elijah Shaw were appointed admins. On 22 Oct 1790 an inventory was filed (£415.14.3) by Philip Cresse and David Hildreth.{NJCW 32:106}

Joshua, son of Joshua, dec. chose as his guardian, Thomas Shaw, on 29 May 1791.{NJCW 32:304; File 563E}

Joshua had the following children: JOSHUA; HUMPHREY; JOHN; and LYDIA, m. John Corson by whom she had Judith, John, Ebenezer, Rachel, Aveline, Jacob Summers, Harriet, James Clark, Charles Henry and William Swain.

Unplaced

A marriage license was issued to ELIJAH SHAW and Jemima Hand, 12 April 1768.{MLNJ}

EXPERIENCE SHAW, b. March 1775, d. 13 Oct 1834, age 69 years, 6 mos, 25 days.{Cold Spring Cemetery}

A marriage license was issued to Thomas Stillwell and HANNAH SHAW, 11 Feb 1761.{MLNJ}

A marriage license was issued to Robert Townsend and JANE SHAW, 4 Oct 1763.{MLNJ}

A marriage license was issued to JOHN SHAW and Mary Eldredge, 4 Jan 1771.{MLNJ}

A marriage license was issued to Gideon Johnston and LYDDA SHAW, 24 April 1767.{MLNJ}

MARY SHAW b. 26 March 1737.{Parsons Account Bk}

RICHARD SHAE had an account with John Parsons, 26 March 1675.{Parsons Account Bk}

A marriage license was issued to RICHARD SHAW and Jerusha Garritson, 19 June 1764.{MLNJ}

Samson Hawk of Great Eggharbour m. SARAH SHAW of Cape May, June 15, 1750.{Baptists}

SARAH SHAW, widow of Edward Shaw (d. 1705), and dau. of Obediah and Elizabeth (Cook) Holmes of Salem Co., m. 1706 Timothy Brandreth (his 3rd marriage).

Jonathan Hildreth* had dau. Silvia, wife of STILLWELL SHAW, as mentioned in deeds dated 1796.{Deeds E: 278}

Stillwell Shaw, b. 19 Sep 1767, d. 29 Aug 1825.{Cold Spring Cemetery} Stillwell and Sylvia were parents of AARON (1795-1856).

George Taylor m. SYLVIA SHAW, 8 May 1720.{First Official Rcds}

THOMAS SHAW m. Hannah Goff 5 July 1770.{Baptists} A marriage license was issued on 5 July 1770.{MLNJ}

In "Diaries of Aaron Leaming," he mentions the death of WILLIAM SHAW's wife Esther in 1760.{Leaming Diaries}

A marriage license was issued to WILLIAM SHAW and Jerusha Hand, 8 March 1762.{MLNJ}

SIMPKINS

1. WILLIAM SIMKINS recorded his ear mark on 18 Sep 1694.{First Public Rcds:271} William was a debtor listed in the inventory (1704) of the estate of John Stubbs.

2. RUTH SIMKINS of Cape May Co. d. leaving a will dated 10 Jan 1735/6, proved 1 June 1736. Son William Simkins, exec. and heir to all her moveable estate.{NJCW Cape May Wills:90E} On 16 Feb 1735/6 an inventory was filed by Ebenezer Newton and Elisha Hand.{NJCW}

Ruth was mother of WILLIAM.

3. MARY SIMKINS, dau. of William Simkins (probably 1. above), was appointed a guardian, Nathaniel Hand. Fellowbondsman: Joshua Hildreth of Cape May Co., Gent. Witness: Zeruiah Hughes.{NJCW 13:495}

4. WILLIAM SIMKINS, son of Ruth (2) Simkins, m. Mary Edmunds by license dated 10 Dec 1759.{MLNJ}

William d. prior to 12 March 1766 when John Conner and Hannah Simkins were appointed admins. of his estate. Fellowbondsmen: Christopher Foster and Richard Stites of Cape May Co. Witnesses: John Shaw and Jer. Leaming. On 7 March 1766 an inventory was filed by Christopher Foster and Richard Stites.{NJCW 12:357}

5. SARAH SIMKINS, dau. of William Simkins, possibly William (4) above, m. John Connell. (Book of Mortgages A: 78, dated 1769).

Unplaced

HANNAH SIMPKINS m. Thomas Pratten on 28 Aug 1766.{Baptists} A marriage license was issued on 27 Aug 1766.{MLNJ}

A marriage license was issued to Isaac Willets and MARY SIMKINS, on 7 Oct 1771.{MLNJ}

JOHN SMITH

1. JOHN SMITH, son of John Smith of Long Island, b. 17th day, 12th mo., 1700, d. 10th day, 1st mo., 1760, m. Mary (N) (b. 30th day, 1st mo., 1703, d. 15th day, 2nd mo., 1771). They were the parents of the following children{GEMM}: ELIZABETH, b. 6th day, 12th mo., 1720/21; JESSE, b. 13th day, 10th mo., 1723, d. 15th day, 10th mo., 1808 near 79 years of age; NOAH, b. 27th day, 9th mo., 1725, d. 30th day, 11th mo., 1790; JAMES, b. 4th day, 2nd mo., 1730; FELIX, b. 27th day, 10th mo., 1732; JOHN, b. 21st day, 12th mo., 1735/6; MARY, b. 9th day, 5th mo., 1738; EPHRAIM, b. 27th day, 2nd mo., 1741; ISAAC, b. 4th day, 10th mo., 1745.

2. JESSE SMITH, probable son of John (1) Smith, m. Elizabeth (N). They were the parents of the following children{GEMM}: RACHEL, b. 22nd day, 2nd mo., 1745; ANN, b. 26th day, 8th mo., 1747, d. 28th day, 10th mo., 1813, m. (N) Bowen; ESTHER, b. 31st day, 6th mo., 1750; 5th day,

5th mo., 1826, m. (N) Higbee; REBECKAH, b. 13th day, 10th mo., 1753, d. 5th day, 10th mo., 1763; SARAH, b. 5th day, 6th mo., 1756, d. 25th day, 10th mo., 1763; MARY, b. 9th day, 7th mo., 1759, d. 4th day, 10th mo., 1763; JOSHUA, b. 1st day, 1st mo., 1762, d. 23rd day, 9th mo., 1763.

3. NOAH SMITH, probable son of John (1) Smith, m. Judith (N) who was b. 15th day, 2nd mo., 1726, d. 7th day, 1st mo., 1778. They were the parents of the following children: PETER, b. 24th day, 5th mo., 1748, d. 13th day, 7th mo., 1751; SUSANNAH, b. 23rd day, 9th mo., 1750; CATHRINE, b. 13th day, 11th day, 1754; SAMUEL, b. 7th mo., 1st mo., 1757, d. 28th day, 2nd mo., 1826; MELISENT, b. 11th day, 4th mo., 1761, d. 6th day, 3rd mo., 1780; ANDREW, b. 18th day, 7th mo., 1763, d. 29th day, 7th mo., 1763; JOHN, b. 20th day, 8th mo., 1764; twin daus. b. 20th day, 12th mo., 1767, d. 23rd day, 12th mo., 1767; JUDITH, b. 6th day, 8th mo., 1769; NAOMI, b. 9th day, 3rd mo., 1759.{GEMM}

On 7th day, 4th mo., 1760, Noah Smith requested advice regarding disposing of a woman slave, as admin. to his father's estate.{GEMM}

WILLIAM SMITH

1. WILLIAM SMITH, Sr., of Cape May Co., yeoman, d. leaving a will dated 18 Feb 1743/4, proved 3 Aug 1744. Mentioned were sons John William, Richard, Jonathan, Daniel and Jeremiah. Dau. Elizabeth, wife of Samuel Foster. Granddau. Ruth Osborn. Execs. were sons Richard and Jonathan. The will was witnessed by Michael Iszard, Mary Conner and Nathl. Jenkins, Jr. On 30 July 1744 an inventory of the estate was filed which included a Negro man, cattle, horses, sheep, etc.; appraised by Jeremiah Hand and Nathl. Jenkins.{NJCW}

William Smith recorded his ear mark on 4 April 1694; he gave the mark to his son William in 1722.{First Public Rcds:272}

William Smith, Esqr., recorded his ear mark 28 May 1722 and on 3 Nov 1749 it was recorded for his son Richard Smith.{First Official Rcds: 334}

William Smith was the father of the following children: JOHN; WILLIAM, b. Oct 1699[108]; RICHARD; JONATHAN; DANIEL;

---

108 William Smith says that he was born in October 1699. {Leaming Diaries}

JEREMIAH; ELIZABETH, m. Samuel Foster.

2. THOMAS SMITH, of Cape May Co., yeoman, possible brother of William (1) Smith, m. Abigail Johnson*, widow of Samuel Johnson, d. leaving a will dated 28 Dec 1731, proved 13 May 1732. Mentioned were wife Abigail; sons: Thomas, Christopher and Anthony; daus.: Margery, Jerusha, Ruth and Alathare. Execs. were friends and brother, William Smith and Henry Young. The will was witnessed by Elizabeth Crowell, John Thomson and John Thompson, Jr.{NJCW 3:217} On 13 April 1732 an inventory was filed which included cattle and half a shallop and a canoe; appraised by Benjamin Hand and John Ingrum. On 20 June 1741 an account of the estate was submitted.{NJCW}

Abigail Smith of Cape May Co., widow of Thomas Smith, d. prior to 11 Dec 1732 when Aaron Leaming was appointed admin. Witnesses: Saml. Bustil and Robert Davis. On 17 Nov 1732 Ebenezer Johnson, Phebe Johnson and Abigail Johnson, children of the said dec. by her former husband, Samuel Johnson, renounced their right in favor of Aaron Leaming.{NJCW 3:227}

Thomas Smith was father of the following children: THOMAS; CHRISTOPHER; ANTHONY; MARGERY; JERUSHA; RUTH; ALATHARE.

3. WILLIAM SMITH, Cape May Co., son of William (1) Smith, d. prior to 12 Jan 1756 when an inventory was filed by John Leonard and Jeremiah Hand. On 20 May 1756 a bond was issued for widow, Phebe, of Cape May Co., as admx.{NJCW 8:307}

4. JONATHAN SMITH, probable son of William (1) Smith, m. Abigail Ludlam by license dated 27 June 1747{MLNJ}.

He d. leaving a will dated 25 Oct 1765, proved 19 April 1766. He left 1/2 of his moveable estate to wife Abigail and use of plantation until son Thomas was 21. Also mentioned were daus.: Sarah Smith, Hannah Smith and three youngest sons: Jonathan, Carmon and Jeremiah. Son Thomas was to have the land, he to pay son Constantine, £100 when 21. Brother Daniel was to have a suit of clothes. Execs. were wife, brother Daniel and son Thomas. The will was witnessed by Joshua Smith, Thomas Richardson, Abigail Hewit and John Bliss. On 2 May 1766 an inventory was filed (£554.16.5 1/2) by Thomas Smith and Joseph Savage. On 17 Sep 1767 an account was filed by Daniel Smith and Abigail Smith, surviving execs.{NJCW 12:349}

Jonathan was father of the following children: THOMAS;

SARAH; HANNAH; JONATHAN; CARMON; JEREMIAH; CONSTANTINE.

5. RUTH SMITH, probable dau. of Thomas (2) Smith, m. James Pharo. On 2nd day, 6th mo., 1731 James Pharo of Little Egg Harbor Monthly Meeting, Monmouth Co., and Ruth Smith of Cape May announced their intentions to marry.{GEMM} On 1st day, 1st mo., 1741, Ruth Pharo was received by certificate to Little Egg Harbor from Cape May (and Great Egg Harbor) Monthly Meeting.{LEMM}

On 9th day, 8th mo., 1759, it was reported that Elizabeth Pharo, dau. of James, had a bastard child and was disowned.{LEMM}

James was the father of ELIZABETH.

6. RICHARD SMITH, son of William (1) Smith, was probable father of DANIEL (10) who was an orphan on 16 Jan 1769; and JAMES, son of Richard who was made a ward of Philip Cresse on 23 June 1772{NJCW 14:506}; and JOHN, son of Richard, dec., who was made a ward of Philip Cresse on 7 March 1774{NJCW 15:530}.

7. JOHN SMITH of Cape May Co., yeoman, probable son of William (1) Smith, d. leaving a will dated 15 Sep 1752, proved 15 Nov 1752. Mentioned were children: Carman, Uriah, Elihu, John and Judith Chesnut. Home farm on Gravely Run Creek; land back of it; a cedar swamp. Execs. were sons Carman and Uriah. The will was witnessed by Shamgar Hand, Joseph Hewit, Nathaniel Jenkins, Jr.{NJCW Cape May Wills:161E} On 14 Nov 1752 an inventory was filed by Nathaniel Jenkins, Jr. and Jeremiah Hand.{NJCW}

John Smith was the father of the following children: CARMAN[109]; URIAH; ELIHU; JOHN; JUDITH Chesnut (last name?).

Third Generation

8. CARMAN SMITH of Cape May Co., yeoman, probable son of John (7) Smith, d. leaving a will dated 7 Dec 1760, proved 6 May 1761. Mentioned were dau. Martha Smith to whom he devised all his lands; wife Lydia, use of lands; dau. Mary, 5 shillings. Execs. were wife and brother John Smith. The will was witnessed by Nathaniel Jenkins, Thomas Stites and Nathan Stites. On 4 June 1761 an inventory was filed (£122.8.10) by Joshua Hildreth and James Cresse.{NJCW 10:222}

---

109 In "Diaries of Aaron Leaming," he mentions the death of Carman Smith in 1760.

Carman was father of the following children: MARTHA; MARY.

9. URIAH SMITH, son of John (7) Smith, m. Mary Sommers (Gloucester Co.), 24 Aug 1758.{MLNJ}

Uriah d. leaving a will dated 10 May 1761, proved 17 May 1764. Mentioned was son Joseph to whom he devised the home plantation at age 21 and wife Mary to whom was given use of the lands and what she brought to the marriage. Joseph was to be put to a trade at age 14. Daus. Neome and Experience were to receive the rest of the moveable estate. Execs. were wife and friend Elihu Smith. The will was witnessed by Jonathan Smith, Shamgar Hand and Richard Osborne. Inventory was filed (£305.10.6) by John Shaw and Lewis Cresse on 28 April 1764.{NJCW 12:331}

Uriah was father of the following children: JOSEPH; NEOME, m. 1 Aug 1744, George Hand*, son of George; EXPERIENCE.

10. DANIEL SMITH, son of Richard, chose Philip Cresse as his guardian on 16 Jan 1769. Fellowbondsman was Nathan Hand of Cape May Co., Gent. Witnesses: Jacob Hughes, Jr. and Elijah Hughes.{NJCW 13:495}

Unplaced

A marriage license was issued to Andrew Godfrey and ABIGAIL SMITH, 5 Jan 1770.{MLNJ}

A marriage license was issued to Joseph Ludlam and ALATHAN SMITH, 23 Jan 1732.{MLNJ}

On 7th day, 5th mo., 1746, the marriage of Edmund Cordrey and CHRISTIAN SMITH was reported as orderly accomplished.{GEMM}

CHRISTOPHER SMITH m. Lydia Badcock, 25 Oct 1774.{Baptists} The marriage license was issued on 24 Oct 1774.{MLNJ}

A marriage license was issued to CHRISTOPHER SMITH and Esther Ludlam, 2 Sep 1768.{MLNJ}

On 4th day, 9th mo., 1751, DANIEL SMITH produced a certificate from Haddonfield Monthly Meeting.{GEMM}

DAVID SMITH m. Hannah Norton of Cape May, 11 Aug 1752.{Baptists}

Rev. David Smith who first preached in publick April 1773 was ordained March 1776 and d. Feb 1784, aged 54 years. His wife Hannah d. 26 Feb 1789 in her 48th year. He and his wife were natives of Cape May Co., baptized into membership of the Baptist Church, married by the Baptist minister.{"The Historic Baptist Burial Yard - Cape May Court House New Jersey," *The Cape May County Magazine of History and Genealogy*, p. 63. June 1956. By M. Catharine Stauffer; Baptist Burials}

David Smith of Cape May, minister of the Gospel, d. leaving a will dated 17 Jan 1784, proved 15 March 1784. To wife all the goods agreeable to the contract with her, then Hannah Shepherd, and John Jones her surety, in consequence of which the rents of the lands said John Jones lives on were to be paid to testator and now to be paid to widow. Eldest son Daniel to have cedar swamp. The rest of estate to go to wife Hannah and children: Phebe, Silvia, Daniel, David, Judith, Lidia, Mark, Norton, William, Jacob, Hannah and the child wife may have. Son Mark to be bound to Jeremiah Smith, to learn to be a shoemaker and son Norton to be put to Thomas Yates to learn to be a shoemaker. Son William was to still live with Philip Godfrey, Jr. until age 14. Exec. was Jonathan Hildreth. The will was witnessed by John Holmes, Nathaniel Holmes and John Cresse. Letters were granted to Jonathan Hildreth, the exec. on 15 March 1784. On 25 Feb 1784 an inventory was filed (£199.13.1) by Joseph Hildreth and John Cresse.{NJCW 38:68}

David and Hannah were parents of the following children: PHEBE; SILVIA; DANIEL; DAVID; JUDITH; LIDIA; MARK; NORTON; WILLIAM; JACOB; HANNAH.

ELIHU SMITH and Judith Billings, Sep 20, 1774.{Baptists} The marriage license was issued on 20 Sep 1774.{MLNJ}

A marriage license was issued to Joseph Sowe and ELIZABETH SMITH, 3 Dec 1737.{MLNJ}

EVI SMITH m. Mary (N). They were the parents of the following children: MARTHA, b. 26th day, 11th mo., 1746; HENRY, b. 10th day, 8th mo., 1749; ROBERT, b. 26th day, 10th mo., 1752, d. 17th day, 2nd mo., 1802; DAVID, b. 26th day, 7th mo., 1755; ELIZABETH, b. 18th day, 6th mo., 1757; JERUSHEA, b. 18th day, 9th mo., 1759; JONATHAN, b. 17th day, 5th mo., 1762. (See ROBERT SMITH){GEMM}

On 5th day, 5th mo., 1755 EVI SMITH acknowledged his outgoing in marriage and unchaste freedom that he took with her that is now his wife, before marriage.{GEMM}

Child of Evi and Mary Smith: Evi Smith, b. 8th day, 3rd mo.,

1768, d. 24th day, 8th mo., 1804.

A marriage license was issued to Elisha Hand* and EXPERIENCE SMITH, 22 Jan 1731.{MLNJ}

A marriage license was issued to Philip Cresse and EXPERIENCE SMITH, 20 Feb 1763.{MLNJ}

A marriage license was issued to Richard Osborne and HANNAH SMITH, 3 May 1762.{MLNJ}

Henry Ludlam m HANNAH SMITH, 30 June 1772.{Baptists} A marriage license was issued to them the same day.{MLNJ}

ISAAC SMITH, b. 1771, d. 1 July 1822.{Cold Spring Cemetery}

JACOB SMITH and Rachel Hand, 29 --- 1758.{Baptists}

JOHN SMITH & Mary Jenkins* of Cape May, m. Oct 2, 1753.{Baptists}

John d. leaving a will dated 10 Dec 1770, proved 29 May 1771. Mentioned were wife Mary and son and daus. (unnamed). On 24 May 1771 an inventory was filed (£193.16.6) by Thomas Smith and Philip Cresse.{NJCW 15:181}

In the deed book is shown Thomas Moore, wife Johanna only heir and dau. of JONAH SMITH (1720).{Deeds B:190}

JONATHAN SMITH m. Alathar Ludlam, on 26 Jan 1761.{MLNJ}

Jonathan Smith of Cape May Co. d. leaving a will dated 26 July 1775, proved 19 May 1776. Mentioned were wife Alathei to whom he left the land until children came of age. Daus.: Phebe, Alatheia and Sylpa Smith; child the wife was big with; sons: Jonathan and Rubin to whom were devised all the lands when age 20. Execs. were wife and friend Jonathan Jenkins. The will was witnessed by Joseph Hildreth, Joshua Smith and Zibiah Hildreth. On 9 Oct 1775 an inventory was filed (£124.19.16) by Joseph Hildreth and Thomas Ludlam. [Wife signed her name as Alathair Smith.]{NJCW 17:383}

JONATHAN SMITH & Mary Golden, at Tuckehoo, Aug 15, 1764.{Baptists}

On 8 Feb 1772 Thomas Stites was appointed guardian for CONSTANTINE SMITH, son of JONATHAN SMITH of Cape May County, dec. Fellowbondsmen: Nathan Hand and Nathaniel Jenkins, gent. Witnesses: Jacob Harris, Ephraim Jenkins and Simeon Billings.{NJCW 14:506}

JOSHUA SMITH and Naomi Osborn, 16 Feb 1762.{MLNJ}

JOSHUA SMITH & Charity Billings, 4 Dec 1770.{Baptists} A marriage license was issued on 3 Dec 1770.{MLNJ}

Charity Smith of died of "Bloody flux" ca. June 1775.{Leaming Diaries}

LOUISA SMITH, b. 9 Nov 1756, d. 4 Nov 1821.{Cold Spring Cemetery}

A marriage license was issued to Shamgar Hand and LYDIA SMITH, 5 Sep 1761.{MLNJ}

Elija Mathews m. MARTHA SMITH 10 Oct 1770.{Baptists} A marriage license was issued to them on the same day.{MLNJ}

A marriage license was issued to Jesse Hand and MARY SMITH, 7 Nov 1759.{MLNJ}

A marriage license was issued to John Iszard and MARY SMITH, 11 Dec 1770.{MLNJ}

The following entries are contradictory.
A marriage license was issued to Abner Corson and MARY SMITH, 5 April 1773.{MLNJ}
Abner Corson m. MARY SMITH 8 March 1773.{Baptists}

A marriage license was issued to Samuel Foster and MARY SMITH, 25 April 1774.{MLNJ}

A marriage license was issued to George Hand and NAOMI SMITH, 1 Aug 1774.{MLNJ}

A marriage license was issued to Samuel Crowell and PHEBE SMITH, 7 Nov 1759.{MLNJ}

A marriage license was issued to Philip Godfrey and PHEBE SMITH, 4

Feb 1775.{MLNJ}

A marriage license was issued to John Willets and REBECCA SMITH, 25 June 1763.{MLNJ}

A marriage license was issued to Frederick Modlaer and REBECCA SMITH, 26 April 1774.{MLNJ}

A marriage license was issued to Henry Foster and RHODAY SMITH, 18 Sep 1777.{MLNJ}

RICHARD SMITH and Rachel Hand, 1 Dec 1737.{MLNJ}

Mrs. RACHEL SMITH, dau. of Abraham Hand, d. 7 Aug 1773, aged 68 years.{Baptist Burials}

Rachel Smith d. leaving a will dated 1 Aug 1773, proved 19 Aug 1773. Mentioned were granddau. Hannah Corey; granddaus.: Rachel Hand, Jr., Martha Taylor and Hannah Swain; children: Richard Swain, Hannah Taylor, Rachel Hand and Nathan Hand; granddau. Joannah Cory. Exec. was Jesse Hand. The will was witnessed by John Cobb, Job Davis and Seth Whilldin. On 19 Aug 1773 an inventory was filed (£328.4.1) by Thomas Smith and Nathaniel Hand. Legacies were made to Nathan Hand, Hannah and Benjamin Taylor, and Elijah and Rachel Hand, and Aaron Crossley.{NJCW 17:38, 24:87}

A marriage license was issued to RICHARD SMITH and Hannah Somers* (Gloucester Co.), 20 Aug 1745.{MLNJ}

ROBERT SMITH m. Elizabeth Belangee. They were the parents of the following children{GEMM}: EVI, b. 12th day, 7th mo., 1721, d. 29th day, 1st mo., 1786; CHRISTIAN, wife of Edmond Cordrey, b. 9th day, 9th mo., 1723; ROBERT, b. 27th day, 2nd mo., 1731; DANIEL, b. 22nd day, 4th mo., 1732.

Elizabeth Smith, wife of Robert Smith and dau. of James Belangee, d. 11th day, 7th mo., 1747.{GEMM}

On 7th day, 9th mo., 1748, the marriage of Robert Smith and Ann Cordrey was reported as orderly accomplished. On 2nd day, 8th mo., 1756 the monthly meeting was informed that Robert Smith and his wife have differed to the degree that it's become a publick scandal. On 3rd day, 1st mo., 1757 Robert and Ann Smith acknowledged their sorrow regardingthe difference that had been between them.{GEMM}

Anne Smith, wife of Robert Smith, d. 16th day, 11th mo., 1763.{GEMM}

Robert Smith, d. 4th day, 5th mo., 1765.{GEMM}

On 4th day, 3rd mo., 1762 ROBERT SMITH acknowledged striking his neighbor.{GEMM}

On 6th day, 9th mo., 1756 ROBERT SMITH, Jr., was spoken to concerning his outgoing in marriage and other disorders.{GEMM}

ROBERT SMITH m. Rebecka (N). They were the parents of ROBERT, b. 11th day, 9th mo., 1773.{GEMM}

ROBERT SMITH m. Dorothy (N). They were parents of the following children: REBEKAH, b. 21st day, 1st mo., 1776, d. 5th day, 2nd mo., 1798, age 23 yrs; DANIEL, 25th day, 4th mo., 1795; LETITIA, b. 21st day, 6th mo., 1790, d. 12th day, 8th mo., 1790; JOSIAH, b. 30th day, 9th mo., 1797.{GEMM}

SAMUEL SMITH of Cape May Co., shipwright, d. leaving a will dated 30 Jan 1720/1, proved 9 Jan 1724/5. Mentioned were wife Elizabeth and children: Armstrong, Samuel, Katherine, Elizabeth, Sarah. Wife extx. The will was witnessed by Joseph Whillden, Joseph Whillden, Jr., Geo. Oatway. On 5 Sep 1724 inventory was made of the estate by Humphrey Hughes and John Taylor.{NJCW}

SARAH SMITH, b. 1775, d. 25 Sep 1811.{Cold Spring Cemetery}

A marriage license was issued to John Scull and SARAH SMITH, 22 Nov 1776.{MLNJ}

THOMAS SMITH of Cape May Co. d. prior to 5 June 1767 when Daniel Smith was appointed admin. of his estate. Fellowbondsman: Shamgar Hand of Cape May Co. Witness: John Cresse. On 5 June 1767 an inventory was filed (£81.2.3) by John Cresse and Shamgar Hand.{NJCW 13:147} On 17 Sep 1767 an account was filed by admin.

A marriage license was issued to THOMAS SMITH and Sarah Cresse, 15 Nov 1739.{MLNJ}

WILLIAM SMITH, Jur. m. Phebe Jenkins of Cape May, 19 Aug 1750.{Baptists}

WILLIAM SMITH and Rachel Hand on 2 Aug 1762.{MLNJ}

WILLIAM SMITH and Margaret Rogers on 27 Dec 1768.{MLNJ}

WILLIAM SMITH d. leaving a will dated 1 Nov 1775. Mentioned were sons: David, Jacob, Joshua; grandson Enoch Smith, Elijah Smith,William Smith; granddau. Phebe Godfrey; son Jonathan's 5 children: Phebe Smith, Allither Smith, Zilpah Smith, Jonathan Smith and Reubin Smith who were to receive part of the estate when of age. The will was witnessed by Nathan Corson, Shamgar Hewit and James Smith. On 3 June 1777 an inventory was filed (£239.17.9) by Thomas Smith and Joseph Hildreth.{NJCW 21:245}

SOMERS

The Somers lived primarily in Gloucester County. The name of John Somers of Gloucester Co. appears in the long list of debtors of the inventory of the estate of John Stubbs in 1704.

Several entries in the following section dealing with the Somers family were published in *Philadelphia & Great Egg Harbor Journal & Ledger* of 28 Oct 1782 as reprinted *Genealogies of New Jersey Families*, published by Genealogical Publishing Co. (1996), Vol. 1, p. 790. Hereafter cited as{*Phila ... Ledger*}.

First Generation

1. JOHN SOMERS of England (d. 19 Dec 1723), m. Hannah (N).

John Somers of Great Egg Harbor left a will dated 8 Jan 1720/21, affirmed 14 Jan 1739. Mentioned were wife Hannah; sons: Richard, James, Samuel, Job, Isaac, Edmond; daus.: Bridget. Reference was made to three daus. Richard, exec. was devised the home land except for 400 acres. James was to have 350 acres where he lived. Samuel and Job to have 800 acres. Isaac was devised 400 acres at Gilbert's Pond. Edmond to have 350 acres. The will was witnessed by Peter White, Jonathan Addomas and Thomas Green.{NJCW 4:216}

Hannah Somers of Egg Harbor, Gloucester Co., d. leaving a will dated 12 Oct 1737, affirmed 24 Feb 1737/8. Mentioned were sons: Richard, James, Samuel, Job and Edmond; dau. Millicent; grandchildren: children of Hannah Ingerson, dec. and Hannah, dau. of James Somers. Reference was made to the three daus. of said Hannah Ingerson, dec. Exec. was son Richard. The will was witnessed by Daniel Ireland, Judith Steelman and Ruth Ireland.{NJCW 4:128} On 7 Jan 1738 an inventory was filed (£278) by Daniel Ireland and John Sculle.

John was father of the following children: BRIDGET; MILISCENT, b. Dec 1685, m. 16 June 1704 Richard Townsend*, son of John and Phebe Townsend; HANNAH, b. ca. 1691, d. 24th day, 2nd mo., 1737, m. 1st Joseph Dole* and m. 2nd Benjamin Ingersul*; RICHARD, b. 1st day, 3rd mo., 1693, d. 27th day, 10th mo., 1760; JAMES, b. 15th day, 1st mo., 1695, d. 22nd day, 2nd mo., 1761; JOHN, b. 26 March 1715; SAMUEL; JOB; ISAAC; EDMOND, b. 7th day, 7th mo., 1737, d. 7th mo., 1743{Dates from Townsend Family Record and GEMM}.

Second Generation

2. RICHARD SOMERS, son of John (1) and Hannah Somers, b. 1st day, 3rd mo., 1693, d. 27th day, 10th mo., 1760, m.[110] in 1726 Judith Letart (b. 26th day, 3rd mo., 1712, d. 10th day, 1st mo., 1761). They were parents of the following children{GEMM}: JOHN, b. 14th day, 10th mo., 1727, d. 28th day, 8th mo., 1799; SARAH, b. 21st day, 7th mo., 1729; JUDITH, b. 5th day, 6th mo., 1731; ELIZABETH, b. 4th day, 3rd mo., 1733; HANNAH, b. 22nd day, 12th mo., 1735/36; RICHARD, b. 24th day, 11th mo., 1737; JAMES, b. 7th day, 2nd mo., 1739; MILICENT, 12th day, 4th mo., 1743; JOSEPH, 4th day, 5th mo., 1743; EDMUND, b. 20th day, 5th mo., 1745.

Richard Somers of Great Egg Harbor, Gloucester Co., d. leaving a will dated 18 April 1752, proved 15 April 1761. He left his wife Judith £200 and use of 1/2 the plantation where he lived, that is to say, the half of the 1000 acres which his father left him. Son John, 1/2 the plantation with the islands, flats and waters adjoining, about 120 acres, and 1/2 the right to the island below the house, about 200 acres, and 20 acres of marsh at Tookhow Marsh. Son Richard to receive all the land that joins James

---

110 On 6th da., 12th mo., 1726 at the monthly meeting of Great Eggharbor the marriage of Richard Somers and Judeth Letart was reported orderly accomplished. {GEMM}

Steelman and the right that was taken up below it by three surveys on the north side of the channel of Great Egg Harbor Inlet, 426 acres, and 1/2 the right on Peck's Beach - he to pay his younger brother Edmund Somers, £34 when 21. Son James was devised the land at Grederes Neck which was taken up by five surveys; also 13 acres at Cedar Hammock; also 200 acres in Tookahow Meadows; also all of Garits Island of 138 acres; he to pay £34 to his brother Edmund. Son Joseph to receive the land bought of John Price on 21 Dec 1749 on South River in two surveys and one on Miere Run and other lands; he to pay his brother Edmund, £30. The rest of the moveable estate was to go to his four daus.: Sarah, Judith, Elizabeth and Hannah. Execs. were wife Judith and son John. The will was witnessed by Isaiah Scull, Fredrick Steelman, Recompence Scull and David Covenover. On 2 April 1761 an inventory was filed (£479.10.10) by Joseph Mapes and Fredreck Steelman. {NJCW 10:379}

Judith Somers of Great Egg Harbor d. leaving a will dated 28 April 1761, proved 7 Sep 1761. Mentioned were eldest son John Somers, sons: Richard Somers, James Somers, Joseph Somers, Edmund Somers; daus.: Sarah Somers, Elizabeth Somers, Judith Risley, wife of Samuel Risley, Hannah Somers; Judith Somers, dau. of son John Somers. Exec. was dau. Sarah Somers. The will was witnessed by Richard Dole, Gideon Scull and Judith Scull. On 5 Sep 1761 an inventory was filed (£228.7.3 1/2) by Joseph Mapes and Gideon Scull.{NJCW 11:110}

3. HANNAH SOMERS, dau. of John (1) and Hannah Somers, wife of Joseph Dole* and Benjamin Ingersul*, b. ca 1691, d. 24th day, 2nd mo., 1737. She was the mother of three daus. by Benjamin Ingersul.{See her mother's will.}

4. JAMES SOMERS, son of John (1) and Hannah Somers, b. 15th day, 1st mo., 1695, d. 22nd day, 2nd mo., 1761, m. Abigail (N) (b. 21st day, 7th mo., 1695, d. 5th day, 9th mo., 1772). They were the parents of the following children{GEMM}: SARAH, b. 1st day, 11th mo., 1720, d. 3rd day, 12th mo., 1809, m. Frederick Steelman*; HANNAH, b. 9th day, 7th mo., 1722, m. by license dated 20 Aug 1745{MLNJ}, Richard Smith; JOHN, b. 30th day, 2nd mo., 1723; JUDITH, b. 8th day, 12th mo., 1725, d. 30 June 1791{Cold Spring Cemetery}, m. Capt. Silas Swain, son of Ebenezer Swain*; ABIGAIL, b. 25th day, 10th mo., 1726; JAMES, b. 25th day, 3rd mo., 1728; REBECKAH, b. 5th day, 3rd mo., 1730; MARY, b. 7th day, 2nd mo., 1732; RACHEL, b. 27th day, 1st mo., 1734; ISAAC, b. 15th day, 2nd mo., 1736; MILLISENT, b. 25th day, 1st mo., 1738, d. 8th day, 7th mo., 1743.

James of Great Egg Harbor, d. leaving a will dated 30 April 1758, proved 15 April 1761. Mentioned was son John, to whom was devised a tract on Great Egg Harbor River, 450 acres. One acre to the Quakers where the meeting house stands. To son James, Jr., the homestead, 449 acres, with the grist mill, dam and one acre purchased of Return Badcock. To son Isaac land on the southwest side of Peter Covenover's of 250 acres. To son John land on the Beach of 100 acres known by the name of Great Hammock at the east end of the beach. Mentioned were daus.: Sarah Steelman, Hannah Smith, Judith Swain, Abigail Smith, Rebekah Badcock, Mary Somers and Rachel Somers. Exec. wife Abigail and son James. The will was witnessed by Joseph Mapes, James Robison and Mathew Dennis. On 10 April 1761 an inventory was filed (£416.0.1) by Joseph Mapes and James Robison.{NJCW 10:376}

Abigail Somers of Great Egg Harbor d. leaving a will dated 20 Oct 1769, proved 17 Nov 1772. Mentioned were dau. Sarah Steelman, Judith Swain, Abigail Smith, Mara Smith, Rachel Somers and Hannah Smith; John Badcok's three youngest children: Margaret Badcok, Rebekah Badcok and Nicholas Badcok to have their mother's share. The exec. was son John Somers. The will was witnessed by Richard Dole, Jacob Somers and Phebe Hakney. On 10 Sep 1772 an inventory was filed (£189.6.9) by Richard Dole. Bonds of James Somers, Silas Swain, Mary Smith, Benjamin Ingalson, Noah Smith, Joseph Dole. Notes of Isaac Somers, Fredrick Steelman and John Somers.{NJCW 14:466}

5. SAMUEL SOMERS, probable son of John (1) Somers, d. leaving a will dated 18 Sep 1761, proved 24 May 1768. Mentioned were wife Mary; eldest son John; son Isaac to whom was devised a plantation lately bought of William Jarret and 2/3 of sawmill; son Jacob, home plantation, right in Peck's Beach and 1/3 of sawmill; dau. Millesent Doughty; son-in-law James Somers; granddau. Martha Somers. Execs. were sons John and Isaac. The will was witnessed by David Lee, Hannah Price and Gideon Scull. On 24 May 1768 an inventory was filed (£253.11.7} by Thomas Pedrick and Moses Hoffman.{NJCW 13:403}

6. EDMOND SOMERS, probable son of John (1) and Hannah Somers, m. Mary Steelman*, dau. of Andrew Steelman.

On 7th day, 5th mo., 1735, Edmund Somers condemned his marrying out.{GEMM}

Edmund Somers of Egg Harbor, d. leaving a will dated 21 Aug 1743, affirmed 15 Sep 1744. Mentioned were wife Mary, extx.; son

Edmund who would have the whole estate after his mother's death; daus.: Hannah, Judith and Mary Somers who would have land about Mapel Swamp when 18 and another 200 acres of marsh at Great Egg Harbor Inlet. The will was witnessed by Richard Somers, Judith Dinge and Abigail Somers.{NJCW 5:170} On 13th day, 10th mo., 1744 an inventory was filed (£189.10.2) by Richard Somers and James Somers.

Edmond was the father of the following children: HANNAH, b. 2nd day, 11th mo., 1733; JUDITH, b. 9th day, 3rd mo., 1740; MARY, b. 28th day, 12th mo., 1742, m. John Falkenburg[111]; EDMOND.

7. JOB SOMERS of Egg Harbor, probable son of John (1) and Hannah Somers, d. leaving a will dated 26 March 1744, affirmed 15 Sep 1744. Mentioned were sons: Job and John to have he devised the home plantation; daus.: Hannah and Eunets. Exec. was brother Richard Somers. The will was witnessed by John Bond, Ezekill Harcort and Daniel Harker.{NJCW 5:172} On 10th day, 2nd mo., 1744, an inventory was filed (£130.2.0) by James Somers and David Cownover.

Job was father of the following children: JOB; JOHN; HANNAH; EUNETS.

Third Generation

8. EDMUND SOMERS of Great Egg Harbor Township, Gloucester Co., son of Richard (2) Somers, d. before 3 Oct 1772 when Richard Somers was appointed admin. of his estate. On 1 Feb 1773 an inventory was filed (£26.4.11) by Fredrick Stellman and James Steelman.{NJCW 14:512, 16:483}

9. JOHN SOMERS, son of James (4) Somers, on 4th day, 7th mo., 1757, was spoken to concerning his going out in marriage and bearing arms in military service.{GEMM}

10. ISAAC SOMERS, probable son of James (4) Somers, b. 15th day, 2nd mo., 1736. On 3rd day, 3rd mo., 1760, was disowned for his going out in marriage.{GEMM}

---

111 On 5th da, 1st mo, 1760, the marriage of John Falkenburgh of Little Egg Harbor and Mary Somers was reported orderly accomplished. {CEMM}

11. RICHARD SOMERS, son of Richard (2), b. 24th day, 11th mo., 1737, d. 22 Oct 1794, aged 56 years, 10 months, 28 days{*Phila ... Ledger*}, m. Suffiah Stillwell*, dau. of Nicholas and Sarah Stillwell, by license dated 3 Dec 1761.{MLNJ} On 2nd day, 8th mo., 1762 members of the monthly meeting spoke to him concerning his going out in marriage.

Richard and Sophia his wife appeared at October Court 1787 along with Moses Griffin and Sarah his wife, James Willets and Rebecca his wife, Rem Corson and Hannah his wife, Phebe Stillwell and Eli Eldredge, execs. to the estate of Sarah Stillwell, dec.{Ltrs&Inv A(Rev):16}

According to Price, Sophia d. 3 Feb 1797 and Richard Somers d. 22 Oct 1794. Richard Somers resided at Great Egg Harbor; moved his family to Philadelphia. Sophia and Richard Somers were the parents of the following children: CONSTANT, b. 14 Oct 1763{*Phila ... Ledger*}, d. 1797, m. 20 Aug 1790 Sarah Hand*, dau. of Jesse Hand; SARAH, b. 31 Dec 1772[112], d. 21 Jan 1850, m. Capt, Wm. Jonas Keen of Philadelphia; RICHARD, b. 15 Sep 1778, d. 4 Sep 1804, Naval hero of the war with Tripoli (See Cape May Co. Mag. Hist. & Gen., Vol. 1, No. 8, p. 307.); EDWARD, d. young; JANE, b. 8 Jan 1774{*Phila ... Ledger*}, d. young.[113]

12. JOSEPH SOMERS of Great Egg Harbor Township, probable son of Richard (2) Somers, d. by 3 Oct 1772 when Richard Somers was appointed admin of his estate. On 8 March 1773 an inventory was filed (£154.15.0) by Frederick Steelman and James Stellman. Land was sold by Sheriff for £150.{NJCW 14:513, 16:482}

13. According to John P. Dornan[114], HANNAH SOMERS, dau. of Richard (2) and Judith (Letart) Somers m. 1765, Peter Andrews, son of Peter Andrews. She d. at Philadelphia, 2nd mo., 21st day, 1821. Dornan notes that her husband was often confused with his first cousin Peter Andrews and she with her first cousin Hannah Somers, dau. of Edward

---

112 b. 30 Dec 1772 according to *Phila ... Ledger*.

113 This latter information is taken directly from "The Stillwells - A Patriotic Family, And Their Descendants," *The Cape May County of History and Genealogy*, p. 51. June 1940, by William Evans Price.

114 *Genealogical Magazine of New Jersey*, Vol. XXIV - XXVI.

[Edmund][115] and Mary Steelman) Somers. They were parents of the following children: AMY, b. 8th day, 5th mo., 1768 at Evesham; PETER, b. 31st day, 1st mo., 1770 at Evesham; TIMOTHY, b. 30th day, 1st mo., 1772 at Tuckerton, m. 1796 Sarah Townsend (b. 27th day, 4th mo., 1776, d. 3rd day, 1st mo., dau. of Isaac, Jr. and Keturah (Albertson) Townsend; ESTHER, b. 18th day, 10th mo., 1774, at Tuckerton, d. 16th day, 7th mo., 1793, at Somers Point; HANNAH, b. 4th day, 2nd mo., 1778, at Tuckerton, d. 20th day, 12th mo., 1848, at Philadelphia; JOSHUA, b. 1781/2 at Mount Holly, d. 15th day, 5th mo., at Philadelphia, m. 15 Feb 1806, Elizabeth Risley.

14. According to Dornan, HANNAH SOMERS, dau. of Edward [Edmund] and Mary (Steelman) Somers, m. Peter Andrews (b. 28th day, 8th mo., 1732, d. intestate 23 Dec 1762), son of Samuel Andrews. On 5th day, 5th mo., 1755, the marriage of Peter Andrews of Little Egg Harbor and HANNAH SOMERS was reported as orderly accomplished.{GEMM} Both Hannah and her husband have been confused with their cousins by the same name [see Hannah (13) above]. Peter Andrews was father of the following children: JESSE; MARY; SARAH, named in the will of Samuel Andrews, their grandfather, dated 7 March 1763.{NJCW 11:324}

Hannah Andrews of Gloucester Co. d. by 4 Jan 1761 when Benajah Andrews was appointed admin. of her estate.{NJCW 10:171}

Unplaced

A marriage license was issued to John Butler and ELIZABETH SOMMERS, 5 Aug 1762.{MLNJ}

On 2nd day, 8th mo., 1767, JACOB SOMERS was disowned for marrying his first cousin.{GEMM}

JACOB SOMERS d. 3rd day, 10th mo., 1772.{GEMM}

Jacob Somers of Great Egg Harbor Township, Gloucester Co., d. leaving a will dated 21 Sep 1772, proved 17 Nov 1772. Mentioned were sons Samuel and Jesse Somers to whom was devised land which testator's father bought of Amariah Lake, Samuel to have the part joining to his uncle Job Somers; son Jephet; child wife is likely to have; wife Eunice to have use of plantation until children are 21. Execs. were Isaac Townsend,

---

115 In most references the name appears as Edmund.

Jr. and Richard Dale. On 19 Oct 1772 an inventory was filed by Noah Smith and Joseph Mapes.{NJCW 14:470}

On 4th day, 2nd mo., 1760, it was reported that JAMES SOMERS, Jr., had sometime earlier married his first cousin contrary to good order of the Society (Quakers).{GEMM}

JAMES SOMERS d. by 29 Sep 1772 when John Somers of Great Egg Harbor Township was appointed admin of his estate. On 9 Oct 1772 an inventory was filed (£148.16.7) by John Hinchman and Joseph Ellis.{NJCW 14:513, 15:519}

JAMES SOMERS of Great Egg Harbor d. leaving a will dated 9 Aug 1777, proved 16 June 1779. Mentioned were son James to whom was devised the farm where testator's father lived, 480 acres and other land; 4 daus.: Elsey Somers, Sarah Somers, Rebecca Somers and Hannah Somers; sons: Aron, to whom was devised land and mills bought of William Allen, 311 acres and other land; dau. Abigail Steelman to receive £40 from Aron when his is 21; wife Rebecca; son-in-law Japhet Clark. On 6 Sep 1777 an inventory was filed by John Somers and Richard Somers.{NJCW 21:39}

On 6th day, 12th mo., 1743 JOB SOMERS condemned his outgoing in marriage.{GEMM}

JOB SOMMERS of Great Egg Harbor m. Eunice Cresse.{Gloucester Co. Court records dated 2 Jan 1732}

Job Somers of Great Egg Harbor d. leaving a will dated 28 April 1775, proved 26 Dec 1777. Dau. Eunice was bequeathed £300. Exec. was cousin Richard Somers, Esq. On 6 Sep 1777 an inventory was filed (£1,336.14.6) by Thomas Champion and Christopher Rape.{NJCW 19:420}

On 3rd day, 10th mo., 1763, JOB SOMERS was disowned for going out in marriage with his first cousin.{GEMM}

JOB SOMERS b. 26 Dec 1777. Job Somers aged 5 years & 6 month when bound out to James Hepborn to serve 15 years & 6 months. Indenture dated 27 June 1783. On another page: Easter Somers, dec. 1 June last [1783].{p. 67 of Richard Somers' Old Ferry Store, Philadelphia, day book, p. 790, *Genealogies of New Jersey Families.*}

On 30th day, 5th mo., 1757, the marriage of JOHN SOMERS and Rachel

Willets was reported accomplished. On 7th day, 11th mo., 1757 John Somers, son of Samuel Somers, and Rachel his wife acknowledged their unchaste freedom before marriage.{GEMM}

On 2nd day, 1st mo., 1758 a certificate was requested for John Somers, son of Samuel, to Salem Monthly Meeting for himself and wife.{GEMM}

This is probably the same John Somers who d. leaving a will dated 5 May 1768, proved 30 May 1768. Mentioned was wife Rachel who would have use of plantation for 7 years and she to bring up the children until they are of age. Sons Jacob and John were devised the plantation. Daus. Hannah Somers and Rachel Somers to have use of the house and plantation until son Jacob was age 21. A child that was yet unborn was provided for. Hannah and Rachel to have £50 each, when 21. On 28 May 1768 an inventory was filed (£395.0.4) by Isaac Somers and Thomas Pedrick.{NJCW 13:401}

On 1st day, 5th mo., 1751, the marriage of Samuel Risley and JUDETH SOMERS was reported as orderly accomplished.{GEMM}

On 5th day, 1st mo., 1760, the marriage of JUDITH SOMERS and Nathan Bartlett of Little Egg Harbor was reported orderly accomplished.{GEMM} On 2nd day, 2nd mo., 1761, a certificate was approved for Judith Bartlett, lately removed to Little Egg Harbor.{GEMM}

A marriage license was issued to Uriah Smith and MARY SOMMERS (Gloucester Co.), 24 Aug 1758.{MLNJ}

On 28th day, 3rd mo., 1750, the marriage of SAMUEL SOMERS, Jr., and Hannah Willets was reported orderly accomplished.{GEMM}

Child of SAMUEL SOMERS, Jr.: MARTHA SOMERS, b. 20th day, 6th mo., 1751.{GEMM}

On 6th day, 9th mo., 1762 SAMUEL SOMERS requested a certificate for himself and wife to Salem Monthly Meeting.{GEMM}

On 7th day, 2nd mo., 1763 ISAAC SOMERS, son of SAMUEL SOMERS, requested a certificate to Salem Monthly Meeting.{GEMM}

SPICER

First Generation

1. SAMUEL SPICER, Gravesend, L.I., m. Ester [Esther, Hester] Tilton, dau. of John. {New York Monthly Meeting} William Nelson in *New Jersey Biographical and Genealogical Notes* (1916)[116] states that Esther was dau. of John and Mary Tilton. He states Samuel removed from Gravesend, Long Island in 1686 to Gloucester, near Cooper's Creek.

Samuel and Esther were the parents of the following children (according to the records of New York Monthly Meeting): Abraham, b. 8th mo., 27th day, 1666, d. 5th mo., 25th day, 1679; Jacob, b. 1st mo., 20th day, 1668; Mary, b. 8th mo., 20th day, 1671; Sarah, b. 4th mo., 19th day, 1674, d. 1st mo., 5th day, 1677; Martha, b. 11th mo., 27th day, 1676, 2nd mo., 29th day, 1677; Sarah 2nd, b. 12th mo., 16th day, 1677/8; Abigail, b. 1st mo., 26th day, 1683.

Samuel Spicer of West New Jersey d. leaving a will dated 13 Sep 1692. Mentioned were sons: Jacob, Thomas, Samuel; daus.: Mary, wife of Jeremiah Bates, Sarah Spicer, Martha Spicer, Abigail Spicer. Land at the Fast Landing and at Pounsokin and beyond Francis Collins. Extx. was wife. Overseers: Wm. Bates, John Keey and Joseph Cooper. The will was witnessed by Samuel Jennings, James (N) and John White. Between 1699 and 12 March 1700 Letters testamentary were granted to Hester Spicer, the widow and extx. During the same period an inventory of the estate (personal estate - £481.19.0) was filed by Archebell Michell, John Cowperthwaite and Joseph Anstell. {Gloucester Wills}

Ester Spicer of Gloucester Co., widow of Samuel, d. leaving a will dated 27 July 1702. Mentioned were sons: Jacob and Thomas; daus.: Martha and Abigall. Grandchildren: Mary, Sarah, Martha and Abigall, children of dau. Mary, wife of Jeremiah Bate; Samuel, son of dau. Sarah, wife of Daniel Cooper. Legacies were given to Samuel, son of John Kay, and to the monthly meeting of women at Newtown. Execs. were son Jacob and son-in-law Cooper. The will was witnessed by John Kay, Mordecai Howell and James Wood. {NJCW}

Samuel was father of the following children: ABRAHAM; JACOB; THOMAS, b. prior to 1686; SAMUEL; MARY, m. Jeremiah Bates; SARAH 1ST; SARAH 2ND, m. Daniel Cooper; MARTHA; ABIGALL.

---

116 Hereafter cited as Nelson.

Second Generation

2. JACOB SPICER of Cape May, yeoman, son of Samuel (1) Spicer, was mentioned in the return of survey for Jacob Spicer, 400 acres of Society land, Bayside, first creek south of Cedar Hammocks on 9 April 1696.{Deeds A:11, reverse} He m. Sarah, widow of Ezekiel Eldredge*, on 6 March 1715. He d. 17 April 1741, aged 73 years,[117] leaving a will dated 4 Nov 1732, proved 9 April 1742. Mentioned were wife Sarah and son Jacob to whom was devised all lands but if Jacob died before 23 "which will be the tenth of April, or thereabout 1739," without lawful issue, then my brother, Thomas Spicer, shall hold my land in the county of Gloucester, he to have 1/2 of the benefit of the fishery on my plantation in Gloucester County, during life and the same to revert to my son Jacob, in case her survives him. Execs. were wife Sarah and son Jacob. The will was witnessed by Jacob Spicer, William Coats, Joshuay Grainger and Joseph Sleigh.{NJCW4:318}

Sarah Spicer, d. 25 July 1742, age 65.{Cold Spring Cemetery}

Jacob was the father of JACOB, b. 10 April 1716, d. 17 Sep 1765. {Cold Spring Cemetery}

3. THOMAS SPICER, SR. of Waterford, Gloucester Co., son of Samuel (1) Spicer, d. leaving a will dated 4 Jan 1759, proved 7 Nov 1759. Mentioned were wife Abigail and sons: Jacob, Thomas and Samuel; grandchildren: Abigail Rudderow, Jacob Spicer, Abigail dau. of Samuel, and Thomas Spicer. Mentioned was a farm in Greenwich in Gloucester Co., land and meadow in Waterford on Cooper's Creek adjoining Abel Nicholson; land bought of Samuel Nicholson; two farms between Samuel Burrough, John or Joseph Osler, cousin Jacob Spicer and Richard Wood; land in Waterford Township; home farm. Execs. were Jacob and Samuel with kinsman, Jacob Spicer of Cape May Co.{NJCW 9:308} On 17-18 1759 an inventory was taken (£1421.0.8) including a Negro man and 2 Negro boys, by Henry Wood and Joseph Morgan.

Thomas m. Abigail, dau. of Francis and Sarah Davenport.[118]

---

117 According to Lewis T. Stevens in *History of Cape May County*, his remains lie on the Vincent Miller Homestead with the inscription, In Memory of Col. Jacob Spicer who died April 17, aged 73 years. According to Stevens he was a grandson of Thomas and Michael Spicer, New England Puritans. Today there is a tombstone for Col. Jacob Spicer next to that of his wife at Cold Spring Cemetery.

118 According to Nelson the Davenports came from Willington, Debyshire, England, in 1691 and settled in Burlington Co. {Nelson:195}

Thomas was father of the following children: JACOB, m. Mary Lippincott, d. 31 Oct 1779 without issue {Nelson:195}; THOMAS; SAMUEL, b. 29 Oct 1720.{Nelson:195}

Third Generation

4. JACOB SPICER, b. 10 April 1716, son of Jacob (2), d. 17 Sep 1765, {Cold Spring Cemetery}, m. 1st Judith Hughes*, dau. of Humphrey Hughes, by license dated 10 June 1738.{MLNJ} She was b. 1715, d. 7 Sep 1747.{Cold Spring Cemetery} They were parents of the following children: SYLVIA, b. 1736, d. Philadelphia on 23 July 1802, m. 10 Nov 1764 Rev. Samuel Jones in Philadelphia[119]; SARAH, b. 13 July 1738, d. 5 Sep 1806, m. 8 Aug 1761, Christopher Leaming 3rd*{MLNJ}; JUDITH, buried at Cold Spring Cemtery, m. 26 Oct 1773 by license, Elijah Hughes*, Jr.{MLNJ}

Jacob m. 2nd Deborah Leaming, widow of Christopher Leaming*, by license issued 16 Dec 1752.{MLNJ} Jacob Spicer and wife Deborah were living in 1761.{Deeds A:84}

Jacob d. 17 Sep 1765{Stevens:137}, leaving a will dated 6 May 1762, proved 9 Oct 1765. Personal estate was to be sold to pay debts, and, if needed, the 250 acres bought of Robert and Sarah Ewing, except 10 acres reserved, and the 200 acres bought of Christiana Peterson (now Grover), and the plantation bought of Gabriel Powell (and many others). Son Jacob was to be educated. Wife Deborah by marriage agreement was to receive £100. Dau. Sarah Leaming, a wood lot. Silvia Spicer, a bed; dau. Judith Spicer, a bed. In the will Jacob said that he had married the widow of Christopher Leaming and had administered but as yet no settlement had been made which he ordered his execs. to do. He stated that the son Christopher Leaming had made him his guardian; Thomas Spicer, Sr., had made him one of his execs.; Lydia Hand had made him exec. to her will and gave her personal estate to her dau. Experience Hand who married John Robertson to whom Jacob had given the proceeds of Lydia's estate, and Experience had since died. He appointed John Townsend and Aaron Leaming, Esq., the appraisers of his personal estate. Dau. Silvia Spicer to received 1/2 of Two Mile Beach. Dau. Judith Spicer to have land. Dau. Sarah Leaming, land, Dau. Judith Spicer to dwell with her mother-in-law, so long as she is his widow. He desired that wife, children-in-law and own children, to live in union with each other. Execs. were Abel James, Jacob Spicer, Sr., of Gloucester Co., wife Deborah, son-in-

---

119 Raymond Hughes in the Hughes genealogy says Rev. Jones was b. Carnarvonshire, North Wales, 14 Jan 1735. They were parents of Sarah, b. 23 July 1744.

law Christopher Leaming, his wife Sarah Leaming, Silvia Spicer and Judith Spicer. Overseers: Daniel Lawrence, Nicholas Stillwell and John Eldredge. The will was witnessed by Ebenezer Johnson, Henry Hand, Henry Stites and Christopher Church.{NJCW 12:256}

5. THOMAS SPICER of Gloucester Co., son of Thomas (3) Spicer, m. Rebecca Day[120] by license dated 29 Dec 1740.{MLNJ}

Thomas Spicer of Waterford Township, Gloucester Co. d. leaving a will dated 14 May 1760, proved 6 Dec 1760. Mentioned were wife Rebecca and dau. ABIGAIL. Execs. were wife and Henry Wood. The will was witnessed by James Johnson, Samuel Osler and John Daniel.{NJCW 10:386} An inventory was taken on 27 Oct 1760 (£371.1.6) by William Stone and Samuel Osler.

6. SAMUEL SPICER of Gloucester Co., son of Thomas (3) Spicer, b. 29 Oct 1720, m. 16 Nov 1743 by license dated 3 Aug 1743, Abigail Willard.{MLNJ}

Samuel Spicer of Waterford, Gloucester Co., surveyor, d. leaving a will dated 1770, sworn 16 May 1777. Mentioned were Abigail Spicer[121] to whom he left the entire estate, she paying to dau. Sarah Spicer when 18, £100 and to dau. Rebecca Spicer when 18, £30.{NJCW 18:380}

Samuel was father of the following children: ABIGAIL; SARAH; REBECCA.

STEELMAN

This family was situated primarily in Old Gloucester County.

1. ANDREW STEELMAN of Great Egg Harbor Township, Gloucester Co., d. leaving a will dated 2 Jan 1731, proved 5 Feb 1736/7. Wife Judith was extx. Mentioned were sons: Frederick to whom was devised 420 acres bought of John Budd and 100 acres bought of Samuel Ward between South River and Stephen's Creek, joining to Great Egg Harbor River; James, 450 acres adjoining John Rambo's on the west side of Great Egg

---

120 According to Nelson she was dau. of Humphrey and Jane Day.{Nelson:195}

121 Nelson:195 states Abigail d. 24 April 1752 and that Samuel then m. 2nd Sarah Potter of Shrewsbury.

Harbor River, joining upon west side of Stephens' Creek; Peter, 250 acres of the home plantation, joining Daniel Ireland's; Andrew, plantation of 250 acres joining James Sommer's on the west side. Andrew and Peter to have 130 acres near Seader Swamp Bridge. Daus.: Mary Somers, Judith, Susanna (the last two not of age). The will was witnessed by Daniel Ireland, John Wells, Alexander Fish and Thos. May.{NJCW 4:84} On 3 Feb 1736/7 an inventory was filed (£286.14.0) including 83 head of cattle. Appraised by Daniel Ireland and Alexander Fish.

Andrew was the father of the following children: FREDERICK; JAMES; PETER; ANDREW; MARY, b. 15th day, 6th mo., 1714, d. 21st day, 5th mo., 1797, m. 1st Edmund Somers* and m. 2nd Joseph Mapes; JUDITH, probably m. Charles Dingee[122]; SUSANNA, may have m. John Kelle[123].

2. FREDERICK STEELMAN of Great Egg Harbor, son of Andrew (1) Steelman, m. Sarah Somers*.

He d. leaving a will dated 22 March 1773, proved 29 April 1778. Mentioned were wife Sarah; eldest son JAMES to whom he devised the saw mill on Gravely Run; sons: FREDERICK and ANDREW; daus.: SARAH, ABIGAL, JUDETH, MARY, HANNAH and RACHEL Steelman; Elias, son of dau. Abigal. The will was witnessed by Thomas Morris, Noah Smith and Jeremiah Robinson.{NJCW 20:82}

3. JAMES STEELMAN of Egg Harbor, Gloucester Co., Gent., probable son of Andrew (1) Steelman, d. leaving a will dated 2 Aug 1734, proved 10 Jan 1734/5. Wife Katharine to have the estate during her widowhood. Mentioned were sons: Andrew and Hance (who had plantation); John, the land and marsh bought of John English where the mill stood, "at the day of his mother-in-law, Katharine Steelman's death or marriage, he to pay £10 to granddau., Susannah, dau. of son John; James, 200 acres where he lived which was mortgaged to the Loan Office; Elias (had plantation); Peter (not 21) to have after the death or marriage of widow and his mother, Katharine Steelman, the home plantation bounding upon Pattcunk's Creek, also 200 acres bought of James Adams and Judiah Allen and land bought of Peter Scull. Daughters: Susannah Kean (had portion), Mary Blackman

---

122 Charles Dingee and JUDITH STEELMAN announced their intentions to marry on 7th da., 6th mo., 1738. {GEMM}

123 A marriage license was issued to John Kelle and SUSANA STEELMAN, 24 Oct 1764. {MLNJ}

(had portion). Execs. were wife Catherine and son John Steelman. Trustee: Nathan Lake. The will was witnessed by Nathan Lake, Edward Orser, Solomon Manery.{NJCW 3:452} On 4 Jan 1734/5 an inventory was filed (£322.3.4} which included cattle and sheep. Appraisers: Nathan Lake and Solomon Manaring.

James Steelman of Gloucester Co. was named as a debtor in the 1704 inventory of the estate of John Stubbs, mariner.

James was father of the following children: ANDREW; HANCE; JOHN; JAMES; ELIAS[124]; PETER; SUSANNAH, m. (N) Kean; MARY, m. (N) Blackman.

4. PETER STEELMAN, son of Andrew (1) Steelman, b. 1st day, 5th mo., 1723, d. 21st day, 4th mo., 1762. On 5th day, 9th mo., 1750, the marriage of Peter Steelman and Hannah Leeds was reported as orderly accomplished. Hannah was b. 18th day, 2nd mo., 1726, d. 24th day, 11th mo., 1762.{GEMM}

Peter and Hannah Steelman were the parents of the following children{GEMM}: JAPHET, b. 10th day, 1st mo., 1752, d. 1st day, 11th mo., 1754 (new style); JUDETH, b. 20th day, 9th mo., 1754, d. last da of 10th mo., 1754 (new style); ISAAC, b. 5th day, 1st mo., 1756 (new style); DEBORAH, b. 9th day, 11th mo., 1757 (new style); MARY, b. 20th day, 3rd mo., 1760, d. 29th day, 7th mo., 1760; SUSANNAH, b. 12th day, 4th mo., 1762, d. 3rd day, 10th mo., 1819.

5. MARY STEELMAN, dau. of Andrew (1) Steelman, m. 1st (N) Somers and m. 2nd Joseph Mapes ca. 3rd mo. 1746. On 26th day, 3rd mo., 1746 the marriage of Joseph Mapes and Mary Somers was reported as orderly accomplished.{GEMM}

Joseph Mapes, son of Joseph Mapes, b. 25th day, 7th mo., 1714 and Mary, his wife, dau. of Andrew Steelman, b. 15th day, 6th mo., 1714, d. 21st day, 5th mo., 1797 were parents of the following children: EDMOND, b. 6th day, 2nd mo., 1747; MELISENT, b. 14th day, 5th mo., 1752, d. 14th day, 7th mo., 1806.

6. JAMES STEELMAN, probable son of James (3) Steelman, d. by 19 May 1767 when Andrew Steelman of Great Egg Harbor was appointed admin. Fellowbondsman: John Lawrence, City of Burlington. Witness:

---

124 Elias Steelman of Great Eggharbour m. Comfort Cresse. {Gloucester Co. Court records dated 16 Dec 1732};

Robert Burchan.{NJCW 13:103}

6. ELIAS STEELMAN of Gloucester Co., probable son of James (3) Steelman, d. by 12 April 1774 when his son Elias, under age of 14, was made a ward of Frederick Steelman.{NJCW 15:521}

7. ISAAC STEELMAN, son of Peter (4) Steelman, was a ward of Japhet Leeds of Great Egg Harbor of Great Egg Harbor, being under 14, Japhet being his uncle.{NJCW 11:280}

8. DEBORAH STEELMAN, dau. of Peter (4) Steelman, was a ward of Japhet Leeds of Great Egg Harbor on 10 Dec 1762, she being under age 14, said Japhet being her uncle on her mother's side. Fellowbondsmen: Noah Smith and Jesse Smith, yeomen.{NJCW 11:279}

9. SUSANNAH STEELMAN of Gloucester Co., dau. of Peter (4) Steelman, was a ward of Japhet Leeds of Green Egg Harbor, she being under age 14, the said Japhet being her uncle. Fellowbondsmen: Noah Smith and Jesse Smith, yeomen.{NJCW 11:280}

Unplaced

ANDREW STEELMAN of Egg Harbor d. by 11 March 1772 when Hannah Steelman, widow, was appointed admx. Fellowbondsman: Joseph Edwards of Cape May, yeoman. On 24 Feb 1772 an inventory was filed (£746.8.3) by Noah Smith and Joseph Edwards.{NJCW 14:427}

David Richman m. ELLONER STEELMAN (both of Gloucester), at Tuckehoo, Aug 15, 1764.{Baptists}

Jeremiah STEELMAN m. Rebecka Cownover of Great Eggharbour on 7 May 1750.{Baptists}

STEVENS

DANIEL STEVENS, b. 17 July 1771, d. 17 Jan 1828.{Cold Spring Cemetery}

EZEKIEL STEPHENS m. Rebeckah Stillwell by license dated 30 April 1763.{MLNJ}

Ezekiel d. prior to 9 Jan 1781 when his widow, Rebecca Stevens, was appointed admx. of his estate. Fellowbondsman: Jacob Hughes of

Cape May Co. Witnesses: Henry Stevens and Elijah Hughes. An inventory was made on 9 Jan 1781 (£7,251.5.0) by Jacob Hughes and Henry Stevens.{NJCW}

A marriage license was issued to Abraham Bennet and LEVICE STEVENS, 6 Nov 1759.{MLNJ}

PHILOMELIA STEVENS, b. 1773, d. 5 Feb 1833.{Cold Spring Cemetery}

A marriage license was issued to HENRY STEPHENS and Jane Iszard, 8 Aug 1764.{MLNJ}

STEPHEN STEPHENS m. Mary Matthews on 8 Sep 1774.{Baptists} A marriage license was issued to them on 5 Sep 1774.{MLNJ}

STEWART (STEWARD)

Jacob Hewet and ELIZABETH STEWARD m. 26 Jan 1773.{Baptists}

EZEKIEL STEWARD and Rachel Garison, May 4, 1773.{Baptists}

Doctor PATRICK STEWART of Cape May d. prior to 28-29 April 1758 when an inventory of the estate was filed by Jeremiah Hand and Jacob Spicer; it included apparel, cash, medicines, surgical instruments, etc. A bond was issued on 2 Oct 1758 to William Smith as admin; Jacob Spicer fellow bondsman, both of Cape May Co.{NJCW 9:313} On 13 Nov 1760 an account was submitted by William Smith, admin.{NJCW}

STILLWELL/STILLWILL

Stevens in his *History of Cape May County* states John Stillwell came to Cape May County from Long Island about 1692.

The information on Nicholas (5) Stillwell and his family is chiefly based chiefly on "The Stillwells - A Patriotic Family, And Their Descendants, *The Cape May County of History and Genealogy*, p. 51. June 1940, by

William Evans Price.[125] For more details on this family and its role in the Revolutionary War see this article and a follow-up article in which the author adds information discovered after the earlier article.

First Generation

1. JOHN STILLWELL of Cape May Co. d. leaving a will dated 1 June 1752, proved 9 May 1753. Mentioned were children: Daniel, Richard and Patience Shaw; grandchildren: Nicholas Stillwell, John Evans, David Evans and Elizabeth Evans (now Skull). Execs. were sons Richard and Daniel. The will was witnessed by Susannah Hand, Isaiah Hand and John Leek.{NJCW 8:180}

John was father of the following children: DANIEL; RICHARD; PATIENCE, m. Richard Shaw*, son of William and Lydia Shaw.

Second Generation

2. DANIEL STILLWELL, probable son of John (1) Stillwell, d. leaving a will dated 26 Sep 1793, proved 4 Dec 1794. Mentioned were son THOMAS; grandson Daniel Stevens; son JOHN. Witnesses: Ann Hughes, Naomi Cresse and Hannah Ingrum.{NJCW 35:101} On 3 Dec 1794 an inventory was filed (£216.3.7) by Ebenezer Newton and Joshua Crowell.{NJCW File:613E}

3. RICHARD STILLWELL, yeoman, probable son of John (1) Stillwell, d. leaving a will dated 2 May 1759, proved 7 June 1759. Mentioned were wife Mary and children: Elijah, Elizabeth, Zerviah Stites and Phebe. Grandson, John Foster. Estate included a Negro man. Execs. were son Elijah and son-in-law Richard Stites. The will was witnessed by Benjamin Laughton, David Bancraft and William Simkins.{NJCW 9:245} On 6 June 1759 an inventory was filed by Christopher Foster and John Leek which included a Negro and books.{NJCW}

In "Diaries of Aaron Leaming," he mentions the death of Mary Stillwell, widow of Richard Stillwell in 1760.

Richard Stillwell had the following children: ELIJAH; ELIZABETH, m. Aaron Eldredge*, son of Samuel Eldredge; ZERUIAH (dec.), m. Richard Stites* by license dated 9 Sep 1748.{MLNJ} The last named had children Elijah (seaman) and John (wife Jean). (Book of Mortgages A: 211, dated 1785){Deeds A:28-30}

---

125 The author was then living at 41 Davis Ave., Bloomfield, NJ.

Third Generation

4. ELIJAH STILLWELL, probable son of Richard (3) Stillwell, d. prior to 29 Oct 1765 when Richard Stites and Aaron Eldredge, gent., were appointed admins. Fellowbondsmen: Isaac Newton, Gent. of Cape May Co. Witnesses: Job Young and Jacob Hughes. On 22 June 1764 an inventory was filed (£66.2.10) by Jacob Hughes and Isaac Newton.{NJCW 12:358}

5. CAPT. NICHOLAS STILLWELL, probable grandson of John (1) Stillwell,[126] b. 1714, m. ca. 1738 Sarah --- (b. 1718, d. 1777, probable dau. of George Hand*, Sr.). Nicholas Stillwell d. 2 April 1771, leaving a large estate; bur. at Beeseley's Point. They were parents of the following children: HANNAH, m. Rem Corson* by license dated 17 Jan 1759{MLNJ}; SOPHIA, b. 7 April 1741, m. 3 Dec 1761{*Phila ... Ledger*}, Richard Somers* by license dated 3 Dec 1761{MLNJ}; NICHOLAS, JR.; AMELIA, b. 1744, d. 22 Aug. 1759; ENOCH; REBECCA m. James Willets*, Jr.; SARAH, m. Moses Griffing*; DAVID; RHUHAME, b. 1757, d. 25 June 1759.[127]

Nicholas left a will dated 1 Feb 1771, proved 4 May 1771. Mentioned were children: Enoch to whom was left land in Gloucester Co. at Tuckaho River, bought of John Champion and Joseph Champion and Jonathan Smith and 20 acres of salt marsh; David, to whom was devised a tract bought of Joseph Camp and other land; Nicholas and Enoch; Sophia Summers; Hannah Corson; Rebeckah Willets; and Sarah Griffin. Also mentioned were grandson Constant Summers; Charity Corson, wife of Jacob Corson. Execs were wife Sarah and sons Nicolas and Enoch. The will was witnessed by Joseph Badcock, Hugh Hathorn and Hannah Hand. On 12 June 1795 Moses Griffing and Sarah Griffing of Cape May were appointed admins. Fellowbondsman: Nicholas Willets. Witnesses: Stephen Hand, Tryphena Bancraft and Thomas J. Curtis. [The execs. appointed by the testator died after administering part of the estate; therefore said Moses and Sarah Griffing were appointed admins, to settle the rest of estate.] On

---

126 The name Nicholas is mentioned as grandson in the will of John (1). There are two sons mentioned, Daniel and Richard. Richard's children are named in his will in 1759 suggesting that Nicholas was son of Daniel.

127 In the article "The Stillwells -- A Patriotic Family and Their Descendants," The Cape May County of History and Genealogy, p. 51, June 1940, the author notes the opinion of H.C. Campion, Jr., that Nicholas Stillwell, Sr., may have had a 10th child, Charity. Charity Stillwell m. 15 Oct 1750, Jacob Corson.

13 Feb 1772 an inventory was filed (£4,839.19.4) by James Godfrey and Eli Eldredge.{NJCW 15:182; 36:276}

Sarah, widow of Nicholas Stillwell, d. leaving a will dated 16 March 1774, proved 22 April 1777. Mentioned were daus. Hannah Corson, Sophia Somers, Rebekah Willets and Sarah Griffin; granddaus.: Armela Corson; sons: Nicholas, Enoch and David.{NJCW 38:77}

Fourth Generation

6. NICHOLAS STILLWELL, son of Nicholas (5) and Sarah Stillwell, b. 20 Sep 1742, d. 23 June 1792, m. 11 Feb 1771 Rhuhamah (b. 22 Sep 1755), dau. of Cornelius Hand. Rhumah m. 2nd 9 April 1801 Matthew Whilldin; she d. 24 Feb 1839, bur. in the old cemetery at Cape May Court House.

Nicholas Stillwell of Cape May Co. d. by 24 July 1792 when Jeremiah Hand, son of Nathaniel Hand, was appointed admin. of his estate. On 23 July 1792 Ruhamah Stillwell, the widow, renounced the will.{NJCW 34:466} On 26 July 1792 an inventory was filed (£195.17.5) by Eli Townsend and Joseph Hildreth.{NJCW File:582E}

Nicholas and Rhuhamah were parents of the following children: NICHOLAS 3rd, b. 26 May 1772, d. 11 Dec 1798, probably without issue; OLIVE, b. 8 March 1775, d. 28 March 1782; LUDLAM HAND, b. 6 July 1777, d. 20 Dec 1800 at sea; AMELIA, b. 23 Oct 1779, d. without issue 30 Jan 1798, m. John H. Kean; JANE, d. 17 Nov 1782, d. 1829, m. 7 March 1802 Daniel Whilldin*; RHUHAMAH, b. 15 Aug 1785, d. June 1793; OLIVE, b. 10 Dec 1788, d. Aug 1794; RICHARD, b. 21 March 1792, d. 28 Feb 1814, without issue.

7. ENOCH STILLWELL[128], son of Nicholas (4) and Sarah Stillwell, b. 5 April 1747, d. 31 Jan 1787, m. 28 Aug 1768[129] Sarah (b. 9 May 1750, d. 19 March 1782), dau. of Joseph and Martha Savage. On 27 Feb 1787 Phebe Stillwill and Eli Eldredge were appointed as admins. An inventory was filed (£2,552.9.10) by Jesse Hand and Thomas Shaw.{NJCW 29:241}

Enoch and Sarah Stillwell were the parents of the following children: MARTHA, b, 28 April 1770, d. 17 March 1791, m. 28 Jan 1789, Joseph Hildreth*; SAVAGE, b. 7 July 1773, m. 27 Jan 1800 Susanna Mason of Perkiomen; SARAH, b. 20 Feb 1776; ANNA, b. 28 July 1778, d. 10 Nov 1820, m. 1 April 1793 Joseph Hildreth* (husband of her dec.

---

128 See Williams Evans Price, "The Stillwells - A Patriotic Family, And Their Descendants, *The Cape May County Magazine of History and Genealogy*, p. 51. June 1940.

129 Marriage license issued 26 Aug 1768.{MLNJ}

sister Martha); SOPHIA, b. 6 March 1781.

Sophia and Anna, daus. of Enoch Stillwell chose Richard Somers of Philadelphia as their guardian on 23 May 1787 and their brother, Savage, chose Richard Somers of Philadelphia as his guardian on 28 May 1788.{NJCW 29:242; 31:94}

At February court 1789 at the request of Mr. Van Leuveneigh in behalf of Joseph Hildreth who m. Martha Stillwell, dau. of Enoch Stillwell, dec. and one of the heirs of Joseph Savage, Esqr., dec. the court appointed Elijah Hudges, Persons Leaming and Philip Hand, auditors to make division of the real estate of said Joseph Savage.{Ltrs&Inv A(Rev):30}

On 23 May 1787 Colonel Richard Summers applied for the appointment of guardianship to himself to take care of the persons and estate of Anna and Sophia Stillwell, daus. of Colonel Enoch Stillwell, dec.{Ltrs&Inv A(Rev):11}

On 27 May 1789 Richard Summars, guardian to the estates of Anna and Sophia Stillwell, daus. of Enoch Stillwell, dec., complained in court against Phebe Stillwell now Daniels and John Daniels her husband, admins. of the estate of Enoch Stillwell, dec. Next court.{Ltrs&Inv A(Rev):32}

At May Term 1791 the account of John Daniel and Phebe his wife late Phebe Stillwell surviving admin. of the estate of Enoch Stillwell, dec. was submitted; £186.16.6 to be distributed.{Ltrs&Inv A(Rev):67}

At October Court 1787 Richard Sumers and Sophia his wife, Moses Griffin and Sarah his wife, James Willets and Rebecca his wife, Rem Corson and Hannah his wife, Phebe Stillwell and Eli Eldredge, were acting as execs. to the estate of Sarah Stillwell, dec.{Ltrs&Inv A(Rev):16}

At October Term 1795 Joseph Hildreth applied for a division of lands late of Joseph Savage, dec., between the said Joseph Hildreth on the part of his late wife Martha Stillwill, Savage Stillwill and Sarah Stillwill which lands the afsd. Joseph bought of Nathan Hand. So ordered.{Ltrs&Inv A(Rev):1112}

8. DAVID STILLWELL, son of Nicholas (4) and Sarah Stillwell, b. ca. 1755, mentioned in his grandfather's will (1771), d. 1788. He m. Jane Jones, dau. of Abraham. In the Revolutionary War he was a private, late an ensign in the Gloucester Foot Company. They had a son ENOCH. Following the death of David Still his widow Jane, m. John Champion. David and Jane Still were parents of a son ENOCH who m. by license 10 Oct 1810 Rany Champion, believed to be from Gloucester Co.

Fifth Generation

9. SAVAGE STILLWELL, son of Enoch (7) and Sarah Stillwell, b. 7 July 1773, m. 27 Jan 1800, Susanna Mason of Perkiomen, became a merchant in Philadelphia. They had a dau. SOPHIA SOMERS STILLWELL.

UNPLACED

Jacob Corson & CHARITY STILLWELL of Cape May m. 15 Oct 15, 1750.{Baptists}

A marriage license was issued to Aaron Eldridge and ELIZABETH STILLWELL, 25 Jan 1761.{MLNJ}

A marriage license was issued to Ezekiel Stephens and REBECKAH STILLWELL, 30 April 1763.{MLNJ}

A marriage license was issued to RICHARD STILLWELL and Sarah Hand, 1 Jan 1736.{MLNJ}

THOMAS STILLWELL, b. 24 Sep 1732, d. 24 Jan 1820.{Cold Spring Cemetery}

A marriage license was issued to THOMAS STILLWELL and Hannah Shaw, 11 Feb 1761.{MLNJ}

STITES

The name is often misread as Stiles. In research of the Stites family also check Stiles entries.

Edmund J. James describes early generations of the Stites family in his article in *The New York Genealogical and Biographical Record*, "The Stites Family," p. 123, Vol. XXVIII (July 1897), 165-166; (Oct 1897), 237-239; Vol. XXIX (April 1898), 93-98. See this article for more details.

According to Edmund J. James:

> John Stites, M.D., was b. in England, 1595, and settled at first in New England, later at Hemstead, L.I., where he d. in 1717. His

son Richard, b. 1640 in England, d. 1702 at Hemstead, L.I. He had three sons: HENRY; BENJAMIN; WILLIAM.

Henry Stites, son of Richard, b. at Hemstead, L.I., removed ca. 1680 to Cape May Co., m. Hannah Garlick of East Hampton, L.I., ca. 1692. James lists children of Henry as Richard and others. Below I show no evidence of children of Henry (1). I show the same Richard as probable son of Richard (2).

According to Lewis Townsend Stevens in *The History of Cape May County* ... Dr. Beesley gave the following information (1857): "Henry Stites, ancestor of all in the county of that name, came to the country about or in the year 1691. He located 200 acres of land, including the place now belonging to the heirs of Eli Townsend. ... a justice in 1746. He left a son, Richard, who resided at Cape Island, and he a son, John, from whom the Lower Township Stites have descended. His son, Isaiah, who died in 1767, and from whom the Stites of the Upper and part of the Middle Township have descended, lived on the place now occupied by his grandsons, John and Townsend Stites, at Beesley's Point. The Middle Township Stites, below the court house, are descendants of Benjamin Stites, who was probably a brother of Henry, and was in the county in 1705."

First Generation

1. HENRY STITES, m. 15 Feb 1693/4, Hannah Garlick*, dau. of Joshua Garlick, before Samuell Crowell, Justice. Witnesses: John Carman, John Shaw, Caleb Carman, Ruth Daton, William Sharwood, Jacob Spicer, Ezekiel Eldredge, Jonathan Pine, Jonathan Osborne, Shamger Hand, Timothy Brandreth.{First Public Rcds:280}

The name Henry Stites, whaleman, appears in the land records of Cape May Co. on 22 April 1695 as owning 200 acres.{Deeds A:450}

2. RICHARD STITES, brother of Henry (1) Stites, m. Abigail Garlick, dau. of Joshua Garlick*. Reference was made to Abigail Stites, widow of Richard Stites on 19 April 1743.{First Official Rcds}

Richard Stites of Cape May Co. d. leaving a will dated 26 Dec 1739, proved 22 May 1740. Mentioned were son Richard, to whom was devised all lands when age 14 (excepting 1/2 the land which was given to wife Abigail during her widowhood). Sons: Henry and Abishai, £80 at age 21. Henry was to be given to brother Henry Stites until of age and Abishai to brother, John Stites until age 20. Daus.: Hannah, Zerviah and Abigail (all under age 18 and unmarried). Execs. were Henry Stites and brother John Stites and wife Abigail.{NJCW 4:238} On 15 May 1740 an inventory including cash, apparel, cattle, sheep and swine, was filed; appraised by Elisha Hand and Joshua Stites.{NJCW}

Richard was the father of the following children: RICHARD; HENRY; ABISHAI; HANNAH; ZERVIAH; ABIGAIL, m. David Bancroft*.

3. JOHN STITES, brother of Henry (1) and Richard (2) Stites, d. leaving a will dated 29 June 1743, proved 1 Aug 1743. Mentioned were cousin Abisha Stites [nephew], son of Richard Stites of Cape May, dec., to whom a tract was devised when age 20, between the land of Richard Shaw and John Garlick, Cape May Co.; also 50 acres, bought of the Commissioners of the Loan office (as a legacy left him by his father, I being one of the executors). Wife Prissila extx., received use of the lands unsold until cousin Abisha was age 20 and the remaining lands until dau. Margrit was age 20. The will was witnessed by Joshua Stites, Elijah Hughes and Cornelius Schillink, Jr.{NJCW 5:7} On 1 Aug 1743 an inventory of the estate was filed which included cooper tools and plantation tools and stock; appraised by Elisha Hand.{NJCW}

John Stites m. Priscilla Leaming* (b. 15 June 1710, d. 21 Sep 1758), dau. of Thomas and Hannah Leaming. He and Priscilla had the following issue: MARGARET, b. at Cape May 1740, d. Cape May 22 Oct 1764, m. at Cape May on 3 March 1763 by license issued 25 Jan 1763{MLNJ}, Jonathan Leaming, son of Aaron Leaming the second, b. 1738; they had one child: Priscilla, b. 9 Oct 1764, d. 4 April 1821, m. Humphrey Stites* (d. 11 June 1827).{Baptist Burials}

4. RICHARD STITES, probable son of Richard (2) Stites, m. by license of 9 Sep 1748{NJCW}, Zeruiah (Zerviah) Stillwell*, dau. of Richard Stillwell, noting that Richard Stillwell had children: Elijah, Elizabeth who m. Aaron Eldredge and Zeruiah (dec.) who m. Richard Stites. The last named had children Elijah and John (wife Jean). {Book of Mortgages A: 211, 1785}

Zerviah Stites d. prior to 21 May 1746 when Richard Stites was appointed admin. Fellow bondsman, Elisha Hand, of said county.{NJCW 5:248} On 10 April 1746 an inventory was filed by Elisha Hand and Cornelius Schillinks.{NJCW}

Richard Stites d. leaving a will dated 23 Sep 1772, proved 23 Jan 1773. Mentioned were wife Zeruiah, dau. of Richard Stillwell whose land descended to his only son Elijah Stillwell. Elijah d. intestate and the lands descended to said Zeruiah and Elizabeth, wife of Aaron Eldredge. Richard had by his wife Zeruiah, 3 sons: John, Richard and Elijah, Zeruiah now being dead (at the time the will was written) her land descended to their son John. At the time the will was written Richard Stites had married Ruth Mulford, 28 Nov 1770, widow of Daniel Mulford, and before that marriage took place a deed of settlement was made dated 25 Sep 1770. Daus. Zeruiah Stites, Philomela Stites, Mary Stites, Abigail Stites and Hannah Stites to whom personal estate was left. Execs. were wife Ruth and Aaron Eldredge and Elijah Hughes. The will was witnessed by James Whilldin, Ezekiel Eldrredge, Henry Stites, Levi Eldredge, Jonathan Eldredge and Aaron Leaming. On 23 Jan 1773 an inventory was made (£463.7.2) by James Whilldin and Levi Eldredge.{NJCW 16:126}

Richard and Zeruiah had the following children: JOHN; RICHARD; ELIJAH; ZERUIAH; PHILOMELA; MARY; ABIGAIL; HANNAH.

5. ISAIAH STITES, probable son of John (3) Stites, m. Rhoda Crowell* by license issued 29 April 1738.{MLNJ}

Mathew Crowell had sisters Elishaba, Mary, Experience and Rhoda who m. Isaiah Stites (1799).{Deeds B:182}

This is probably the same Isaiah Stites who d. leaving a will dated 22 Jan 1764, proved 23 May 1768. Mentioned were wife Elizabeth; son Esaiah to whom was devised 1/2 of tract in Middle Precinct which formerly belongs to testator's father. Son Henry to have the west 1/2 of said tract. Sons John and Israel to have land that their father lived on. Daus. Sarah Stites and Hannah Stites to receive rest of the moveable estate. Execs. were son Isaiah Stites, wife, and dau. Sarah Stites. The will was witnessed by John Goldin, Joseph Badcock and Daniel Gerretson. On 23 May 1768 an inventory was filed (£235.10.3) by Nicholas Stillwill and Reuben Ludlam.{NJCW 13:442}

Isaiah was father of the following children: ESAIAH; HENRY; JOHN; ISRAEL; SARAH; HANNAH.

6. ELIJAH STITES of Elizabeth Borough, Essex Co., probable son of Richard (4) Stites, d. leaving a will dated 30 Oct 1765, proved 9 Nov 1767. Mentioned were wife Mary; daus.: Rebecca Scodder and Rachel Hand; dau. Nancy. Six daus.: Nancey, Mary, Hannah, Providence, Chloe and Asenah. Sons: Elijah and Abner were devised that part of the farm on the southeast of the road, 70 acres. Exec. brother John Stites, who was to be guardian of the children: Witnesses: John Whitehead, Margaret Stites.{NJCW I:173}

Elijah was father of the following children: REBECCA, m. (N) Scodder; RACHEL, m. (N) Hand; NANCY; MARY; HANNAH;

PROVIDENCE; CHLOE; ASENAH; ELIJAH; ABNER.

7. JOHN STITES, son of Richard (4) Stites, b. 1756, d. 12 Dec 1840; m. Jane (N) who d. 3 Aug 1817, age 65. She was a native of the city of Philadelphia.{Cold Spring Cemetery} John was placed as ward of John Stillwell, mariner, on 20 April 1773.{NJCW 15:530}

8. RICHARD STITES, son of Richard (4) Stites, was placed as ward of William Schellinger, pilot, appointed guardian on 6 Nov 1773. Fellowbondsmen: Abraham Bennet and Christopher Leaming. Witnesses: Henry Schillinger and Elijah Hughes.{NJCW 18:623}

9. JOHN STITES, son of Isaiah (5) Stites, was appointed a guardian, Isaiah Stites, on 26 Oct 1768. Fellowbondsman: Joseph Ludlam of Cape May Co. Witnesses: Jonathan Jenkins, Joshua Hildreth and James Townsend.{NJCW 12:523}

BENJAMIN STITES

1. BENJAMIN STITES of Cape May Co., yeoman, d. leaving a will dated 6 Sep 1732. Mentioned were wife Elizabeth to whom was devised the house and 40 acres and 10 acres of marsh near Fishing Creek, except two apples trees and land under them which was given to his two youngest sons; also debt due from Shamgar Hand. Son George was given the remainder of the land, he to pay a bond due the West Jersey Society and after wife's marriage or death, he to pay each of his brothers, Benjamin and Jonathan, £20 when they arrived at age 21. Daus.: Deborah Paig and Martha Ludlum. Execs. were wife Elizabeth and son George Stites. Overseers of two youngest sons, sons-in-law, Joseph Paige and Jeremiah Ludlam.{NJCW 3:335} An inventory was filed on 18 Sep 1732 by Nathaniel Rusco and John Paige.{NJCW}

Benjamin Stites recorded his ear mark on 17 May 1707; later recorded for Jonathan Stites.

Benjamin was the father of the following children: GEORGE; BENJAMIN; JONATHAN; DEBORAH, m. Joseph Page; MARTHA, m. Jeremiah Ludlam.

2. GEORGE STITES of Cape May Co., yeoman, probable son of Benjamin (1), d. leaving a will dated 23 Sep 1754, proved 27 Sep 1754.

Mentioned were wife Esther; sons: WILLIAM, GEORGE, THOMAS, NATHAN, ADONIJAH[130] and DANIEL, all but the first two under age. Execs. were wife and son George. The will was witnessed by Mary Taylor, Jane Doubedee and Francis Taylor.{NJCW 8:67} An inventory was filed on 15 Oct 1754 by Christopher Foster and Joshua Shaw.{NJCW}

3. BENJAMIN STITES, Jr., son of Benjamin (1) Stites, m. Sarah Hand, dau. of Daniel Hand, by license issued 14 Jan 1779.{MLNJ} Sarah Stites and Martha, wife of Absolom Hand, were daus. of Daniel Hand dec. (1795).{Deeds A:122; B:29-35}

Benjamin Stites had the following children: HUMPHRY, probably m. Priscilla Leaming*; PHILIP; JOSHUA; PATIENCE, m. David Cresse*; ELIZABETH, m. Eli Eldredge* (1791). Benjamin also had two grandchildren: Silsby and Eli, both sons of Nathaniel Jenkins.{Deeds A:137}

4. GEORGE STITES, probable son of George (2) Stites, d. leaving a will dated 10 March 1774, proved 13 Aug 1777. Mentioned were son George to whom was devised the plantation whereon the testator lived, when he is 20 years of age; son Joshua; daus. Eadith Stites, Rowena Stites and Abigail Stites to whom were left lands at Dennis Creek. Wife to have her dower right and 12 acres. The will was witnessed by John Foster, Nathaniel Philips and Thomas Prather. On 13 Aug 1777 an inventory was filed (£590.1.7) by Thomas Smith and Benjamin Stites.{NJCW 21:120}

George was father of the following children: GEORGE; JOSHUA; EADITH; ROWENA; ABIGAIL.

5. THOMAS STITES, son of George (2) and Esther Stites, m. Hannah Jenkins of Cape May, June 19, 1756. She was a dau. of Nathaniel (2) and Elizabeth (Seeley) Jenkins*, b. ca. 1736, (*Cape May Co. Mag. of Hist and Gen.*, June 1955, p. 24). Hannah m. 2nd (N) Young.

6. PHILIP STITES, probable son of Benjamin (3) Stites, m. Rachel (N) (d. 20 Nov 1817 in her 53rd year.{Baptist Burials} On 3 Aug 1786 Philip complained that Jesse Hand as exec. to estate of Rachel Smith detained a legacy due to his wife given to her as a legacy of dec.{Ltrs&Inv A(Rev):6}

---

130 In "Diaries of Aaron Leaming," he mentioned the death of Adonijah Stites in 1760.

HENRY STITES

1. HENRY STITES of Cape May Co. d. leaving a will dated 6 Feb 1748/9, proved 8 May 1749. Mentioned were son Esaiah, exec., to have the tract on which the testator lived, joining Richard Smith and the land that was formerly John Reeves; also 1/2 personal estate. Dau. Mary Skillinger, 1/2 of movables. The will was witnessed by Richard Smith, Hannah Smith and Daniel Hand.{NJCW 6:62} On 25 May 1749 an inventory was filed which included cattle, sheep and swine; appraised by Joseph Savage and Zebulon Swaine.{NJCW}

Henry was father of the following children: ESAIAH; MARY, m. Cornelius Skillinger* on 10 June 1715{First Official Rcds}.

2. HENRY STITES, Jr., Cape May Co., probable son of Henry (1), d. leaving a will dated 1 Sep 1746, proved 27 Nov 1746. Mentioned were cousin Zebulon Swaine, son of Zebulon Swaine, late of Cape May, dec., exec. and to have the entire estate. The will was witnessed by Daniel Smith, Martha Smith and Willm. Evans.{NJCW 5:495} On 3 Dec 1746 the inventory of the estate was filed including horses, cattle, sheep, swine, whale boat and tackling; appraised by John Leonard and Joseph Savage.{NJCW}

Unplaced

A marriage license was issued to --- STITES and Sarah Eldridge, 30 Oct 1727.{MLNJ}

A marriage license was issued to David Bancroft and ABIGAIL STITES, 6 Nov 1752.{MLNJ}

A marriage license was issued to ELI STITES and Temperance Bowen, 22 July 1769.{MLNJ}

ELI STITES of Cape May Co. d. prior to 2 June 1770 when Temperance Stites was appointed admx. Fellowbondsman: Thomas Matthews of Cape May Co. Witnesses: Joshua Hildreth and Zeruiah Hughes. On 26 May 1770 an inventory was filed (£44.15.10) by Joshua Hildreth and Thomas Mathews.{NJCW 14:399}

A marriage license was issued to Jeremiah Mills and ELIZABETH STITES on 18 Feb 1757.{MLNJ}

A marriage license was issued to Richard Janvier and ELIZABETH STITES, 24 Dec 1761.{MLNJ}

A marriage license was issued to Nathaniel Jenkins and ESTHER STITES, 15 May 1753.{MLNJ}

A marriage license was issued to Elijah Hughes and HANNAH STITES, 28 Oct 1740.{MLNJ}

HANNAH STITES of Cape May Co., widow, d. leaving a will dated 21 July 1791, proved 5 Nov 1795. Mentioned were eldest dau. Edith Townsend, son George Stites and daus.: Kowanna and Abigail; son Joshua. The will was witnessed by Sarah Carll, Martha Hand and Constantine Carll.{NJCW 36:266} On 30 Oct 1795 an inventory was filed (£61.4.8} by Jeremiah Richardson and Constantine Foster.{NJCW File:632E}

A marriage license was issued to HENRY STITES and Pheby Swain, 11 July 1769.{MLNJ}

ISAIAH STITES m. Hannah Cressey by license issued 19 Dec 1770.{MLNJ}

A marriage license was issued to ISRAEL STITES and Phebe Scull (Great Egg Harbor), 11 April 1775.{MLNJ}

JONATHAN STITES m. Elizabeth Lawrence, 10 Feb 1774.{Baptists}

JOSHUA STITES of Cape May Co. d. prior to 21 May 1746 when Abigail Stites was appointed admx. Fellow bondsman, Henry Stites. Witness: Cornelius Schillinks.{NJCW 5:248} An inventory was filed on 7 May 1746 which included cattle, horses and sheep; appraised by Joseph Savage and Elisha Hand.{NJCW}

Joshua probably m. Abigail PARSONS*.

A marriage license was issued to Jonathan Leaming and MARGARET STITES, 25 Jan 1763.{MLNJ}

A marriage license was issued to John Nicholson and MARTHA STITES, 25 Oct 1763.{MLNJ}

A marriage license was issued to Silas Lupton and MARY STITES, 11 May 1756.{MLNJ}

NATHAN STITES, d. 6 Aug 1823, age 54 years, 6 mos., 9 days. He m. Charlotte (N) (b. 2 or 5 July 1776, d. 2 or 5 Jan 1826.{Cold Spring Cemetery}

A marriage license was issued to David Cresse and PATIENCE STITES on 27 Sep 1769.{MLNJ}

A marriage license was issued to Matthew Whildin and RHODA STITES, 8 Dec 1768.{MLNJ}

Samuel Matthews and TEMPERANCE STITES m. 10 Aug 1771.{Baptists}

A marriage license was issued to Samuel Matthews and Temperance Stites, 10 Aug 1771.{MLNJ}

THOMAS STITES, b. 3 April 1777, d. 9 Dec 1867, m. Rhoda (N) (d. 8 Oct 1841, age 50 years, 5 mos., 28 days).{Baptist Burials}

THOMAS STITES of Cape May Co., son of Jacob Stites, dec., chose William Flowers as his guardian on 13 March 1792. Fellowbondsman: Isaiah Hand.{NJCW 34:467, File:583E}

A marriage license was issued to Nathaniel Jenkins and WILLERAMINA STITES, 15 Aug 1765.{MLNJ}

WILLIAM STITES & Rachel Crowell of Cape May m. 8 May 1751.{Baptists}

STORER

John Storer of Cape May, now of Burlington, d. leaving a will dated 28 Oct 1687 and proved 6 Dec 1687 which divided property between Daniel England of Burlington and Thomas Potts of the same place. Exec. was Daniel England. The will was witnessed by Sara Sherwine, Martha Hill and James Hill. On 9 Nov 1687 the estate was inventoried by John Brigs and Alexander Humphrey. On 6 Dec 1687 a bond was issued to Daniel England, sailor, as admin. Thomas Gardner fellow bondsman.{NJCW Cape May Wills} In 1687 Letters of administration on the estate were granted to Daniel England.{NJCW}

STUBBS

JOHN STUBS of Cape May, mariner, d. leaving a will dated 29 Aug 1702 and proved 4 Sep 1702 and 26 July 1705 in which was divided his personal estate between Richard Downes, Richard Carr, Deborah Hand, Peter Procter. Execs. were John Taylor, Thomas Hand and John Hickman. The will was witnessed by John Downes, Tho: Hand and George Hand. On 24 July 1704 an inventory was taken of the estate (£529.12.7 1/2) of which £20 stands for the plantation of John Tailor's; the rest was personal including debts due [listed]. On 5 Sep 1702 bonds had been issued to John Hickman, John Taylor and Shamger Hand as admin. of the estate. Account of Shamger Hand against the estate of John Stubbs. In 1704 a bond of Shamger Hand as admin. (and principal creditor). Joshua Barkestead and George Willis fellow bondsmen.{NJCW 1:77 and Cape May Wills}

Letters of administration granted to John Hickman, Shamger Hand and John Tayler on the effects of John Stubbs, 5 Sep ---, ca. 1708? {First Official Recds}

SWAIN

For additional detils see "Swain Family," *The Cape May County Magazine of History and Genealogy*, p. 251, June 1953, by Margaret Irwin McVickar.

According to Ms. McVickar,

> RICHARD SWAIN came to this country in the ship, *Truelove* in 1635. He m. 1st Elizabeth called Brasilla (N). She and several of their children preceded him to the colonies. The family first lived in Rowley, MA and then moved to Hampton, NH. Richard and Brasilla were the parents of the following children: FRANCIS, b. in England, m. Martha (N); WILLIAM, m. Prudence Marston in NH and later drowned; DOROTHY, m. 1st Thomas Abbott, m. 2nd Edward Chapman, m. 3rd Archelaes Woodman; ELIZABETH, m. 1656, Nathaniel Wier (Weare); JOHN, m. Mary Wier (Weare);

GRACE, m. Nathaniel Boulton (or Boulter).

Richard Swain m. 2nd in 1658, Jane Bunker, widow, and dau. of John Godfrey of Ipswich.[131] Richard and Jane were the parents of a son RICHARD, b. 13 Jan 1660 in Hampton, NH. Richard Swain and seven other men, including his son John, purchased the island of Nantucket from Thomas Mayhew.[132] Jane Swain, wife of Richard, d. 31 Oct 1662 on Nantucket Island. Richard Swain d. 14 April 1682.

2. RICHARD SWAIN, son of Richard and Jane Swain, was father of the following children: ABIGAIL, b. 7 Feb 1683; JONATHAN, b. 23 Dec 1685; EBENEZER, b. 1686; LEMUEL, b. 1689. Richard Swain and his family probably moved to Cape May ca. 1686.

Richard Swaine (2) of Cape May d. prior to 22 May 1707 when administration of his estate was granted to his eldest son Jonathan Swane.{NJCW 1:179} On 22 Aug 1707 an account was made of the estate by Andrew and John Belcher of Boston, New England, against the estate. On 21 Oct 1706 an inventory of the estate was made by Humphry Hughes and Samuel Foster. On 6 Oct 1706 an account was made by Jonathan Swaine, admin. On 28 July 1707 Letters of administration were granted to Jonathan Swayne, son of Richard, formerly of Nantucket, late of Cape May, husbandman, by Isaac Addington, Judge of Probate for Suffolk Co., MA. An additional inventory was made on 13 May 1708. A final account was made on 6 Sep 1708. On 25 Oct 1708 Ebenezer, 19 years old and Alamuwell (Lemuel), age 16, sons of Richard, petitioned that their brother Jonathan be appointed their guardian.{NJCW}

Richard m. Sarah, widow of Thomas Jacocks. Following the death of Richard, Sarah m. William Mason. Sarah Mason of Cape May d. leaving a will dated 16 Feb 1714/5. Mentioned were sons: Jonathan Swain, Ebenezer Swain, Joshua Jacocks and James Jacocks, granddau. Joanna Swain, and "my own daughter." A legacy to Nathaniel Jencens. Son-in-law Jonathan Swain and Elizabeth Swain to be "overseers of my own sons and executors." The will was witnessed by Humphrey Hughes, Joseph Welden, Debrow Russell.{NJCW 2:56}

---

131 See the McVickar article for more on John Godfrey.

132 The McVickar article gives more details on the Swains in Nantucket.

3. JONATHAN SWAIN, son of Richard (2) Swain, Jr., b. 23 Dec 1685, m. Ruth Jeacocks, dau. of William and Sarah Jeacocks. In the deeds of 1715 is shown Jonathan Swaine, cooper, and wife Ruth.{Deeds B:95}

4. EBENEZER SWAIN, son of Richard (2) Swain, Jr., b. 1686, m. Mary Jeacocks*, dau. of William and Sarah Jeacocks.

Ebeneser Swaine recorded his ear mark on 18 Jan 1707; later recorded for Silas Swain.{First Official Rcds}

Ebenezer Swain of Cape May Co., mariner, d. leaving a will dated 12 Dec 1755, proved 18 May 1756. Mentioned were wife Mary and children: Daniel, James, Silas, Mary Townsend and Ruth Mulford. Home farm; land adjoining Timothy Hand; interest in Five-Mile Beach; part of a mill; land between Reuben and Daniel Swaine. Execs. were sons Daniel and Silas. The will was witnessed by Ruth Swain, Mary Forkland and Francis Taylor.{NJCW Cape May Wills:179E}

Ebenezer was the father of the following children: MARY, m. ca. 1st month, 1732/3, Silvanius Townsend*[133]; SARAH; DANIEL; JAMES; RUTH, d. 21 Oct 1790, age 65, m. 1st Daniel Mulford* and m. 2nd Richard Stites*; SILAS, d. 8 May 1795, age 73{Cold Spring Cemetery}, m. Judith Somers.

5. SILAS SWAIN, son of Ebenezer (4) and Mary Swain, m. Judith Somers*, dau. of James and Abigail (Adams) Somers.{"The Pierson Family," The Cape May County Magazine of History and Genealogy, p. 63, June 1956} Silas Swain was father of JEREMIAH, b. 6 Feb 1770, who m. 14 March 1790, Mary Pierson.{Swain Bible as transcribed in Pierson article}

6. JEREMIAH SWAIN, son of Silas (5) and Judith Swain, b. 6 Feb 1770, d. 5 Nov 1806, m. 14 March 1790, Mary Pierson* (b. 14 Feb 1775), dau. of Stephen Pierson. They were the parents of the following children: ROXANNA, b. 4 April 1794; MARY, b. 14 Dec 1796; ANN, b. 20 July 1799; ELIZA LINN, b. 7 Dec 1801, d. 26 Aug 1802; ANN ELIZA, b. 31 Aug 1803, d. 21 Oct 1805; RUTH MILLS, b. 12 Dec 1806.{Swain Bible as transcribed in Pierson article}

Mary (Pierson) Swain, widow of Jeremiah, m. 2nd Dr. Robert Coleman Schenck; she d. 10 June 1812.

---

133 On 12th da., 1st mo., 1732/3, the marriage of Silvanius Townsend and Mary Stites was reported as orderly accomplished. {GEMM}

7. LEMUEL SWAIN, son of Richard Swain, Jr., b. 1689, m. Jerusha Hand.

Lemuel Swaine of Cape May Co. d. leaving a will dated 21 Sep 1733, proved 2 March 1733/4. Mentioned were wife Jerusha; son Samuel at age 21 to have 60 acres back of William Johnson; son Reuben land whereon testator lived. Daus.: Abigail, Elizabeth, Marcy, Lydia and Phebe, 2/3 of personal estate. If wife with child, it is to have equal part in personal estate. Execs. were wife Jerusha and son Reuben. The will was witnessed by Humphrey Hughes, Ebenezar Swaine and Daniel Swaine. {NJCW 3:408} On 2 March 1733/4 an inventory of the estate was filed by John Stillwell and Joshua Stites. {NJCW}

Lemuel was father of the following children: SAMUEL; REUBEN; ABIGAIL; ELIZABETH; MARCY; LYDIA; PHEBE.

8. REUBEN SWAIN, probable son of Lemuel (7) Swain, d. prior to 21 Feb 1758 when an inventory was filed for his estate by Amos Johnson and Richard Stites which included a Negro man. On 22 Feb 1758 a bond was issued for George and Judith Taylor as admins.; Amos Johnson fellow bondsman, all of Cape May Co. On 27 Oct 1758 an additional inventory was filed which included a pilot boat and tackle, made by the same appraisers. {NJCW Cape May Wills:193E}

9. ZEBULON SWAINE of Cape May, son of Hannah Stites, yeoman, d. leaving a will dated 10 April 1739 [apparently 1729 was intended], proved 22 April 1730. Brother Henry Stites was exec. and guardian of testator's son Zebulon. Dau. Martha was placed in the charge of mother Hanah Stites. The will was witnessed by John Stites, Hope Willets, Jacob Crowell. Inventory of the estate was made on 21 April 1730 by John Stilwell and Nathaniel Rusco. {NJCW}

Zebulon Swain recorded his ear mark on 9 Sep 1723, later recorded by James Swain. {First Public Rcds:272}

Zebulon was the father of the following children: ZEBULON; MARTHA.

10. REUBEN SWAIN, son of Reuben (8) Swain, of Cape May Co. chose his brother-in-law, George Taylor as his guardian. [George Taylor m. Jude (Judith) Swain by license dated 9 Feb 1758.] On 23 July 1760 a bond was issued for George Taylor as guardian. John Taylor, fellow bondsman, both of Cape May Co. {NJCW 10:602}

Reuben d. leaving a will dated 15 April 1780, proved 14 July 1780. He stated in his will that he had considerable landed estate and have but 2 daus., now in infancy and desired his lands to be rented until eldest dau. Elizabeth Swain was 21 and if she did not live then to dau. Martha Swain at age 21. Wife Edith to have rents. Execs. were wife Edith and friend Henry Hand. The will was witnessed by Silas Swain, Nezer Swain and Catherine Swain. On 14 July 1780 an inventory was filed (£13,594.7.5) by Silas Swain and Jonathan Leaming.{NJCW 24:83}

At the February Term 1790 Richard Townsend, Esqr. in behalf of Martha Swain, minor, and Daniel Swain in behalf of his wife, the heirs of Ruben Swain, dec. requested the land be divided.{Ltrs&Inv A(Rev.):45}

At August Term 1790 auditors were appointed to divide the lands of Reuben Swain, late dec. between his two daus.: Elizabeth, wife of Daniel Swain and Martha Swain, minor.{Ltrs&Inv A(Rev):51} (plats shown). Martha petitioned on 14 March 1794 to have Eleazer Hand as her guardian.{NJCW 35:110, File 614E}

Reuben was father of the following children: ELIZABETH, m. Daniel Swain; MARTHA.

11. ZEBULON SWAIN, probable son of Zebulon (9) Swain, d. leaving a will dated 14 March 1794, proved 8 Jan 1795. Mentioned were wife Abigail and sons Zebulon and John; daus.: Phebe Stites, Martha Godfrey, Sarah Townsend and Hannah Leaming.{NJCW 36:186, File 634E}

Zebulon was father of the following children: PHEBE, m. Henry Stites by license dated 11 July 1769{MLNJ}; MARTHA, m. Elijah Godfrey by license dated 8 Nov 1769{MLNJ}; SARAH, m. John Townsend*, Jr, by license dated 8 Jan 1777{MLNJ}; HANNAH, b. 3 March 1767, d. 14 Sep 1857, m. in 1784, Spicer Leaming*{County Clerk's recds, Book B, Cold Spring Cemetery}.

Unplaced

DANIEL SWAIN m. Keziah, dau. of John Cresse (1761).{Deeds A:84}

Daniel of Cape May Co. d. leaving a will dated 26 April 1771, proved 21 July 1774. Mentioned were wife Kezia, all the cedar swamp (except that what he had by his brother Neazer Swain, dec.), also the use of the plantation. To son William the land where testator lived. To son Aaron the plantation at wife's death. To son Daniel the cedar swamp that testator had by his brother Neazer Swain. To daus.: Jane Swain, Mary Swain and Kezia Swain; and to son Daniel, the moveable estate. To sons William and Aaron, all the navigation books, seal and other instruments of navigation. Rights to five mile beach to be sold. Boat to be sold. Execs. are wife Kezia and son William. The will was witnessed by Ezekiel Hand,

Ezra Hand, Elijah Hughes. On 8 Aug 1774 an inventory was filed (£192.12.3) by James Whilldin and Henry Hand.{NJCW 17:167}

DANIEL SWAIN, d. 4 June 1834, age 72 years, 2 mos., m. Elizabeth (N), d. 26 Aug 1849, age 81 years, 13 days.{Cold Spring CEMETERY}

A marriage license was issued to John Yates and ELIZABETH SWAIN, 9 April 1768.{MLNJ}

George Croslee m. HANNAH SWAIN April 16, 1750, of Cape May.{Baptists}

A marriage license was issued to JACOCKS SWAIN and Hannah Townsend, 10 Feb 1774.{MLNJ}

JAMES SWAIN of Cape May d. by 17 Feb 1773 when Jacob Crowell was appointed admin. Fellowbondsman: Daniel Crowell. On 11 Feb 1773 an inventory was filed (£88.13.7) by Henry Hand and Daniel Crowell.{NJCW 14:521}

A marriage license was issued to George Taylor and JANE SWAIN, 3 Oct 1775.{MLNJ}

A marriage license was issued to JOHN SWAIN and Rebecca Hand, 6 June 1760.{MLNJ}

A marriage license was issued to George Taylor and JUDE SWAIN on 9 Feb 1758.{MLNJ}

LEMUEL SWAIN d. prior to 20 May 1766 when Elizabeth Swain was appointed admx. of his estate. Fellowbondsman: Robert Parson of Cape May Co. Witnesses: James Whilldin and David Townsend. On 4 April 1766 an inventory was filed (£137.0.5) by Robert Parson and James Whilldin.{NJCW 12:357}

Dr. John Hunt m. MARY SWAIN, Feb 14, 1773.{Baptists}

A marriage license was issued to John Hunt, Jr. and Mary Swain, 13 Feb 1773.{MLNJ}

NEZER SWAIN, b. 1756, d. 18 June 1796.{Cold Spring Cemetery}

Nezer Swain d. leaving a will dated 26 Sep 1793, proved 21 June 1796. Mentioned were wife Catharine; children mentioned but not named.{NJCW 36:264} On 1 July 1796 an inventory was filed (£987.1.5) by Matthew Whilldin and Ebenezer Newton{NJCW File:664E}

A marriage license was issued to REUBEN SWAIN and Martha Hughes, on 3 Nov 1766.{MLNJ}

A marriage license was issued to REUBEN SWAIN and Elizabeth Eldridge, 12 May 1772.{MLNJ}

Silas Young m. TABITHE SWAIN 13 Dec 1749, of Cape May.{Baptists}

TAYLOR

The following is partially based on Parsons Account Book and First Public Records.

First Generation

1. GEORGE TAYLOR was in Cape May Co. as early as 10 May 1692 when he was appointed clerk by the Justices. On 4 April 1694 his name was noted in the deed book A:14.

An inventory of George Taylor's estate, appraised by John Crafford and William Golding, was filed on 9 Sep 1701.{First Public Rcds}

On 5 Sep 1693 George Taylor recorded his ear mark (later Benjamin Taylor's){First Public Rcds:270}

Second Generation

2. JOHN TAYLOR, son of George (1) Taylor of Cape May Co., and Elisabeth Belsher, late of Boston, in New England, m. after the manner of the Church of England, on 5 April 1697. Recorded 14 April 1697. Witnesses: Elisabeth Taylor, Jno. Worledg, Tim. Brandreth.{First Official Rcds} John was father of the following children: MARGERY, b. 16 Aug 1698, m. James Briggs* on 22 March 1713; GEORGE, b. 11 Dec 1699; JOHN, b. 14 June 1704; MARY, b. 25 April 1707, d. 11 Oct 1711; SAMUELL, b. 27 March 1710, d. 11 Oct 1711; JEREMIAH, b. 14 Aug 1713, d. 22 Dec 1713.{First Official Rcds:325}

3. GEORGE TAYLOR, probable son of John (2) Taylor, m. 8 May 1720, Lydia Shaw, dau. of William and Lydia Shaw*, by Rev. Nathaniel Jenkins.{First Official Rcds}

George Taylor of Cape May Co., yeoman, d. leaving a will dated 11 Aug 1738, proved 14 July 1739. Mentioned were wife Lydia and children: William, George, John, Matthias, Daniel and Lydia (all under age). Execs. were wife and son William, "now very ill." The will was witnessed by Joshua Shaw, Nathan Shaw and Francis Taylor. A codicil was written on 14 Aug 1738 devising a plantation to son William and another to son George. The codicil was witnessed by the same witnesses. On 19 May 1739 an inventory of the estate was filed by Ebenezer Swaine and John Stites.{NJCW Cape May Wills:95E}

Lydia Taylor, spinster, d. leaving a will dated 4 Oct 1764, proved 20 Nov 1766. Mentioned were sons George Taylor and John Taylor, to whom she devised her back land, lying at the head of the plantation where she lived, of 140 acres. Son Daniel Taylor was left her land at Prince Morrises River in Cumberland Co., about 300 acres. Grandson William Taylor to receive 100 acres in Middle Precinct. Should Lydia Skellinks outlive her husband, Cornelius Skellinks, then Daniel Taylor was to give his sister, Lydia Skellinks, moveable estate, and, if Lydia should choose not to live with her husband, then she to have it. Execs. were George Taylor and Daniel Taylor. The will was witnessed by Henry Hand, Joshua Shaw, Jr. and Jonathan Leaming.{NJCW 13:472}

They were the parents of the following children: WILLIAM b. 7 June 1722; eldest dau. b. 22 Feb at nite 1723/4; dau. b. 24 Jan in the night 1726/7; GEORGE, probably m. Sarah Hand, dau. of Elias Hand; LYDIA, b. Aug 1730, m. Cornelius Schellinger* (Skellinks); JOHN, b. 25 Dec 1732; MATTHAIS, b. Sep 1734; --- b. 6 April 1737; DANIEL.{First children based on First Official Rcds. Lydia and subsequent children based on Parsons Account Bk; in addition the wills mention GEORGE and DANIEL.}

4. JOHN TAYLOR, probable son of John (2) Taylor m. Lydia Schillinx* 14 Oct 1722 by Rev. Nathaniell Jenkins. Their dau. Mary Taylor was b. 5 Aug 1723. Lydia d. Nov 1725. John m. again to Deborah Garrison by Mr. Jenkins, 8 May 1726. {First Official Rcds}

John Tayler of Cape May Co. d. prior to 20 Sep 1728 when his estate was inventoried by Henry Young and George Taylor. The estate included a Negro boy. On 30 Sep 1728 administration of the estate was granted to Deborah Taylor. A bond was issued to her on 30 Sep 1728. Henry Young fellow bondsman, both of Cape May Co. on 4 June 1737 an account of the estate was made by Deborah, late widow of Cornelius Hand

and now wife of Jeremiah Hand, who had charges "for dyetg & cloathg ye decds child Deborah 3 yrs at £5 p. a. and for 3/4 a year's Schooling." {NJCW}

John was father of the following children: MARY; DEBORAH.

Third Generation

5. JOHN TAYLOR, son of George (3) Taylor, had children: MERCY Curry, JUDITH Taylor and DANIEL Taylor, mentioned in the will of Lydia Schellenger, sister of John (5) Taylor. {NJCW 34:463}

Unplaced

A marriage license was issued to BENJAMIN TAYLOR and Hannah Holden, on 3 Oct 1768. {MLNJ}

A marriage license was issued to DANIEL TAYLOR and Rebecca Paulling on 3 Sep 1760. {MLNJ}

ELIAS TAYLOR of Cape May Co., Gent., d. leaving a will dated 4 July 1751, proved 7 March 1752. Mentioned were children: Thomas, Elias and Mary Flowers. Exec. was Ebenezer Johnson with Elisha Hand as assistant. The will was witnessed by John Eldredge, John Bock (Buck) and John Crandel. {NJCW 9:53} On 31 Dec 1757 an inventory of the estate was filed by William Simkins and John Eldredge. On 4 Jan 1758 a bond was issued for Mary Taylor as admin. (estate being intestate), William Simkins fellow bondsman, both of Cape May Co. {NJCW}

Elias was father of the following children: THOMAS; ELIAS; MARY, m. (N) Flowers [possibly William Flowers].

A marriage license was issued to FRANCIS TAYLOR and Rachel Hewet* on 1 June 1770. {MLNJ}

GEORGE TAYLOR and Elizabeth Donkor (black), 13 June 1679. {First Official Recds}

GEORGE TAYLOR and Jude Swain, 9 Feb 1758. {MLNJ}

GEORGE TAYLOR and Jane Swain, 3 Oct 1775. {MLNJ}

A marriage license was issued to JOHN TAYLOR and Sarah Townsend, on 8 Nov 1760. {MLNJ}

A marriage license was issued to JOHN TAYLOR and Marcy Buck, on 29 Dec 1759.{MLNJ}

MARTHA TAYLOR of Cape May Co. d. prior to 30 March 1759 when an inventory was filed by Jonathan Smith and Carman Smith. On 2 April 1759 a bond was issued for Joshua Hildreth as admin; Amos Johnson, fellow bondsman, both of Cape May Co., Gent.{NJCW 9:314}

A marriage license was issued to John McCormick and MARY TAYLOR, on 20 April 1759.{MLNJ}

A marriage license was issued to Elisha Hand and RUTH TAYLOR, on 26 Jan 1774.{MLNJ}

At the monthly meeting on 6th day, 6th mo., 1733, THOMAS TAYLOR requested a certificate to the Philadelphia Monthly Meeting.{GEMM}

THOMPSON

MARSEY THOMPSON m. Isaac Hand by license dated 3 April 1730. {MLNJ}

RICHARD TOMSON m. Raamah Corsen, 19 Dec 1741.{MLNJ}

RICHARD TOMSON m. Marget Nickerson, 31 Dec 1764.{MLNJ}

RICHARD THOMPSON of Cape May Co. d. by 8 June 1773 when Naomi Thompson was appointed admx. On 10 May 1773 an inventory was filed (£64.17.9) by Joseph Edwards and Hugh Hathorn.{NJCW 15:529}

RICHARD THOMPSON, m. Charlotte (N) (d. 3 Dec 1812, age 47 years, 7 mos., 9 days).{Cold Spring Cemetery}

DEBORAH THOMSON m. David Edwards by license dated 20 Jan 1772.{MLNJ}

Simeon Iszard and MARGARET TOMPSON m. Jan 26, 1774.{Baptists}

A licens was issued to Margaret Tompson and Simeon Iszard by on 26 Jan 1774.{MLNJ}

TOWNSEND (TOWNSHEND)

See *The Cape May County Magazine of History and Genealogy*, 1931, "John Townsend: An Historical and Genealogical Record of One of the Original English Settlers of Cape May County," p. 122. By Lewis Townsend Stevens. See this article for more on the English and New England ancestry of this Townsend family. See also "Comments on Townsend," *The Cape May County Magazine of History and Genealogy*, p. 174. June 1942. By H. C. Campion, Jr., in which some earlier statements by Stevens on Townsend English origins are challenged.

See "Townsend Family Record," in Vol. 58 (1983), pp. 113-116, *Genealogical Magazine of New Jersey*. This is a transcription of "an ancient Book" written mostly by John Townsend, son of Richard Townsend and Milliscent Somers, made by Reuben Townsend, probably in the early 1800s. It is filed in Folder 9 of a manuscript box labelled "Townsend, Joshua (1786-1868)," Ac 2091, in the Special Collections Department, Rutgers University Library, New Brunswick. Later this article was published in *Genealogies of New Jersey Families*, by Genealogical Publishing Co., 1996. [Herein cited as{Townsend Family Record}.]

First Generation

1. RICHARD TOWNSEND, father of Cape May John Townsend, first appears in Jamaica, Long Island, in 1656, but his name does not appear in the Oyster Bay records until 1668, when he bought the land of Luslum, of Robert Williams, whose dau., Phebe Williams, became the first wife of John Townsend, the ancestor of Cape May. Richard Townsend m. Elizabeth Weeks.[134]

---

134 Lewis Townsend Stevens, "John Townsend: An Historical and Genealogical Record of One of the Original English Settlers of Cape May County," *The Cape May County Magazine of History and Genealogy*, 1931.

Second Generation

2. JOHN TOWNSEND, son of Richard (1) and Elizabeth Townsend, and his wife Phebe, dau. of Robert and Sarah Williams[135], came from Long Island to Cape May in 1675.[136]{Townsend Family Record}

Phebe Townsend d. 9 Aug 1704. John m. 2nd Mary (Mercy) Willitts*, widow of Hope Willets in 1707, they declaring their intentions to marry at Haddonfield Monthly Meeting[137].

John Townsend of Cape May Co., Gent., d. 5 Jan 1721.{Townsend Family Records} He left a will dated 24 Nov 1715, proved 10 Jan 1721/2. Mentioned were wife Mercy and sons: Richard and Robert, son-in-law (stepson), John Willis (Willets). Land at Goshen, Cape May Co. Execs. were the wife and two sons, with Colonel Jacob Spicer, John Page and Nathaniel Jenkins as trustees. The will was witnessed by Richard Downes, Andrew Godfrey and Joseph Lydlow.{NJCW 2:206} On 8 Dec 1721 inventory of the estate was made by Nathaniel Jenkins and Thomas Gandy. On 8 Dec 1721 his personal estate was appraised at £174.3.9.5.

John and Phebe Townsend had the following children: SYLVANUS, d. 25 Sep 1711; RICHARD, b. 1681, d. 30 May 1737 in Philadelphia; ROBERT, b. June 16850; SARAH, d. 22 Sep 1711 unmarried.[138]

---

135 Sarah Williams, widow of Robert Williams, d. leaving a will dated 16 Feb 1693, making her son-in-law John Townsend an overseer of her estate along with Thomas Powell and John Dewsberry.

136 H. Clifford Campion in an article titled, "Comments on Townsend," noted that John Townsend is mentioned several times as a witness and makes several sales of real estate in the records of Queen County, L.I. up into 1698 and on that account suggests that Townsend came to Cape May later than 1690, thus refuting an earlier claim by Lewis Townsend Stevens. {"Comments on Townsend," The Cape May County Magazine of History and Genealogy, p. 174. June 1942.} However David Townsend, great-great grandson of John Townsend, wrote that his ancestor came from Long Island in 1675. {Townsend Family Record}

137 John Townsend of Cape May, son of Richard and Elizabeth (Wickers) Townsend of Oyster Bay, Long Island, NY and Mercy Willits, widow, announced the continued intentions of marriage as reported in the Haddonfield Monthly Meetings of 8th mo, 9th da, 1707.

138 Paul H. Townsend, in the article, Comments on Townsend, finds no evidence that John Townsend had a dau. Sara; it was his belief that Sarah was the wife of Silvanus Townsend.

Mary (Mercy) Townsend had the following children by Hope Willets: JOSEPH; RICHARD; JAMES; JOHN, b. 29 Oct 1698[139]; and triplet daus.: HANNAH, PATIENCE and ABIGAIL, all b. 8 March 1696.{H. C. Campion, Jr. believed Hannah m. David Cresse, son of Arthur Cresse, Sr.; Patience m. Thomas Creamer of Little Egg Harbor; and had no information on Abigail. He noted that John the youngest of the sons, was the only one son to remain in Cape May County.}

Third Generation

3. RICHARD TOWNSEND, son of John (2) and Phebe Townsend, d. of dropsy on 30 May 1737 in Philadelphia. He m. 16 June 1704 Millicent Somers* (d. 20 Sep 1762, in her 77th year){Townsend Family Record}, dau. of John and Hannah Somers of Somers or Leeds Point. In 1705 he and his father were the owners of the sloop *Adventurer*. He and his brother Robert and their father were owners of the sloop *Dolphin* in 1709.

According to the Quaker records, Richard Townsend, son of John Townsend from Long Island, b. 7th day, 12th mo., 1681, d. 3rd mo., 1737, m. Millicent Somers (b. 7th day, 10th mo., 1685, d. 20th day, 9th mo., 1762). They were the parents of the following children: PHEBE, b. 8th day, 7th mo., 1704, d. 16th day, 11th mo., 1705/06; JOHN, b. 29th day, 8th mo., 1706; HANNAH, b. 7th day, 9th mo., 1708, d. 3rd day, 9th mo., 1794; RICHARD, b. 27th day, 6th mo., 1710; SILVANUS, b. 5th day, 1st mo., 1713, d. 3rd day, 3rd mo., 1788; ISAAC, b. 10th day, 5th mo., 1715, d. 25th day, 2nd mo., 1788; JACOB, b. 6th day, 9th mo., 1717; MILISENT, b. 1st day, 5th mo., 1720; ROBERT, b. 23rd day, 7th mo., 1723, d. 28th day, 10th mo., 1723; SAMUEL, b. 12th day, 12th mo., 1725/26; DANIEL, b. 12th day, 10th mo., 1728.{GEMM}

In "Townsend Family Record," John Townsend gives the dates of his sister's birth and death as "my sister Phebe Townsend, was born the 8th day of September 1705. My Sister Phebe, deceased the 16th of February 1706." He also gave the date of marriage of his parents as "16th day of June, in the year 1704." Although the day and months are the same as those given above in the Quaker records, the year of his sister's birth and death are a year later which would be more acceptable perhaps to the date of marriage of his parents. John gave his date of birth and the dates of his other siblings the same as those shown in the Quaker records, except brother Richard whose birth date he gives as 7 Nov 1710[above given as

---

139 Mentioned as son-in-law, John Willetts, in the will of John Townsend.

27 Aug 1710 and Miliscent as born 1 May 1720 whereas her above birth date is given as 1 July 1720. Noting of course that March was first month in the contemporary calendar, etc.]{Townsend Family Record}

Richard Townsend of Cape May Co., yeoman, d. leaving a will dated 30 day, 2nd mo., 1737, proved 29 Sep 1737. Mentioned were wife Millicent; sons: John (eldest), Samuel, Daniel, Richard, Isaac, Silvanus, Jacob, John; daus.: Hannah Gregory, Millecent Townsend. Eldest son John to have the tract of land and marsh where testator lived (wife to have during widowhood use of the house and mill and half the barn to keep what creatures she may have on the plantation) he to pay £15 each to two younger sons, Samuel and Daniel, when 21. Son Richard to have 200 acres whereon he lives, he to pay two younger sons, Samuel and Daniel each £8 when 21. Son Isaac to have 200 acres joining son Richard on the north which land was bought of Timothy Brandeth. Son Silvanus, land and marsh bought of Thomas Gandy, between lands of Joseph Ludlum and Henry Young, he to pay sons Samuel and Daniel, each £8 when 21. Samuel and Daniel to have land and marsh (663 acres) on the west end of Peck's Beach, bought of Lewis Morris. They to have schooling and at 15 to be put to trades. Son Jacob, £15 when he sets up his trade. Movables to dau., Hannah Gregory, and to dau. Millecent Townsend when 21. Grist mill to be shared equally by sons John, Richard, Silvanus and Isaac. The will was witnessed by Robert Townsend, Ebanr. Swaine and Jacob Corson.{NJCW 4:119} On 13 Oct 1737 admins. were appointed: Millicent Townsend, widow, and John Townsend, eldest son. On 21 Sep 1737 an inventory of the estate was filed by Henry Stites and Daniel Brandeth.{NJCW}

4. JAMES TOWNSEND, probable son of John (2) Townsend, m. Abiah Hand, 7 Jan 1740.{MLNJ}

This is probably the same James Townsend who d. leaving a will dated 20 Jan 1775, proved 20 May 1786.[140] Mentioned were eldest son, James, to whom was devised the land where he lived, except 40 acres, on the southwest side, which was given to youngest son Elijah. Son Eli was devised land where testator lived, between land of John Townsend and Silvanus Townsend. Son Elijah to receive land at head of tract given to son James which was bought of Clement Daniels; also right in cedar swamp which testator bought in partnership with Isaiah Stites and Zebulon

140 Noting especially that he had a dau. named Abiah, the same name as the wife of above James.

Swain at a place called Wiggens Neck, and the above said 40 acres. Dau. Abiah Foster, a Negro girl. Youngest dau. Rhuhamah Townsend, a Negro girl. Execs. were sons James, Eli and Elijah. The will was witnessed by Silvanus Townsend, Jr., Robert Townsend, Elisha Hughes and Jonathan Townsend.{NJCW 36:270}

At May Term 1797 Elijah Townsend, Esq., applied for a division of Cedar Swamp late of James Townsend, dec., between the heirs of Eli Townsend, Esq., Elijah Townsend, Esq., and Ruhamah Townsend.{Ltrs&Inv A(Rev):147}

James was father of the following children: JAMES; ELIJAH; ELI; ABIAH, m. Charles Foster by license dated 16 Oct 1764; RHUHAMAN.

5. ROBERT TOWNSEND, son of John (2) and Phebe Townsend, was b. ca. 1685, noting that he witnesed a will of Daniel Wells, dated 26 Jan 1714/5. He m. 1st (N); he m. 2nd 1735 Mary Abbott Tyler, widow of William Tyler of Salem. On 7th day, 5th mo., 1735 a certificate was received for Mary Townsend from Salem Monthly Meeting.{GEMM}

The deeds of 1787 of Cape May Co. show that John Townsend had a son Robert who had a son SILVANUS whose heir was Jonathan Townsend (wife Mary).{Deeds} On 12 Jan 1755 the monthly meeting was informed that Robert Townsend had allowed his dau. to be married out.{SAMM}

Fourth Generation

6. JOHN TOWNSEND, son of Richard (3) and Miliscent Townsend, b. 29th day, 8th mo., 1706. He m. 1st on 6 Sep 1733, Sarah Champion who d. 9 Feb 1740. They were parents of the following children: AMY, b. 13 May 1734; DAVID, b. 16 July 1735, d. 6 March 1802; RACHEL (d. 11 Nov 1738) and MILISCENT (d. 30 Sep 1738), twins, b. 24 Sep 1737; RICHARD, b. 23 Jan 1740, d. 7 March 1802.{Townsend Family Record; GEMM}

Shown in the deeds of Cape May Co. are John Townsend, wife Sarah; Richard Townsend; Joshua Townsend (d. without issue); and Henry Townsend; children of John Townsend (1783-7).{Deeds A:90-96}

John m. 2nd, 1 Dec 1740, Tobitha Young*, dau. of Henry Young. John and Tobitha were parents of the following children: TOBITHA, b. 28 July 1742, d. 6 July 1743; HENRY YOUNG TOWNSEND, b. 7 May 1744 ("under the rule and Government, of the Planet Saturn"), d. 13 May 1789; HANNAH, b. 28 Dec 1746, m. Jacocks Swain by license dated 10 Feb 1774; TOBITHA and SARAH, b. 7 Feb 1749, m. (N) Stites; JUDITH, b. 15 Oct 1752; JOHN, b. 8 May 1755; JOSHUA, b. 28 Dec

1757, d. 13 May 1789[141]; PRISSILA, b. 15 Aug 1760, d. 7 Sep following.{Townsend Family Records; GEMM}

"John Townsend, Son of Richard Townsend and grandson to John Townsend the Ancestor ... " on 23 Sep 1785, "being aged 78 years 10 months and 26 days, leaving issue ... David, Richard, Henry, Hannah, Tabitha, Sarah, Judith, John and Joshua."{Townsend Family Record}

John Townsend (living 1745 and 1783) had a son Henry Young Townsend.{Deeds A:221}

Tabitha Townsend of Cape May Co. d. leaving a will dated 10 June 1786, proved 22 Aug 1793. Mentioned were sons: Henry and John Townsend; daus.: Hannah Swain, Tabitha Townsend, Sarah Stites and Judith Townsend. The will was witnessed by Joseph Wheaton, Jeremiah Youngs and Henry Corson.{NJCW 33:278, File 597E}

7. RICHARD TOWNSEND, son of Richard (3) and Millicent Townsend, b. 27th day, 6th mo., 1710.

On 6th day, 7th mo., 1731 the marriage of Richard Townsend, Jr., and Sarah Ludlam*, both of Cape May Monthly Meeting, was reported orderly accomplished.{GEMM}

Sarah Townsend, first wife of Richard Townsend, d. 28th day, 6th mo., 1732.{GEMM} On 7th day, 2nd mo., 1735, the marriage of Richard Townsend, Jr., and Sarah Brandrath was reported accomplished.{GEMM}

Children of Richard Townsend: TIMOTHY, b. 12th day, 9th mo., 1735, d. 26th day, 11th mo., 1741; LEVI, b. 7th day, 8th mo., 1738, d. 12th day, 11th mo., 1741; JACOB, b. 13th day, 11th mo., 1741; JUDAH, b. 20th day, 8th mo., 1743; CATHRINE, b. 20th day, 8th mo., 1746; DANIEL, b. 24th day, 2nd mo., 1753.{GEMM}

8. SAMUEL TOWNSEND, probable son of Richard (3) and Millicent Townsend, m. Rachael Godfrey* (b. 22nd day, 8th mo., 1732, d. 28th day, 2nd mo., 1798). On 3rd day, 8th mo., 1752, the marriage of Samuel Townsend and Rachael Godfree was reported as orderly accomplished.{GEMM}

Rachel Townsend of the Upper Precinct, Cape May Co., d. leaving a will dated 28 Sep 1796. Mentioned were daus.: Elizabeth Townsend, Millescent Young, Phebe Godfrey, Hannah Cathcart, Edith

---

141 He died "... after running a horse along a road, in the woods and was thrown against a tree, and in less than 2 hours, Expired, being Aged 28 years three Months and 28 Days." {Townsend Family Record}

Corson and Rachel Townsend; son: Samuel Townsend.{NJCW 37:426} An inventory was filed on 3 April 1798 (£104.14.7) by Cornelius Corson and John Mackey.{NJCW File:715E}

Samuel and Rachel were parents of the following children: ELIZABETH, b. 16th day, 3rd mo., 1753, d. 8th day, 11th mo., 1800; MILLISENT, b. 16th day, 4th mo., 1756, (N) Young.{GEMM}

Samuel was also father of the following children: PHEBY, b. 13th day, 10th mo., 1758, m. James Godfrey*; HANNAH, b. 15th day, 8th mo., 1762, m. (N) Cathcart; JOSHUA, b. 5th day, 12th mo., 1766; SAMUEL, b. 29th day, 9th mo., 1771, d. 30th day, 11th mo., 1800; EDITH, b. 12th day, 2nd mo., 1776, m. (N) Corson; RACHEL.{GEMM}

9. ISAAC TOWNSEND, probable son of Richard (3) Townsend, probably m. Sarah Willets*, since on 2nd day, 11th mo., 1737 Isaac Townsend and Sarah Willets announced their intentions to marry and she is named in her father's will as Sarah Townsend.{GEMM}

Isaac Townsend (of Upper Precinct) d. leaving a will dated 10 March 1782, proved 15 April 1788. Wife was to have 1/2 of the land. Son Mark to have looms and lands and to pay son Isaac's children, £70 when age 21: Josiah, Samuel, Jesse, Isaac, Sarah and Anne. The rest of estate was to go to wife and daus.: Hannah Willis and Lydia Baner. Execs. were Mark Townsend, Jordan Willis and Elisha Baner. The will was witnessed by David Townsend, Daniel Townsend and Henry Y. Townsend. Letters granted to Mark Townsend, the only surviving exec. On 15 April 1788 an inventory was filed (£297.9.9) by David Townsend and Henry Y. Townsend.{NJCW 31:88}

Isaac Townsend was the father of the following children{GEMM}: ISAAC, b. 27th day, 9th mo., 1738; HANNAH, b. 23rd day, 10th mo., 1741, d. 12th day, 6th mo., 1793, m. Jordan Willis; LYDIA, b. 23rd day, 1st mo., 1748, m. 1774, Elisha Baner; MARK, b. 5th day, 10th mo., 1756.

10. SILVANIUS TOWNSEND, son of Robert (4) Townsend, m. 1739, Marcy Willets*, dau. of John Willits. She was b. 11th day, 11th mo., 1721, d. 12th day, 2nd mo., 1785.{GEMM} Their children: JOHN, b. 9th day, 1st mo., 1740; JOB, b. 15th day, 1st mo., 1742; MILLISENT, b. 5th day, 6th mo., 1744, d. 3rd day, 2nd mo., 1783, age 37 years; JACOB, b. 5th day, 1st mo., 1747; MARCY, b. 5th day, 12th mo., 1749/50, d. 6th day, 8th mo., 1762; RACHEL, b. 9th day, 10th mo., 1752; SILVANUS, b. 6th day, 3rd mo., 1755; THOMAS, b. 7th day, 10th mo., 1757; PRUDENCE, b. 3rd day, 3rd mo., 1761; AMOS, b. 9th day, 3rd mo., 1765.{GEMM}

On 3rd day, 3rd mo., 1761, Silvenus Townsend requested a certificate for his son Jacob, lately bound to a trade in Philadelphia.{GEMM}

11. SILVANUS (Silvanius) TOWNSEND, son of Richard (3) Townsend, b. 5th day, 1st mo., 1713, d. 3rd day, 3rd mo., 1788. On 12th day, 1st mo., 1732/3 the marriage of Silvanius Townsend and Mary Swain* was reported as orderly accomplished.{GEMM}

Silvanus d. leaving a will dated 28 Feb 1788, proved 29 March 1788. He wished to be buried near his wife in friends' burying ground in Upper Precinct. To son-in-law William Hawkins, his right in a note of £28 due from Drusilla Townsend of Currytuck Co., North Carolina. To Augustus Hawkins and his brother Immanuel, £92, which is due from a statement of accounts from John Townsend, late husband to the said Drusilla. His only child RACHEL received the residue of the estate. On 28 March 1788 an inventory was filed (£150.18.9) by Henry Y. Townsend and Nathan Cresse.{NJCW 31:89}

12. DANIEL TOWNSEND, son of Richard (3) and Millicent Townsend, b. 12th day, 10th mo., 1728.

On 2nd day, 2nd mo., 1756, the marriage of Daniel Townsend and Rebekah Corson* was reported as orderly accomplished.{GEMM}

Daniel and Rebecca were parents of the following children{GEMM}: DANIEL, b. 21st day, 9th mo., 1756; PETER, b. 1st day, 10th mo., 1758; RACHEL, b. 26th day, 12th mo., 1760; HANNAH, b. 15th day, 8th mo., 1762; MELISENT, b. 17th day, 1st mo., 1772.

13. HANNAH TOWNSEND, dau. of Richard (3) Townsend, b. 7th day, 9th mo., 1708, d. 3rd day, 9th mo., 1794, was probably the Hannah Townsend who m. Joseph Wade by 27th day, 9th mo. 1727.{GEMM}

Fifth Generation

14. DAVID TOWNSEND, son of John (6) and Sarah Townsend, b. 16 July 1735, d. 6 March 1802.{Townsend Family Record}

On 7th day, 4th mo., 1760, David Townsend requested a certification order for marriage to a person of Salem Monthly Meeting.{GEMM}

On 2 July 1760 David m. Elizabeth Brandrith*, dau. of Daniel Brandrith of Salem.{Townsend Family Record} The monthly meeting register read that David Townsend of Cape May Co. and Elizabeth Brandreth of Salem Co., having consent of parents, m. 2nd day, 7th mo., 1760.{SAMM}

In "Diaries of Aaron Leaming," he mentioned the death of the wife of David Townsend from childbirth on 6 March 1761.

From Townsend Family Record:

"Our Daughter Elizabeth Townsend, David Townsend's wife departed this life on the 5th Day of March, in the year 1761 after a long illness of an excessive cold, and yellow jaundice And being delivered of a child it being a Daughter, which child expired a few minutes after its birth, and the Mother lived about 2 hours after and expired also!! and they were both buried in one coffin on the 7th Day of March following, 1761."

David m. 2nd on 26 March 1767, Hannah Smith* (b. 22 March 1745, d. 29 Nov 1796), dau. of Thomas and Sarah Smith.[142] David and Hannah were parents of the following children: THOMAS, b. 8 Oct 1767, d. 3 July 1799, m. Rebecca Mattocks 6 Aug 1789; SARAH (Sally), b. 6 Nov 1769, m. Jeremiah Hand on 21 Jan 1790; DAVID, b. 13 April 1775, m. Nancy Swain on 16 Feb 1800 by whom he had a dau. Tabitha, b. 15 Nov 1800.{Townsend Family Record}

Thomas (wife Rebecca), David and Sarah (wife of Jeremiah Hand), children of Hannah, wife of David Townsend and only dau. of Thomas Smith (1797).{Deeds B:59}

15. HENRY YOUNG TOWNSEND, son of John (6) and Tobitha Townsend, b. 7 May 1744, m. Priscilla Leaming, probably dau. of Christopher Leaming, by license dated 9 May 1769.{MLNJ} His dau. Tabitha d. 10 Dec after a long illness of the consumption in 1793.{Townsend Family Record}

Henry Young Townsend d. by 29 June 1789 when Richard Townsend and Reuben Townsend were appointed admins. The will was witnessed by Sarah Hand and Mary Harris. On 24 June 1790 an inventory was filed (£481.19.8) by Eli Townsend and Parmenas Corson. "Debt due from the estate of Tobitha Willets, as allowed on the settlement." Henry Young Townsend was father of the following children: HENRY YOUNG; TABITHA; PRISCILLA; REUBEN.

16. JOHN, son of John (6) and Tobitha Townsend, b. 8 May 1755, m. Sarah Swain*, by license dated 8 Jan 1777.{MLNJ}

---

142 See will of Sarah Smith of Cape May Co., widow, who mentioned dau. Hannah, wife of David Townsend; also sons Christopher and Levi Smith. {NJCW 32:289}

17. ISAAC TOWNSEND, son of Isaac (9), m. Keturah, dau. of Josiah and Ann (Austin) Albertson[143]. They were the parents of the following children{GEMM}: JOSIAH, b. 17th day, 2nd mo., 1768, d. 27th day, 10th mo., 1785; SAMUEL, b. 15th day, 4th mo., 1770, d. 5th day, 10th mo., 1798, a minister; JESSE, b. 4th day, 11th mo., 1771; SARAH, b. 7th day, 4th mo., 1776, m. Timothy Andrews{Deeds B:88}; ANN, b. 18th day, 3rd mo., 1778, d. 5th day, 3rd mo., 1797; ISAAC (mentioned in the will of his grandfather Isaac Townsend).

Ketturah Townsend, widow of Isaac Townsend, the younger, dau. of Josiah and Ann Albertson, d. 27th day, 10th mo., 1797, 54 yrs. Ketturah Townsend was an elder.{GEMM}

18. MARK TOWNSEND, son of Isaac (9) Townsend, b. 5th day, 10th mo., 1756, m. 1777, Elizabeth Clement. They were the parents of the following children: HANNAH, b. 17th day, 8th mo., 1778; JACOB, b. 7th day, 12th mo., 1780, d. 1st day, 3rd mo., 1797; MARK, b. 9th day, 4th mo., 1783; ELIZABETH, b. 13th day, 11th mo., 1786; REBECAH, b. 18th day, 5th mo., 1789; LYDIA, b. 16th day, 1st mo., 1792, d. 16th day, 10th mo., 1793; LYDIA, b. 29th day, 9th mo., 1794; SARAH, 23rd day, 8th mo., 1797; RUTH, b. 11th day, 12th mo., 1800.{GEMM, Deeds B:88}

Mark Townsend (wife Elizabeth), son of Isaac. Jesse Townsend, wife Judith. Isaac Townsend, wife Hannah. (1800){Deeds B:88}

Sixth Generation

19. HANNAH TOWNSEND, possible dau. of Mark Townsend (18), m. Christopher Leaming by license dated 6 Sep 1798.{Co. Clerk Rcds - Book A}

20. JESSE TOWNSEND, son of Isaac (17) and Keturah Townsend, b. 4th day, 11th mo., 1771, is probably the Jesse Townsend who m. Judith (N). They were the parents of the following children{GEMM}: twin daughters, not named b. 22nd day, 1st mo., 1794, both died the 22nd day, 1st mo., 1794; JOSIAH, b. 28th day, 8th mo., 1795; KETTURAH, b. 2nd day, 6th mo., 1798.

---

143 For more details on Albertson family see *New Jersey Genealogies*, Vol. 2, p. 104.

21. SARAH TOWNSEND, dau. of Isaac (17) Townsend, m. Timothy Andrews (30th day, 1st mo., 1772 at Tuckerton, son of Peter and Hannah Andrews.{Genealogies of New Jersey Families, Vol. 2, p. 109}

22. TABITHA TOWNSEND of Upper Precinct of Cape May Co., dau. of Henry Young (15) Townsend, d. leaving a will dated 6 Nov 1793, proved 1 May 1795. Mentioned were uncle Richard Townsend, half-sister Priscilla Townsend (under age 21); brother Reuben Townsend; father Henry Y. Townsend. Reference was made to her part of a tract of woodland given to her by her grandfather Reuben Ludlam which being 1/2 of a tract which said Reuben and Anthony Ludlam purchased of Deborah Sreet, Christopher Leaming, Sarah Leaming and Samuel Jones, containing 450 acres. Exec. was brother Reuben Townsend. The will was witnessed by Eli Townsend, John Townsend, Henry Swain and Joshua Swain.{NJCW 36:185} On 30 Dec 1793 an inventory was filed (£70.1.11) by Richard Townsend and Jacocks Swain.

Unplaced

A marriage license was issued for AMOS TOWNSEND and Martha Hand, 10 Oct 1745.{MLNJ}

Child of DAVID and REBECCA TOWNSEND: Caleb Townsend, b. 5th day, 12th mo., 1764.{GEMM}

A marriage license was issued to ELIJAH TOWNSEND and JUDITH TOWNSEND, 20 April 1775.{MLNJ}

On 5th day, 7th mo., 1756, JOHN TOWNSEND was spoken to concerning his outgoing in marriage.{GEMM}

A marriage license was issued to JOHN TOWNSEND and DRUZELLAH TOWNSEND, 10 Oct 1770.{MLNJ}

On 21 April 1777 JOSHUA TOWNSEND died.{Leaming Diaries}

A marriage license was issued to JOTHAM TOWNSEND and Rachel Cressey, 14 Nov 1768.{MLNJ}

A marriage licenses was issued to JOTHAM TOWNSEND and Elizabeth Corson, 21 May 1776.{MLNJ}

A marriage license was issued to Jeremiah Hand and MARTHA TOWNSEND, 12 July 1763.{MLNJ}

A marriage license was issued to Elnathan Sheppard (Cumberland Co.) and MARY TOWNSEND, 8 March 1766.{MLNJ}

On 2nd day, 9th mo., 1741, the marriage of Edward Holinshead and MILLISENT TOWNSEND was reported as orderly accomplished.{GEMM} On 30th day, 3rd mo., 1743 Millisent submitted a paper regarding her outgoing.{GEMM}

A marriage license was issued to James Godfrey* and PHEBE TOWNSEND, 26 Feb 1765.{MLNJ}

A marriage license was issued to Giles Worth and RACHEL TOWNSEND, 14 March 1770.{MLNJ}

On 7th day, 5th mo., 1753 a certificate was requested for RICHARD TOWNSEND and his wife to Salem Monthly Meeting.{GEMM}

ROBERT TOWNSEND of Cape May Co. d. before 16 Dec 1772, the day on which James Townsend and Eli Townsend, yeomen, were appointed admins. Fellowbondsman: John Townsend, Esqr., all of said county. Witnesses: James Godfrey and Ruhamah Townsend. On 19 Nov 1772 an inventory was made by John Townsend and James Godfrey. On 15 Dec 1773 the account was filed by Eli Townsend, admin.{NJCW 14:508, 538}

A marriage license was issued to ROBERT TOWNSEND and Rebecca Richardson, 1 June 1767.{MLNJ}

A marriage license was issued to ROBERT TOWNSEND and Jane Shaw, 4 Oct 1763.{MLNJ}

A marriage license was issued to John Taylor and SARAH TOWNSEND 8 Nov 1760.{MLNJ}

Joseph Gooden and SARAH TOWNSEND announced their intentions to marry on 1st day, 3rd mo., 1738.{GEMM}

VAN GELDER/GILDER

1. JOHN VAN GELDER of Upper Precinct d. leaving a will dated 8 Oct 1772, proved 3 Dec 1773. Mentioned were son Abraham Van Gelder to whom was devised 1/4 of the land which joined land sold to Joseph Corson and Isaac Bowes; son John, 1/4 where testator lived; son Isaac, 1/4 between Abraham and John; son Jeremiah, 1/4 that is between John and the land of Samuel Townsend; dau.-in-law Margret van Gelder, a bed that was her mother's; grandson William Robenson. Execs. were sons John and Jeremiah. The will was witnessed by John Mackey, Abel Moslander and Samuel Townsend. On 9 Nov 1773 an inventory (£87.15.8) was filed by John Mackey and Samuel Townsend.{NJCW 17:30}

John was the father of the following children: ABRAHAM, m. Martha Hand by license dated 22 Aug 1757{MLNJ}; JOHN, m. Margaret (N); ISAAC, m. Mary (N); JEREMIAH, m. Sarah Bishop by license dated 1 Aug 1780{MLNJ} [144] [The following persons were mentioned in the deed book: Abraham Van Gilder, wife Martha. John Van Gilder, wife Margaret. Isaac Van Gilder, wife Mary. (1791){Deeds B:72}]

A marriage license was issued to John VAN GILDER and Hannah Scull, on 21 July 1757.{MLNJ}

---

144 Mentioned in the deeds dated 1787. {Deeds E: 39}

2. JOHN VAN GILDER of the Upper Precinct, Cape May Co., son of John (1) Van Gilder, d. leaving a will dated 2 Feb 1799, proved 9 April 1799. Mentioned were brothers Abraham and Isaac Van Gilder; Robert and James Mickle, sons of James Mickle. Execs. were nephews: John Van Gilder, Jr. and Isaac van Gilder, Jr. {NJCW 38:420} On 18 March 1799 an inventory was filed (£281.4.4) by John Mackey and Nicholas Willets.{NJCW File:729E}

WELLS

DANIEL WELLS of Cape May, Cape May Co. d. leaving a will dated 26 Jan 1714/5, proved 18 April 1715. Mentioned were wife Mary sole heiress and extx. until children (unnamed) were of age. Legacy to brother David. The will was witnessed by Robert Townsend (29 years old) Abraham Hand and Mary Hand. An inventory of the estate was made on 9 Feb 1714/5 by John Taylor and Robert Townsend. On 15 Aug 1715 a bond was issued to Mary Wells as admx. of the estate. David Wells fellow bondsman.

DAVID WELLS of Cape May Co., joiner, d. leaving a will dated 13 Jan 1714/5, proved 17 May 1720.{NJCW 2:150} On 3 May 1720 inventory of the estate was made by John Taylor and Aaron Leaming. On 1 Oct 1723 account of the estate was made by the extx. Elizabeth, now wife of Humphrey Hughes.{NJCW}

WESTON

ABRAHAM WESTON of Cape May d. prior to 20 May 1690 when a bond was issued to John Reeves of Cape May, cooper, as admin. of the estate. James Wills, cooper, and James Hill, cordwainer, both of Burlington, fellow bondsmen. On 24 Nov 1687 inventory of the estate was made by John Brigs and Alexr. ---. On 20 May 1690 the inventory was exhibited and attested by John Reeves, admin.{NJCW Burlington Records:15}

WHEATON

A marriage license was issued to Jeremiah Goff and ASSINAH WHEATON on 14 May 1739.{MLNJ}

A marriage license was issued to John Buck and ELIZABETH WHEATON on 25 Jan 1766.{MLNJ}

JOSEPH WHEATON m. Esther Willets*, dau. of James Willets, by license dated 24 Oct 1768.{MLNJ}

August Term 1789. Division of the land of James Willets, dec. among his several devisees: Nicolas Willets, son and minor; Esther Wheaton, late Esther Willets and dau. of said James, now wife of Joseph Wheaton; Enoch Willets, son of said James Willets; James Willets, son of said James Willets; Rachel Corson, late Rachel Willets and dau. of James Willets dec., and now wife of Parmanus Corson, Esqr.; Sarah Edwards, late Sarah Willets, and dau. of James Willets, dec., and now wife of Joseph Edwards. {Ltrs&Inv A(Rev):33} (plats shown)

Joseph Wheaton, wife Esther.{Book of Mortgages A: 199, dated 1793}

WILLETS WHEATON and Rebecca Willets m. 18 March 1799.{Co. Clerk Rcds - Book A}

WHILLDIN

Much of the following information was taken from Rev. Paul Sturtevant Howe, *Mayflower Pilgrim Descendants In Cape May County New Jersey. A Record of the Pilgrim Descendants who early in its History settled in Cape May County, and some of their children throughout the several States of the Union at the present time.* (1921). Reprinted Genealogical Publishing Co., Inc., Baltimore, 1977.

First generation

According to Rev. Howe,

1. JOSEPH WHILLDIN of Yarmouth, Plymouth Colony, was b. 1656-60, d. at Cape May ca. 1725, m. before 1683 Hannah Gorham. She was b. at Barnstable, Plymouth Colony 28 Nov 1663, d. at Cape May ca. 1728. They had issue as follows: HANNAH, b. at Yarmouth 1683, m. Thomas Leaming; JOSEPH, b. 1690, d. 18 March 1748[145] at Cape May; MARY, m. 17 Dec 1708, Josiah Crowell{First Official Rcds}; EXPERIENCE, m. William Foster; ISAAC.

145 Cold Spring Cemetery.

Hannah Gorham was the dau. of Capt. John Gorham and his wife Desire Howland, dau. of the Pilgrim John Howland and his wife Elizabeth Tilley, who came with her father in the Mayflower. John Gorham was b. at Benefield, Northamtonshire, England, bapt. 28 Jan 1621, d. of a fever after the Great Swamp fight. He d. 5 Feb 1675/6.

Second generation

2. JOSEPH WHILLDIN, son of Joseph (1) and Hannah (Gorham) Whilldin, b. 1690, d. at Cape May, 18 March 1748, bur. Cold Spring Cemetery, m. Mary Wilson, b. 1689, d. Cape May, 8 April 1743.{Cold Spring Cemetery}

Joseph Whilden of Cape May Co., yeoman, d. leaving a will dated 16 March 1747/8, proved 30 March 1748. Mentioned were wife Abigail; sons: Mathew, James, David; daus.: Hannah, Rachel and Loes; dec. dau., Mercy's children, Ellis and Judith; grandsons: Memukin Hughes, Willman and Isecar Crafford. Son Mathew to have land and marsh purchased of Isaac Whildin and interest in Five Mile Beach and 20 acres of Cedar Swamp. James to have home plantation and 20 acres of Cedar Swamp. David to have 10 acres of Cedar Swamp and price of Negro man Asse and Negro woman, he to pay each dau. £5 and £2 each to dec. dau. Mercy's children. Execs. were James Whillden and Richard Crafford. The will was witnessed by William Mulford, Charity Mulford and Elijah Hughes.{NJCW 5:454} On 26 April 1748 an inventory was filed which included farm stock and 3 Negroes; appraised by Thomas Hand and Elisha Hand. An account was submitted on 19 May 1748 showing payments to Elijah Hughes, Elisha Crowell, Will'm Mulford, Elisha and Thomas Hand, Henry Young, Elisha Eldridge, Uriah Hughes, Ephraim Seeley, David Bancraft, Ellis Hughes, James Whilldin, Richard Crawford, Abigail Whildin, David Whilldin, Mathew Whilldin, Loes Whilldin, etc.{NJCW}

Joseph was father of the following children: MATHEW; JAMES[146], b. 1714, d. 5 Nov 1780{Cold Spring Cemetery}; HANNAH, b. ca. 1719, m. 1st before 1739, Ellis Hughes* who was b. 1708 and d. at Cape May, 1752 and Hannah m. 2nd (N) Elldredge; DAVID, b. 1725, d. 17 March 1762{Cold Spring Cemetery}; RACHEL, m. 1st Richard Crawford* and m. 2nd (N) Mills; LOIS, b. 1730, d. March 1756{Cold Spring Cemetery}, m. (N) Mills; MERCY (Mary), m. Uriah Hughes*.

---

146 Joseph Whilden, Jr. recorded his ear mark on 11 April 1715; later James Whillden's. {First Court Rcds: 336}

Third generation

3. MATTHEW WHILLDIN, son of Joseph (2) and Mary Whilldin, d. prior to 6 Aug 1751 when James Whilldin was appointed admin. Bondsman: Jeremiah Hand of said county. Witnesses: Jacob Hughes and Jonathan Smith. On 11 Oct 1750 an inventory was filed by Thomas Hand and Jeremiah Hand.{NJCW Cape May Wills:157E}

4. JAMES WHILLDIN, son of Joseph (2) and Mary Whilldin, b. 1714, d. 5 Nov 1780{Cold Spring Cemetery}, m. 1st Jane Hand* who was b. 1719, d. 8 Nov 1760{Cold Spring Cemetery}, bur. at Cold Spring Cemetery, m. 2nd by license of 20 July 1761{MLNJ}, Jane Izard*, m. 3rd by license of 13 Jan 1766{MLNJ}, Susannah Hand, who survived him.

James Whilldin d. leaving a will dated 11 Oct 1780, proved 21 Nov 1780. Mentioned were wife Susannah; son Jonathan; son James; grandson Seth Whilldin; son of dau. Jane known as Humphrey Hughes; son Matthew; daus. Mary Hughes, Jane Edmonds, Loes Teates and Rachel Whilldin; son-in-law Thomas Hand. Execs. were wife Susannah and sons Matthew and James. The will was witnessed by James Watt, Elias Tylor and Robert Harris. On 23 Nov 1780 an inventory (£35,922.14.0) was filed by Jeremiah Eldredge and Henry Hand and later on 3 Nov 1785 by Jeremiah Eldredge and Henry Hand.{NJCW 27:496}

James was father of the following children: JAMES, b. 20 Aug 1742, m. 1st by license of 8 Dec 1774, Rhoda Mulford, who was b. 1755, d. 9 Sep 1801, bur. Cold Spring Cemetery and m. 2nd Martha Hand and moved to Ohio where he d.; SETH, d. 1778, m. 25 Dec 1776, Rebecca Goldin of Maurice River, Cumberland Co. by whom he had a dau. Ruth who d. in 1791[147] and a son Seth Whilldin, Jr., b. 1778; MATTHEW, b. 1749, d. 16 July 1828{Cold Spring Cemetery}; JONATHAN, b. 1755, d. 13 Feb 1796; JANE, b. 15 June 1756, d. 26 Dec 1790, m. 1st Humphrey Hughes* and m. 2nd Jeremiah Edmunds*; MARY, m. (N) Hughes; LOES, m. (N) Teates; RACHEL.

5. DAVID WHILLDIN, son of Joseph (2) and Mary Whilldin, d. leaving a will dated 13 Feb 1762, proved 13 May 1762. In his will he provided that a head and foot stone be bought for the graves of his mother, Mary Whillden, sister Lois Mills (both dead) and himself. Also mentioned were

---

147 Ruth Whilldin, dau. of J. and R., d. 7 March 1791, in her 4th year. (Perhaps the S. was misread for J.) {Cold Spring Cemetery}

brother James Whillden, Esq., sister Hannah Eldredge, sister Rachel Mills, Ellis Hughes, Judith Hughes and Mary Hughes (the legal representatives of sister Mary Hughes, dec.) His right in Five Mile Beach bought of James Swaine to be sold. To Matthew Whillden, son of brother James, cedar swamp. To Seth Whilldin, the 2nd son of brother, the use of testator's homestead until said Matthew Whillden was 21. Execs. were said James Whillden and Ezekiel Eldredge. The will was witnessed by William Flower, John Hughes, Mary Edwards and Jacob Spicer. On 14 May 1762 an inventory was filed (£482.3.5) by John Eldredge and Richard Stites.{NJCW File 237 E}

Fourth generation

6. JAMES WHILLDIN, son of James (4) and Jane (Hand) Whilldin, b. 20 Aug 1742, m. 1st by license of 8 Dec 1774{MLNJ}, Rhoda Mulford, b. 1755, d. 9 Sep 1801, bur. Cold Spring Cemetery and James m. 2nd Martha Hand and moved to Ohio where he d. They were the parents of Capt. DANIEL, lost at sea 23 Dec 1811, age 36{Cold Spring Cemetery}, m. Jane Stillwell* (b. 17 Nov 1782, d. 13 Sep 1829) and they were the parents of the following children: RHODA, b. 2 June 1806; ALEXANDER, b. 28 Jan 1808; AMELIA STILLWELL, b. 29 Oct 1809, d. 9 July 1889, m. Samuel Springer; DANIELA, b. 27 Feb 1812.

7. MATTHEW WHILLDIN, son of James (4) and Jane (Hand) Whilldin, was b. 1749, d. 16 July 1828, bur. Cold Spring Cemetery, m. 1st by license of 22 April 1771{MLNJ}, Phebe Hildreth*, who was b. 1753, dau. of James Hildreth, and d. 14 June 1798.{Cold Spring Cemetery} He m. 2nd 1 Sep 1799, Ruhama Hand, widow of Nicholas Stillwell, who survived him; she d. 24 Feb 1839 in her 84th year and was bur. in the Methodist Cemetery, Cape May Court House.

Matthew and Phebe Whilldin were the parents of the following children: ISAAC, d. 13 May 1867, age 82 years, 2 mos., 28 days, m. Mahala Edmunds (d. 12 Nov 1840 in her 58th year); LYDIA, b. 19 Jan 1790, d. 13 Feb 1856, m. 1st 22 March 1808, James Schellenger, m. 2nd James Leaming; DAVID, b. 1792, d. 10 Dec 1813.{Cold Spring Cemetery}

8. JONATHAN WHILLDIN, son of James (4) and Jane (Hand) Whilldin, b. 1755, d. 13 Feb 1796, m. by license issued 16 Nov 1772{MLNJ}, Hannah Crowell. They were the parents of the following children: WILMON, b. 1773, d. at Philadelphia, 2 April 1852; DEBORAH, b. 1780, d. before 10 June 1808, m. 1799, Joseph Ware (b. Cumberland Co.,

NJ, 27 Aug 1771, d. 13 Feb 1827 - he m. 2nd Harriet Whilldin, sister of his first wife); HARRIET, b. 1785, d. 3 Aug 1851, m. 10 June 1808, Joseph Ware (see above).

9. SETH WHILLDIN, son of James (4) Whilldin, m. 25 Dec 1776, Rebecca Goldin of Maurice River, Cumberland Co.

Seth Whilldin of Cumberland Co. d. by 7 April 1777 when Matthew Whilldin was appointed admin. of his estate. Fellowbondsman: James Whilldin of Cape May Co. Witness: John Burchan. On 10 June 1777 an inventory was filed (£405.8.10) by Joshua Brick and David Lose at Maurice River.{NJCW 18:208, 25:422}

Seth was father of the following children: RUTH d. in 1791[148]; SETH, b. 1778.

Unplaced

A marriage license was issued to Jeremiah Ludlam and ANNA WHILDIN, 16 Feb 1774.{MLNJ}

A marriage license was issued to Jonathan Foster* and HANNAH WILLDEN, 28 July 1759.{MLNJ}

A marriage license was issued for Ellis Hughes and MARY WILLDIN on 2 Oct 1761.{MLNJ}

A marriage license was issued to MATTHEW WHILDIN and Rhoda Stites, 8 Dec 1768.{MLNJ}

A marriage license was issued to WILMON WHILDIN and Eleanor Hurst, 8 Aug 1764.{MLNJ}

WILLITS

Arthur S. Wardwell, in *The New York Genealogical and Biographical Records*, Vol. LXXX (1949) and subsequent volumes, describes the early

148 Ruth Whilldin, dau. of J. and R., d. 7 March 1791, in her 4th year. (Perhaps the S. was misread for J.) {Cold Spring Cemetery}

generations of the Willets Family in his article entitled, "The Willets Family of Hempstead and Jericho, Long Island." He begins with Richard Willets who had the following children: THOMAS, HOPE, b. 7th mo., 1652; JOHN; RICHARD; MARY. According to Wardwell, Hope, son of Richard, was b. in Hempstead, m. ca. 1676, Mary or Mercy Langdon, dau. of Thomas Langdon. For more details on the early generations see this article.

According to Lewis Townsend Stevens in *The History of Cape May County* ... Dr. Beesley gave the following information (1857): John Willits was the son of Hope Willets, and was born here in 1688, married Martha Corson in 1716, left three sons, Isaac, James and Jacob. He was judge of the court many years, a member of the Legislature in 1743, and was living in 1763.

According to Mr. Wardwell,

> 1. HOPE WILLETS m. Mercy Langdon{Wardwell} and had the following children: JOSEPH; RICHARD; JAMES; JOHN, b. 29 Oct 1698[149]; and triplet daus.: HANNAH, PATIENCE and ABIGAIL, all b. 8 March 1696; MARY, ELIZABETH, HESTER, TIMOTHY, HOPE and PHEBE.{H. C. Campion, Jr. believed Hannah m. David Cresse, son of Arthur Cresse, Sr.; Patience m. Thomas Creamer of Little Egg Harbor; and had no information on Abigail. He noted that John, youngest of the sons, was the only one son to remain in Cape May County.}
>
> Mercy, widow of Hope Willets m. John Townsend* in 1707.

Second Generation

2. JOHN WILLITS, son of Hope (1) Willets, m. Martha Corson*, dau. of John Corson, 5 Oct 1716.{First Public Recds} before John Townsend, Justice of the Peace. Witnesses: David Cresse, Benjamin Holdin, David Hildreth, Samuell Eldrige, William Goldin, William Midellton, Henry Young, Ezekiel Eldredg, George Taylor, J. Townsend, Marcy Townsend, John Corson, Jacob Corson, Hannah Corson, Hannah Cresse, Martha Willitts, Robert Townsend.{First Public Rcds}

An entry in the Leaming diaries dated 1 July 1777 shows, Died, Captn. John Willits, Esq., aged 78, the 29th day of last October. Thus he was born 29 Oct 1698.{Leaming Diaries}

---

149 Mentioned as son-in-law [step-son], John Willetts, in the will of John Townsend.

John Willets of Cape May left a will dated 2 Jan 1775, proved 11 Aug 1777. In it were mentioned sons James and Isaac to whom he devised all that part of Pecks Beach which he bought of John Townsend and Richard Smith. His personal estate was left to daus.: Sarah Townsend, Massah Townsend, Hannah Corson and Rachel Sparks. Execs. were Isaac Townsend of Cape May Co. and sons James and Isaac. The will was witnessed by Hugh Hathorn, Elizabeth Hathorn and Rem Corson. On 9 Aug 1777 an inventory of the estate £645.5.2 1/2) was filed by Rem Corson and Hugh Hathorn.{NJCW 21:233}

John Willets was father of the following children{GEMM}: JAMES, b. 24th day, 8th mo., 1717; SARAH, b. 14th day, 8th mo., 1719, d. 24th day, 4th mo., 1796, m. Isaac Townsend* in 1737/8[150]; MARCY [Massah], b. 11th day, 11th mo., 1721, d. 10th day, 2nd mo., 1775, m. 1739 Silvanus Townsend, son of Robert Townsend*[151]; JACOB, b. 22nd day, 11th mo., 1724, d. 13th day, 6th mo., 1746; ISAAC, b. 11th day, 8th mo., 1727; HANNAH, b. 4th day, 3rd mo., 1730, d. 26th day, 7th mo., 1777, m. Darias Corson*{GEMM}; RACHEL, b. 22nd day, 2nd mo., 1737, m. (N) Sparks.

Third Generation

3. JAMES WILLETS, son of John (2) Willits, b. 24th day, 8th mo., 1717, m. Esther Hand in 1740 by license.(MLNJ}

James d. leaving a will dated 10 Jan 1775, proved 5 Dec 1788 by Elizabeth Watson, one of the witnesses. To son James, the plantation where he (son James) lived and 1/2 of cedar swamp bought of Nathan Golden. To son Enoch, the plantation bought of Nathan Golden and the overplus lands bought of Jacob Spicer and 2 small lots bought of Benjamin Scull and land in Cumberland Co. bought for the use of a pond and mill dam; also the salt marsh bought of Nathan Golden in Gloucester Co. on north side of Tuckaho River; also salt marsh bought of John Willets, Sr. Sons, Enoch, Amos and Nicholas, the other part of the cedar swamp given to son James. Sons, Amos and Nicholas, the homestead plantation and rights of land on Pecks Beach. Children: James, Ester Wheaten, Martha Willets, Enoch, Amos, Rachel Willets, Sarah Willets

---

150 On 2nd da., 11th mo., 1737, Isaac Townsend and Sarah Willets announced their intentions to marry. {GEMM}

151 On 2nd da., 5th mo., 1739, the marriage of Silvanus Townsend and Marcy Willets was reported orderly accomplished. {GEMM}

and Nicholas, moveable estate. Execs. were Jonathan Hand and brother Isaac Willets, who were to be guardians of the children. The will was witnessed by John Willets, Hugh Hathorn and Elizabeth Hathorn.{NJCW 31:90}

At August Term 1789 division of the land of James Willets, dec. was made among his several devisees: Nicolas Willets, son and minor; Esther Wheaton, late Esther Willets and dau. of said James, now wife of Joseph Wheaton; Enoch Willets, son of said James Willets; James Willets, son of said James Willets; Rachel Corson, late Rachel Willets and dau. of James Willets dec., and now wife of Parmanus Corson, Esqr.; Sarah Edwards, late Sarah Willets, and dau. of James Willets, dec., and now wife of Joseph Edwards. {Ltrs&Inv A(Rev):33} (plats shown)

James was the father of the following children: JOHN; JAMES; ESTER (Esther), m. Joseph Wheaton* by license dated 24 Oct 1768{MLNJ}; MARTHA; ENOCH; AMOS; RACHEL, b. 9 Aug 1762{Corson Sampler}, m. Parmanus Corson*; SARAH, m. Joseph Edwards*; NICHOLAS.

4. ISAAC WILLETS of Upper Precinct, probable son of John (2) Willits, d. leaving a will dated 26 Sep 1775, proved 26 Jan 1776. Mentioned were son Isaac (lived in Cumberland Co.) to whom was devised the salt marsh that was bought of Jacob Homestead, lying in Gloucester Co., 10 acres; son Jacob to whom was devised the homestead and tracts adjoining; son Hope (not of age), to whom was devised land called the Old Field; dau. Phebe Willets, who was left £100 when 18; Jonathan (not yet 14) (£150). Son Jacob was to be guardian of son Jonathan. Execs. were Joseph Edwards of Cape May and son Jacob. The will was witnessed by Hugh Hathorn, Samuel Homestead and Stephen Young. On 26 Jan 1776 an inventory (£1,191.10.4) was filed by John Golden and Hugh Hathorn.{NJCW 17:385}

Isaac was father of the following children: ISAAC; JACOB; HOPE; PHEBE; JONATHAN.

Fourth Generation

5. AMOS WILLETS, son of James (3) and Ester Willets, d. by 25 Oct 1780 when Enoch Willets, Gent., was appointed admin.{NJCW 38:79}

6. JOHN WILLETS of Upper Precinct, son of James (3) and Ester Willets, d. leaving a will dated 20 Aug 1771, proved 17 Nov 1772. Mentioned were brother James Willets; brother-in-law Joseph Wheaton to whom he left the use of his saw mill and grist mill for 3 years after his lease; father James Willets to whom he left his plantation, saw mill and grist mill. Execs. were father James Willets and mother Ester Willets and brother

James Willets. The will was witnessed by Jacob Harris, Isaac Willets and Jeremiah Smith. On 21 Nov 1772 an inventory of the estate (£206.11.2) was filed by John Willets and Hugh Hathorn.{NJCW 16:45}

7. NICOLAS WILLETS, son of James (3) Willets, was a minor in 1789.

At February Court 1789 Jonathan Hand, exec. to James Willets, requested in behalf of Nicolas Willets, minor son of sd. James that auditors be appointed to divide and allot the lands of sd. Willets among sd. Willet's respective devisees.{Ltrs&Inv A(Rev):29}

Nicolas is probably the same Nicolas Willets who m. Experience Stillwell Griffing*.

8. JAMES WILLETS, son of James (3) Willets, m. prior to 1771, Rebecca Stillwell*, dau. of Nicholas and Sarah Stillwell (b. ca. 1750).[152]

At October Court 1787 Richard Sumers and Sophia his wife, Moses Griffin and Sarah his wife, James Willets and Rebecca his wife, Rem Corson and Hannah his wife, Phebe Stillwell and Eli Eldredge were execs. to the estate of Sarah Stillwell, dec. [widow of Nicholas Stillwell].{Ltrs&Inv A(Rev):16}

9. ISAAC WILLETS of Cumberland Co., son of Isaac (4) Willets, d. before 8 June 1776, when Jacob Willets was appointed admin. of his estate. Fellowbondsman: Joseph Edwards. Witnesses: Esther Wheaton and Hugh Hathorn. On 28 May 1776 an inventory (£334.1.1) was filed by Joseph Edwards and Hugh Hathorn.{22:42}

10. HOPE WILLETS of Cape May Co., probable son of Isaac (4) Willets, d. prior to 15 June 1784 when Tabitha Willets was appointed admx. of his estate. Fellowbondsman: Henry Y. Townsend of Cape May Co. Witnesses: Hugh Hathorn and Jonathan Hildreth.{NJCW 38:79}

At court during the February Term 1790 Martha Corson laid an account before the court for keeping and maintaining Hopewell Willets, dau. of Hope Willets, dec., 4 years and 3 months.{Ltrs&Inv A(Rev):44}

Unplaced

On 28th day, 3rd mo., 1750, the marriage of Samuel Somers, Jr., and HANNAH WILLETS was reported orderly accomplished.{GEMM}

---

152 See her father's will.

HOPE WILLETS of Burlington m. Mary Buck* by license dated 20 June 1730.{MLNJ}

A marriage license was issued to ISAAC WILLETS and Mary Simkins on 7 Oct 1771.{MLNJ}

A marriage license was issued to JAMES WILLETS and Rachel Young on 9 Dec 1776.{MLNJ}

Rachel d. leaving a will dated 16 Dec 1796, proved 8 Feb 1797. Mentioned were nieces: Tabitha Young, Ann Young, Elizabeth Young, Eugenia Young; nephews: Reuben Young, Dan Young; brother: Uriah Young.{NJCW 37:162} On 6 Feb 1797 an inventory was filed (£66.1.0) by John Baker and Lewis Corson.{NJCW File:697E}

A marriage license was issued to JOHN WILLETS and Rebecca Smith on 25 June 1763.{MLNJ}

WOOLSON

1. HANCE WOOLSON d. prior to 16 March 1769 when Abraham Woolson was appointed admin. of his estate. Fellowbondsman: Isaac Newton, Sr. of Cape May Co. Witness: John Eldredge. On 14 March 1769 an inventory was filed (£100.6.4) by John Eldredge and Isaac Newton.{NJCW 13:532}

2. ABRAHAM WOOLSON, possible son of Hance (1) Woolson, m. Judith Robens by license dated 29 May 1769.{MLNJ} Judith Woolson d. 17 Feb 1777.{Leaming Diaries} Abraham m. 2nd Mary (N).

Abraham d. leaving a will dated 23 Oct 1784, proved 13 April 1791. Mentioned were wife Mary; sons: Abraham, John, Aaron and Caleb; dau. Judith. Execs. were wife Mary and friends, Philip Cresse and David Hildreth. The will was witnessed by Tho. Curtis, John Cochran, Leodosha Izard.{NJCW 32:281} An inventory was filed (£328.7.10) by Eben Kewon and Robert Edmunds.{NJCW File:568E}

At October Term 1796 in pursuance of an order of the Orphans Court the lands of Abraham Woolson were divided between his five children: ABRAHAM, JUDITH, JOHN, AARON and CALEB, agreeable to the last will of said dec.{Ltrs&Inv A(Rev):138}

3. CAPT AARON WOOLSON, possible son of Abraham (2) Woolson, b. 1778, d. 11 Oct 1824.{Cold Spring Cemetery}

Unplaced
A marriage license was issued to Eli Daniels (Cumberland Co.), and POLLEY WOOLSON, 20 March 1776.{MLNJ}

YATES

See "Bible Records, *The Cape May County Magazine of History and Genealogy*, p. 111. June 1957. By Margret Irwin McVickar.

1. WILLIAM YATES, b. 30 Aug 1732, m. Sarah Iszard (b. 23 Aug 1735) by license dated 24 Aug 1762.{MLNJ} She was the dau. of Michael Iszard III and his wife Sarah Reeves. They were the parents of the following children: SARAH, b. 9 Dec 1768, m. 7 Jan 1792 Edward Irwin, Jr. (b. 20 March 1760); ELIZABETH, b. 15 Sep 1772; WILLIAM, b. 8 Nov 1775; THOMAS.

William Yates d. leaving a will dated 23 April 1783, proved 10 Sep 1783. Mentioned were wife Sarah; sons: William and Thomas. Son William was to be put to a trade when 15. Execs. were son Thomas and Jesse Hand. The will was witnessed by Amos Cresse, John Swain, Zebulon Swain, Jr. and Silvanus Church.{NJCW 38:73}

Sarah Yates of Cape May Co., widow, d. leaving a will dated 8 Aug 1790, proved 21 May 1791. Mentioned were son-in-law Thomas Yates; dau.-in-law Ruth Crawford; and testatrix's children: Sarah Yates, Elizabeth Yates and William Yates (William not 21). Exec. was friend Phillip Cresse, Esq. The will was witnessed by John Hancliff, Samuel Sringer, Marcy Iszard and Rebecca Swaine.{NJCW 32:294} An inventory was filed (£53.7.4) by Amos Cresse and John Swain{NJCW 569E}

2. WILLIAM YATES, probable son of William (1) Yates, m. Hannah Hand by 7 May 1799.{Co. Clerk Rcds - Book A}

INDEX

-E-

-F-

-G-

-K-

-L-

-M-

-N-

-O-

-P-

-T-

-V-

-W-

APPENDIX

ADDITIONS TO FIRST EDITION

Most of the following additions were based on the recent book titled, *New Jersey Bible Records, Volume 1: Atlantic, Burlington, Cape May, and Gloucester Counties*, edited by Anna Miller Watring. (Colonial Roots: 2002), hereafter cited as NJBR1.

CROWELL

p. 39. Add the following:
6. BARNABAS CROWELL, b. 19 Dec 1766, d. 5 March 1819, son of Daniel (3) Crowell, m. Elizabeth (N) (b. 11 Aug 1768, d. 15 Jan 1836.{Cold Spring Cemetery; NJBR1}

Barnabas and Elizabeth were parents of the following children: THOMAS, b. 15 Jan 1789; HANNAH, b. 2 Oct 1790; JUDITH, b. 6 Sep 1793; BARNABAS, b. 6 April 1802. {NJBR1}

7. HANNAH CROWELL, b. 2 Oct 1790, m. 17 Dec 1809, dau. of Barnabas (6) and Elizabeth Crowell, m. Jonathan Crawford.

They were parents of the following children: JONATHAN CRAWFORD, b. 15 May 1811; WILLIAM CRAWFORD, b. 15 May 1811, m. 27 Jan 1835, Eliza Cresse; ELIZABETH CRAWFORD, b. 22 July 1814, m. 15 Aug 1836, Aaron Garretson; REBECCA CRAWFORD, b. 4 Sep 1818, m. 1st 3 Feb 1833, Jacobs S. Hughes and m. 2nd 22 Oct 1836, Stillwell Stevens; BARNABAS CROWELL CRAWFORD, b. 27 Aug 1820; SARAH CRAWFORD, b. 7 May 1823, m. 31 March 1846, S... Hoffman; ISAAC OGDEN CRAWFORD, b. 14 April 1826; ANNA MARIA CRAWFORD, b. 24 Oct 1828, m. 16 Oct 1854, Silvanus Willets; MARTHA CRAWFORD, b. 16 April 1831. {NJBR1}

EDMUNDS

p. 46 and 47. Change to read:
5. JEREMIAH EDMUNDS, son of Downes (2) Edmunds, b. 2 Oct 1760, d. 22 Nov 1807, m. 1st 1 July 1780, Mrs. Jane Hughes (d. 26 Dec 1790), dau. of James Whilddin*, and were the parents of ELIZABETH, b. 4 Dec 1780, d. 11 Jan 1868, m. 10 April 1799, Levi Eldredge (b. 17 Oct 1776, d. 23 Nov 1822); MAHALAH, b. 10 Jan 1783, m. Isaac Whilldin*. Jeremiah later m. Mrs. Ann Hughes, widow of Jacob Hughes*; JEREMIAH, b. 15 April 1785. {Sheppard Papers, Cold Spring Cemetery; NJBR1}

MAHALA EDMUNDS, dau. of Jeremiah (5) and Jane Edmunds, b. 10 Jan 1783, d. 12 Nov 1840, m. Isaac Whilldin (b. 20 Feb 1764 (1784?). {NJBR1}

They were parents of the following children: JANE WHILLDIN, b. 24 Dec 1809; DANIEL WHILLDIN, b. 2 Oct 1812, d. 3 March 1813; MATTHEW WHILLDIN, b. 3 May 1814, d. 4 Oct 1814; MATHEW, b. Dec 1815; MARY, b. Dec 1820; ISAAC, b. 5 Sep 1823, d. 20 Dec 1823; ISAAC, b. 3 April 1825. {NJBR1}

7. JEREMIAH EDMUNDS, b. 15 April 1785, son of Jeremiah (5) and Jane Edmunds, m. 13 April 1791, Ester Eldredge.

They were parents of the following children: JANE, b. 15 May 1792.

Jeremiah Edmunds d. 22 Nov 1807. {NJBR1}

Humphrey Edmunds b. 10 Nov ... (torn). {NJBR1}

NATHANIEL FOSTER

p. 65. Change the entry to read as follows:

4. GEORGE FOSTER, son of Capt. Salathiel (2) Foster, b. 11 Aug 1754, d. 30 Dec 1788, m. 30 March 1790, Rachel Edmonds (b. 5 Jan 1758, d. 20 Sep 1822)*. They were parents of the following children: MARCH; CORNELIA, b. 29 Aug 1785, m. 15 Feb 1815, Jesse Hand*; RACHEL.{Sheppard Papers; NJBR1}

GODFREY

p. 78. Add the following:

10. MATTHEW GODFREY, b. 27 ___ 1797, probable son of James (7) Godfrey, m. 18 Jan 1818, Angelina Miller (b. 12 March 1796?). {NJBR1}

They were parents of WILLIAM M., b. 6 June 1820; AARON T., b. 4 Aug 1822?, d. 13 Oct 1822; AARON F., b. 14 1823?; CAROLINE, b. 23 Oct 1826; MATTHEW, b. 13 April 1828?, d. 28 Nov 1836; GILBERT, b. 28 May 1830; ROBERT STEVENS, b. 24 Oct 1832; RICHARD TOWNSEND, b. 1 Feb 1838, d. 25 April 1861. {NJBR1}

HAND

p. 100. Change the entry to read as follows:

31. ELISHA HAND, son of Silas (17) and Sarah Hand, b. 17 Jan 1752, d. 18 Nov 1814, m. 25 March 1783, Esther Teal who was b. 10 Nov 1762, d. 4 June 1802.[57] They were the parents of the following children: SARAH, b. 4 Dec 1786; NOAH, b. 24 March 1789, d. 12 June 1725; AARON B., b. 5 May 1791, d. 23 Dec 1861, m. 18 Feb 1818 Jane Hand Bancroft (b. 20 Aug 1793, d. 14 Jan 1864[58]); EXPERIENCE, b. 14 Feb 1794; ELIAS, b. 15 Jan 1797, 14 Aug 1798; RHODA, b. 4 Sep 1799; JESSE, b. 26 May 1802. {NJBR1}

p. 103. Make the following addition:

39A. NOAH HAND, b. 24 March 1789, d. 12 June 1725, son of Elisha (31) and Esther Hand, m. 15 Feb 1815, Cornelia Foster (b. 29 Aug 1785), dau. of George and Rachel Foster.

Noah and Cornelia were parents of the following children: JACOB FOSTER, b. 1 Oct 1815; ESTHER, b. 21 April 1817, d. Oct 1833; NOAH, b. 7 Aug 1823, d. 14 Oct 1824; GEORGE, b. 12 Nov 1824, d. 20 Nov 1824.

---

p. 104.

46. SHAMGAR HAND, probable son of Shamgar (also Shangar) (14) Hand, m. 1st (N), m. 2nd (N) and m. 3rd Priscilla Hildreth [probably widow of Daniel Hildreth*], 28 Feb 1772.{Baptists} The license was issued on 27 Feb 1772.{MLNJ} {Bible records show Priscilla as 3rd wife of Shangar Hand. NJBR1}

Ephraim Hildreth and Miss Abigail hand, dau. of Shangar Hand by his 3rd wife Priscilla, m. 14 Nov 1794. {NJBR1}

Shamgar was father of the following children: JONATHAN; STEPHEN; CORNELIUS, chose Stephen Hand as his guardian on 12 Oct 1793{NJCW 33:280, File 587E}; SARAH; ABIGAIL, b. 6 Jan 1775, m. 14 Nov 1794, Ephraim Hildreth*. {NJBR1}

---

p. 112. Add the following unplaced entry:

PHILIP HAND, b. 28 Aug 1756, m. 15 Feb 1781, Lavisia Hand (b. 17 Nov 1762, d. 13 May 1794).

They were parents of the following children: HULDAH, b. 1 Nov 1781, d. 8th of the next Dec; NATHANIEL, b. 8 Nov 1782; HULDAH, b. 19 March 1785,

d. 12 March 1826, m. (N) Cresse; LUDLAM, b. 5 May 1787; PHILIP, b. 27 April 1790, d. 3 Aug 1794; PRISCILLA, b. 28 April 1791, d. 14 Feb 1877, m. (N) Stites; ELIZABETH, b. 6 Dec 1793, d. July 1794.

HILDRETH

p. 120. Add a son underJoshua Hildreth as follows:

2. JOSHUA HILDRETH, probable son of David (1) Hildreth, m. Alice (N) and had a son JOSEPH, mentioned in the will of Joseph (4) Hildreth; DAVID [based on Ephraim Hildreth Bible. {NJBR1}

p. 122. Show David (6) Hildreth as son of Joshua (2) vice David (1).

6. DAVID HILDRETH, b. 14 Feb 1748, son of Joshua (2) and Alice Hildreth, m. Jane Edwards by license dated 21 April 1769.{MLNJ} Jane dau., of Ephraim and Mary Edwards, b. 25 July 1750. Jane Hildreth m. 19 Sep 1827 Levi Hand. {NJBR1}

David and Jane Hildreth were parents of EPHRAIM, b. 22 Jan 1770, d. 21 March 1841; MARY, b. 10 March 1772. {NJBR1}

p. 124. Add the following prior to Unplaced:

13. EPHRAIM HILDRETH, b. 22 Jan 1770, d. 21 March 1841, son of David (6) and Jane Hildreth, m. 14 Nov 1794, Miss Abigail Hand (b. 6 Jan 1775, d. 30 Oct 1856), dau. of Shangar Hand by his 3rd wife Priscilla. Abigail Hand, dau. of Shangar and Priscilla hand, b. 6 Jan 1775. {NJBR1}

Ephraim and Abigail were parents of MARY, b. 20 Jan 1795; EPHRAIM, b. 30 Sep 1796, d. 18 Sep 1842; DAVID, b. 7 Nov 1798, d. 23 Jan 1839; SHANGAR, b. 6 July 1801, d. 18 Sep 1841; ABIGAIL, b. 6 March 1804; JANE, b. 21 Sep 1808 at 2:00 a.m.; DANIEL EDWARDS, b. 23 Sep 1811 at 2:00 a.m.; ALEXANDER, b. 19 Sep 1814 between 10 and 11 a.m. {NJBR1}

Fourth Generation

14. EPHRAIM HILDRETH, b. 30 Sep 1796, son of Ephraim Hildreth, m. 16 Jan 1822, Judith Hildreth, dau. of Joshua and Judith Hildreth.

Ephraim and Judith were parents of GEORGE, b. 28 May 1822.

LEAMING

p. 165. Add the following entry:

13. HUMPHRY LEAMING, son of Christopher (9) and Sarah (Spicer) Leaming, b. 6 Dec 1780, m. Mary Stites (b. 10 Jan 1785, d. 6 Dec 1839).

They were parents of the following children: MARY, b. 16 Sep 1811, d. 9 Feb 1874; HUMPHREY, b. 12 Oct 1813; RACHEL, b. 30 Nov 1815; PHILIP, b. 30 May 1818; DEBORAH, b. 17 Feb 1821; CHRISTOPHER, b. 1 July 1827, d. 8 May 1888.

LUDLAM

p. 171 (unplaced). Following is additional information (underlined) on unplaced Henry Ludlam.

HENRY LUDLAM m. Hannah Smith, 30 June 1772.{Baptists; MLNJ}

In the land records are shown Henry Ludlam and wife Hannah (1800).{Deeds B:43}

Daniel Ludlam, son of Hnnah Ludlam and Henry her husband, b. 20 Nov 1774. {NJBR1}

DANIEL LUDLAM, b. 20 Nov 1774, son of Henry and Hannah Ludlam, m. 2 Feb 1806, Phebe Lawrence (b. 27 May 1785), dau. of James and Sarah Lawrence. {NJBR1}

Daniel and Phebe were parents of JULIAN, b. 21 Jan 1812; GEORGE, b. 13 Nov 1816; EMELINE, b. 5 March 1819. {NJBR1}

PAIGE

p. 187 (unplaced). Following is additional information (underlined) on unplaced Thomas Paige.

THOMAS PAIGE, b. 3 July 1742, m. 1st 10 Aug 1766, Lydia Church (b. 10 May 1745) {NJBR1} and m. 2nd Rachel Parsons.

A marriage license was issued to Thomas Paige and Lydia Church, 7 Aug 1766.{MLNJ}

Lydia Paige, wife of Thomas Paige, d. 15 May 1767. {NJBR1}

A marriage license was issued to Thomas Paige and Rachel Parsons, 12 April 1773.{MLNJ}

Thomas Paige [Page] of Cape May Co. d. by 1 Feb 1777 when Rachel Paige was appointed admx. of his estate. Fellowbondsman: Robert Parsons of Cape May Co. On 1 Feb 1777 an inventory was filed (£299.10.8) by Daniel Stillwell and Downes Edmunds.{NJCW 22:41}

LYDIA, dau. of Thomas and Lydia Paige, b. 12 May 1767. {NJBR1}

LYDIA PAIGE, b. 12 May 1767, d. 3 May 1828, dau. of Thomas and Lydia Paige, m. 3 Dec 1788, Thomas H. Hughes (b. 10 Jan 1769).

See Hughes section of this vol.

RICHARDSON

pp. 195, 196. Add the following entry:
5. JEREMIAH RICHARDSON, son of Jacob (4) Richardson, m. Susannah Church (license dated 8 Sep 1764. {MLNJ}

6. JEREMIAH RICHARDSON, son of Jeremiah (5) and Susannah Richardson, b. 30 March 1785, m. 10 Jan 1816, Lydia Holmes, by Rev. David Jenkins. {NJBR1}

Jeremiah and Lydia were parents of the following children: CHARLOTTE, b. 23 May, d. 23 June 1817, aged 1 mo.; JEREMIAH, b. 1 Dec 1818; MARTHA ANN S., b. 4 Sep 1821, d. 23 Feb 1825; LYDIA H. b. 19 Feb 1824; JOSEPH H., b. 17 July 1825; MARTHA ANN STILLWELL, b. 5 April 1829. {NJBR1}

SCHELLINGER

p. 203 (unplaced). Following is additional information on unplaced Enos Schellenger.

A. ENOS SCHELLINGER b. 28 Feb 1752, d. 16 Jan 1809, m. Sarah (N) (b. 3 June 1758, d. 7 March 1822). {NJBR1}

Enos (Schellenger), b. 1752, d. 16 Jan 1809{Cold Spring Cemetery}

Enos and Sarah were parents of the following children: REBECCA, b. 10 Feb 1774; JOSEPH, b. 20 Sep 1775; SARAH, b. 27 Dec 1780; REBECCA, b. 9 Oct 1782; MARY, b. 20 June 1784; ENOS, b. 16 April 1786; JOSEPH, b. 26 Aug 1787; ANNA, b. 18 Oct 1789; CHARLES, b. 225 Sep 1792; JOANAH, b. 10 Jan 1793; JOSEPH, b. 20 Nov 1795; JOANNA, b. 10 Oct 1797; MARIAH, b. 20 Dec 1799. {NJBR1}

B. ENOS SCHELLINGER, b. 16 April 1786, d. 1 Sep 1832, son of Enos (A) and Sarah Schellinger, m. Eliza (N) (b. 12 Oct 1793.

They were parents of the following children: SARAH C., b. 25 Aug 1811; MARY, b. 6 Feb 1814, d. 5 April 1814; CHARLES COX, b. 23 April 1815; MARY MILLS, b. 16 Feb 1817; EPHRAIM MILLS, b. 6 Feb 1820, d. 23 May 1826; SAMUEL McK., b. 15 Oct 1822; ELISA, b. 17 Feb 1825, d. 23 Sep 1846; WILLIAM MILLS, b. 20 Aug 1828; JOSEPH COX, b. 22 Dec 1830. {NJBR1}

C. CHARLES SCHELLINGER, b. 25 Sep 1792, d. 9 July 1823, son of Enos (A) and Sarah Schellinger, m. Jane Edmunds[1] (b. 14 May 1792).

They were parents of the following children: ELIZABETH, b. 7 May 1816, d. 14 April 1844; ENOS, b. 28 Sep 1818; ABIGAIL, b. 3 Oct 1820; JANE, b. 8 Aug 1823. {NJBR1}

STEVENS

p. 239-240. This entire section may be re-organized as follows:

1. EZEKIEL STEVENS b. 5 May 1739, m. by licenses dated 30 April 1763, Rebecca Stillwell (b. 9 April 1741). {MNLN; NJBR1}

Daniel Stevens, son of Ezekiel and Rebecca Stevens, b. 17 July 1771, on Wednesday.

Ezekiel d. prior to 9 Jan 1781 when his widow, Rebecca Stevens, was appointed admx. of his estate. Fellowbondsman: Jacob Hughes of Cape May Co. Witnesses: Henry Stevens and Elijah Hughes. An inventory was made on 9 Jan 1781 (£7,251.5.0) by Jacob Hughes and Henry Stevens.{NJCW}

Ezekiel and Rebecca were parents of DANIEL.

2. DANIEL STEVENS, b. 17 July 1771, d. 5 Feb 1833, son of Ezekiel (1) Stevens, m. Philamelia (N) (b. 11 Dec 1774) {Cold Spring Cemetery; NJBR1}.

Daniel Stevens, b. 17 July 1771, d. 17 Jan 1828.{Cold Spring Cemetery}

Philamela Stevens, w/o Daniel Stevens, d. 5 Feb 1833. {NJBR1}

Philomelia Stevens, b. 1773, d. 5 Feb 1833.{Cold Spring Cemetery}

Daniel and Philamelia were parents of REBECCA, b. 25 Aug 1794; HANNAH, b. 4 Sep 1795; WILLIAM, b. 21 Jan 1776; REBECCA, b. ---- March 1799; HENRY, b. 8 Oct 1802; DANIEL, b. 5 March 1805, d. 25 Dec 1828; STILLWELL, b. 3 March 1807; JOHN, b. 1 Oct 1812. {NJBR1}

3. STILLWELL STEVENS, b. 3 March 1807, son of Daniel (2) and Philamelia Stevens, m. 22 Oct 1836, Rebecca Hughes, dau. of Jonathan and Hannah Crawford, and widow of Jacob Stillwell Hughes. {NJBR1}

Jacob Stillwell Hughes and Rebecca Crawford m. 3 Feb 1833. They had a dau. Mary Higbee Hughes, b. 5 May 1834. Jacob S. Hughes d. 22 Oct 1835, in his 32nd yr. {NJBR1}

Hannah Elizabeth Stevens, dau. of Stillwell and Rebecca Stevens, b. 15 March. 1837. {NJBR1}

Philamelia Stevens b. 15 Nov 1839. {NJBR1}

Thomas Stillwell Stevens b. 24 May 1841. {NJBR1}

Jonathan Crawford Stevens, son of Stillwell and Rebecca Stevens, b. 7 Aug 1843. {NJBR1}

Rebecca Stillwell Stevens, dau. of Stillwell and Rebecca Stevens, b. 16 July 1845. {NJBR1}

Martha Jane Stevens, dau. of Stillwell and Rebecca Stevens, b.1 April 1849.

William Henry Stevens, son of Stillwell and Rebecca Stevens, b. 12 Mar. 1851, d. 18 May 1851, aged 8 weeks. {NJBR1}

Caroline F. (or T.?) Smith Stevens, dau. of Stillwell and Rebecca Stevens, b. 22 May 1852, d. 28 March 1852, aged 10 mos., 6 days, sick and week.. {NJBR1}

Emily Hughes Stevens and Anna Pierce Stevens, twin daus. of Stillwell and Rebecca Stevens, b. 5 Mar. 1854. {NJBR1}

Fanny Schellinger Stevens, dau. of Stillwell Stevens, b. 16 Oct 1857.

Harriet B. Stevens, dau. of Stillwell and Rebecca Stevens, b. 1 April 1859, d. 1 Aug, aged 4 mo. {NJBR1}

4. DANIEL STEVENS, son of Daniel (2) and Philamena Stevens, d. 3 Sep. 1830, on the Island of St Jago De Cuba. {NJBR1}

5. WILLIAM STEVENS, son of Daniel (3) and Philamela Stevens, d. 20 Oct 1828, in Philadelphia. {NJBR1}

Unplaced

A marriage license was issued to Abraham Bennet and LEVICE STEVENS, 6 Nov 1759.{MLNJ}

A marriage license was issued to HENRY STEPHENS and Jane Iszard, 8 Aug 1764.{MLNJ}

STEPHEN STEPHENS m. Mary Matthews on 8 Sep 1774.{Baptists} A marriage license was issued to them on 5 Sep 1774.{MLNJ}

TOWNSEND

p. 268. Under 6. JOHN TOWNSEND, add the following:

Tabitha Townsend d. 2 April 1793 after an illness of 15 weeks, aged 74-5-4. {Sarah Townsend Stites Bible, NJBR1}

p. 272. Under 15. HENRY YOUNG TOWNSEND, add the following:

Priscilla Townsend, wife of Henry Young Townsend, d. 18 Aug 1881. {Sarah Townsend Stites Bible, NJBR1}

p. 272. Create entries 15A and 15B following the entry for Henry Young (15) Townsend:

15A. TOBITHA/TABITHA TOWNSEND, dau. of John (6) Townsend, b. 7 (or 3?) Feb 1749 (1750?), m. 1 Jan 1773, Eli Townsend (b. 3 Feb 1749) Tabitha d. 26 March 1804, aged 55 years.

Tabitha and Eli were parents of PRISCILLA, b. 14 Jan 1782, d. 23 Feb 1807, m. Joshua Swain (b. 2 Feb 1778) and had children: Tabitha Swain, b. 28 Aug 1802, d. 13 May 1803; Henry Swain, b. 12 May 1806; Joshua Swain, b. 2 June 1804. Joshua Swain m. 2nd Susan Mattox (d. 18 Jan 1865, in her 87th year), dau. of Robert and Sarah Mattox; ELI, b. 5 Oct 1778, d. 4 March 1797, in his 19th year; ABIAH, b. Oct 1773, d. 3 Nov 1774; HANNAH, b. 10 Aug 1775, d. 27 May 1799; PRISCILLA, b. 14 Jan 1782; ABIAH, b. 9 Feb 1784, d. 10 Sep 1785; twins, unnamed, b. 7 Feb 1786, one d. 8th and the other the 27th of same month; JAMES, b. 12 April 1788?; REUBEN, b. 12 April 17–, d. 4 Oct 1790. {NJBR1}

15B. SARAH TOWNSEND, dau. of John (6) and Tobitha Townsend, b. 7 Feb 1749, m. 1 Jan 1773, John Stites, on the same day as her twin sister, Tabitha m. Eli Townsend. {NJBR1}

Richard Stites, 1st son of John and Sarah Stites, b. 8 Feb 1774, d. 12 March 1797, after an illness of 8 days. {NJBR1}

Rhoda Stites, 1st dau. of John and Sarah Stites, b. 26 Sep. 1776 and d. 13 Sep. 1779 after a sickness of 3 days. {NJBR1}

Rhoda Stites, 2nd dau. of John and Sarah Stites, b. 23 Oct 1779.

24 June 1792, Rhoda Stites, dau. of John and Sarah Stites, m. Thomas Beesley and went to live at Morris River 16 Oct following. {NJBR1}

Tabitha Stites, 4th dau. of and 7th child of John and Sarah Stites, b. Sunday, 18 April 1790, 11:00 at night, d. 18 Oct 1801. {NJBR1}

John Stites d. Sunday, 24 Sep. (no year given), aged 47-4-6. He left 5 children, 2 sons and 3 daughters, namely: his sons John and Townsend and his daughters Rhoda, Sarah and Tabitha, Rhoda the eldest child and Tabitha the youngest. He went unwell with fever on Saturday and went from home on Monday (date unknown) to go up the Delaware with a load of rails and continued unwell and on this day he went out of Dennisses Creek and stood up the Delaware to Grub's Landing, then sold part of his load and then went to Kingston and sold the rest and set off for home, and was taken worse and went into Wilmington on Sat., 23 Sep., and the next day died and was bur. in the Methodist Churchyard in Wilmington. {NJBR1}

Sarah Stites d. 17 Sep. 1824, aged 74-7-10. {NJBR1}

John and Sarah were parents of RICHARD; RHODA (1st); RHODA (2nd); SARAH; TABITHA; JOHN; TOWNSEND.

RHODA STITES, dau. of Sarah (15B) and John Stites, m. 24 June 1792, Thomas Beesley.

Sally Beesley, 1st child of Rhoda and Thomas Beesley, b. 13 July 1801.

---

p. 270. Correct the last entry to read,
10. SILVANIUS TOWNSEND, son of Robert (5) Townsend, ...etc. vice Robert (4) Townsend ...

---

p. 271. Create a new entry below 13. HANNAH TOWNSEND:
13A. ELIJAH TOWNSEND, son of James (4) and Abiah Towsend, b. 20 April 1751, m. 20 April 1775 Judith Townsend (b. 15 Oct 1752).

They were parents of the following children: ENOCH, b. 1 Feb 1776; JOHN, b. 22 Feb 1778; JOHN, b. 7 Dec 1780; ELIJAH, b. 8 July 1783; JUDITH, b. 22 Dec 1790; ELI, b. 13 June 1799. {NJBR1}

---

p. 275 *(unplaced). Following is additional information on unplaced Jotham Townsend:*

A. JOTHAM TOWNSEND m. Rachel Cresse (b. 11 July 1764), dau. of Philip Cresse.

A marriage license was issued to Jotham Townsend and Rachel Cressey, 14 Nov 1768.{MLNJ}

Jotham and Rachel were parents of CRESSE.

B. CRESSE TOWNSEND, b. 1 Oct 1769, d. 28 Jan 1841, son of Jotham (A) and Rachel Townsend, m. 1st 26 July 1791, Phebe Godfrey* (b. 16 April 1771), dau. of Philip and Ruth Godfrey. Cresse Townsend m. 2nd 3 July 1808, Rachel Godfrey, widow of Nathan Godfrey and dau. of Philip Godfrey, by Shangar Hewit, Esq. Cresse Townsend m. 3rd 4 July 1826, Elizabeth Tomlin (b. 30 Dec 1777), widow of Jediah Tomlin and dau. of Hugh Hathorn, by Rev. John Townsend.

Phebe Townsend d. 29 June 1806, aged 35-3-12.

Elizabeth Townsend d. 30 Oct 1837, aged 59 years, 10 mos.

Cresse and Phebe were parents of the following children: RACHEL, b. 20 March 1792; AMELIA, b. 19 Oct 1793; SETH, b. 12 Feb 1795, d. 29 June 1806; SYLVIA, b. 25 Feb 1798; JOTHAM, b. 26 May 1799 at 1:30 a.m., d. 4 Sep 1828; SIXTH CHILD (boy), b. stillborn 3 March 1801; GODFREY, b,. 30 Oct 1802, d. 9 Feb 1837; DANIEL C., b. 15 Sep 1804, d. 4 Sep 1887.

C. RACHEL TOWNSEND, dau. of Cresse (B) and Phebe, b. 20 March 1792, d. 17 June 1833, m. Philip Hand (d. 17 Dec 1836).

D. AMELIA TOWNSEND, dau. of Cresse (B) and Phebe, 19 Oct 1793, m. 15 July 1810, Enoch Godrey*.

INDEX TO APPENDIX (Additions to First Edition)

Heritage Books by F. Edward Wright:

18th Century Records of the German Lutheran Church at Philadelphia, Pennsylvania (St. Michael's and Zion): Volume 1, Baptisms, 1745–1769
Robert L. Hess and F. Edward Wright

18th Century Records of the German Lutheran Church at Philadelphia, Pennsylvania (St. Michael's and Zion): Volume 2, Baptisms, 1770–1786
Translated by Robert L. Hess, Ph.D. Edited by F. Edward Wright

18th Century Records of the German Lutheran Church of Philadelphia, Pennsylvania (St. Michael's and Zion): Volume 3, Baptisms, 1787–1800
Translated by Robert L. Hess, Ph.D. Edited by F. Edward Wright

18th Century Records of the German Lutheran Church at Philadelphia, Pennsylvania (St. Michael's and Zion): Volume 4, Marriages and Confirmations
Robert L. Hess and F. Edward Wright

18th Century Records of the German Lutheran Church at Philadelphia, Pennsylvania (St. Michael's and Zion): Volume 5, Burials
Robert L. Hess and F. Edward Wright

Abstracts of Bucks County, Pennsylvania, Wills, 1685–1785

Abstracts of Cumberland County, Pennsylvania, Wills, 1750–1785

Abstracts of Cumberland County, Pennsylvania, Wills, 1785–1825

Abstracts of Philadelphia County, Pennsylvania, Wills, 1682–1726

Abstracts of Philadelphia County, Pennsylvania, Wills, 1726–1747

Abstracts of Philadelphia County, Pennsylvania, Wills, 1748–1763

Abstracts of Philadelphia County, Pennsylvania, Wills, 1763–1784

Abstracts of Philadelphia County, Pennsylvania, Wills, 1777–1790

Abstracts of Philadelphia County, Pennsylvania, Wills, 1790–1802

Abstracts of Philadelphia County, Pennsylvania, Wills, 1802–1809

Abstracts of Philadelphia County, Pennsylvania, Wills, 1810–1815

Abstracts of Philadelphia County, Pennsylvania, Wills, 1815–1819

Abstracts of Philadelphia County, Pennsylvania, Wills, 1820–1825

Abstracts of South Central Pennsylvania, Newspapers, Volume 1, 1785–1790

Abstracts of South Central Pennsylvania, Newspapers, Volume 3, 1796–1800

Abstracts of the Newspapers of Georgetown and the Federal City, 1789–99

Abstracts of York County, Pennsylvania, Wills, 1749–1819

Adams County [Pennsylvania] Church Records of the 18th Century

Baltimore Directory of 1807

Berks County, Pennsylvania, Church Records of the 18th Century, Volume 1

Berks County, Pennsylvania, Church Records of the 18th Century, Volume 2

Berks County, Pennsylvania, Church Records of the 18th Century, Volume 3

Berks County, Pennsylvania, Church Records of the 18th Century: Volume 4

Bible Records of Washington County, Maryland

Bucks County, Pennsylvania, Church Records of the 17th and 18th Centuries, Volume 1: German Church Records

Bucks County, Pennsylvania, Church Records of the 17th and 18th Centuries, Volume 2: Quaker Records: Falls and Middletown Monthly Meetings
Anna Miller Watring and F. Edward Wright

Bucks County, Pennsylvania, Church Records of the 17th and 18th Centuries, Volume 4

Caroline County, Maryland, Marriages, Births and Deaths, 1850–1880

Citizens of the Eastern Shore of Maryland, 1659–1750

Colonial Families of Cape May County, New Jersey, Revised 2nd Edition

Colonial Families of Delaware, Volume 1

Colonial Families of Delaware, Volume 2: Kent and Sussex Counties

Colonial Families of Delaware, Volume 3 (2nd Edition): Kent and Sussex Counties

Colonial Families of Delaware, Volume 4: Sussex County

Colonial Families of Delaware, Volume 5: New Castle

Colonial Families of Delaware, Volume 6: Kent

Colonial Families of New Jersey, Volume 1: Middlesex and Somerset Counties

Colonial Families of Northern Neck, Virginia, Volume 1
Holly G. Wright and F. Edward Wright

Colonial Families of Northern Neck, Virginia, Volume 2
Holly G. Wright and F. Edward Wright

Colonial Families of the Eastern Shore of Maryland, Volume 1
Robert W. Barnes and F. Edward Wright

Colonial Families of the Eastern Shore of Maryland, Volume 2
Robert W. Barnes and F. Edward Wright

Colonial Families of the Eastern Shore of Maryland, Volume 4
Christos Christou and F. Edward Wright

Colonial Families of the Eastern Shore of Maryland, Volume 5
Henry C. Peden, Jr. and F. Edward Wright

Colonial Families of the Eastern Shore of Maryland, Volume 6
Henry C. Peden, Jr and F. Edward Wright

Colonial Families of the Eastern Shore of Maryland, Volume 7
Henry C. Peden, Jr. and F. Edward Wright

Colonial Families of the Eastern Shore of Maryland, Volume 8
Henry C. Peden, Jr. and F. Edward Wright

Colonial Families of the Eastern Shore of Maryland, Volume 9
Henry C. Peden, Jr. and F. Edward Wright

Colonial Families of the Eastern Shore of Maryland, Volume 10
Vernon L. Skinner, Jr. and F. Edward Wright

Colonial Families of the Eastern Shore of Maryland, Volume 11
Henry C. Peden Jr. and F. Edward Wright

Colonial Families of the Eastern Shore of Maryland, Volume 12
Henry C. Peden, Jr. and F. Edward Wright

Colonial Families of the Eastern Shore of Maryland, Volume 13
Henry C. Peden, Jr. and F. Edward Wright

Colonial Families of the Eastern Shore of Maryland, Volume 14
Henry C. Peden, Jr. and F. Edward Wright

Colonial Families of the Eastern Shore of Maryland, Volume 15
Ralph A. Riggin and F. Edward Wright

Colonial Families of the Eastern Shore of Maryland, Volume 16
Henry C. Peden, Jr. and F Edward Wright

Colonial Families of the Eastern Shore of Maryland, Volume 17
Ralph A. Riggin and F. Edward Wright

Colonial Families of the Eastern Shore of Maryland, Volume 18
Vernon L. Skinner, Jr. and F. Edward Wright

Colonial Families of the Eastern Shore of Maryland, Volume 19
Henry C. Peden, Jr. and F. Edward Wright

Colonial Families of the Eastern Shore of Maryland, Volume 20
Vernon L. Skinner, Jr. & F. Edward Wright

Colonial Families of the Eastern Shore of Maryland, Volume 22
Vernon L. Skinner, Jr. and F. Edward Wright

Colonial Families of the United States of America, Volume II
Holly G. Wright and F. Edward Wright

Cumberland County, Pennsylvania, Church Records of the 18th Century

Delaware Newspaper Abstracts, Volume 1: 1786–1795

Early Charles County, Maryland, Settlers, 1658–1745
Marlene Strawser Bates, F. Edward Wright

Early Church Records of Alexandria City and Fairfax County, Virginia
F. Edward Wright and Wesley E. Pippenger

Early Church Records of Bergen County, New Jersey, 1740–1800

Early Church Records of Dauphin County, Pennsylvania

Early Church Records of Lebanon County, Pennsylvania

Early Church Records of New Castle County, Delaware, Volume 1: 1701–1800

Early Church Records of Rockingham County, Virginia

Early Lists of Frederick County, Maryland, 1765–1775

Early Records of the First Reformed Church of Philadelphia, Volume 1, 1748–1780

Early Records of the First Reformed Church of Philadelphia, Volume 2, 1781–1800

Frederick County, Maryland, Militia in the War of 1812
Sallie A. Mallick and F. Edward Wright

Henrico County, Virginia, Marriage References and Family Relationships, 1654–1800

Inhabitants of Baltimore County, Maryland, 1692–1763

Judgment Records of Dorchester, Queen Anne's, and Talbot Counties [Maryland]

Kent County, Delaware, Marriage References and Family Relationships

King George County, Virginia, Marriage References
and Family Relationships, 1721–1800
Anne M. Watring and F. Edward Wright

Lancaster County Church Records of the 18th Century, Volume 1

Lancaster County Church Records of the 18th Century, Volume 2

Lancaster County Church Records of the 18th Century, Volume 3

Lancaster County Church Records of the 18th Century, Volume 4

Lancaster County, Pennsylvania, Church Records of the 18th Century, Volume 1
F. Edward Wright and Robert L. Hess

Lancaster County, Pennsylvania, Church Records of the 18th Century, Volume 3

Lancaster County, Pennsylvania, Church Records of the 18th Century, Volume 5

Lancaster County, Pennsylvania, Church Records of the 18th Century: Volume 6
Robert L. Hess and F. Edward Wright

Lancaster County, Virginia, Marriage References and Family Relationships, 1650–1800

Land Records of Sussex County, Delaware, 1769–1782

Land Records of Sussex County, Delaware, 1782–1789: Deed Book N No. 13
Elaine Hastings Mason and F. Edward Wright

Marriage Licenses of Washington, District of Columbia, 1811–1830

Marriage References and Family Relationships of Charles City, Prince George, and Dinwiddie Counties, Virginia, 1634–1800

Marriages and Deaths from Eastern Shore Newspapers, 1790–1835

Marriages and Deaths from the Newspapers of Allegany and Washington Counties, Maryland, 1820–1830

Marriages and Deaths from the York Recorder, *1821–1830*

Marriages and Deaths in the Newspapers of Frederick and Montgomery Counties, Maryland, 1820–1830

Marriages and Deaths in the Newspapers of Lancaster County, Pennsylvania, 1821–1830

Marriages and Deaths in the Newspapers of Lancaster County, Pennsylvania, 1831–1840

Marriages and Deaths of Cumberland County, [Pennsylvania], 1821–1830

Marriages, Births, Deaths and Removals of New Castle County, Delaware

Maryland Calendar of Wills, Volume 9: 1744–1749

Maryland Calendar of Wills, Volume 10: 1748–1753

Maryland Calendar of Wills, Volume 11: 1753–1760

Maryland Calendar of Wills, Volume 12: 1759–1764

Maryland Calendar of Wills, Volume 13: 1764–1767

Maryland Calendar of Wills, Volume 14: 1767–1772

Maryland Calendar of Wills, Volume 15: 1772–1774

Maryland Calendar of Wills, Volume 16: 1774–1777

Maryland Eastern Shore Newspaper Abstracts, Volume 1: 1790–1805

Maryland Eastern Shore Newspaper Abstracts, Volume 2: 1806–1812

Maryland Eastern Shore Newspaper Abstracts, Volume 3: 1813–1818

Maryland Eastern Shore Newspaper Abstracts, Volume 4: 1819–1824

Maryland Eastern Shore Newspaper Abstracts, Volume 5: Northern Counties, 1825–1829
F. Edward Wright and Irma Harper

Maryland Eastern Shore Newspaper Abstracts, Volume 6: Southern Counties, 1825–1829

Maryland Eastern Shore Newspaper Abstracts, Volume 7: Northern Counties, 1830–1834
Irma Harper and F. Edward Wright

Maryland Eastern Shore Newspaper Abstracts, Volume 8: Southern Counties, 1830–1834

Maryland Eastern Shore Vital Records, Book 1: 1648–1725, Second Edition

Maryland Eastern Shore Vital Records, Book 2: 1726–1750

Maryland Eastern Shore Vital Records, Book 3: 1751–1775

Maryland Eastern Shore Vital Records, Book 4: 1776–1800

Maryland Eastern Shore Vital Records, Book 5: 1801–1825

Maryland Militia in the War of 1812, Volume 1: Eastern Shore

Maryland Militia in the War of 1812, Volume 2: Baltimore City and County

Maryland Militia in the War of 1812, Volume 3: Cecil and Harford Counties

Maryland Militia in the War of 1812, Volume 4: Anne Arundel and Calvert Counties

Maryland Militia in the War of 1812, Volume 5: St. Mary's and Charles Counties

Maryland Militia in the War of 1812, Volume 6: Prince George's County

Maryland Militia in the War of 1812, Volume 7: Montgomery County

Maryland Militia in the Revolutionary War
S. Eugene Clements and F. Edward Wright

Maryland Militia, War of 1812: Volume 6–Prince George's County

Middlesex County Virginia, Marriage References and Family Relationships, 1673–1800

Middlesex County, New Jersey, Records of the 17th and 18th Centuries

New Castle County, Delaware, Marriage References and Family Relationships, 1680–1800

Newspaper Abstracts of Allegany and Washington Counties [Maryland], 1811–1815

Newspaper Abstracts of Cecil and Harford Counties [Maryland], 1822–1830

Newspaper Abstracts of Frederick County [Maryland], 1811–1815

Newspaper Abstracts of Frederick County [Maryland], 1816–1819

Northampton County, Virginia, Marriage References and Family Relationships, 1634–1800

Northumberland County, Virginia, Marriage References and Family Relationships, 1645–1800

Orphans' Court Proceedings of New Castle County, Delaware, 1742–1761

Quaker Minutes of the Eastern Shore of Maryland: 1676–1779

Quaker Records of Henrico Monthly Meeting and Other Church Records of Henrico, New Kent and Charles City Counties, Virginia

Quaker Records of South River Monthly Meeting, 1756–1800

Richmond County, Virginia, Marriage References and Family Relationships, 1692–1800

Sketches of Maryland Eastern Shoremen

St. Mary's County, Maryland, Marriage References and Family Relationships, 1634–1800

Stafford County, Virginia, Marriage References and Family Relationships, 1661–1800

Supplement to Maryland Eastern Shore Vital Records, Books 1–3

Sussex County, Delaware, Marriage References, 1648–1800

Sussex County, Delaware, Wills: 1800–1813

Tax List of Chester County, Pennsylvania, 1768

Tax List of York County, Pennsylvania, 1779

The Maryland Militia in the Revolutionary War
S. Eugene Clements and F. Edward Wright

Vital Records of Kent and Sussex Counties, Delaware, 1686–1800

Washington County [Maryland] Church Records of the 18th Century, 1768–1800

Western Maryland Newspaper Abstracts, Volume 1: 1786–1798

Western Maryland Newspaper Abstracts, Volume 2: 1799–1805

Western Maryland Newspaper Abstracts, Volume 3: 1806–1810

Wills of Chester County, Pennsylvania, 1766–1778

York County, Pennsylvania, Church Records of the 18th Century, Volume 1
Marlene S. Bates and F. Edward Wright

York County, Pennsylvania, Church Records of the 18th Century, Volume 2
Marlene Strawser Bates and F. Edward Wright

York County, Pennsylvania, Church Records of the 18th Century, Volume 3

York County, Virginia, Marriage References and Family Relationships, 1636–1800

York County, Virginia, Wills Inventories and Accounts, 1760–1783

www.ingramcontent.com/pod-product-compliance
Lightning Source LLC
Chambersburg PA
CBHW070545270326
41926CB00013B/2204

* 9 7 8 1 5 8 5 4 9 4 4 3 9 *